D1707108

Urban and Landscape Perspectives

Volume 7

For further volumes:
http://www.springer.com/series/7906

Aims and Scope

Urban and Landscape Perspectives is a series which aims at nurturing theoretic reflection on the city and the territory and working out and applying methods and techniques for improving our physical and social landscapes.

The main issue in the series is developed around the projectual dimension, with the objective of visualising both the city and the territory from a particular viewpoint, which singles out the territorial dimension as the city's space of communication and negotiation.

The series will face emerging problems that characterise the dynamics of city development, like the new, fresh relations between urban societies and physical space, the right to the city, urban equity, the project for the physical city as a means to reveal *civitas*, signs of new social cohesiveness, the sense of contemporary public space and the sustainability of urban development.

Concerned with advancing theories on the city, the series resolves to welcome articles that feature a pluralism of disciplinary contributions studying formal and informal practices on the project for the city and seeking conceptual and operative categories capable of understanding and facing the problems inherent in the profound transformations of contemporary urban landscapes.

Multimedia Explorations in Urban Policy and Planning

Beyond the Flatlands

Leonie Sandercock and Giovanni Attili
Editors

 Springer

Editors
Leonie Sandercock
University of British Columbia
School of Community &
Regional Planning
433-6333 Memorial Road
Vancouver BC V6T 1Z2
Canada
leonies@interchange.ubc.ca

Giovanni Attili
University of Rome "La Sapienza"
Dipt. di Architettura e
Urbanistica
Via Eudossiana, 18
00184 Rome
Italy
giovanni.attili@gmail.com

ISBN 978-90-481-3208-9   e-ISBN 978-90-481-3209-6
DOI 10.1007/978-90-481-3209-6
Springer Dordrecht Heidelberg London New York

Library of Congress Control Number: 2009943615

Cover illustration: Graphic elaboration of the photos in this book, by Giovanni Attili

Printed on acid-free paper

Springer is part of Springer Science+Business Media (www.springer.com)

Preface: Intersecting Journeys in the Fields of Planning

> A rhyme's
> a barrel of dynamite.
> A line is a fuse
> that's lit.
> The line smoulders,
> the rhyme explodes –
> And by a stanza
> a city
> is blown to bits.
> (Mayakovsky, 1925 in Blake 1960, p. 195)

I had an epiphany on the road to Wollongong in 1984. I was doing research on the social impacts of economic restructuring in the coastal steel and coal mining town of Wollongong (a 100 miles south of Sydney, Australia) when I realized, with a power of epistemological detonation akin to Mayakovsky's poem, that the research as formulated wasn't going anywhere. My political economy framework appeared to me as a ghostly ballet of bloodless categories (class, labour, capital). Listening, in homes and pubs and union offices, to the stories of the men who had lost their jobs, I realized that the research could only be animated through the telling of their stories. I changed the research plan, hired a research assistant to help with in-depth interviews, read a book of poems by a Wollongong lad who told obliquely of the ordeals of some of the retrenched miners and steelworkers. But after 2 years of a research grant I was unable to write the expected academic book. I had a macro-political economic framework (that carried one narrative) and a micro-sociological and psychological set of field data (that carried a myriad of individual stories), and I didn't know how to put the two together. I didn't know how to make a good academic story out of these two seemingly incompatible sources. I didn't even have a clue where to look for illumination. I gave up on the project and my sense of failure and guilt was such that I started to ask that potentially transformative, uh-oh question, 'what am I doing here?'

Within a year I had resigned from my professorial position in Urban Studies in Sydney and moved to Los Angeles, where I enrolled in a masters in Screenwriting at UCLA. My experience of the social sciences in general and of planning education in particular, up to that point (the intolerance of diverse ways of knowing and writing), convinced me that my epistemological crisis could not be resolved from within academia. Film making, on the other hand, spoke directly to the emotions yet also, in the hands of directors like John Sayles, involved 'thinking in pictures' (Sayles, 1987). Perhaps, I thought, film could bridge the unbridgeable, intellect and emotions. Sayles, the writer/director/editor of such politically charged feature films as *Matewan, The Brother from Another Planet, City of Hope, Lone Star,* would be my role model.

For a half dozen years after I'd graduated from Film School, I led two very different lives: one as a part-time screenwriter in Hollywood, the other as part-time academic at the University of California's Graduate School of Architecture and Urban Planning. Despite an early 'success' in getting my first post-film school script bought and produced as an ABC TV Movie of the Week (Sandercock, 1992), by 1995 I felt I was losing my moral compass, second guessing what producers might want to buy instead of writing what I wanted to write. I decided to return full-time to academic life, but I made myself a promise. I would apply what I learned in film school to my academic teaching and writing, concentrating on the power of story as a way of learning and as a communicative device. At this time, I *believed in* the power of stories, but in a completely fuzzy and stubbornly un-analytical way. Like good sex, I was afraid I might spoil the magic if I *thought too much* about why story is important, how it works, in what circumstances, and what kind of work stories do.

I've told this story before (Sandercock, 2003). I tell it again here as a segue to the autobiographical sequel which, in turn, explains 'why this book.' After a less than happy stint as a department head of Landscape, Environment and Planning (dealing with budget crises and administrative reorganizations) back in Australia, I returned to North America in 2001, to a new home in the graduate School of Community and Regional Planning at the University of British Columbia, in Vancouver. Still teaching planners. As a newcomer to Canada, I was eligible for funding from the federal government's Canadian Foundation for Innovation (CFI), which was typically used to fund electron microscopes, cyclotrons and other expensive laboratory equipment, as well as to build laboratories. The grants were generous. My Head of Department, Tony Dorcey, encouraged me to apply. But, I said, I don't need all that money, let alone a laboratory. I just need time, peace, to do my research and write my academic stories.

Now, stage left, enters Serendipity.

I gave a keynote at the International Network of Urban Research and Action conference in 2001. For the first few days, the conference took place in a derelict factory (these are true urban activists!) in Florence. Then we moved to a villa in the Tuscan countryside, recently taken over by organic farmers trying to start an *agriturismo* business. At the end of the week, PhD students were given a brief chance to display their wares. Resisting the temptation to take a much needed nap in the shade of an olive tree, I attended their session. And that day I saw a presentation by Giovanni Attili, a doctoral student in Planning at the University of Rome, La Sapienza. As part of his doctorate, Attili was constructing a 2-h interactive hypermedia CD-ROM (a project described in Chapter 10) depicting refugee landscapes in a neighbourhood in inner Rome.

'And by a stanza, a city is blown to bits' (Mayakovsky, 1925 in Blake, 1960, p. 195). Here was my second epistemological detonation. While I was still toiling around the campfire of storytelling as the written and spoken word, Attili's feet were firmly planted in twenty-first century storytelling modes. With the impact of his handful of dynamite thrown into the campfire, I was being shown the cascading potentialities of multimedia in depicting a complex and unsettled urban reality composed of many stories, images, sounds, music, a multi-sensory experience, a complex tapestry, artfully woven together. I was awed. We talked. I suggested keeping in touch. And 3 years later we were working on our first collaborative film project. (But now I'm jumping ahead to the story I tell in Chapter 4.)

I returned to Vancouver and applied for that CFI grant. My 'laboratory' could be a multimedia/film studio and my equipment would be digital video cameras, microphones, servers, laptops and editing software. I needed these twenty-first century tools to get students more attuned to the city of spirit, the city of memory and the city of desire; to explore the complexities of the mongrel (multicultural) cities now emerging globally; and to think through the challenges that such cities pose to planners and planning. My educational mission was to nurture a planning imagination for the twenty-first century, which I defined as creative, audacious, political and therapeutic.

My research partnership with Giovanni Attili was one answer to this personal as well as educational yearning for the 'juice' that could help animate this wonderful vocation of planning. When he finished his doctorate, I invited Giovanni to Vancouver as a post-doctoral fellow, and we set about teaching a class on 'digital ethnography' to 15 masters students. Giovanni taught the videography skills in my laboratory (which had been grandiosely named the Vancouver Cosmopolis Laboratory in the successful grant application), but the research which I orchestrated took place in the low-income Collingwood neighbourhood in the City of Vancouver, with 45,000 residents of whom only 27% speak English as their first language. Here was our first 'experiment' with multimedia as a means of social research, a form of meaning making, a tool in community engagement and community development and as a catalyst for policy dialogue.

And it was such an intense experience, so rewarding in so many ways, and has had so much 'fall-out' (see Chapter 4) that we started other experiments, here in our School, and began to search for a network of folks engaged in similar pursuits.

This book is the result of that search. It unabashedly reflects our own and others' excitement about the ways in which multimedia can be used by activists, NGOs, immigrant and indigenous communities, planning scholars and educators, wherever urban policies are being debated.

I had a dog, whose name was Kilim. Every day, after school, I used to go to a park close to my parents' house, Villa Pamphili. Even if Kilim was really disobedient, I hated holding him on a leash. The first few times I did nothing but running after him and despairing because he suddenly disappeared. It took me one year to find a tacit agreement with him: every time that I reached Villa Pamphili and Kilim was free to wander around, he had the permission to disappear. But he had to come back exactly where I left him in 2 h time.

Those endless hours were the occasion for me to enjoy the incredible nature surrounding me: to sense the wind blowing through the trees, to smell pollens in the air, to touch rough barks and humid grass, to hear colourful chirpings. In my little paradise I started feeling a close connection with mother earth. I used to wait for Kilim in a little spot and lay down, looking at the sky. The earth was beneath me. In those moments a strange short circuit was taking place: I was superimposing the love for my philosophy professor on that precious and magical embroidery of living nature. This fusion evoked Spinoza. I started perceiving a pantheistic sense of life. If God existed, he couldn't be confined in some transcendental world. He had to be *there*. In Villa Pamphili and in whatever I was sensing in my blessed spot. I started breathing the immanence of something sacred in nature. I started feeling a sense of belonging. I was part of that nature. Immanence and pantheism became my two main references.[1]

At that moment I had to choose which University I wanted to go to. I wanted that choice to reflect the deep sensations I was living. Spinoza and Villa Pamphili were there to remind me that I should choose something connected with nature. I started looking at different Faculties and finally I decided: Environmental Engineering.

Naïvely, what attracted me was the adjective 'environmental'. Miserably, what I found was the noun 'engineering'. It was a hard discovery made of quadratic equations, thermodynamics laws, redox reactions, first derivatives, integration of rational functions, magnetic axis and asymptotic curves. A world of numbers and rigid laws that were waiting for uncritical application. That magical yet childish world vanished into a prison of quantities, structures and rigid formulae that suffocated me. I was very good at resolving all the mathematical problems, but I was not satisfied. I started hating Kilim.

The parliament of diverse selves which inhabited me at that time started shouting. One of the members of this tumultuous parliament planned a coup d'état. He couldn't stand being devoured by the aridity and the presumptuousness of numbers. This unruly parliamentarian wanted to save me and made me enroll in a School of Theatre. There I met Perla Peragallo: one of the most important landmarks of my formative journey.

Perla has been one of the most prominent figures in the Italian theatrical scene of the second half of the twentieth century. Together with Leo De Berardinis and Carmelo Bene, she led a revolutionary and transformative process of the very concept of theatre. In the 1970s, Perla was a true experimenter and a bold opponent of the official theatre. She nurtured an avant-garde artistic wave that ended up sweeping away the traditional and bourgeois products of that period. Together with her lifetime partner Leo, she started working in marginalized spaces where they performed the utopia of a *cognitive theatre*: a 'diagnostic' approach aimed at addressing the rottenness and the damages of the society. The reverberation of their performances was extraordinary. But their success risked absorbing them into the official theatre system. This is the reason why they left Rome and founded the so-called 'Teatro di Marigliano' in the neglected hinterland of Naples. Here the couple succeeded in intermingling with the local subproletariat who became the main characters in their performances. Marigliano represented a gesture of artistic and political rebirth. A gesture of criticism of the status quo.

In their theatre, it was not only the contents that were revolutionary but also the languages and the new expressive codes. They succeeded in mixing fragments of popular narratives with educated quotations; dialects and invented languages; avant-garde jazz and Shakespearian fragments; Schönberg and poetical pieces from Rimbaud, Mayakovsky and Artaud. They used videos, which they personally edited in astonishing experimental and contemporary ways. They were musicians, actors and directors.

In 1979 Perla's mother died. That same year, Perla performed her last piece: Annabel Lee. She said, 'When theatre faces the real world, it is disillusioned. I came out from the coma where theatre imprisoned me. In the last performances, I couldn't abandon myself anymore. During Annabel Lee, I said: It is not fair that I fake. The circle is now closed'.

I never saw Perla on the stage. Except one time. A few minutes. If God existed, he was not in a transcendental world, nor in Villa Pamphili. He must have lived inside that visceral and primal energy which gushed out of her.

Years later, she founded a School of Theatre: 'Fiora's mill'.[2] This is the school that I attended to survive the suffocation of Engineering. And it was a transformative personal experience whose seeds are still growing inside me. Perla's maieutic[3] method invited us to give expression to our own inner world. In order to achieve this goal, she helped us with an involving and mind-blowing pedagogy. Every 2 months we had to prepare an 'invented scene'. We had to create a short theatrical piece from scratch. We had to write it. We had to organize the lighting, playing with a variety of stage floodlights, colours and atmospheres. We had to think about the music, selecting recorded pieces or inviting musicians to play on the stage. We had to invent the stage design, creating and reshaping the space with whatever was meaningful for our piece of work. We had to think about video projections, editing film clips, if we needed them. We had to act in this piece and be director at the same time: which meant selecting the other actors and guiding them. We had to concretize the suggestions we received from a parallel class of dance theatre. We could use and invent everything that was functional to our artistic project: water, fire, antiques, plastic, tents, masks, scents and costumes. We could overturn the stage/spectators space or definitively explode it into itinerant performatory events. We could select and build personal ways of communicating ourselves without being subordinated to any imposed rule. The only rules were to rigorously and skillfully assemble whatever we needed in order to expressively create and communicate our theatrical story.

In other words, we were encouraged to play with a wide range of skills, to contextually use multiple expressive languages, to think globally about an artistic gesture as the result of a sensitive dance of very different elements. A 'total work of art' which was able to incorporate diverse codes, semantics and representations. It was my first multimedia and storytelling experience. Perla tore aside a veil, creating a space for my creativity, empowering and enabling me to take full responsibility for my own creations.

I used to attend Engineering classes in the morning. After that, I used to go to Perla's theatre where I spent countless hours and sleepless nights working on my own creations. I experienced the fatigue and the beauty of it. That same period was also the most productive in terms of the excellent grades I was receiving at the University.

My parliament of selves was not frustrated anymore because each parliamentarian finally had his own space. At the same time, the items on my agenda began to appear really ambitious. How could I get those different selves together?

My Urban Planning PhD program was the opportunity to find a possible answer. But there was a further complication: another voice inside me was starting to think about social justice and it needed to be listened to. I started working on immigration issues but I found that the analytical tools that the urban planning discipline was providing were totally inadequate to properly address these complex phenomena. Objectifying cartographies and quantitative methods were not able to portray a conflicted, pulsating world (see Chapters 3 and 10). These analytical approaches were not able to capture the *pluriverses* of irreducible inhabitants characterized by relations, expectations, feelings, reminiscences, bodies, voices and stories which are stratified in living urbanities. Cartographies meticulously succeed in representing the silenced shapes of an objectified city, but they ignore life through space. They don't consider what is invisible, what loves hiding and elusively pulsates in the interstices of maps and of the morphological design of the city. Beyond what is already told and done. Beyond plans and cartographies.

I faced a crisis. The research exchange that my Department (Architecture and Urban Planning) was building with the Anthropology School of Bologna seemed to be a promising path to follow. Through that exchange, I progressively understood what I was looking for: a toolkit of methodologies and interpretative lenses which had already been explored and critically organized within the anthropological field: the biographical approach, ethnographic analysis, visual anthropology. A set of qualitative methods that I started to study in depth.

My PhD committee was deeply hostile. Most of the professors didn't like the content of my research. They thought that planners shouldn't try to address everything. And migrants were not part of their interest, their definition of planning. Moreover, they contested the analytical approach I was trying to follow. In their opinion, it was not getting me anywhere. This conflict was tough. But retrospectively it was fruitful. I spent a lot of time studying and trying to demonstrate to them that both contents and methodologies were not extraneous to our discipline. I had to find appropriate and persuasive arguments. I had to structure my research in a rigorous way. I had to immerse myself in the history of urban planning and analyze a variety of case studies which made me feel more secure: I was headed in a good direction, even if I was isolated.

The seeds Perla planted in me began germinating. My aversion for traditional planning tools was amplified by the consciousness that planning needed to expand the horizons of its language. My idea was that planners had to learn how to communicate in more deep and evocative ways. I thought that the aesthetics of planning's communicative dimension had to be expanded to reach wider audiences and to involve and engage people at more profound levels, using imaginative and poetical languages.

Digital languages helped me in achieving this goal. Together with the written PhD dissertation I started elaborating an interactive hypermedia. In this tool, textual language is substituted for, integrated with and expanded by a variety of other languages and expressive codes: texts, films, music, graphic animations, numbers, sounds, photographs. The mingling of these various languages offered the promise of accounting for the complexity of our cities, where the centrality of private memories, emotional dimensions, the meshing of intersecting spaces and lived times requires a plurality of representational grammars.

The hypermedia represented the perfect encounter of an academic research journey and the nourishment provided by the experimental and pluri-linguistic approach embedded in the theatre of Perla. The symbolic and metaphorical languages started intermingling with the rigorousness of the life stories I captured in the neighbourhood I was studying. The poetical gestures I used to create on the stage matched with the statistics I've been using in the hypermedia. The multiplication of expressive codes and the variety of skills I developed during my theatrical experience were applied in the representation of the migrants' city.

But again this expressive urgency seemed a little too unconventional in the eyes of my PhD committee.

In 2001, I attended the INURA[4] conference in Florence. I showed a part of the hypermedia I was working on. And there happened another of those encounters which profoundly affected my life. Leonie was there. She saw my work. I was intimidated by her reputation. I had read her books. I knew her work. She is a well-known international scholar. At that time I was just a shy PhD student who could barely speak a word of English. Unexpectedly our paths intersected. And we recognized each other. We were interested in the same research topics, and she was impressed by the storytelling potentialities that my hypermedia had shown. We talked. I was happy because I felt that I was no longer alone. There was someone else in the world who was on my same wavelength. This encounter gave me the energy to accomplish my research goals, to face my PhD committee with greater confidence.

In the same period that I was finishing my hypermedia, I heard that Leonie was in Bari for a conference. It is not my nature to advertise myself. I fought with me (always the same parliament) and I decided to send her a copy of this digital product. That was THE moment. Leonie saw it and asked me to come to Vancouver as a postdoctoral fellow. It was 2004. Since then, we have been synergistically working together on projects which enhance storytelling potentialities through the use of digital languages within the planning field. We are a perfect working team, with shared values and curiosity, and with complementary skills. Since then Leonie has been nurturing what Perla had sown. She is not just watering that farmed field. She has the constant capability to fill my life and my research path with luminous epiphanies. Our encounter gave me the opportunity to explore and experiment. The most beautiful thing I could have ever asked for.

Most of my students think I'm a sort of architect/anthropologist/artist and are completely astonished in discovering that I'm an engineer. I confess I'm quite proud of that. Not that I think engineers are bad people. But the rigidity and violent oppression I felt when I was a student of Engineering created this prejudice in me. At the same time I have another confession to make. I'm happy to have chosen Engineering and I thank Kilim for that. Without Engineering I would have not felt the urgency to nurture other parts of me. I would have not met Perla. I would have not embraced the path which led me to Leonie.

I will always be thankful to those lighthouses I met in my life. They showed me a way, illuminating and nourishing who I was. And am.

Notes

1. If now I look back at that shy teenager and his naive discovery, I feel the nostalgia of his disenchanted and magical view of the world. What would he have thought of me today?
2. Fiora is Perla's mother. She owned a mill. After her death, Perla sold the mill to build her new Theatre School.
3. Perla used the word 'maieutic' the first time we met. She referred to the Socratic maieutic art (Gk. *maieutikos*, of midwifery), which solicits and helps people to express a knowledge they already have, to give birth to what is already present within themselves. It is a facilitation process aimed at self-educating people.
4. International Network for Urban Research and Action.

References

Mayakovsky, V. (1925). Conversation with a tax collector about poetry. In P. Blake (Ed.), (1960) *The bedbug and selected poetry of Vladimir Mayakovsky*. Bloomington, IN: Indiana University Press.

Sandercock, L. (1992). *Captive. ABC TV movie of the week*. Produced by Ten Four Productions, distributed by Disney.

Sandercock, L. (2003). *Cosmopolis 2: Mongrel cities of the 21st Century*. London: Continuum.

Sayles, J. (1987). *Thinking in pictures: The making of the movie Matewan*. Boston: Houghton Mifflin Company.

Vancouver, BC, Canada   Leonie Sandercock
Via Eudossiana, Rome, Italy   Giovanni Attili

Contents

Contributors

Giovanni Attili
Dipartimento di Architettura e Urbanistica per l'Ingegneria
Università "La Sapienza" di Roma, Roma, Italy
giovanni.attili@gmail.com

Giovanni Attili obtained his master's degree in environmental engineering (summa cum laude) and his PhD from the University of Rome, La Sapienza, in 2003. He has been a researcher in the same Department as well as a Postdoctoral Fellow in the School of Community & Regional Planning at the University of British Columbia. He works with Leonie Sandercock on documentaries about planning issues and is co-author with Leonie Sandercock of the book and DVD package Where strangers become neighbours: the integration of immigrants in Vancouver, Canada *(2009).*

Sheri Blake
University of Manitoba, Winnipeg, MB, Canada
blakes@cc.umanitoba.ca

Sheri Blake was educated at the Universities of Waterloo, Canada, and Tokyo, Japan (D. Eng. (Arch) 1995). She has taught at Temple University Tokyo and is currently a professor in the Department of City Planning at the University of Manitoba. In addition to teaching planning and design studios and theory courses, she provides technical assistance to non-profit community development initiatives in Winnipeg's inner city. Her research focuses on the role of citizen participation and the development of documentary films as tools for literacy building among planners, designers and local residents to engage more effectively and collaboratively.

Leonardo Ciacci
Department of Town Planning, University IUAV of Venice, Venice, Italy
ciacci@iuav.it

Leonardo Ciacci is Associate Professor of Town Planning and Theories of Town Planning at the Faculty of Architecture of Venice. His research works are focused on filmed representation and communication of town planning projects; he is author of some video products on planning items. He is scientific curator of the Videoteca IUAV and the editor of "Archive Movies" in «<http://www.planum.net/>www.Planum.net»

Anuttama Dasgupta
Urban Design and Planning Consultant
Cherokee Dr, Richardson, TX, USA
anudg94@gmail.com

Anuttama Dasgupta earned her bachelor's degree in architecture in 1999 from the Birla Institute of Technology and practiced 6 years in the south Indian city of Chennai where she worked with DakshinaChitra, a museum of the traditional arts and architecture of South India. She earned her masters degree in Urban Planning from the University of Illinois in 2007, winning the AICP Outstanding Graduate Student Award. She lives in Dallas, pursuing a career in planning and urban design.

Lidia Decandia
Department of Architecture and Planning
University of Sassari, Alghero, SS, Italy
decandia@uniss.it

Lidia Decandia is Associate Professor of Urban Planning at the Architecture Faculty of the University of Sassari where she coordinates the group of courses, "Planning in the Social Context" and teaches Regional Planning and Urban and Regional History. In the same Faculty she founded and is in charge of "Matrica: a laboratory of urban fermentation." She is part of the Urban Planning PhD committee at the University La Sapienza of Rome. Her most recent publication is Polifonie urbane. Oltre i confini della visione prospettica *(2008).*

Michael Q. Dudley
Institute of Urban Studies, University of Winnipeg
Winnipeg, MB, Canada
m.dudley@uwinnipeg.ca

Michael Q Dudley holds masters degrees in Library and Information Studies (1993) and City Planning (2001). He has taught environmental and urban studies at the University of Winnipeg and environmental design and city planning at the University of Manitoba. Since 2001, he has been a Research Associate and Library Coordinator at the Institute of Urban Studies.

Penny Gurstein
School of Community and Regional Planning
University of British Columbia, Vancouver, BC, Canada
gurstein@interchange.ubc.ca

Penny Gurstein is a Professor and Director of the School of Community and Regional Planning at UBC. She obtained her PhD from UC Berkeley (1990). She specializes in the socio-cultural aspects of community planning with particular emphasis on those who are the most marginalized in planning processes. She also produces documentaries and researches multimedia as a tool for social learning.

Jessica Hallenbeck
Ear to the Ground Planning, Vancouver, BC, Canada
jessica@eartotheground.ca

Jessica Hallenbeck is a Project Manager at Ear to the Ground Planning, a Vancouver-based planning firm that specializes in using multimedia to enable positive social change. Jessica's areas of focus include participatory planning, youth engagement and First Nations planning. Jessica holds a Bachelor's from Queen's University in Film Studies, and master's degree in Planning from the University of British Columbia.

Susy Hemphill
Department of Urban and Regional Planning
University of Illinois, Champaign, IL, USA
hemphil1@illinois.edu

Susy Hemphill is pursuing a Masters in Urban Planning at the University of Illinois. She earned both a Bachelor of Arts in women's studies and a Bachelor of Business Administration in economics from the University of Iowa. At Illinois, she is a community liaison in the East St. Louis Action Research Project.

Andrew Isserman
Department of Urban and Regional Planning
University of Illinois, Champaign, IL, USA
isserman@illinois.edu

Andrew Isserman is professor of regional economics, planning and public affairs at the University of Illinois. His current research focuses on federal programme analysis and place policies, what makes prosperous places and effective storytelling for planning analysis and engaging the future. He has received two National Planning Awards from the American Planning Association. He earned a B.A. in economics from Amherst College and an MS in economics and PhD in City and Regional Planning from the University of Pennsylvania.

Mallory Rahe
Department of Agricultural and Resource Economics
Oregon State University, Corvallis, OR, USA
mallory.rahe@oregonstate.edu

Mallory Rahe was raised on a small farm in central Illinois and earned a masters degree in agricultural economics from the University of Illinois in 2009. In 2008 she won the AICP Outstanding Graduate Student Award. She is doing fieldwork on the links between community engagement and economic outcomes for her doctoral dissertation in Regional Planning.

Elihu Rubin
Yale School of Architecture, 180 York Street
New Haven, CT 06511, USA
elihu.rubin@yale.edu

Elihu Rubin is an architectural historian, city planner and documentary filmmaker based in Brooklyn and New Haven. Since 2007 he has served as the Daniel Rose Visiting Assistant

Professor of Urbanism at the Yale School of Architecture. He received a PhD in Architecture and a master's in City Planning, both from the University of California, Berkeley, and a BA from Yale. His documentary films include On Broadway: A New Haven Streetscape *and* Rudolph and Renewal.

Leonie Sandercock
School of Community and Regional Planning
The University of British Columbia, Vancouver, BC, Canada
leonies@interchange.ubc.ca

Leonie Sandercock is a Professor in the School of Community & Regional Planning at the University of British Columbia where she teaches planning theory and history, and cross-cultural planning. She has published eleven books, written one produced feature film and is working with Giovanni Attili on their second documentary film. Her research is now focusing on multimedia, storytelling and planning.

Wendy Sarkissian
Sarkissian Associates Planners P/L, Nimbin, NSW, Australia
wendy@sarkissian.com.au

Wendy Sarkissian seeks spirited ways to nurture an engaged citizenry. Initially trained as an educator, she holds a Masters of Arts in literature, a Masters of Town Planning and a PhD in environmental ethics. She has pioneered innovative planning and development approaches in a wide variety of contexts. Her most recent publication is Kitchen Table Sustainability; Practical Recipes for Community Engagement with Sustainability *(2008).*

Jacob A. Wagner
Department of Architecture, Urban Planning and Design
University of Missouri-Kansas City, Kansas City, MO, USA
wagnerjaco@umkc.edu

Jacob A. Wagner is an assistant professor of Urban Planning and Design at the University of Missouri-Kansas City. His research focuses on cultural heritage, place identity and partici-patory design processes in the recovery of urban neighborhoods in New Orleans and Kansas City. Through his teaching and scholarship, he seeks to create more sustainable commu-nities that are connected to a deep understanding of place, public memory and the urban environment.

Multimedia, Policy and Planning: New Tools for Urban Interventions

Leonie Sandercock

In 1882, Edwin Abbott wrote *Flatland*, a novel about an imaginary two-dimensional reality: a completely level world, a vast sheet of paper in which houses, inhabitants and trees are straight lines, triangles, polygons and other geometric figures. Through a compelling narrative, Abbott invents a place and fills it with entities characterized by abstract and linear contours. These figures move freely on a surface, but without the capacity to rise above or sink below it. In this imagined world nobody has the perception of a third dimension until a sphere enters this space, and the plot thickens (see Chapter 3).

There is an interesting analogy between the level world invented by Abbott and the representations of urban space which are traditionally produced in the urban planning field, where a sort of cartographic anxiety (akin to the Cartesian anxiety known to philosophers) converts the city into a two-dimensional surface intersected by lines, partitioned by geometries and filled with homogenous colours. These stylized grammars flatten urbanity as lived and experienced into an isotropic and gridded space. As in Abbott's novel, cartographies are overfilled with geometrically detailed, yet dimensionally limited languages. A bird's eye perspective captures the physical shape of the city and projects it onto graphed surfaces according to a logic which gives sense only to those aspects of urban life which can be expressed in this kind of legible shape, within a visible and two-dimensional rendering. The city is sterilized, frozen, vivisected and objectified through quantitative lenses and panoptic and standardizing views: tools which have become essential to the administering of the modern state (Scott, 1998). Like *Flatland*, the mapped and measured city lacks *other* dimensions. What is missing from these urban planning cartographies are the plural worlds and multiple stories of irreducible inhabitants whose lives are characterized by relations, expectations, feelings, reminiscences, bodies, voices and histories, all layered into living urbanities. Traditional planning cartographies do not, and cannot, represent what is invisible, what is hiding and yet elusively pulsating in the interstices of maps and of the morphological design of the city.

Thus we feel an urgency to invent new descriptive and analytical tools which can give centrality to people, focusing on the individual and collective practices through which inhabitants create their own meaningful living environments. It is important to find a dense way to read a relational space which connects different situated and embodied subjectivities. In finding ways of doing this, we are not denying the relevance of the physical, morphological dimensions of the city. But we want to emphasize the importance of an expressive and analytical path which can intersect and connect physical and relational spaces and challenge conventional modes of spatial thinking, transcending the *flatlands* that traditionally permeate our disciplinary field and expanding the languages available to us. We want to create tools which not only capture everyday experiences but which also give citizens more opportunities to participate in conversations about the city and to shape their own life spaces.

This book explores the potential applications of multimedia – the combination of multiple contents (both traditional and digital: texts, still images, animations, audio and video productions) and interactive platforms (offline interactive CD-ROMs, online websites and forums, digital environments) – in the urban policy and planning fields. This is an epistemological, historical, pragmatic and pedagogic exploration, probing the capacities of multimedia as a mode of inquiry, as a form of meaning making, as a tool of community engagement and as a catalyst for public policy dialogues. This is not a totally new epistemological excavation. What is new are the tools that we are exploring.

The beginning of an epistemological shift in the field of planning was foreshadowed in the early 1970s in the works of Churchman (1971) and Friedmann (1973). Friedmann outlined a 'crisis of knowing' in which he skewered the limitations of 'expert knowledge' and advocated a new approach which he called 'mutual learning' or 'transactive planning', an approach which could appreciate and draw on local and experiential knowledge in dialogue with expert knowledge. At the same time, Churchman's inquiry into knowing was exploring the value of stories. 'The Hegelian inquirer is a storyteller, and Hegel's Thesis is that the best inquiry is the inquiry that produces stories' (Churchman, 1971, p. 178). Over the next several decades, the termites kept eating away at the Enlightenment foundations of modernist planning, anchored as it was in an epistemology that privileged scientific and technical ways of knowing. Accompanying a broader post-positivist movement in the social sciences (Stretton, 1969; Geertz, 1983; Rabinow & Sullivan, 1987; Bourdieu, 1990; Flyvbjerg, 2002), pushed further along by feminist and postcolonial critiques (Said, 1979; Hooks, 1984; Kelly, 1984; Trinh, 1989; Lerner, 1997; Sandercock, 1998), planning scholars have begun to see the need both for an expanded language for planning and for ways of expanding the creative capacities of planners (Landry, 2000, 2006; Sandercock, 2005a, 2005b; Sarkissian & Hurford, 2010) by acknowledging and using the many other ways of knowing that exist: experiential, intuitive and somatic knowledges; local knowledges; knowledges based on the practices of talking and listening, seeing, contemplating and sharing; and knowledges expressed in visual, symbolic, ritual and other artistic ways.

The 'story turn' in planning (Chapter 2) has been one response to this epistemological crisis. In the past two decades a growing number of planning scholars have been investigating the relationship between story and planning (Forester, 1989; Mandelbaum, 1991; Marris, 1997; Sandercock, 1998, 2003; Eckstein & Throgmorton, 2003; Attili, 2007). These investigations highlight how planning is performed through stories, how rhetoric and poetics are crucial in interactive processes, how the communicative dimension is central to planning practices and how stories can awaken energies and imaginations, becoming a catalyst for involving urban conversations, for deep community dialogues.

This epistemological shift in planning emphasizes the need for an expanded language for planning; necessarily encourages the creative capacities of planners; and foregrounds the value of story and storytelling in planning practice (Sandercock, 1998, 2003, 2005a, 2005b; Sarkissian, Stenberg, Hirst, & Walton, 2003; Attili, 2007). An 'epistemology of multiplicity' (Sandercock, 1998) would nurture these other ways of knowing without discarding or dismissing more traditional forms of scientific and technical reasoning.

In planning's post-World War II rush to join the social sciences (then dominated by the positivist paradigm), some of its capacity to address important urban issues was lost because it turned its back on questions of values, of meaning, and on the arts of interpretation and of place making. The intellectual and emotional universes of planning were thus choked and caged. The notion of an expanded language for planning is a way to blow open this cage and release the chokehold. Some scholars and practitioners have been searching for a language that can encompass the lived experience of our 'mongrel cities' (Sandercock, 2003): the joys, hopes, fears, the senses of loss, expectation, adventure (Sarkissian & Hurford, 2010). In this book, we explore ways for the urban professions (planners, architects, landscape architects and urban designers) to be more attuned to 'the city of spirit, the city of memory, and the city of desire' (Sandercock, 1998). These are what animate life in cities, and also animate the urban conflicts in which we as professionals are engaged. In the same vain, in stressing the importance of a creative sensibility as central to a planning imagination for the twenty-first century, various scholars and practitioners are seeking to make planning processes less constipated and more playful (Landry, 2000, 2006; Sandercock, 2005a; Sarkissian & Hurford, 2010).

This book explores the ways in which multimedia can advance all of these agendas, thus becoming 'a new frontier' in the policy and planning fields. Our contributors demonstrate the incredibly rich potential, through multimedia, for manifesting an epistemology of multiplicity, for providing multiple forms of voice and thus participation. There is great potential, too (in the form of persuasive storytelling) for stimulating dialogue, opening up a public conversation and influencing policy. There are diverse ways in which multimedia can nurture community engagement and community development, as well as oppositional forms of planning. Multimedia tools create the opportunity for urban researchers to discover new realities, to expand the horizons of both qualitative and quantitative research and to represent the city in multidimensional and polyphonic ways. And multimedia products can offer transformative learning experiences, 'educating the heart' through mobilizing a democracy of the senses. The chapter overviews that follow highlight what we regard as remarkable about the pioneering efforts we've assembled.

In Part I, we frame the subject of multimedia in relation to the urban field both historically and epistemologically as well as explaining the philosophy and methodology of digital ethnography. Leonardo Ciacci, a scholar of the uses of film since the 1920s in the planning field (Ciacci, 1997, 2002), provides an analytical and critical overview of the history of this relationship between cinema and planning. What his historical research uncovers is provocative. Ever since planners began to make films in 1928, films whose ostensible purpose was to contribute to debate within the field, usually on the occasion of a public exhibition for the circulation of ideas of resolving issues of urban change, their actual mission has been to persuade 'the public' of a particular planning scheme which has already been thought through and is being proposed as 'the solution' by the 'experts'. The documentaries in this body of work that Ciacci calls 'Town Planners' Cinema' adopted an approach to the story of the proposed plan that is deductive and presents the choices contained within the plan as proposals consistent with a correct reading of reality: 'a kind of filmed propaganda'. The composition of the discourse of these films was, at a more fundamental level, intended to convince 'the public' of the social duties and potential of town planning. In other words, the tools of cinema were in the service of a thoroughly modernist, expert-driven approach to place making and managing urban change. Ciacci cites examples from various countries (Germany, France, Italy, the United States) in support of this argument. And like all good historians, his final reflections concern the contemporary situation, and the ongoing question as to whether film necessarily serves the purposes of those in power or whether it may yet have the potential to extend participation in the project for urban change to the largest possible number of people. It is that very question which is addressed in each of the chapters in Part II.

Urbanist/academic and film maker Leonie Sandercock's contribution in Part I is an argument about the role of story (in its various forms) in planning. Stories are central to planning practice: to the knowledge it draws on from the social sciences and humanities, to the knowledge it produces about the city, to ways of acting in the city. Planning is *performed* through story, in a myriad of ways. And since storytelling has evolved from oral tales around a campfire to the technologically sophisticated forms of multimedia available in the early twenty-first century, it is surely time for the urban professions to appreciate the multifarious potential of these new media. All the more so since the planning and design fields have been forced by the demands of civil society to be more engaged with communities, more *communicative*. This chapter covers two issues: first, an unpacking of the many ways in which we use stories in planning and design: in process, as a catalyst for change, as a foundation, in policy, in pedagogy, in critique, as justification of the status quo, as identity and as experience. Second, a tracing of the evolution of storytelling techniques 'from the campfire to the computer', leading to the suggestion that multimedia is fast becoming the twenty-first century's favoured form of storytelling, and illustrating its many applications to the planning field.

Reaching into the epistemological heart of planning, Sandercock is always critically aware of the politics of knowing, the politics of voice and cautions that stories' ability 'to act as transformative agents depends on a disciplined scrutiny of their forms and uses' (Eckstein, 2003). We still need to question the truth of our own and others' stories. We need to be attentive to how power shapes which stories get told, get heard, carry weight. We need to understand the work that stories do, or rather that we ask them to do, in deploying them, and to recognize the moral ordering and value-driven motives involved in the conscious and unconscious use of certain plots and character types, as well as visual and representational aesthetics.

In the final essay in Part I, planning researcher and film maker Giovanni Attili poetically evokes the potential of what he calls 'digital ethnographies' to enhance qualitative research and practice in planning, offering a multidimensional and polyphonic antidote to planning's traditional cartographic and elite-controlled representations. Digital ethnographies offer an interconnected patchwork of evocative images imbued with ambiguity, creating a field of comprehension open to diverse interpretations and possibilities. This level of interpretive openness transforms ethnographies into possible catalysts for interaction inside planning processes. In other words, they represent a different way of provoking dialogue, suggestions and inclusiveness in decision-making contexts, a world away from the old 'Town Planners' Cinema'. It is a way of opening up a public conversation. Digital languages, Attili argues, strengthen the expressive possibilities of ethnographies, connecting a qualitative study of the city to the potentialities of deeply communicative languages. Digital ethnographies can be creative and delicate interventions that reveal meaning without seeking to define it: they embody a transition from rhetoric to poetics, a different form of meaning making, a capacity for arousing astonishment and fresh interrogation. As the fulcra of genuinely interactive events, digital ethnographies can be inserted in urban space through psycho-geographical projections on the faces of buildings, interactive installations or involving digital games.

The eight chapters in Part II describe and reflect on a variety of applications of multimedia, particularly documentary film and video, in planning practice and policy debates. This section opens with Leonie Sandercock's account of a 3-year, three-stage research and action project that began with the making of the film 'Where strangers become neighbours: the story of the Collingwood Neighbourhood House and the integration of immigrants in Vancouver' (Attili & Sandercock, 2007). The second stage involved the research and writing of a manual to accompany the film, for public education purposes, and a series of workshops in four Canadian cities which used the film as a catalyst for community dialogue. The third stage was the writing and preparation of a book/DVD package designed to make the Vancouver story a learning experience for cities and regions beyond Canada (Sandercock & Attili, 2009). The research began with the sociological and political questions: how do strangers become neighbours in a city which has been undergoing rapid transformation from a predominantly Anglo-European demographic to one in which immigrants whose first language is not English are now a demographic majority? How does a transition from fears and anxieties about immigrants to acceptance and integration come about, and how are conflicts managed? The film researched a specific neighbourhood in the City of Vancouver and focused on a specific local institution which has an inspiring story to tell. This chapter then assesses the effectiveness of film both as a mode of inquiry/social research and as a tool for social learning, community engagement and policy dialogue.

The planner's ability to produce compelling images of the city has been tightly bound with the profession's claim to 'expert' knowledge. From City Beautiful renderings of boulevards and civic centres to the most sophisticated GIS tools for mapping statistical information, the planner employs visual techniques to assert mastery over urban space (see also Attili, Chapter 3). Urbanist and videographer Elihu Rubin's chapter presents the process of video-making as a dynamic tool in a planning approach that is focused on engaging with the city's spaces and people rather than asserting dominance. Rubin describes video as an invitation to urban sociability and a means of producing qualitative (re)presentations of streets and other places. He argues that many of the planner's visual techniques are designed to *perceptually stabilize* the urban realm. But what if the city is not a stable entity? If this is true, *stable* images may actually serve to estrange the professional from the unsettled and contested social realities of the urban 'life-world.' In this frame-work, Rubin suggests that video-making can be a fruitful method of reasserting the primacy of the street and street-life itself.

Video is certainly not immune from a critique of visual methods as pos-itivist or objectifying, a theme elaborated upon in his paper. However, the planner-videographer may draw on the medium's representational strengths and the attributes of montage, to embrace and not to homogenize the disjointed and sometimes disorienting qualities of urban experience. Rubin's chapter first situ-ates video-making within a history of visual methods in planning practice. Then, drawing from his case study of transportation planning in Oakland, California, he proposes a model for using video as a form of engagement and documentation. This technique emphasizes the capacity of video to record both the fragmentary yet richly detailed urban 'moment' as well as interpersonal encounters. In fact, the video cam-era can sometimes act as a catalyst for otherwise unlikely encounters. Finally, he addresses the ethics of video-making and its public re-presentation, which demand a self-consciously reflexive approach; one which recognizes the complex issues of participation, authorship and patronage (a theme elaborated by Gurstein in the final chapter in Part II of this book).

Shifting from the use of video in a transportation planning investigation insti-gated by a state representative in Oakland, California, to the chaotic context of disaster recovery in New Orleans, planning academic Jacob Wagner's chapter explores the uses of digital communication tools to provide a forum for a critique of the state-driven recovery planning process. Specifically, his chapter documents the political dimensions of digital media and their uses in both the official and unofficial planning processes following Hurricane Katrina. In the absence of a well-organized state planning process, Wagner argues, the most significant aspect of the New Orleans experience has been 'the recovery activism and unofficial planning led by citizens' in what he describes as 'the most digitally mediated planning process to date'. He provides a staggering array of examples of the uses of digital media (for example, internet, websites, blogs, data bases, list serves, on-line surveys, mapping programmes and discussion groups), by individuals and groups, non-profit agencies and other advocacy groups, to communicate, critique, participate in and literally invent a disaster recovery process in the absence of adequate government or private sector responses. Wagner reveals two very different approaches to the use of digital media in the recovery process: those that were citizen-driven compared with those used in the official planning process. He then asks whether and how the use of these tools enhanced democratic planning. His chapter raises significant questions about the digital mediation of planning information (in particular, web-based tools) and highlights fundamental issues for planning theory and ethics regarding how digital media are employed and to what ends, whether such processes increase planning literacy and social learning among residents and whether digital communication tools have contributed to the empowerment of local citizens as they developed collective responses to the disaster.

Empowerment was an explicit theme in the decision to use video in a participatory planning exercise in the Downtown Eastside (DTES) of Vancouver, the most socially disadvantaged postal code in Canada. Planner/videographer Jessica Hallenbeck's chapter examines the relationships among the right to the city, social justice and video, using as an example a short film that was conceived as a participatory video project focusing on a particular street in the DTES. The video was a collaboration between students and street-oriented youth, intended to elicit residents' desires for this particular pivotal street (pivotal in the city planners' scheme), via a film-making process, and conveying those desires to city planners. And it was simultaneously an action research project *and* a vehicle for reflecting on the potential of video in contributing to social justice in the city. Hallenbeck's argument is that the right to the city starts with an imagining of the city in question being different from the *status quo* and that video can foster this essential act of imagining by engaging people in a dialogue over their rights to participation and to the appropriation of space. Hallenbeck's short film established a dialogue based on utopian imagining and visual appropriation and thereby can make a claim of contributing to the struggle for social justice. Nevertheless, Hallenbeck critically reflects on the shortcomings of this process and the broader implications for planning institutions as well as communities when it comes to incorporating video in urban governance structures.

The multiple-award-winning Australian social planner, Wendy Sarkissian, has been as pioneering in experimenting with the uses of video as she has been in so many other dimensions of planning practice (see Sarkissian, 2005, Sarkissian, Hofer, Shore, Wilkinson, & Vadja, 2008, Sarkissian & Hurford, 2010). Here she writes about her evolving experimentation since 1990, often in collaboration with community artist and activist Graeme Duncan, and the ways in which their work has been influenced by the theories and philosophies of Gregory Bateson (1972, 1979) and Jean Houston (1982, 1987). The various projects that she discusses, all for paying clients, have ranged from innovative approaches to community engagement with children to a flamboyant workshop (which she called 'The Gods Must Be Crazy') for a state road planning agency, from redesigning the foyer of a state library to a community cultural development project in a low-income neighbourhood, in which the videotaped record of the process reveals an epiphany of empowerment that words could not have expressed.

Architetto-urbanista and film maker Leonardo Ciacci reappears in this section to discuss a film that he made in 2000 as part of his research into regional change processes in the Veneto region of Italy. This film was commissioned by the Italian Association of Planners, for screening at their national conference in 2000, and was reproduced on VHS in a modest edition of 100 copies. The primary purpose of the film was to show the significant changes to the landscape of the Veneto region in north-east Italy in the previous decade. But this simple representation in turn had two larger ambitions: one was to demonstrate to town planners the importance of taking care of physical changes and not only of the administrative conditions of planning, and the other was to raise public awareness and focus attention on the importance of what was happening outside the city (in its traditional sense), to highlight a collective, implicit spontaneous project of a regional urbanizing environment.

Using the making of the film initially as part of a research process produced surprising results, revealing a different and more complex reality than what was apparently known. Ciacci envisages film as an instrument in planning practice and this indeed became reality with 'The countryside that becomes metropolis'. The film held up a mirror to the planners and politicians as well as inhabitants of the region and resulted in expanding circles of public dialogue. As evidence of this, in 2004, the administrative office of the regional government of the Veneto commissioned a new edition of the film, with a new introduction, for distribution among local politicians and the general public. For this second edition of the film, 5000 DVD copies were made, indicative of the film's success in generating awareness and dialogue among urbanists as well as between urbanists and politicians and inhabitants. The language of film, Ciacci argues, can be non-didactic, non-demonizing, telling a story through which people are able to see things in a new way, construct new meanings and interpretations of what is in front of them, perceive changes that they themselves are creating (through their individual decisions, which are not necessarily in the collective interest) and to reflect on the desirability and consequences of those changes. This chapter is a revealing account of how film is indeed a research tool through which we can come to see things in new ways, as well as a tool for informing and communication.

In the penultimate chapter in this section, Giovanni Attili discusses an experiment in hypermedia,[1] working in a particularly complex neighbourhood of Rome: the Esquilino district. This neighbourhood is widely recognized as the most culturally diverse area of the city. It is characterized by a significant presence of immigrants (newcomers who plan to settle down in this part of the city) and transitory migrants: people who don't have fixed addresses and live in the district on a temporary basis. Attili focuses on these transient inhabitants who have progressively transformed the Esquilino into a *caravanserai*: a crossroad of different migratory projects; a crucial junction that is part of an intricate erratic geography; the stratification of different *circulatory territories* produced by the collective memory; and the social exchange practices of migrant populations.

Attili's representational experiment aims at portraying this pulsating landscape, transgressing traditional urban planning analysis which has always been focused on permanencies, persistencies and fixity of contexts (see also Rubin, Chapter 5). Adopting a wide range of analytical tools (mainly qualitative), Attili succeeded in getting in touch with these populations who would not have been reached through the traditional panoptic and morphological analysis. Moreover, he assembled a multilayered representation of the district (its social and political dimensions) using the tools of hypermedia, a versatile and interactive mechanism, constructed at the point of intersection and hybridization between different languages: texts, films, graphic animations, statistics, sounds, moving maps and photographs. Attili's intention, in mixing these multiple languages, is a richer portrayal of the multifaceted nature of our cities. He argues that the collective practices, the self-centred nature of private memories, the emotional dimensions, and the fusion of spaces crossed and time experienced demand pluralistic codes of expression. The hypermedia is the space where these different codes and analytical approaches can find their expressive dimension. It is a representational space which can be explored in non-linear ways: choosing knowledge paths according to the interests of the user. These characteristics transform this hypermedia, made of provocative images and stories, into a tool which can potentially activate an urban dialogue: the incubator of an involving conversation on our 'mongrel cities' (Sandercock, 2003).

Architect/planner/film producer Penny Gurstein's chapter appropriately closes this section of the book with an overview, a number of cautions and a recommendation about the centrality of reflexivity in the use of multimedia in planning. In her overview, Gurstein cites specific examples of the positive contributions of multimedia: from opportunities for social learning and community empowerment to an enhanced understanding of place; from the uncovering of countervailing stories that challenge dominant discourses to critical and interpretive forms of policy analysis; and in fostering better community development and planning through the creation and use of new forms of knowledge. Gurstein leads us through some practical examples of multimedia as a change agent, before posing the second big issue: what are the limitations of multimedia in generating change and is there a potential 'dark side'? While there is no doubt about the power of multimedia to shape the communication of ideas and visions, that power comes with multiple dangers, which leads Gurstein into an analysis of the power relations that impact the production and use of multimedia. Her own normative framework is grounded in the central importance of dialogue and reflexivity in planning processes. Given that framework, she argues that if multimedia is to be effective as a change agent, its use must be integrated within agreed-upon protocols and processes that allow opportunity for mutual trust, and a commitment from stakeholders not only to engage in meaningful dialogue but also to act on its outcome. Her chapter is an important reminder of the power relations always already embedded in multimedia and therefore the importance of a reflexive and ethically driven approach to its use. These crucial issues will be taken up again by the editors in the concluding chapter.

All four contributors in Part III have been exploring the diverse ways in which multimedia might enrich teaching, through the use of film and other digital technologies. While three of these chapters share their experiences in working with planning and design students, designer/planner/academic and film maker Sheri Blake has targeted design practitioners as her audience. Her normative mission is the democratizing of place making through participatory design. Through film, she hopes to reach design professionals and change design practices. Her account of the making of her film, 'Detroit Collaborative Design Center... amplifying the diminished voice', is a beautiful example of what Gurstein is calling for in Chapter 9: a reflexive approach to film making and to planning methodology. Blake tells us of the initial negative reaction from design professionals in rough cut screenings of her story of the work of the Detroit Collaborative Design Center's inspiring participatory design practice. Architects, in particular, became highly defensive about the critique of traditional design practice (the Howard Roark approach) that initially occupied the first 10 min of the film, and as a result they shut themselves down to the rest of the film. After testing the film with a range of audiences, and thinking especially about her target audience of architects, Blake reconfigured the film in such a way as to seduce rather than alienate architects. Exactly how she re-thought her approach becomes a fascinating account of a film maker's reflexive attention to the question of audience and contains important lessons not only for film makers but also for would-be urban reformers. Blake describes her own learning about the education of planners/designers through this film-making process thanks to the feedback she received from practitioners, and she ends on a note of caution about the use of film, reminding us that it is just one mode of education and communication, and needs to be combined thoughtfully with other modes. Along the way, we learn a lot about the complexity of participatory design through reading her chapter.

Lidia Decandia teaches regional planning, in its social context, in the Faculty of Architecture in Alghero, Sardinia. Her chapter describes a deeply thoughtful approach to teaching territorial analysis, based on Dewey's 'learning by doing' and, more specifically, requiring of her students a full sensory immersion in the local field work context. She asks her students to become 'pilgrims', taking a metaphorical journey on foot, with many pauses for refreshment (of mind, body and spirit) and reflection. She demands no less than an existential encounter with territories, their inhabitants and the emotions and passions of those inhabitants. In an extension of the metaphor of travel, Decandia acknowledges the importance of a map, for new exploration, and a suitcase of tools. Her maps include some of the historic thought in our field, from Geddes to Kropotkin, and her tools include the traditional forms of analysis in planning, but above all, she seeks to transgress these more Cartesian, cartographic, linear and two-dimensional tools, enhancing them with digital technologies. In a very poetic essay (translated by Giovanni Attili), Decandia evokes the potential of digital languages to create involving situations and environments in which it is possible to produce vital and expressive knowledges that are intended as sensory resources, generating energy and motivation. These digital technologies, she argues, play a crucial role in two specific moments: when students start on their own pilgrim's journey and then, when they need to tell the story of that experience, at which point the digital tools will enable them to assemble and interconnect diverse languages and a wide variety of expressive codes (such as texts, films, graphic animations, statistics, sounds, cartographies, contemporary and historical images) through which they can give expression to their own creativity.

Decandia's text is a rich description of an immersive teaching/research process in a regional social context. The images which parallel her text tell their own story of one such course, which investigated the ancient village of Santu Lussurgiu in central Sardinia. Here is an elegant example of what Attili is proposing in Chapter 3, that digital representations are able to transgress the perspectival and cartographic views that have dominated our discipline (the flatlands), making walls and stones speak, giving life to monuments and signs which can no longer be verbally interrogated, emitting germinative energies and destabilizing the most familiar assumptions in our field. The challenge is to replace the supremacy of intellectual and rational learning with a learning based on the five senses, based on the consciousness that the communicative function of aesthetic pleasure is a crucial moment of every learning process.

The final two chapters in this section are written by planning educators with quite different backgrounds (economics and city planning) who both use mainstream feature films in the classroom to connect theory with practice and individual student life experiences with larger questions of justice, ethics, belonging and place making. Michael Dudley uses films in a required undergraduate theory course in environmental design for student designers and planners. Faced with the challenge of teaching abstract theoretical concepts of environmental psychology (human–environment transactions) to design students who are primarily visual thinkers, Dudley came up with an ingenious solution. He matched a selection of popular feature films with appropriate readings from environmental psychology and asked students to identify the concepts from the literature in the films. His chapter describes how what started as an experimental assignment ultimately became the core of the course, appealing to the students' visual orientation and allowing them to assimilate and apply environment and behaviour research theory in creative ways. The chapter first outlines the body of knowledge that goes under the label 'environment and behaviour research' (EBR), explaining why this constitutes an important component of planning knowledge. The goal of the course is to locate in the films and in the associated EBR readings insights into the meaning of place and the process of place making, drawing on cinema's power to metaphorically understand or represent the human condition. Drawing also on film theory, and making connections between film theory and environmental psychology, Dudley understands that film can render visible what we did not see before its advent. Or, as Kracauer put it, film 'effectively assists us in discovering the material world and its psychophysical correspondences' (Kracauer, 1960, p. 300). Audiences negotiate meaning in a film, just as the inhabitants of a place negotiate meaning in and through the built environment. The balance of Dudley's chapter takes us into the classroom, into some of the 'texts' being explored (EBR theory goes to the movies), and uses quotes from student assignments to demonstrate the insights generated through this approach to learning. Interestingly, the immediacy and immersive nature of cinema provides a similar learning experience to that which Decandia is aiming for in her 'pilgrim's journey' of knowledge through local field work: new ways of yielding profound insights for planning scholarship, education, and practice.

Another extraordinary teacher, Andrew Isserman, an economist teaching planners, pulls off an engaging experiment in his contribution. Isserman teaches a course on 'US Cultures and Economies' by screening two feature films each week and then discussing them with his students in ways that connect with profound issues of race and class, heritage and identity, belonging and alienation. Isserman throws down as a gauntlet at the start of the course the words of Robert Frost:

> Tell us something so stinging real that we wouldn't think you'd dare to tell it... Tell us something about your life and surroundings that no newspaper man could imagine – that I couldn't imagine. Inside stuff (Frost, 1933, quoted in Chapter 15).

The intent is that through the films, and the essays and discussions about those films, students learn about the United States, about themselves and their values, and through this process, become more complete human beings, better writers and better planners. Instead of telling us himself what this course achieves, Isserman shows us, by inviting three students to write about their learning experience. Anuttama Dasgupta, Mallory Rahe and Susy Hemphill then take us on their own 'pilgrim's journeys', as Decandia would describe it, sharing their insights into what they got out of taking 'a film watching course with a professor of economics instead of something more practical that I could apply to my future planning career'. Films such as 'Powwow Highway', 'The Namesake', 'Country', 'Boyz n the hood' and 'North Country' became catalysts for explorations and discoveries of a sense of pride in a lost heritage, an outsider's lifelong quest for a sense of belonging, claiming the right to take the road less travelled, developing an empathy for that which appears strange and recognizing that 'we are all in the company of strangeness'. They discovered themselves and their values and what they wanted to fight for. Above all, they discovered story: the power of stories and why planners need storytelling.

Watching movies, and reading and writing stories inspired by those movies, ultimately enabled these students to learn how much is missing from traditional planning documents and processes. Personal stories became connected with federal policies and policy failings. People, their dreams, hopes, fears, were brought back into the centre of planning education.

> I thought of the data tables I worked with in my planning courses and how each number in a column was made up of living, breathing people that I would never meet or who would pass me by indifferently on a bus. The characters that we so deeply identify with or empathize with on a screen would go unnoticed if we happened to pass them on the street, given our tendency to generalize, label and negate individuals (Dasgupta, Chapter 15).

In their search for the 'stinging real', and ways to write about it, via film watching, these students received something of the same intense planning education that Decandia outlines in her chapter: where the emphasis is put not only on the world of ideas but also on relationships between people, unique concrete individuals with stories and bodies, subjects who are able to think and to feel emotions at the same time. There is no better way to describe this than *educating the heart*.

In a revelatory and rewarding final section of this chapter, Andy Isserman's own journey unfolds, from regional economist teaching methods and policy to planning students, to something like life coach or mentor, eliciting more than creative writing from planning students. 'What I do might look like editing, but really I am helping the self-discovery process'. But Isserman's learning has been palpable too, as we glean from his own 'stinging real' account. He too has been captivated, and brought more alive, by the power of storytelling. In the process of creating this safe space of self-discovery for his students, he has also enabled his own soul to grow.

This book reflects the way that the editors' intersecting personal journeys in the planning field evolved into a search for a network of like-minded multimedia enthusiasts: folks committed to the urban planning field yet dissatisfied both with the traditional ways of researching and representing the city *and* with the processes and opportunities available to citizens to shape their own living conditions. It unabashedly reflects our own and others' excitement about the ways in which multimedia can be used by activists, NGOs, immigrant and indigenous communities, planning scholars and educators, wherever urban policies and planning strategies are being debated and communities are struggling to shape, improve or protect their life spaces. The book is an exploration of a new frontier in the urban planning and policy fields, a frontier 'beyond the flatlands'. It reveals a new set of tools and diverse ways to use them. But it goes beyond enthusiasm for the new, incorporating a critical stance about the power relations embedded in these new information and communication technologies as well as the limitations of each of the applications we discuss.

So, by the end of this, our pilgrim's journey in the exploration of multimedia in urban policy and planning, we have not produced a new 'atlas' for twenty-first century urbanists. Rather, in our concluding chapter, we reflect on the rewards and risks of this infant forum and its capacity, among other things, to enable us to think with all of our senses.

Note

1. 'Hypermedia' is a digital and interactive tool that can host and connect different languages and expressive codes. Users/viewers can navigate through the hypermedia in non-linear ways, according to their own interests.

References

Attili, G. (2007). Digital ethnographies in the planning field. *Planning Theory and Practice, 8*(1), 90–97.

Attili, G., & Sandercock, L. (2007). *Where strangers become neighbours: the story of the Collingwood Neighbourhood House and the integration of immigrants in Vancouver* (*50 minute documentary*). Montreal, QC: National Film Board of Canada.

Bateson, G. (1972). *Steps to an ecology of mind*. New York: Ballantine Books.

Bateson, G. (1979). *Mind and nature*. Toronto, ON: Bantam Books.

Bourdieu, P. (1990). *In other words: Essays towards a reflexive sociology*. Cambridge: Polity Press.

Churchman, C. W. (1971). *The design of inquiring systems*. New York: Basic Books.

Ciacci, L. (Ed.). (1997). *Il Cinema degli Urbanisti* (Vol. 1). Modena, Italy: Comune di Modena.

Ciacci, L. (Ed.). (2002). *Il Cinema degli Urbanisti* (Vol. 2). Modena, Italy: Comune di Modena.

Eckstein, B. (2003). Making space: Stories in the practice of planning. In B. Eckstein & J. Throgmorton (Eds.), *Story and sustainability: Planning, practice, and possibility for American cities*. Cambridge, MA: MIT Press.

Eckstein, B., & Throgmorton, J. (Eds.). (2003). *Story and sustainability*. Cambridge, MA: MIT Press.

Flyvbjerg, B. (2002). *Making social science matter*. Cambridge, UK: Cambridge University Press.

Forester, J. (1989). *Planning in the face of power*. Berkeley, CA: University of California Press.

Friedmann, J. (1973). *Retracking America*. New York: Doubleday Anchor.

Frost, R. (1933). *Letter to Hugh Saglio in "Your success is my success" Robert Frost to Hugh Saglio*. Amherst, MA: The Friends of the Amherst College Library (2004).

Geertz, C. (1983). *Local knowledge: Further essays in interpretive anthropology*. New York: Basic Books.

Hooks, B. (1984). *Feminist theory: From margin to center*. Boston: South End Press.

Houston, J. (1982). *The possible human*. Los Angeles: JP Tarcher.

Houston, J. (1987). *The search for the beloved: Journeys in sacred psychology*. Los Angeles: JP Tarcher.

Kelly, J. G. (1984). *Women, history, and theory*. Chicago: University of Chicago Press.

Kracauer, S. (1960). *Theory of film: The redemption of physical reality*. Oxford: Oxford University Press.

Landry, C. (2000). *The creative city*. London: Earthscan.

Landry, C. (2006). *The art of city making*. London: Earthscan.

Lerner, G. (1997). *Why history matters*. Oxford: Oxford University Press.

Mandelbaum, S. (1991). Telling stories. *Journal of Planning Education and Research, 10*(1), 209–214.

Marris, P. (1997). *Witnesses, engineers, and storytellers: Using research for social policy and action*. Maryland: University of Maryland, Urban Studies and Planning Program.

Rabinow, P., & Sullivan, W. M. (Eds.). (1987). *Interpretive social science: A second look*. Berkeley, CA: University of California Press.

Said, E. (1979). *Orientalism*. Vantage Books, New York.

Sandercock, L. (1998). *Towards cosmopolis: Planning for multicultural cities*. Chichester: Wiley.

Sandercock, L. (2003). *Cosmopolis 2: Mongrel cities of the 21st Century*. London: Continuum.

Sandercock, L. (2005a). A planning imagination for the 21st century. *Journal of the American Planning Association, 70*(2), 133–141.

Sandercock, L. (2005b). A new spin on the creative city: Artist/Planner collaborations. *Planning Theory and Practice, 6*(1), 101–103.

Sandercock, L., Attili, G., Cavers, V., & Carr, P. (2009). *Where strangers become neighbours: The integration of immigrants in Vancouver, Canada*. Dordrecht, The Netherlands: Springer.

Sarkissian, W. (2005). Stories in a park: Giving voice to the voiceless in Eagleby, Australia. *Planning Theory and Practice, 6*(1), 103–117.

Sarkissian, W., Hofer, N., Shore, Y., Wilkinson, C., & Vadja, S. (2008). *Kitchen table sustainability*. London: Earthscan.

Sarkissian, W., Hurford, D., & Wenman, C. (2010). *Creative community Planning: Transformative engagement methods for working at the edge*. London: Earthscan.

Sarkissian, W., Stenberg, B., Hirst, A., & Walton, S. (2003). *Community participation in practice: New directions*. Perth, WA: Murdoch University, Institute for Sustainability and Technology Policy.

Scott, J. C. (1998). *Seeing like a state. How certain schemes to improve the human condition have failed*. New Haven, CT: Yale University Press.

Stretton, H. (1969). *The political sciences*. London: Routledge and Kegan Paul.

Trinh Minh-ha. (1989). *Woman native other*. Bloomington, IN: Indiana University Press.

Part I
Ethnography, Epistemology, History

Chapter 1
Film Works Wonders: Analysis, History and Town Plan United in a Single Representation

Leonardo Ciacci

1.1 Introduction: A Problem That Is Repeated over Time

The capacity of film, and moreover of photography, for description is generally recognised and demonstrated by the role it has had in political propaganda and social communication. Little recognition, however, is given to the planning aspect of the filmed interpretation of events and situations, evident not only in film's capacity to propose a specific point of view but primarily in its power to stimulate the audience through stories capable of changing the meanings of the situations shown.

This includes the role that the tools of film have had almost since its inception, and may with all the more reason have today, in dealing with two critical and never-resolved town planning questions: How to reconcile three different planning tools: historic interpretation of the city, quantitative analysis of urban processes, and design of the inhabited space and how to extend participation in the project for urban change to the largest possible number of people.

Some of the more recent experiences, and a review of the occasions when town planners became involved in film over the course of the last century, show how the language and tools of film can provide the necessary means for positively responding to both these old questions.

1.2 The Filmed Representation of the Town Plan in the Twentieth Century

Within the planning field there has been perpetual tension between the analysis of urban issues, on the one hand, and the plans that are produced to address those same issues, on the other. But if this same question is looked at using film as a mode of research, the picture defined above seems to offer a different prospect.

L. Ciacci (✉)
Department of Town Planning, University IUAV of Venice, Venice, Italy
e-mail: ciacci@iuav.it

L. Sandercock, G. Attili (eds.), *Multimedia Explorations in Urban Policy and Planning*, Urban and Landscape Perspectives 7, DOI 10.1007/978-90-481-3209-6_1,
© Springer Science+Business Media B.V. 2010

In an essay of some years ago I proposed a reading of a film genre I defined as *Il cinema degli urbanisti* (Town Planners' Cinema).[1] Starting from 1928 it is possible to find various films made by town planners, whose purpose was to contribute to the disciplinary debate in support of a theoretical orientation taken as the basis of the town plan.[2] All the films in the series obviously have the nature of documentaries and were originally used as tools of political-cultural and disciplinary persuasion, or what some might call "propaganda". Almost all these films were made on the occasion of a public exhibition for the mass circulation of ideas, programmes and town plans. The most obvious aim of all was to convince *the public* of the social duties and potential of town planning. All the Town Planners' Cinema documentaries pursue that purpose, proposing the reasons for a specific town plan.

The occasion of a public exhibition was of course necessary to motivate the production of a specialist film, otherwise inadmissible to the cinemas. Producing even a short film, however, is a complex operation, which requires considerable money, preparation, organisation and the participation of a certain number of people with different specialisations. This, combined with the fact that film imposes a difficult to control (that is, non-rational) language, consisting of inevitable simplifications and based on the emotional grasp of the images before the scientific content of the message communicated, makes the decision to make a film a choice laden with special meaning for a town planner. Commenting on the outcome of the Town Planning Exhibition set up at the 10th Triennale of Milan in 1954, Giancarlo De Carlo, one of the curators, clearly intimated that he did not consider the role of the films made as part of the show planned for that occasion exhausted in the context of the exhibition:[3] "...the short films have had an immediate effect – which will certainly be wider when they are screened on the normal circuits" (De Carlo, 1954, p. 24). Unfortunately there is no indication that the three films produced in 1954, or the exhibition itself, were distributed to cinemas.

The public, the great public, is what justifies the production of a film, even a specialist documentary. This *should* make the documentaries of the Town Planners' Cinema different from books on town planning theory. But they seem rather to be constructed in exactly the same way as a theoretical essay, even a manual, is drafted. In all the films of the Town Planners' Cinema, the contrast between different planning scenarios, even if only implied, is an essential component of the screenplay and influences its composition. Not only this, but in general all those films seem to be structured into two parts: a first one dedicated to the interpretation of the object, the city or the house, and a seconds dedicated to the illustration of a plan and a built example of a city or house, or one to be built.

It is obviously a method of composing the message specifically aimed at obtaining the agreement of the audience to a project presented as already thought to be the optimum. The procedure adopted in the story is deductive and tends to present the choices contained in the final plan as proposals consistent with a correct reading of reality: a kind of filmed propaganda.

The plans contained in the images of these films, or better, the plans that these films transfer to the cinema screen for an audience of non-specialists, are already known. They are already known to the specialists through the traditional documents

Fig. 1.1 Video still from "Una lezione di Urbanistica" (1954)

of disciplinary communication, so they were already known at the time of being screened and transferred onto film. How much these unusual disciplinary documents contain must thus be sought in the method of interpretation proposed, in the communicative forms and in the composition of the discourse that in those historic moments was thought useful for creating the conditions of contact between specialist technicians in the sector and users, between "educated" culture and "common sense" culture, between technical-political exponents and possible partners. In the search for a direct relationship with those that in town planning are usually considered users, a town planner may thus find in a highly emotive medium of mass communication the suitable means for imparting his own particular stimulus to a situation in change.

A short film by Marcel Poëte, *Pour mieux comprendre Paris*, strengthens this reading.[4] It is a very short, short film in two parts (the seconds part has not yet been found), filmed to be shown at a town planning exhibition and then possibly intended for screening in cinemas as an interval in the main programme. The rapid images showing Paris apply the concepts already formulated by Poëte for understanding the genesis and development of a city. It is an educated, difficult interpretation and moreover screened on the big screen at high speed in a very few minutes, three

Fig. 1.2 Video stills from "Pour mieux comprendre Paris" (1935) and from "The city" (1939)

to be precise. What did Poëte think would possibly remain of all this in the memory of the average viewer? Certainly not much that could be rationally memorised. Perhaps some images or perhaps some combination of images; perhaps only the idea that Paris, a big modern capital city, was the result of a century-long history and, especially, was a result very different from those produced under the same general conditions in London, Berlin, New York, Chicago, etc., whose layouts were compared with that of Paris in the film. Would the average visitor to the Paris exhibition of 1935 have been able to imagine that such unrepeatable urban individuality could have been erased to make way for a "cité contemporeen"? Was it possible to conceive of violently interrupting the evolution of that living and vital organism to replace it with an entirely new city, specially constructed to remodel the space of modern urban life in the era of the motor car and industry, as the tenacious and genial Le Corbusier had been very evocatively preaching for years?[5] Perhaps, precisely this was the mainspring that convinced a scholar so attentive to detail, as Poëte proved to be, to accept "three minutes" as the maximum time within which to contain his four books on Paris, along with other reflections of quite complex theoretical implication.[6] This is an interesting point. He does not set himself against a project certainly regarded as very dangerous and unacceptable, as Le Corbusier's "la cité pour trois milion d'abitant" must have seemed to Poëte, by attacking its proposals, but rather by indirectly demolishing their historical legitimacy. Le Corbusier had written 10 years earlier that the "city is a tool of work". "The study of a city [thus] comes within the frame of scientific research, having to do with a complex that is sufficiently consistent for its laws to be determined" (Le Corbusier, 1967, p. 79). To Poëte, on the contrary, every city "is a living organism" in constant change, healthy and alive until such time as something intervenes to interrupt its vitality, turning it into a ruin, an archaeological remnant (Poëte, 1958).

To proceed along this road, it must be admitted that in town planning the clash between different positions is a clash between alternative histories of the city prior to being a clash between alternative plans. All the classics of theoretical town planning literature, not without justification, proceed in the same way. A plan that has already

Fig. 1.3 Video stills from "Die Frankfurter Kleinstwohunung" (1928) and from "Die Stadt von Morgen. Ein Film vom Stadtebau" (1930)

been designed, already defined in its general structure, is followed by a rewriting of the history of the city to be placed prior to the new project in the text. In the light of a specially formulated premise, the choices of the proposed project cannot but consequently seem the logical and "natural" consequence of those premises. This is true of Le Corbusier, as it is of Cerdà, Camillo Sitte and all the others who have posed these problems. On the other hand, it must be the fate of every "utopia", of every all-absorbing plan to transform the city-society, if Thomas More also wrote the premise that defines the philosophical and ideal motivations of his *Utopia* only after having defined and described the ideal form of that social organisation. That this then became the first of the two parts of his treatise should leave no doubt as to the order of priority.

When town planners translated their projects into cinematic images, they adopted the same procedure used in the organisation of the index of one of their books of

Fig. 1.4 Video stills from "Some Activities of Bermondsey County Council" (1930) and from "The Social Life of Small Urban Spaces" (1979)

theory. The analysis of the working conditions of housewives in the kitchen, while they move around in old-fashioned spaces with dated equipment, serves to justify the plan for a new functional kitchen: a saving in time and effort for a woman who participates in the general renewal of society.[7] The representation of the squalid living conditions in the industrial suburbs of the city justifies the decentralisation of families of American workers to small *green cities*.[8] An awareness of the ancient roots of social relations in the countryside of southern Italy justifies the idea of the separate, autonomous village.[9] Recognition of the organic nature of the medieval hamlets of central Italy justifies the conservation plan for the old city centres.[10] Finally, the detailed list of urban problems and its meticulous communication to the inhabitants of the city justifies a social town plan for inhabitants who will thus learn to be its citizens.[11]

If the length of the Town Planners' Cinema documentaries was such as to allow the traditional division into two formally separated parts, each one of them would do just that: a first analytical part, mainly dedicated to the history of the city, and a seconds technical part illustrating a plan for the city: a premise and a proposal, difficult to read in a different sequence. The premise in these films is their most important part: that which contains a version of the facts that is already in itself a plan for urban transformation, in search of supporters.

1.3 The 1960s: An Attempt Is Made in Italy to Make Cinema into a Town Planning Tool

Verucchio 1969: The theme of the 16th International Conference of Artists, Critics and Art Scholars was "The Visual Space of the City, Town Planning and Cinema".[12] Italy was entering the heart of its 1968, a decisively more political movement than in other countries, capable of extending to industrial trade unions rather than applying only to youth and student issues. Architects and art historians discussed what could become one of the most suitable means of enlarging the technicians' capacity for intervention in the fate of the cities. Tafuri had written the year before that only a few sector studies try to examine the city using means other than the now self-regarding ones of architecture:[13]

> [...] we are today unable to make an adequate analysis of the ways in which the communication induced by architectural or urban images is received [...]; did not perhaps the architectural avant-gardes start precisely with the aim of influencing the relationships between artistic communications and public reactions? (Tafuri, 1980, p. 117).[14]

One of the references of Tafuri's citation was the book by Kevin Lynch, *The Image of City*, translated into Italian in 1964, and there is no doubt that that book was one of the reasons for the conference. Lynch did not restrict himself to studying the perception that could be found in the daily experience of some inhabitants of Boston, Jersey City and Los Angeles, but from these, and starting from the particular power, the "figurability" of some urban objects, he claimed that the individual and collective mechanisms by which the city was constantly transformed by its own inhabitants had to be recognised. A study of his on the images of the high-way perceived from the driver's seat of the car is well known among town planners (Appleyard, Lynch, & Myer, 1964). "The urban landscape that may be seen from a moving car was revealed to us by the film" seems to echo Argan. And he continues:

> In a broader sense: cinema visualises the urban space in relation to an existential, symbolic or symptomatic fact of overall human existence. The cinema profoundly influences our psychological habits: it places us 'in situation' regarding reality [. . .]. More than 'informing' on the form or on the visual space of the city, cinema provides a key to reading the urban phenomenon (Argan, 1969, p. 11).

How this takes place was still unknown and, alas, was to remain so long after the conference, which was not to have any significant follow-up in the grounds of architectural research for many years to come. In town planning terms, Argan had formulated the problem thus: "To town planning ends it is not so necessary to know what the real historic or aesthetic value of the Coliseum is, as to know what the 'Coliseum' historic-artistic fact means to the Roman community" (Argan, 1969, p. 11). It seems that Argan is proposing the same theoretical purposes as Lynch and wants to study the perception that Romans have of the Coliseum. In reality Argan asks what must be done to induce a particular perception of the Coliseum in the Romans and, more precisely, a perception in line with the plans for the conservation of the historic heritage of the cities, which in those years was starting to become the most urgent town planning agenda in Italy.

Cinema, claimed Argan, had the capacity to propose a "predigested" version of town planning themes. In other words, it allowed an assertion of the interpretation necessary to support a specific project. In Italy the use of cinema in town planning had been talked about for years. Argan himself and Bruno Zevi had written about it in the cinema magazine *Bianco e Nero* in 1949. Ragghianti (1933) had theorised about it first, then put it into practice, along with his town planner friend Edoardo Detti, with the Olivetti *critofilms* of the 1950s, on the plan for the conservation of the old city centres in Italy. Ludovico Quaroni (1963) was to support it some years later, taking part in a conference on "educational television" in 1963, in which Zevi also participated (1963). Italy had emerged from two decades of Fascist propaganda, which had made widespread use of the cinema, and perhaps those scholars, having experienced its power of conviction, thought that that same tool could be used for progressive and politically positive ends. Furthermore, the period of Neorealism, when cinema had shown the most authentic Italians close up, captured in their everyday occupations and stories, had just come to an end. Architecture had also interpreted that cultural period, planning new areas of state housing, in which it was thought possible to reconstruct the conditions of community life.[15] Cinema and architecture had shared a single language: why not make the relationship between the two means of social transformation structural? It was only a question of making interpretation and plan come together in a single language capable of speaking to the public in simple terms, understandable also to the non-expert, and above all capable of transforming passive spectators into active interpreters of the urban and regional transformation that had violently struck the Italy of the economic boom: that same boom whose effects had been dramatically described in 1963 by *Le mani sulla città*, the film made by Franco Rosi on the building mismanagement scandals in Naples.[16]

The articles by Argan and Zevi published by *Bianco e Nero* coincided with an interview with Luigi Piccinato published in *Metron*, the magazine conceived and edited by Zevi, entitled *Invito alla storia dell'urbanistica*, which contains an interesting reference to historical *knowledge*. In a "...completely ahistorical way of thinking, [at the end of the 9th century] the city was not seen as a social product, but only as an aesthetic fact..." (Piccinato, 1949, p. 7).[17] And the position of "looking at the technical aspect, glorifying its strength as the only positive fact ... much in vogue also today..." is also "pseudo historical". It is precisely with reference to the role of the technician that Piccinato uses the term *knowledge*, referring to the action of those building technicians who resolve "problems ... separately, one by one (or at least very rarely reaching that synthesis that architecture represents and almost always without knowledge of it)..." (Piccinato, 1949, p. 7). In the history of the twentieth century,

> in town planning technicians, the *knowledge* that, also materially, the city is a collective fact with its social content that alone can justify it [follows on from] that great experience represented by the ... disaster of the English mining towns, that of the North American metropoli [and] after Howard's apostolic work.... Such *knowledge* appeared first in the spirit of the economists and philologists, then in that of the technicians: the architect Unwin can consider himself the interpreter of the Howard programme more than the creator of the first English garden city (Piccinato, 1949, p. 8).

Piccinato's reference to *knowledge* was not casual, nor an isolated case, given that 30 years later, at the conclusion of his speech to the International Conference on the History of Town Planning in Lucca in 1975, he asserted again that "it is necessary to have historic knowledge".[18]

> ... the crisis in which town planning now struggles [...] has its roots [...] at the very roots of our civilisation and our society [...] if we want to intervene [...] it is primarily necessary that we *acquire knowledge of the city*. Well this acquisition can only be given by the history of town planning (Piccinato, 1949, p. 11).[19]

Continuing in this same direction, however, the town planner cannot remain alone in his action of transforming the world around him and of which he also has historic knowledge; it is necessary that that same knowledge is extended to his partners and becomes a shared and knowing action. This is why a town planner can find in a highly emotive medium of mass communication the suitable means for imparting his own particular stimulus to a situation in change and "acquire knowledge of the city".

1.4 Pasolini: Inadvertent Town Planner

In 1974, as presenter and co-author of a television programme entitled *Pasolini e... la forma della città*,[20] Pier Paolo Pasolini presented a long monologue of about 17 minutes. This seemed to be a reflection on the form of the city of Orte from a film director's point of view, but was actually a very firm stance against the extraordinary lack of reflection with which dramatic damages were being done in Italy to the integrity of historic cities in the 1970s. In the same programme, edited with images shot in Orte, a sequence extracted from a previous documentary of his on the walls of Sana suddenly appears. *Le mura di Sana. Documentario in forma di appello all'UNESCO*,[21] made by Pasolini in 1970, clarifies without any shadow of doubt the nature and the real aims of the subsequent television interview. One Sunday in October 1970 in Sana, the capital of Yemen, the director decided to make a documentary on the destruction of the walls of that city, which he witnessed directly, with the "... film left over from the main shoot ..." of *Il fiore delle mille e una notte* (created between 1973 and 1974). After centuries of perfect conservation, work was proceeding on the gradual demolition of the medieval wall to allow the new road, built "by the Chinese" connecting the desert valley in which Sana stands to the Red Sea, to enter into the city. This drove Pasolini to take a stance, using his tools as a film maker.

> I was too anxious to make this documentary. It is perhaps a professional distortion, but the problems of Sana, the disfigurement that like leprosy is invading it struck me with a pain, an anger, a sense of impotence and at the same time a feverish desire to do something, from which I was peremptorily obliged to film (from the commentary in the film).

In Orte, too, the profile of the city had been ruined by recent constructions and in particular by the presence of a state housing block that, according to the director, defaced the character of the city, upsetting the ancient relationship between its form and the surrounding natural environment.

There are many interesting sections in this film. At the beginning Pasolini turns to Ninetto Davoli, who is with him, saying "... I'll speak to you, because I'm incapable of speaking in the abstract, facing nothing, the television audience, whose location I don't know", showing the strength of his need to tangibly involve the audience in his action. Subsequently, during the long shot of the "ascent" to the city along the cobbled street that leads to one of Orte's oldest gates, Pasolini speaks to the camera, turned this time to the spectator: "... I want to defend something that is not sanctioned, that is not codified, that no one defends; which is the work, let us say, of the people of an entire history, of the entire history of a city's people. Of an infinity of nameless men who worked within an era that then produced the most extreme, most complete fruit in individual works of art. [...] But no one realises that what must be defended is precisely this anonymity, this anonymous past, this nameless past, this popular past". It is essentially as if Pasolini is revealing his role and his responsibility as an intellectual, as one who, possessing the tools to do so, makes himself spokesman for those who have no access to such means of public condemnation. Those who have the means to make themselves heard have the duty to give voice to those who do not, to support projects in the collective interest.

Interpreted with the attention of the specialist on urban questions, in this case, too, history, analysis and plan appear as integrated actions in the film. While Pasolini is launching his appeal to UNESCO, proposing his *plan* for the conservation of the city of Sana "as beautiful as Urbino, Venice", he is making its *history*, and *describing* its specificity, proposing an analysis of that urban reality. This is an eloquent demonstration of the peculiarity of the cinema "language", a language that does not allow the isolation of sections that in the experimental scientific method we are used to confronting and presenting separately in different times and forms. The cinematic representation/interpretation always presents the historic reconstruction of a situation, an analysis of the current one and a possible plan for its future order. All this, of course, takes on meaning if it is shown to the public. Imagine wanting to communicate a conservation plan for the city of Sana, without explaining what the city of Sana is, where it is, how it is made up and what its history is: no one would understand what you were talking about. In the same way, if the history was not directed towards the plan that motivates it, it would take on a different form, and it would have a different effect on the spectator, who would be identified not by his interest in the conservation of historic cities but by a vague geographical-tourism interest in exotic places. Pasolini turns to an audience that he wants to make active, that he provokes with the intention of obtaining its agreement to a cultural and political project, but with precise practical and planning aspects: to provoke concrete action on the part of UNESCO. It took many years, but the project that Pasolini was pursuing 38 years ago has now been activated: UNESCO is actually concerning itself with the protection of the city of Sana, part of our world heritage.

1.5 Conclusion: Film and Propaganda/Persuasion: An Old Tool for New and Necessary Participation

The term *propaganda* has the disadvantage in the common perception of having a meaning *established* by the use made of it in the decades of totalitarian government in the twentieth century. Fascist propaganda in Italy used film widely and instrumentally in the project to change cities and thus brought about its definitive identification as a negative tool of communication. However, even in political exploitation, filmed propaganda is actually an active form of distanced dialogue and no other system of multimedia communication has since been able to replace it in terms of its ability to create the conditions necessary for collective action.

Construction of an active exchange between the parties contributing to the implementation of a plan requires the sharing of a single language and the possibility that the hierarchical distance between the actions that help form a series of choices is not perceived. Drawing up a shared plan requires the adoption of a means of relating between the subjects involved that offers the same conditions of participation to all and avoids the exclusion provoked by specialist languages.

Communication, intended as the pure transmission of information, is actually too "cold" a practice to be associated with the construction of a project for urban change. Communicating an already formalised project is an action that leaves the relations between the subjects of the communication unchanged: the sender does not put himself into a dialogical relationship with the receiver, though a project requires one to be established. The recent and more and more frequent use of this *communication* by public bodies, whose sole aim is to build consensus, does not go beyond the confines of the publicity given to public actions, intended to limit, if not exclude, any genuinely active participation.

The language of film, however, while showing facts and situations, is based on emotional mechanisms and identification: film narrates, offers interpretations, produces expectations and triggers the capacity for judgement in viewers who thus feel included in a project that involves them.

This is precisely the condition that the town plan now needs: the stimulation of many actors who, involved in a situation of urban change, despite being in a distanced relationship, can at the same time access the necessary historical knowledge, analytical information and planning scenarios, to the point of potentially taking on a role of critical and constructive participation in the planning path and/or its implementation. In film narratives, the distance between author and audience is attenuated. The audience participates, even if indirectly, in construction of the narrative and spontaneously places itself in the story (the plan); the hierarchical distinction that the logical succession of actions attributes to the specialist practice is largely erased. The language of film, because of this, presents itself as a precious tool for participation in town planning processes. The necessary condition for its positive use is to abandon the retreat into scientific/technical language, to make the public accept it for what it is and to adopt the construction of a shared meaning as the outcome of the contrast between the plan and the many "irrational" actions that guide the choices of the inhabitants/builders of cities.

Notes

1. The first review of the *Cinema degli urbanisti*, by the author, took place in Modena in 1997, promoted by the Istituto Nazionale di Urbanistica and the Comune di Modena. a second review on the themes of housing was made in 2002. See Ciacci (1997, 2002).
2. These films are the subject of many of the periodical updates of *Movies*, one of the columns at www.planum.net, and of Ciacci (2001).
3. The three documentaries were made for the town planning exhibition at the 10th Triennale of Milan in 1954. The titles of the three films are, in their current order, *Cronache dell'urbanistica italiana*, directed by Nicolò Ferrari, *La città degli uomini*, directed by Michele Gandin, and *Una lezione d'urbanistica*, directed by Gerardo Guerrieri. The subjects are all by Giancarlo De Carlo, Carlo Doglio, Michele Gandin, Billa Pedroni, Ludovico Quaroni and Elio Vittorini; the music by Guido Nascimbene. The films were shot in 35 mm, in black and white, with voice-over narration. Produced by La Meridiana Film, Italy 1954.
4. *Pour mieux comprendre Paris*, directed by Hetienne de Lallier, screenplay by Marcel Poëte, an ATLANTIC FILM production, 35 mm, black and white with narration, length 5 minutes and 18 seconds, Paris 1935. The series that includes this film is presented with the words "*3 minutes pour …*", suggesting a repeated formula for condensing an originally vast and complex subject into a few minutes, as in this case the *description* of the evolution of the city of Paris.
5. The reference is obviously to the project for the "city for three million people", shown at the *Salon d'Automne* in 1923 and subsequently published by Le Corbusier in *Urbanism*, in 1925, along with his proposal to apply these same theoretical and planning principles to the city

of Paris with "*Plan Voisin*", exhibited in Paris in the pavilion of the *Esprit Nouveau* at the *Esposizione delle arti Decorative* of 1925. See Le Corbusier (1967).

6. In 1935 Marcel Poëte (1866–1950) was conservator at the *Bibliothèque des travaux historiques de la ville* in Paris (from 1903) and lecturer in town planning at the *Ecole des hautes études urbains*. The four volumes of *Un vie de cité. Paris de sa naissance à nous jours*(1924–1931) had already been published, as had his *Introduction à l'Urbanisme. L'évolution des villes*, in 1929. The cinema evidently added a new and potentially highly effective tool to those until that time used by Poëte in promotion and pedagogical experimentation and for his plan to make "a service intended for a vast audience..." institutional. See Calabi (1995, 1997).

7. The reference is to Die Frankfurter Kuche, the short documentary that interprets the function and reasonings of the "Frankfurt Kitchen" designed by Grete Schütte Lihotzky for the Siedlung Praunheim planned by Ernst May in Frankfurt, now part of the series of four documentaries Neus Bauen in Frankfurt am Main, made by May for the CIAM of 1929. See http://www.planum.net/archive/movies-frankfurt.htm.

8. The reference is to *The City*, the film made in 1939 by the American Institute of Planners and produced by Ralph Steiner and Willard Van Dyke, on the basis of a commentary written by Lewis Mumford. See http://www.planum.net/archive/movies-city.htm.

9. The reference is to Cronache dell'urbanistica italiana (op cit). See http://www.planum.net/archive/movies-de_carlo.htm.

10. The reference is to the two *critofilm* made in 1954–1955 by Carlo Ludovico Ragghianti: *Città millenarie* and *Lucca città comunale*.

11. The reference is to Deie Stadt von Morgen, the film made in Berlin in 1930 by Maximillian von Golbeck and Erich Kotzer. See http://www.planum.net/archive/movies-die-stadt.htm.

12. The meeting took place in the castle of Verucchio, a Renaissance construction built by Malatesta in the hills near Rimini. See AAVV (1969).

13. Manfredo Tafuri also took part in the meeting. See Tafuri (1969).

14. See Manfredo Tafuri (1980) *Teorie e storia dell'architettura* (p. 117) in the chapter L'architettura come metalinguaggio: il valore critico dell'immagine. See Lynch (1960).

15. The Tiburtino district in Rome, by Quaroni and Ridolfi, is considered an example of neorealist architecture.

16. See Ciacci (2005): the entire first issue of the new magazine was dedicated to Rosi's film.

17. See Piccinato (1949) and Ciacci (1999).

18. See Martinelli and Nuti (1976).

19. ...which removes every possibility of space for a history of town planning to be considered as a simple history of the discipline "There is in fact an important and fundamental law: that of *compliance* of the plan [...] to the structure of the city ... [condition without which] the plan is no more than an object of town planning history, but may concern, if anything, only the history of design" (Piccinato, 1949, p. 11). The italics are mine.

20. The Rai television series "IO E..." was conceived and directed by Anna Zanoli, art critic and film maker who between 1973 and 1975 worked on 30 filmed interviews of figures of culture, politics and entertainment, who were asked to talk about a place or work of art to the television audience.

21. *Le mura di Sana. Documentario in forma di appello all'Unesco*, directed and narrated by Pier Paolo Pasolini; director of photography: Tonino Delli Colli; editing: Tatiana Casini Morigi; production: Rosina Anstalt; producer: Franco Rossellini; 35 mm colour; length: 13'20". Broadcast as part of Rai's "Boomerang", 16 February 1971. First screening: Capitol Cinema, Milan, 20 June 1974. The film was not released for commercial distribution.

References

AAVV. (Eds.). (1969). *Lo spazio visivo della città "urbanistica e cinematografo"*. Bologna: Cappelli.

Appleyard, D., Lynch, K., & Myer, J. R. (1964). *The View from the Road*. Boston: MIT Press.

Argan, C. (1949). Lettura cinematografica delle opere d'arte. *Bianco e Nero, 8,* 39–46.

Argan, G. C. (1969). Lo spazio visivo della città «Urbanistica e cinematografo. In AAVV (Eds.), *Lo spazio visivo della città "urbanistica e cinematografo".* Bologna: Cappelli.

Calabi, D. (1995). Marcel Poëte, un militante della storia urbana. *Urbanistica, 104,* 146–149.

Calabi, D. (1997). *Parigi anni venti. Marcel Poëte e le origini della storia urbana.* Venezia: Marsilio.

Ciacci, L. (Ed.). (1997). *Il cinema degli urbanisti* (Vol. 1). Modena: Comune di Modena.

Ciacci, L. (1999). Urbanistica filmata. Non progetti illustrati, ma trasformazioni della memoria. *Urbanistica, 113,* 128–136.

Ciacci, L. (2001). *Progetti di città sullo schermo.* Venezia: Marsilio.

Ciacci, L. (Ed.). (2002). *Il cinema degli urbanisti* (Vol. 2). Modena: Comune di Modena.

Ciacci, L. (2005). Ancora le mani sulla città? *CINEMACITTA,* $^1/_4$, 295–296.

De Carlo, G. (1954). Intenzioni e risultati della mostra di urbanistica. *Casabella, 203,* 24.

Le Corbusier, (1967). *Urbanistica.* Milano: Il Saggiatore (Paris 1925).

Lynch, K. (1960). *The Image of the City.* Boston: The MIT Press.

Martinelli, R., & Nuti, L. (1976). *La storiografia urbanistica.* Lucca: Ciscu-Marsilio Editori.

Piccinato, L. (1949). Invito alla storia dell'urbanistica. *Metron, 33–34,* 7–12.

Poëte, M. (1958). *La città antica. Introduzione all'urbanistica.* Torino: Einaudi (Paris, 1929).

Quaroni, L. (1963). La TV e l'educazione urbanistica. In Rai come pubblico servizio (Eds.), *Associazione Radio-teleabbonati.* Rome Cinema, Einaudi: Biblioteca dello spettacolo (Turin 1979).

Ragghianti, C. L. (1933). Cinematografo rigoroso. Cine-Convegno, 1(4–5). Now in Ragghianti, C. L. (1979). *Arti della visione* (vol. 1). Torino: Einaudi.

Tafuri, M. (1969). Lo «spazio» e le cose: città, town design, architettura. In AAVV (Eds.), *Lo spazio visivo della città "urbanistica e cinematografo".* Bologna: Cappelli editore.

Tafuri, M. (1980). *Teorie e storie dell'architettura.* Roma-Bari: Laterza.

Zevi, B. (1949). Architettura per il cinema e cinema per l'architettura. *Bianco e Nero, 8,* 60–63.

Zevi, B. (1963). Urbanistica e architettura nei programmi televisivi. In Rai come pubblico servizio (Eds.), *Associazione Radioteleabbonati.* Rome: Biblioteca dello spettacolo.

Chapter 2
From the Campfire to the Computer: An Epistemology of Multiplicity and the Story Turn in Planning

Leonie Sandercock

2.1 Introduction

Not long after joining my present university in 2001, I was shocked to hear that a Native woman who proposed to do her Masters thesis by focusing on the stories of her people had been told that that was not an appropriate topic or methodology. For the longest time, 'story' was thought of in the social sciences (though not in the humanities) as 'soft,' inferior, lacking in rigor, or, worst insult of all, as a 'woman/native/other' way of knowing.[1] There was even a time, in the academic discipline of history (my own starting point as an undergraduate), in which story was demoted and more 'analytical' and quantitative approaches were sought. In response to this kind of marginalizing of story, feminists, historians, and workers in the cultural studies field, not to mention anthropologists, have reasserted its importance, both as epistemology and as methodology (Kelly, 1984; Lerner, 1997; Rabinow & Sullivan, 1987; Geertz, 1988; Trinh, 1989). Yet the struggle to create a legitimate space for the use of stories in planning curricula and scholarship as well as in planning's diverse practices is ongoing, because of the privileging of what are seen as more scientific and technical ways of knowing. (We shouldn't be forced to choose between stories and the so-called more rigorous, typically quantitative research, stories and census data, stories and modeling, because all three 'alternatives' to story are actually each imbued with story). Nevertheless, a 'story turn' is well under way in planning.

Accompanying a broader post-positivist movement in the social sciences (Stretton, 1969; Geertz, 1988; Rabinow & Sullivan, 1987; Bourdieu, 1990; Flyvbjerg, 2002), pushed further along by feminist and postcolonial critiques (see Said, 1979; Hooks, 1984; Trinh, 1989; Sandercock, 1998), planning scholars have begun to see the need both for an expanded language for planning and for ways of expanding the creative capacities of planners (Landry, 2000, 2006; Sandercock,

L. Sandercock (✉)
School of Community and Regional Planning, The University of British Columbia,
Vancouver, BC, Canada
e-mail: leonies@interchange.ubc.ca

L. Sandercock, G. Attili (eds.), *Multimedia Explorations in Urban Policy and Planning*, Urban and Landscape Perspectives 7, DOI 10.1007/978-90-481-3209-6_2, © Springer Science+Business Media B.V. 2010

2005a, 2005b; Sarkissian & Hurford, 2010) by acknowledging and using the many other ways of knowing that exist: experiential, intuitive, and somatic knowledge; local knowledge; knowledge based on the practices of talking and listening, seeing, contemplating, and sharing; and knowledge expressed in visual, symbolic, ritual, and other artistic ways.

The 'story turn' in planning has been one response to this epistemological crisis. In the past two decades, a growing number of planning scholars have been investigating the relationship between story and planning and consciously trying to create the space for this other 'language' (Forester, 1989; Mandelbaum, 1991; Marris, 1997; Sandercock, 1998, 2003; Eckstein & Throgmorton, 2003; Attili, 2007). These investigations highlight how planning is performed through stories, how rhetoric and poetics are crucial in interactive processes, how the communicative dimension is central to planning practices, and how story can awaken energies and imaginations, becoming a catalyst for involving urban conversations, for deep community dialogues.

Fig. 2.1 A planning imagination for the 21st century. Photo by Maurizio Monaci. Graphic elaboration by Giovanni Attili

In order to imagine the ultimately unrepresentable spaces, lives, and languages of the city, to make them legible, we translate them into narratives. The way we narrate the city becomes constitutive of urban reality, affecting the choices we make and the ways we then might act. As Alasdair MacIntyre put it: 'I can only answer the question "What am I to do" if I can answer the prior question, "of what story or stories do I find myself a part?" ' (quoted in Flyvbjerg, 2002, p. 137).

My argument in this chapter will be deceptively simple. Stories are central to planning practice: to the knowledge it draws on from the social sciences and humanities; to the knowledge it produces about the city; and to ways of acting in the city. Planning is *performed* through story, in a myriad of ways. And since storytelling has evolved from oral tales around a campfire to the technologically sophisticated forms of multimedia available in the early 21st century, it is surely time for the urban professions to appreciate the multifarious potential of these new media. All the more so since the planning and design fields have been forced by the demands of civil society to be more engaged with communities, and thus necessarily to be more *communicative*.

In this chapter I perform two tasks. First, I unpack the many ways in which we use stories in planning and design: in process, as a catalyst for change, as a foundation, in policy, in pedagogy, in critique, as justification of the status quo, as identity, and as experience. Second, I trace the evolution of storytelling techniques 'from the campfire to the computer,' leading to the suggestion that multimedia is fast becoming the 21st century's favored form of storytelling and to illustrate its many applications to the planning field.

My approach is not uncritical. Despite increasing attention to and use of story in some of the newer academic fields (feminist and cultural studies, for example), I don't see it as the new religion, and I take to heart Eckstein's caution that stories' ability 'to act as transformative agents depends on a disciplined scrutiny of their forms and uses' (Eckstein, 2003, p. 13). We still need to question the truth of our own and others' stories. We need to be attentive to how power shapes which stories get told, get heard, carry weight. We need to understand the work that stories do, or rather that we ask them to do, in deploying them and to recognize the moral ordering involved in the conscious and unconscious use of certain plots and character

Fig. 2.2 A planning imagination for the 21st century. Video stills from the multimedia production 'A planning imagination for the 21st century' by Giovanni Attili

types. A better understanding of the role of stories can make us more effective as planning practitioners, irrespective of the substantive field of planning. Story and storytelling are at work in conflict resolution, in community development, in participatory action research, in resource management, in policy and data analysis, in transportation planning, and so on. A better understanding of the role of stories can also be an aid to critical thinking, to deconstructing the arguments of others. Stories can sometimes provide a far richer understanding of the human condition, and thus of the urban condition, than traditional social science, and for that reason alone, deserve more attention.

Story is an all-pervasive, yet largely unrecognized force in planning practice. We don't talk about it, and we don't teach it. Let's get this out of the closet. Let's liberate and celebrate and think critically about the power of story and appreciate why there is a 'story turn' underway in the planning field.

2.2 Planning as Performed Story

I turn first to the ways in which I see *planning as performed story*: in process, in foundational stories, in stories as catalysts for change, in policy, and finally, in academic stories, as method, as explanation, and as critique.

2.2.1 Story and Process

For many planning practitioners, the role of story is central, although not always consciously so. Those who do consciously make use of story do so in diverse, and often imaginative and inspiring, ways. The best way to demonstrate this is by using some examples – of story as process and of story being used to facilitate process. These examples are so varied that I'll use subheadings as guides.

2.2.1.1 Community Participation Processes

In community or public participation processes, planners orchestrate an event in such a way as to allow everybody, or as many people as possible, to tell their story about their community, neighborhood, school, or street. We tend to refer to this as drawing on local knowledge, and there are various techniques for eliciting people's stories, such as small group work with a facilitator for each group or doing community mapping exercises.[2] What is not always clear is how these collected stories will be used in the subsequent process, but the belief operating here is that it is important for everybody to have a chance to speak and to have their stories heard. This is linked with an argument about the political and practical benefits of democratizing planning.

When a participatory event is a way of *starting* a planning process, its purpose is most often about getting views and opinions, so the story gathering is likely to be followed by an attempt to find common threads that will help to draw up priorities. But when the participatory event is a response to a preexisting conflict that needs to be addressed before planning can move ahead, then the gathering of *rival* stories takes on more import. In such a situation, practitioners will usually meet separately with each involved person or group and listen to their stories of what the problem is before making a judgment about when and how to bring the conflicting parties together to hear each other's stories. In extreme cases, where the conflict is long-standing, relating to generations or even centuries of oppression or marginalization, this is very difficult work, but when done well can be therapeutic, cathartic, even healing.

2.2.1.2 Mediation, Negotiation, and Conflict Resolution

In one growing branch of planning practice – mediation, negotiation, and conflict resolution – there is a raft of techniques and procedures for facilitating storytelling, and the hearing of stories, in conflict situations.[3] In this kind of work, the ability of a practitioner to make the space for stories to be heard is more important than the ability to tell stories. And it is here that the importance of listening to others' stories, and the skills of listening in cross-cultural contexts, is at a premium:[4]

> In telling stories, parties tell who they are, what they care about, and what deeper concerns they may have that underlie the issues at hand (Forester, 2000, p. 166).

Forester describes a case in Washington State, where the mediator, Shirley Solomon, brought together Native Americans and non-Native county officials to settle land disputes. A critical stage in that mediation was the creating of a safe space in which people could come together and 'just talk about things without it being product-driven' (Solomon, quoted in Forester, 2000, p. 152). Solomon ceremonialized this safe space by creating a talking circle and asking people to talk about what this place meant to them. Everyone was encouraged to tell their story, of the meaning of the land, the place, to them and their families, past, present, and future – the land whose multiple and conflicting uses they were ultimately to resolve. It was this story-ing that got people past 'my needs versus your needs' and on to some 'higher ground,' moving toward some common purpose. Solomon describes this stepping aside to discuss personal histories as both simple and powerful, as a way of opening surprising connections between conflicting parties. Or as Forester has it, storytelling is essential in situations where deep histories of threatened cultural identity and domination are the context through which a present dispute is viewed. Stories have to be told for reconciliation to happen (Forester, 2000, p. 157). In terms of process, too, the design of spaces for telling stories makes participants from different cultures and class backgrounds more comfortable about speaking and more confident about the relevance of the whole procedure. A tribal elder who was present at Solomon's mediation said to her: 'In those meetings where it's Roberts Rules of Order, I know that I either have nothing to say, or what I have to say counts for nothing' (quoted in Forester, 2000, p. 154).

Fig. 2.3 A planning imagination for the 21st century. Video stills from the multimedia production 'A planning imagination for the 21st century' by Giovanni Attili

2.2.1.3 Core Story

Another interesting development of the use of story in practice is what Dunstan and Sarkissian (1994) call 'core story.' The idea of core story as methodology draws on work in psychology, which suggests that each of us has a core story: that we do not merely tell stories but are active in creating them with our lives. We become our stories. When we tell stories about ourselves, we draw on past behavior and on others' comments about us in characterizing ourselves as, say, adventurous, or victims, or afraid of change, or selfish, or heroic. But in telling and re-telling the story, we are also reproducing ourselves and our behaviors. Social psychologists argue that communities, and possibly nations, have such core stories that give meaning to collective life (see Houston, 1982, 1987). Culture is the creation and expression and sharing of stories that bond us with common language, imagery, metaphors, all of which create shared meaning. Such stories might be victim stories, warrior stories, fatal flaw stories, stories of peace-making, of generosity, of abandonment, of expectations betrayed.

In their work in evaluating the success of community development on a new outer suburban estate developed by a public agency in an Australian city, Dunstan and Sarkissian (1994) used an array of research tools: attitude and satisfaction surveys, interviews, focus groups, as well as census and other 'hard' data. When they came to analyze this material, they found contradictions that were not likely to be resolved by collecting more details. In order to go beyond the details and the quantitative scores on 'satisfaction,' they explored the notion of core story, drawing on

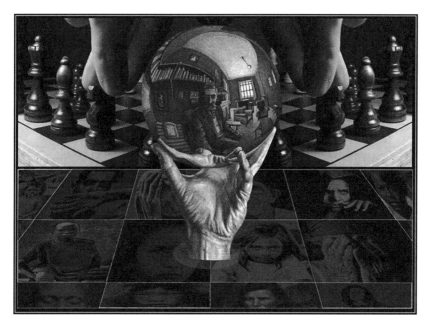

Fig. 2.4 A planning imagination for the 21st century. Video stills from the multimedia production 'A planning imagination for the 21st century' by Giovanni Attili

heroic, mythic, and meta-poetic language. They scripted such a story of heroic settlers, of expectation and betrayal, of abandonment, and took the story back to the community, saying 'this is what we've heard.' The response was overwhelming, and cathartic. 'Yes, you've understood. That's our story.' The task then, as the social planners defined it, was to help the community to turn this doomed and pessimistic story around. They asked them how they thought their story might/could/should be changed. Underlying this was a belief that core stories can be guides to how communities will respond to crisis or to public intervention. As with individuals, some tragic core stories need to be transformed by an explicit healing process or else the core story will be enacted again and again. Renewal and redemption are possible, Dunstan and Sarkissian believe. New 'chapters' can be written if there is the collective will to do so. They suggest four steps toward renewal. The first is a public telling of the story in a way that accepts its truth and acknowledges its power and pain. The second is some kind of atonement, in which there is an exchange that settles the differences. The third is a ceremony or ritual emerging out of local involvement and commitment by government (in this case municipal and provincial) that publicly acknowledges the new beginning. The fourth is an ongoing commitment and trust that a new approach is possible and will be acted on Dunstan & Sarkissian (1994, pp. 75–91).

This fascinating case study offers some illumination to a more general puzzle in participatory planning: how to turn a raft of community stories into a trustworthy plan, one that is faithful to community desires. To turn the light on inside the black box of that conversion surely requires planners to take their plan back to the community and say, 'this is how we converted your stories into a plan. Did we understand you correctly?' In a community or constituency where there is only one core story, this is a more straightforward process than in a situation where what the planners have heard is two or more conflicting stories. In the latter situation there is far more working through to do, in order to prioritize and to reach some consensus about priorities.

2.2.1.4 Non-verbal Stories

Less 'verbal' storytelling approaches have been developed using people with community arts experience to be part of a community development project that creates the opportunity for residents to express their feelings and tell their story vividly and powerfully. The Seattle Arts Commission matches artists with communities to engage in just such projects. At their best, they can create a new sense of cohesion and identity among residents, a healing of past wrongs, and a collective optimism about the future.

A community quilt, and quilting process, has proved to be a successful way to bring people together and for a group to tell their story. Depending on the community involved in an issue, video or music, or other art forms, may be more powerful forms of storytelling. In his violence-prevention work with youth in the Rock Solid Foundation in Victoria, British Columbia, Constable Tom Woods initiated a project to create an outdoor youth art gallery and park site along a 500-m stretch of railway right-of-way between two rows of warehouses. This area, which had a long history as a crime corridor, is now home to the Trackside Art Gallery, where local youths practice their graffiti on the warehouse walls. Woods realized that these teenagers needed a safe site for their graffiti. More profoundly, he realized that they needed a space to express themselves through nonviolent means and that graffiti is a communicative art form, a form of storytelling (McNaughton, 2001, p. 5). The potential of planners working with artists in processes like these that encourage storytelling has only just begun to be tapped (Sarkissian & Hurford, 2010).

2.2.1.5 Future Stories

Peter Ellyard is another consultant who uses story in an imaginative way in his 'preferred futures process.' Working with an array of clients, from institutions and corporations to place and interest-based communities, he helps them to develop their own 'future myth,' a preferred future scenario; he then takes them through a process of 'backcasting' or reverse history, as they unfold the steps from the future back to the present, which got them to where they want to be. On the way, there are missions, heritages, disasters, triumphs, and pitfalls. He consciously employs these narrative devices as an aid to imagination. Once the future myth task is complete, they proceed to SWOT (strengths, weaknesses, opportunities, threats) analyses and to the development of capacity-building strategies and action plans (Ellyard, 2001).

What is emerging then is the use of story in both obvious and imaginative ways in planning processes: an ability to tell, listen to, and invent stories is being nurtured as well as the equally important ability to make the space for stories to be heard. Part II of this book illustrates an explosion of interest in the role of new media in story gathering and storytelling.

2.2.2 Story as Foundation, Origin, Identity

I've already discussed the notion of core story and how it might be used by planners. There's a related notion of foundational story, a mytho-poetic story of origins, a story that cities and nations tell about themselves. This is particularly relevant to planning in multiethnic, multicultural contexts in which conflicting notions of identity are at play. In the winter of 2002 I was working in Birmingham at the invitation of the consulting firm Comedia (Charles Landry and Phil Wood), who had been hired by the City Council. Partly in response to race riots in other northern British cities in the preceding summer, Birmingham's politicians were concerned about 'getting it right' in relation to 'managing' ethnic diversity. As we met with various groups in the city, from the city planning staff to workers in a variety of community development programs, to young black men and Muslim women, we began to hear very different versions of Birmingham's identity. There was a fairly widely accepted founding story on the part of some Anglo residents (who referred to themselves as the 'indigenous' population) that Birmingham was an *English* city (not a multicultural city) and that those who were there first had greater rights to the city than the relative newcomers from the Indian subcontinent, the Caribbean, and so on. This profoundly political question of the city's changing identity clearly needed the widest possible public debate. I suggested that at some point the city was going to have to rewrite its foundational story, to make it more inclusive and open to change. The city's planners were very much implicated in this debate. At the community coalface, and especially in non-Anglo neighborhoods, these predominantly Anglo-Celtic planners were either reproducing the founding story of 'British Birmingham' or helping to change that story by making their policies and programs reflect and respect the diversity of the 'new city.'

This is not an isolated example anymore, but a situation increasingly common across Europe in this age of migrations. The need to collectively change (and represent in the built environment itself) these old foundational stories is one of the contemporary challenges facing planners.

2.2.3 Story as Catalyst for Change

Stories and storytelling can be powerful agents or aids in the service of change, as shapers of a new imagination of alternatives. Stories of success, or of exemplary actions, serve as inspirations when they are retold. I've lost count of the number of times I have told 'the Rosa Parks story,'[5] either in class or in a community or activist meeting, when the mood suddenly (or over time) gets pessimistic and people feel that the odds are too great, the structures of power too oppressive and all-encompassing. When Ken Reardon tells or writes his East St. Louis story (Reardon, 2003), he is among other things conveying a message of hope in the face of incredible odds. This 'organizing of hope' is one of our fundamental tasks as planners, and one of our weapons in that battle is the use of success stories, and the ability to tell those stories well, meaningfully, in a way that does indeed inspire others to act. My chapter in Part II of this book describes how I have been using the documentary, 'Where Strangers Become Neighbours' (Attili & Sandercock, 2007), as an inspirational catalyst in community development workshops in different Canadian cities.

Depending on the context, though, *success* stories may not be enough to disrupt existing habits of thought and bring about profound change, as we've seen in the last two examples. We may need different kinds of stories: stories that frighten, stories that shock, embarrass, defamiliarize (Eckstein, 2003). Giovanni Attili and I are currently making just such a film, about race relations in two small communities in northern British Columbia, Canada (Sandercock & Attili, 2010).

Deciding what stories to tell in what circumstances is part of the planner's art. The puzzle of how to change the stories that people tell themselves everyday, often repeating familiar stories from the media, absorbing and internalizing the messages

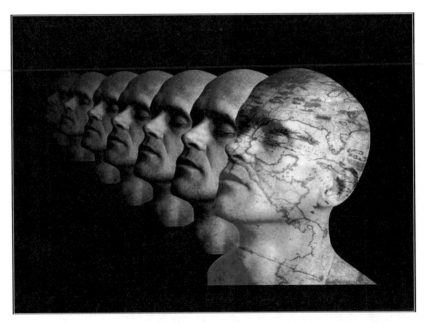

Fig. 2.5 A planning imagination for the 21st century. Video stills from the multimedia production 'A planning imagination for the 21st century' by Giovanni Attili

of the dominant culture or class, is an old one. Faced with a situation where people appear to be telling themselves 'the wrong stories,' there are two things that planners can do. One is, in good conscience and with humility, to suggest alternative stories. The second is to build 'education for a critical consciousness' into their participatory approaches. Planners are, after all, just one of the actors in the force field of public conversation.

I have one more example of the use of story in planning practices – in the process of policy analysis, formulation, and implementation – before I turn to academic storytelling about planning.

2.2.4 Story and Policy

Here I am aided by two scholars, James Throgmorton and Peter Marris, each of whom has done a lot of thinking about the connections between story and policy. In *Witnesses, Engineers and Storytellers: Using Research for Social Policy and Community Action* (1997), Peter Marris argues that the relationship between knowledge and action is not straightforward and that knowledge itself cannot, has not ever, determined policy. In analyzing various types of and approaches to social policy research, Marris asks why so little of the research produced on poverty, for example, has affected policy. His answers are several. One is that academics are powerful critics but weak storytellers. That is, they fail to communicate their findings in a form that is not only plausible but persuasive. (By contrast, he notes that community actors have great stories to tell, but no means of telling them, except to each other. So the wrong stories win the debates.) Storytelling, he says, is the natural language of persuasion, because any story has to involve both a sequence of events and the interpretation of their meaning. A story integrates knowledge of what happened with an understanding of why it happened and a sense of what it means to us. (If it fails to do all this, we say things like 'but I still don't understand why he did that' or 'why are you telling me this?') Stories organize knowledge around our need to act and our moral concerns. The stories don't have to be original, but they must be authoritative (that is, provide reliable evidence marshaled into a convincing argument). The best are both original and authoritative.[6]

To be persuasive, the stories we tell must fit the need as well as the situation. Policy researchers compete with everyone else who has a story to tell, and their special claim on public attention lies in the quality of their observation as well as the sophistication of the accumulated understanding through which they interpret their data. But this truthfulness is not, in itself, necessarily persuasive. Good stories have qualities such as dramatic timing, humor, irony, evocativeness, and suspense, in which social researchers are untrained. 'Worse,' says Marris, 'they have taught themselves that to be entertaining compromises the integrity of scientific work' (Marris, 1997, p. 58). Writing up policy research is hard work: it's hard to tell a good story while simultaneously displaying conscientiously the evidence on which it is based. But, Marris insists, the more social researchers attend to the storyteller's craft, and honor it in the work of colleagues and students, the more influential

Fig. 2.6 A planning imagination for the 21st century. Video stills from the multimedia production 'A planning imagination for the 21st century' by Giovanni Attili

they can be. We have to be able to tell our stories skillfully enough to capture the imagination of a broader and more political audience than our colleagues alone.

There are two notions of story at work here. One is functional/instrumental: bringing the findings of social research to life through weaving them into a good story. The other is more profound: storytelling, in the fullest sense, is not merely recounting events, but endowing them with meaning by commentary, interpretation, and dramatic structure.

While Marris confines his advocacy of storytelling to the publishing of research results, James Throgmorton's work addresses the next step: the arts of rhetoric in the public domain of speech and debate. The lesson he wants to impart is that if we want to be effective policy advocates, then we need to become not only good story creators but also good storytellers, in the more performative sense. In *Planning as Persuasive Storytelling* (1996), Throgmorton suggests that we can think of planning as an enacted and future-oriented narrative in which participants are both characters and joint authors. And we can think of storytelling as being an appropriate style for conveying the truth of planning action.

Throgmorton (1996, p. 48) draws on the concept of 'narrative rationality' in claiming that humans are storytellers who have a natural capacity to recognize the fidelity of stories they tell and experience. We test stories in terms of the extent to which they hang together (coherence) and in terms of their truthfulness and reliability (fidelity). But Throgmorton is unhappy with this, reminding us of situations in which two planning stories, both of which are coherent and truthful on their own terms, compete for attention. What then makes one more worthy than another? Throgmorton suggests that the answer to this question lies in part at least in the persuasiveness with which we tell our stories. Planning is a form of persuasive storytelling, and planners are both authors who write texts (plans, analyses, articles) and characters whose forecasts, surveys, models, maps, and so on act as tropes (figures of speech and argument) in their own and others' persuasive stories. A crucial part of Throgmorton's argument is that this future-oriented storytelling is never simply persuasive. It is also constitutive. The ways in which planners write and talk help to shape community, character, and culture. So a critical question for planners is what ethical principles should guide and constrain their efforts to persuade their audiences.

Marris's and Throgmorton's work has very important implications for policy research. If planners want to be more effective in translating knowledge to action, they argue, then we had better pay more attention to the craft of storytelling in both its written and oral forms. That means literally expanding the language of planning, to become more expressive, evocative, engaging, and to include the language of the emotions. New digital languages give us this capacity, as Attili's chapter in Part I argues, and as all of the chapters in Part II demonstrate.

'Academic story telling,' writes Finnegan, 'is ugly in its stark, clichéd monotone manner. We tell the dullest stories in the most dreary ways, and usually deliberately, for this is the mantle of scientific storytelling: it is supposed to be dull' (Finnegan, 1998, p. 21). What Finnegan alleges of academic storytelling is equally true of bureaucratic storytelling. Policy reports produced by government planning agencies, and also by consultants for those agencies, are cut from the same clichéd cloth. They are dry as dust. Life's juices have been squeezed from them. Emotion has been rigorously purged as if there were no such things as joy, tranquility, anger, resentment, fear, hope, memory, and forgetting, at stake in these analyses. What purposes, whose purposes, do these bloodless stories serve? For one thing, they serve to perpetuate a myth of the objectivity and technical expertise of planners. And in doing so, these documents are nothing short of misleading at best, dishonest at worst, about the kinds of problems and choices we face in cities.

To influence policy, then, as well as to be effective in planning processes, planners need to learn story, or rather an array of storytelling modes.

2.2.5 Story as Critique and/or Explanation

There is a false binary in our heads that separates planning documents, social scientific research, and theorizing from storytelling, rather than allowing us to appreciate the ways in which each of these employs story. Planning documents, from maps, to models, to GIS, to plans themselves, do in fact all tell a story. Sometimes the story is descriptive, or poses as descriptive – 'this is how things are,' 'these are the facts.' But there is no such thing as mere description, or pure facts. There is always an author who is choosing which facts are relevant, what to describe, what to count, and in the assembling of these facts a story is shaped, an interpretation, either consciously or unconsciously, emerges. Facts are usually marshaled to explain something and to draw some conclusions for action.

Scholars also use story in their critical writings about cities and planning, sometimes consciously, but usually not. As with planning documents, the more alert we can be to the underlying story or stories, the better we are able to evaluate them. We need to understand the mechanisms of story (structure, plot, characters), in order to tell good stories ourselves, to be more critical of the stories we have to listen to, and to be able to resist persuasive stories as well as create them. How to do this?

Fig. 2.7 A planning imagination for the 21st century. Video stills from the multimedia production 'A planning imagination for the 21st century' by Giovanni Attili

Eckstein (2003) explains that stories do their work, make themselves compelling, by manipulating time, voice, and space. So we need to attend to all three when hearing or constructing stories. *Time* is 'manipulated' through the device of duration. How much story 'space' is given to specific time intervals or periods of time? Which parts of a chronological story are collapsed into relatively few sentences, pages, or minutes, compared with other parts of the story that are given extended treatment? Paying attention to this issue of duration can allow the listener/reader to hear what matters most to the teller, as can listening for repetition, which produces patterns of significance. *Space* ranks with time as a component of and in story, and is critically important for urban scholars and practitioners. We must be able to ' "see" time in space' (Balzac, quoted in Eckstein, 2003, p. 28). Geographic scale is an important factor in the production of meaning. Stories operate at different geographic scales, sometimes metaphorical, and interpretation requires careful attention to those scales. The most obvious example would be whether one is viewing the city from the windows of a plane or skyscraper (the bird's eye view) or from the street. Stories also sometimes ask us to adopt a different spatial perspective than the one we're most comfortable with. For example, residents and local activists may be most familiar with looking at issues from the local or neighborhood perspective. Some stories ask us to take a regional or even global perspective. If this is beyond our familiarity, the storyteller will have to be very skillful in helping us to do this.

Voice is also central to storytelling. Is the story being told in first person, third person, or first or third person plural (I, she/he, we, they, 'those people'), and what does that signify about who is speaking on behalf of whom? Whose voices are given prominence, whose are repressed? As with the myths of other cultures, our planning and academic stories function not only as sanction and justification for the current order, but also as launching pads for counter-versions. Academic stories about planning usually take sides, although not always overtly. Sometimes this is revealed by asking, of any narrative, what voices are missing here? In other words, a critical perspective on the workings of story is as important as a critical perspective on the workings of power and influence in land-use planning.

2.3 From the Campfire to the Computer: Storytelling in a Digital Age

Getting inside the mechanisms of a story, as outlined above, is rather like getting inside the workings of a fine old clock or an electric motor, in so far as it is a way of understanding what makes it tick, what gives it power. But stories have fuelled human connection, teaching and understanding, and social organization since long before the invention of writing, let alone critical exegesis. The oral traditions of storytelling around a campfire or under the shade of a tree, at the river's edge or inside a cave, were extensions of, or complemented visual representations of, stories that were expressed on the walls of caves or in more ephemeral sand and chalk drawings and bark paintings. The visual element of or approach to storytelling has its stand-alone forms, which include the evolution from sand drawings to narrative paintings, as well as its complementary forms, supporting the verbal, such as the use of 'scenery' in theater and opera. Dance, puppetry, drumming, many genres of music, as well as cartoons and graffiti, are also vehicles for story that find their own audiences and tell us that, for many people, words are not the ultimate conveyors of meaning.

All of these storytelling forms still thrive in their different contexts for particular audiences. But arguably the most potent form of all emerged and evolved in the first half of the 20th century in the shape of 'moving pictures,' from the first black and white, silent films to present-day cinema with its apparently endless possibilities of technological invention, including animation, special effects, even 3-D. Still, filmmaking was, up until the digital revolution, a very expensive business requiring 'specialists' (producers) who knew how to raise large amounts of money, heavy equipment which was difficult and expensive to transport, and still more 'specialists' who knew how to distribute the 'product' to paying audiences, along with fixed capital investment in 'movie houses' or cinemas. These cinemas and, for a time, drive-in movie theaters became a hugely important part of the physical and social landscape of 20th century cities and towns, from the 1920s to the 1980s, when movie viewing was a more or less collective and social experience. Then, with increasing affluence and technological advances, all of that changed. Home entertainment systems started to replace moviegoing, but continued to propel an insatiable appetite for films, while the miniaturizing and digitalizing of cameras as well as advances in editing software and the spread of home computers quite suddenly made it possible and affordable for seemingly everyone to be making videos. And simultaneously the Internet has given people a 'movie house' in which to screen their efforts.

This rapid democratizing of filmmaking technologies offers enormous communicative possibilities to ordinary citizens as well as to planners and designers, for expressing opinions, for making advocacy films, and for providing means of visualizing alternative urban design and planning scenarios, possibilities ranging from full-blown long-form documentaries distributed as DVDs to 30-s raves posted on YouTube, intentionally more ephemeral but not necessarily any less influential. What Part II of this book demonstrates is a burgeoning of invention among urbanist filmmakers over the past decade in how video technologies might be applied to a range of urban interventions and policy discussions. And given what we know about the power of story, and particularly of the power of story expressed through the medium of film, it is important to develop a critical reflexivity about these uses (see Banks, 2001; Back, 2007).

Documentary filmmaking has an almost century-long history now and has evolved with and taken advantage of technological advances in mainstream moviemaking. As Ciacci has shown in Chapter 1, there is a specific history of the use of documentaries in planning and design practice, which he has called 'town planners' cinema.' While potentially or theoretically the tools of cinema could extend participation in the project for urban change to the largest possible number of people, Ciacci's deconstruction of their actual use delivers a sobering message. By and large, town planning films have been primarily made for 'propaganda value,' that is, to explain and persuade an audience of choices already made by the expert urbanists (architects, designers, and planners). This raises profound questions about the purposes of and possible audiences for documentaries and other video interventions in the urban arena.

Within the world of documentarians, a counter-trend developed in reaction to such 'official uses.' What has become known as 'participatory video' (PV) emerged in Latin America, inspired partly by Paolo Freire's thinking (Freire, 1970), and Canada in the 1970s. In Canada, the Fogo Process was part of a 1970s initiative called Challenge for Change, which created a series of films 'that intended to raise public consciousness about the rights and needs of disenfranchised and disadvantaged groups' (Weisner, 1992, p. 68). Challenge for Change did not set out to make progressive films *about* social issues but instead to use the filmmaking process as a

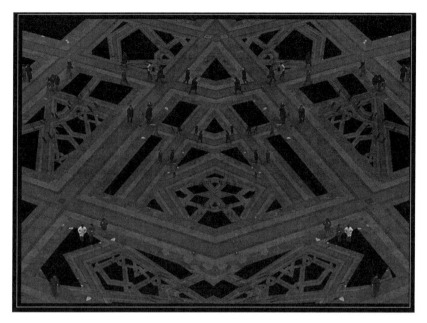

Fig. 2.8 A planning imagination for the 21st century. Video stills from the multimedia production 'A planning imagination for the 21st century' by Giovanni Attili

form of social change. The intent was to use film production and distribution as a means of empowering politically and socially disenfranchised people.

Fogo Island, off the coast of Newfoundland, Canada, was a community of 5.000 people who, by the late 1960s, were facing the collapse of their local fishing economy (leaving 60% of the population on social assistance), public infrastructure was in a state of disrepair, 50% of islanders were functionally illiterate, and differences in religion and tradition socially divided the community. To address the problems Fogo Island was facing, the government at the time proposed to relocate the entire community to a nearby 'development town.' Colin Low, a filmmaker, and Don Snowdon, an academic, came up with the idea of using video as a mechanism to facilitate dialogue between residents and government officials. In doing so, they invented a revolutionary filmmaking process centered on some key community-based concepts. They required every subject to have full editorial rights over their appearance and every effort was made to ensure that the government would respond to the community-produced video (Frantz, 2007, p. 104).

While there was never any formal evaluation of the Fogo project, shortly after the films were produced, a fishing cooperative and a school were established on Fogo Island and the community was not relocated. The question is whether projects like Fogo could work in urban areas if properly designed, and if so, to what ends? (Weisner, 1992, p. 71). Participatory video is an evolving action research methodology and will be discussed further in Part II, as well as in the Conclusions to this book.

The only unchanging thing about documentary over the past 100 years is that it is a form that makes assertions or 'truth claims' about the real world and/or people in that world (including the real world of history). *How* it does that is something that is subject to change and to ongoing debate (Ward, 2005, p. 8). Here I mention just four debates that have particular relevance to the chapters in Part II, which dwell on the use of documentary and video experiments in planning and other urban interventions. Perhaps the most consistent and enduring debate within the world of documentaries concerns the tension between, on the one hand, capturing some aspect of the real world or the people who inhabit it and, on the other hand, the inevitable use of aesthetic and representational devices to achieve that aim. A second hugely interesting area of debate is the way in which the subjects of and in documentary can be said to be 'performing for the cameras': in some instances this means behaving in ways that are a little larger than life, but in other instances can mean that interviewees tell the interviewer/filmmaker what they would like to hear (or perhaps what the interviewee would like to believe) rather than what actually is. A related issue is the way in which being in front of a camera intimidates some potential 'subjects' to the point of depriving them of voice, while apparently liberating others. A third debate is the issue of interpretation versus actuality: the notion that a documentary filmmaker is never simply a scientific or detached or balanced observer but is always, constantly, interpreting what she/he sees, imposing her/his own coherence as well as her/his own value system on the subject matter. And finally, there is the question of audience. To the extent that documentary filmmakers are conscious of a specific audience, their film will be shaped to speak to the particular interests of that audience (developers, investors, politicians, for example), thus necessarily omitting aspects of a topic deemed less relevant (social and environmental impacts on residents, for example). Documentaries can be designed to educate, to explain, to provoke, to shock, and to mobilize. Their purpose and intended audience determine how their story will be told.

Within the last decade we've seen a rapid 'democratizing' of film/video making, along with many other important tools of the digital revolution, all of which amount to technological developments that offer enormous *communicative* and *activist* possibilities for planning and policy, if only we can grasp the centrality of storytelling to our mission and envision equally democratic ways of harnessing this potential. Part II of this book provides an introduction to this potential, while our concluding chapter injects some critical reflexivity into this new frontier of the urban professions (Nichols, 1991, 1994).

My purpose in this chapter has been to establish the power and centrality of story in the planning field. Multimedia offers the latest technologies in the service of the oldest of human devices for understanding and inspiring: that is, stories. The rest of this book is an exploration of the ways in which multimedia can enhance and expand on the wide range of applications of story and storytelling in planning processes, practices, pedagogy, and research.

As cities become undeniably multiethnic and multicultural, the need to engage in dialogue with strangers must become an urban art and not just a planner's art, if we are concerned about how we can coexist with each other, in all our difference.

This most ancient of arts begins with the sharing of stories and moves toward the shaping of new collective stories. 'The storyteller, besides being a great mother, a teacher, a poetess, a warrior, a musician, a historian, a fairy, and a witch, is a healer and a protectress. Her chanting or telling of stories ... has the power of bringing us together' (Trinh, 1989, p. 140).

Notes

1. Here I'm alluding to the title of Trinh's book, *Woman Native Other* (1989). Trinh is a writer, composer, and filmmaker.
2. Doug Aberley is a Vancouver-based practitioner who uses elaborate community mapping techniques in his work with indigenous communities. Maeve Lydon is the founder and director of Common Ground Community Mapping Project, a nonprofit organization in Victoria, BC, that provides mapping and learning resources for schools, neighborhoods, and communities who want to undertake sustainable community development and planning projects.
3. See Susskind, McKearnan, and Thomas-Larmer (1999), LeBaron (2002), Fowler and Mumford (1999), and Thiagarajan and Parker (1999).
4. Eckstein's advice is invaluable: 'if one listens to others' stories with ears tuned to how their stories will serve one's own storytelling, how they will fit in one's grander narrative, then one risks not hearing them at all' (Eckstein, 2003).
5. Rosa Parks was the African American woman who, in Alabama in 1955, refused to move to the back of the bus when white folks boarded. This act of civil disobedience turned into a year-long boycott of the bus service by Blacks, and gave birth to the civil rights movement.
6. Marris cites Herbert Gans' *The Urban Villagers* and Michael Young and Peter Willmott's *Family and Kinship in East London* as good examples.

References

Attili, G. (2007). Digital ethnographies in the planning field. *Planning Theory & Practice, 8*(1), 90–97.

Attili, G., & Sandercock, L. (2007). *Where strangers become neighbours (50 minute documentary)*. Montreal, QC: National Film Board of Canada.

Back, L. (2007). *The art of listening*. New York: Berg.

Banks, M. (2001). *Visual methods in social research*. London: Sage.

Bourdieu, P. (1990). *In otherwords: Essays towards a reflexive sociology*. Cambridge: Polity Press.

Dunstan, G., & Sarkissian, W. (1994). Goonawarra: Core story as methodology in interpreting a community study. In W. Sarkissian & K. Walsh (Eds.), *Community participation in practice. Casebook*. Perth, WA: Institute of Sustainability Policy.

Eckstein, B. (2003). Making space: Stories in the practice of planning. In B. Eckstein & J. Throgmorton (Eds.), *Story and sustainability: Planning, practice, and possibility for American cities*. Cambridge, MA: MIT Press.

Eckstein, B., & Throgmorton, J. (Eds.). (2003). *Story and sustainability: Planning, practice, and possibility for American cities*. Cambridge, MA: MIT Press.

Ellyard, P. (2001). *Ideas for the new millennium* (2nd ed.). Melbourne, VIC: Melbourne University Press.

Finnegan, R. (1998). *Tales of the city. A study of narrative and urban life*. Cambridge, UK: Cambridge University Press.

Flyvbjerg, B. (2002). *Making social science matter*. Cambridge, UK: Cambridge University Press.

Forester, J. (1989). *Planning in the face of power*. Berkeley, CA: University of California Press.

Forester, J. (2000). Multicultural planning in deed: Lessons from the mediation practice of Shirley Solomon and Larry Sherman. In M. Burayidi (Ed.), *Urban planning in a multicultural society.* London: Praeger.

Fowler, S., & Mumford, M. (Eds.). (1999). *Intercultural sourcebook: Cross-cultural training methods* (Vol. 2). Yarmouth, ME: Intercultural Press.

Frantz, J. (2007). Using participatory video to enrich planning process. *Planning Theory and Practice, 8*(1), 103–107.

Freire, P. (1970). *Pedagogy of the oppressed.* New York: Herder and Herder.

Geertz, C. (1988). *Works and lives: The anthropologist as author.* Stanford, CA: Stanford University Press.

Hooks, B. (1984). *Feminist theory: From margin to center.* Boston: South End Press.

Houston, J. (1982). *The possible human.* Los Angeles: Tarcher.

Houston, J. (1987). *The search for the beloved: Journeys in sacred psychology.* Los Angeles: Tarcher.

Kelly, J. G. (1984). *Women, history, and theory.* Chicago: University of Chicago Press.

Landry, C. (2000). *The creative city.* London: Earthscan.

Landry, C. (2006). *The art of city making.* London: Earthscan.

LeBaron, M. (2002). *Bridging troubled waters.* San Francisco: Jossey Bass.

Lerner, G. (1997). *Why history matters.* Oxford: Oxford University Press.

Mandelbaum, S. (1991). Telling stories. *Journal of Planning Education and Research, 10*(1), 209–214.

Marris, P. (1997). *Witnesses, engineers, and storytellers: Using research for social policy and action.* College Park, MD: University of Maryland, Urban Studies and Planning Program.

McNaughton, A. (2001). *Constable Tom Woods – the unlikely planner.* Unpublished Term Paper for PLAN 502, School of Community and Regional Planning, University of British Columbia, Vancouver, BC.

Nichols, B. (1991). *Representing reality.* Bloomington, IN: Indiana University Press.

Nichols, B. (1994). *Blurring boundaries.* Bloomington, IN: Indiana University Press.

Rabinow, P., & Sullivan, W. M. (Eds.). (1987). *Interpretive social science: A second look.* Berkeley, CA: University of California Press.

Reardon, K. (2003). Ceola's vision, our blessing: The story of an evolving community/university partnership in East St. Louis, Illinois. In: B. Eckstein & J. Throgmorton (Eds.), *Stories and sustainability: Planning, practice and possibility for American cities.* Cambridge, MA: MIT Press.

Said, E. (1979). *Orientalism.* New York: Vantage Books.

Sandercock, L. (1998). *Towards cosmopolis: Planning for multicultural cities.* Chichester: Wiley.

Sandercock, L. (2003). *Cosmopolis 2: Mongrel cities of the 21st century.* London and New York: Continuum.

Sandercock, L. (2005a). A planning imagination for the 21st century. *Journal of the American Planning Association, 70*(2), 133–141.

Sandercock, L. (2005b). A new spin on the creative city: Artist/planner collaborations. *Planning Theory & Practice, 6*(1), 101–103.

Sandercock, L., & Attili, G. (2010). *Finding our way: A path to healing native/non-native relations in Canada (90 minute documentary).* Distributor as yet undecided.

Sarkissian, W., Hurford, D., & Wenman, C. (2010). *Creative community planning: Transformative engagement methods for working at the edge.* London: Earthscan.

Stretton, H. (1969). *The political sciences.* London: Routledge and Kegan Paul.

Susskind, L., & McKearnanMand Thomas-Larmer, J. (Eds.). (1999). *The consensus building handbook.* Thousand Oaks, CA: Sage.

Thiagarajan, S., & Parker, G. (Eds.). (1999). *Teamwork and teamplay.* San Francisco: Jossey-Bass.

Throgmorton, J. (1996). *Planning as persuasive storytelling*. Chicago: University of Chicago Press.

Trinh Minh-ha, T. (1989). *Woman native other*. Bloomington, IN: Indiana University Press.

Ward, P. (2005). *Documentary: The margins of reality*. London: Wallflower Press.

Weisner, D. (1992). Media for the people: The Canadian experiments with film and video in community development. *American Review of Canadian Studies, 2*(1), 65–75.

Chapter 3
Beyond the Flatlands: Digital Ethnographies in the Planning Field

Giovanni Attili

New technologies represent a system of constraints and possibilities that constitute the foundation of new rhetorical spaces: the spheres of new communicative and persuasive procedures. Nowadays, urban planning has the chance to critically and rigorously experiment with these new spaces. It has the chance to transgress traditional representational codes and to expand its semantic horizons.

This chapter portrays one such challenging exploration: the fecund crossroads between qualitative analytical approaches and digital languages within the planning field. It is a path that embraces diverse dimensions: media and messages, analysis and rhetoric, ethics and aesthetics.

A path which springs from a visionary metaphor.

3.1 A Methodological Kidnapping

In 1882, Edwin Abbott writes an imaginary novel about a bi-dimensional reality: *Flatland*. It is a completely level world, a vast sheet of paper in which houses, inhabitants, and trees are straight lines, triangles, polygons, and other geometric figures. Through a striking narrative, Abbott invents a place and fills it with entities characterized by abstract and linear contours. These figures move freely on a surface but without the power of rising above or sinking below it. In this reality nobody has the perception of a third dimension. The irruption of a Sphere in Flatland provokes bewilderment in the Square-Narrator who doesn't accept the existence of a world with another dimension. His reaction is violent: a three-dimensional world is not possible. It is a deceit. The Square tries to kill the Sphere. He wants to hand the Sphere over to justice. For its part the Sphere tries to convince the Square with an analogical reasoning, in vain. There is no solution for the Sphere but to kidnap the Square and carry it to a higher position, separated from Flatland, from where it is possible to discern new shapes and dimensions.

G. Attili (✉)

Dipartimento di Architettura e Urbanistica per l'Ingegneria, Università "La Sapienza" di Roma, Roma, Italy

e-mail: giovanni.attili@gmail.com

L. Sandercock, G. Attili (eds.), *Multimedia Explorations in Urban Policy and Planning*, Urban and Landscape Perspectives 7, DOI 10.1007/978-90-481-3209-6_3, © Springer Science+Business Media B.V. 2010

Fig. 3.1 Ethnographic analysis. Photo and graphic elaboration by Giovanni Attili

> An unspeakable horror seized me. There was a darkness; then a dizzy, sickening sensation of sight that was not like seeing. I saw a Line that was not a Line; Space that was not Space; I was myself and not myself. When I could find voice, I shrieked aloud in agony: 'either this is madness or this is hell!' (Abbott, 1993, p. 124).

The coercive action of the Sphere destabilizes the self-referential vision of the Square, leading it to a diverse image of the world. A logical leap makes the Square transit from one world to another, from a consolidated perception to the comprehension of different cognitive laws. This leap is painful. The kidnapping is a methodological kidnapping: "only the violence and the giddiness can crash the unhealthy use of the language" (Manganelli, 1993, p. 165).

Abbott's novel tragically ends with the futile attempt by the Square to convince Flatland's other inhabitants about the existence of a third dimension. The Square is derided and imprisoned.

> Prometheus up in Spaceland was bound for bringing down fire for mortals, but I – poor Flatland Prometheus – lie here in prison for bringing nothing to my countrymen. Yet I exist in the hope that these memoirs, in some manner, I know not how, may find their way to the minds of humanity in Some Dimension, and may stir up a race of rebels who shall refuse to be confined to limited Dimensionality (Abbott, 1993, pp. 150–151).

Flatland's narrative illusionism ends with the sensation that other spaces are conceivable and with the conviction that each language faces a challenge when it accepts new possible descriptive codes: it is a tragic attack on the limitations of language and on the spatial images which are created by it. It is the possibility of thinking about other potential dimensionalities which violates the consolidated ones.

3.2 Senseless Bi-dimensional Surfaces

Why Flatland? There is an interesting analogy between the level world invented by Abbott and the representations of urban space which are traditionally produced in the urban planning field. In this field, a sort of cartographic anxiety ends up turning the city into a bi-dimensional surface which is crossed by lines, marked by geometries, and filled with homogenous colors. These stylized grammars flatten urbanity into an isotropic and metrical space. As in Abbott's novel, cartographies are overfilled with geometrical, detailed, descriptive, and dimensionally limited languages. From above, a triumphant flying-over technique photographs the physical shape of the city through zenithal views which are projected on scaled papery surfaces. The eyes are firmly kept on the ground, according to a logic which gives sense only to the figures which can express themselves in a readable shape and inside a visible and bi-dimensional surface. From this perspective the physical-material dimension of the territory is the only one to be legitimately considered and represented.

Through a rationalist and abstract operation, cartographies reduce urban complexities to morphologies, models, systems, compositions. The result is a flat territory which is inhabited by signs: "texts of an impersonal, inhuman and intelligible narrative; demented and horribly reasonable like impeccable and senseless

grammatical examples" (Manganelli, 1993, p. 166). The city is sterilized and represented like a fictitious geometrical-Euclidean container: a conventional and timeless
space, in which the objects can be tidily placed according to a system of predeter-
mined orthogonal axis. As a result, urban space is frozen and vivisected through
metric-quantitative lenses and panoptic-standardizing views. These representations
embody a simplifying and control anxiety: from above, the city is controllable at a
glance and can be translated into a Cartesian level where nothing seems to escape
from the territorial government.

Nevertheless this kind of city appears surreal and improbable. In this city, humanities, accidents, conflicts, and relational spaces are scientifically removed. As in
Flatland, the cartographed city lacks *other* dimensions. I am not talking about
the geometrical height that is symbolized by the irruption of the Sphere into the
bi-dimensionality of Abbott's world. The missing dimensions of urban planning
cartographies are connected with *pluriverses* of irreducible inhabitants characterized by relations, expectations, feelings, reminiscences, bodies, voices, and stories
which are stratified in living urbanities. In other words, cartographies are meticulously determined in representing the silenced shapes of an objectified city, but
they forget life-through-space. They don't consider what is invisible, what loves
hiding and elusively pulsates in the interstices of maps and of the morphological design of the city. Beyond what is already told and done. Beyond plans and
cartographies.

It is urgent to invent new analytical tools which can give centrality to people. It
is important to focus on the individual and collective signification practices through
which inhabitants create their own living environment. It is important to find a dense
way to read a relational space which connects different situated and embodied subjectivities. In doing this, I'm not denying the relevance of the physical dimension of
the city, rather I'm evoking the need of an expressive and analytical path whose aim
is to intersect the physical and the relational space. I'm evoking an alternative envisioning of spatiality as illustrated in the heterotopologies of Foucault, the trialectics
and thirdings of Lefebvre, the marginality and radical openness of bell hooks, the
hybridities of Homi Bhabha which directly challenge all conventional modes of
spatial thinking: the demolition of all the *flatlands* which traditionally permeate our
disciplinary field.

3.3 Ethnographic Polyphonies

According to these premises, what kind of path should we take? First of all we
should be conscious that the present internal organization of disciplines represents
the result of an historical course. This course, in its evolution, has left aside many
other unexplored and perhaps more fecund knowledge articulations, paradigms, and
approaches. From this perspective it is possible to critically think about some possibilities which have been historically set aside and try to bring them up to date
(Bourdieu, 1995). For example, I'm talking about the revaluation of qualitative

Fig. 3.2 Video stills from "Where Strangers Become Neighbours" (see Chapter 4). Video stills from "Where Strangers Become Neighbours" (Attili & Sandercock, 2007)

analytical tools which historically permeated some 1950s' planning experiences.[1] In the last decades, these qualitative analytical approaches have been progressively sacrificed in favor of more quantitative methods which have influenced many disciplinary sectors, even those which were far away from the hard scientific disciplines. But what is not recognized is that a powerful imaginary is the best one, unless we accept that what's powerful is necessarily the best.

Rather than succumbing to the mermaid's singing of the quantitative analysis (made of numbers, universal laws, matrixes, zoning, and objectifying maps), maybe it's time to embrace a more qualitative view of the city. Ethnographic analysis, for instance, succeeds in expressing what is beyond the surface of maps, objects, classifications, and quantitative-aggregated data. Such analysis intentionally focuses on individual lives that cross urbanities made of changing densities, memories, perceptive, and aesthetic levels. It is an attentive and minute analysis of urban spaces, where existences, intersections, languages, and interstitial freedoms delineate controversial and palpitating landscapes.

Fig. 3.3 Video stills from "Where Strangers Become Neighbours" (see Chapter 4). Video stills from "Where Strangers Become Neighbours" (Attili & Sandercock, 2007)

The goal of this kind of analysis is to get more deeply in touch with inhabitants' life practices, conflicts, and modalities of space appropriation/construction, which reveal principles, rationalities, and potential writings that transgress the ordered text of the planned city. Capturing these multiform practices involves listening to the city's murmurs, to catch stories, to read signs and spatial poetics, all of which are sense generative. It involves researching the invisible, which is intended as something that is not imprisonable in any scheme or form, as something that ends up interrogating our ways of exploring, analyzing, depicting, and planning the space in which we live.

Transgressing the ideology of the transcendental observer, the ethnographic approach privileges the study of collaborative contexts which are intended to produce a collective invention of interconnected stories. In this perspective there is no longer one lonely eye that scans everything, but a multiplicity of situated views based on inhabitants' stories that cannot be thought of as separated monads, but rather as connected and sense-making narratives. Through in-depth interviews and the confrontation of diverse visions of the world, the ethnographic approach becomes a powerful tool to be used for a deeper comprehension of what animates our cities: the diverse souls, the conflicts, and the unexplored resources.

The result is a narrative which is built on the intersection of multiple narratives. It's a story which doesn't pretend to represent the truth, claiming subjectivity and partiality. In each story, before narrating the others, we narrate to ourselves and we narrate ourselves, disclosing invisible threads which hide a desire or its opposite: a fear. A plot connects the narrative elements: fate or mind cannot unravel twisted skeins and misleading perspectives where everything hides some other things.

Fig. 3.4 Video stills from "Where Strangers Become Neighbours" (see Chapter 4). Video stills from "Where Strangers Become Neighbours" (Attili & Sandercock, 2007)

3.4 Situational Ethics

The polyphonic ethnographic narrative is the result of a series of in-depth interviews. This qualitative methodological approach is used to capture a plurality of voices, perceptions, and stories. It is an interpretive practice whose aim is to make sense of phenomena in terms of the meanings people bring to them (Denzin & Lincoln, 2005). It is an activity based on a deep interaction with people who are invited to express themselves and their worlds. It is an involving process that invokes a series of important ethical issues regarding the construction of the interviews and the use of the collected information.[2] These issues have been faced historically by social scientists through the formalized definition of ethical codes and protocols. In many countries review and monitoring organs (such as the Institutional Review Boards, IRBs) have been established to control how this kind of human research responded to universal ethical standards. The assumption was that social research was based on a value-free perspective and its ethical dilemmas had to be addressed through positivistic and standardized procedures. The result was a bureaucratic *gamesmanship* (Blanchard, 2002, p. 11) with severe structural deficiencies: an approach characterized by the rationalist presumption of canonical ethics which was destined to be progressively challenged by new and evolving epistemological consciousnesses.

Nowadays the regulatory systems built to monitor the ethically sensitive issues of social research are increasingly deconstructed in favor of a different approach to knowledge: the research cannot be considered a value-free inquiry formalized through objective rules, but rather a contextualized activity in which values and moral assumptions play a significant role. Moreover researchers and communities cannot be considered as separated and hierarchically organized monads: they are connected by a mutual, collaborative, and pedagogical relationship. In this respect, "participants have a co-equal say in how research should be conducted, what should be studied, which methods should be used, which findings are valid and acceptable, how the findings have to be implemented and how the consequences of such actions are to be assessed" (Denzin, 2003, p. 257). This reflects a different commitment on the part of the researcher, who is no longer subjected to a "remote discipline or institution but to those he or she studies" (Denzin, 2003, p. 258). This approach implies a constant redefinition of what needs to be done to address ethical challenges in social research. The universal basic moral standards (such as respect for people, beneficence, and justice) established by monitoring organs or institutions need to be shaped according to the different contexts, situations, and embodied relationships that embrace the research participants. From this perspective, the research cannot be seen as a preestablished or preapproved set of procedures. It cannot be guided by a monocultural ethical rationalism. Rather, it needs to be built in collaborative ways through a mutual learning process: the different subjects who are part of this process have a co-responsibility in defining the proper strategies to deal with ethically sensitive issues. This approach is particularly relevant in multicultural contexts characterized by a plurality of ethical perspectives, values, and views.

The ethnographic approach requires an evolving and adaptive ethical awareness and practice: the willingness to cooperate with the members of the community to find original and contextualized ways to build the research itself. It is not only the researchers' ethical perspective, or just the one of the community: it is a research path that emerges in a co-learning environment where researchers are "led by the members of the community to discover them" (Denzin, 2003, p. 243). This approach transgresses pre-codified procedures based on rational validation and opens up unexpected synergies that inform the research. The caring values are still central but need to be reshaped according to the specificity of the contexts and of the people involved.

The collaborative mutuality of this approach deconstructs the non-contingent cosmology of universal ethical values in favor of a *situational ethics* rooted in a cooperative and contextualized relationship. What does need to be acknowledged, however, is that the relation between researchers and respondents is not completely symmetrical, contrary to Denzin's argument (1997). There are power positions that cannot be ignored or blurred; rather they need to be recognized through a responsible ethical practice that is rooted in an "asymmetrical reciprocity" (Young, 1997).

3.5 The Power to Narrate Has to Be Framed

Ethnographers have to be extremely conscious about the power they exercise to narrate: the power to give expression to the polyphony of voices that have been captured during the research. Nowadays there is a widely recognized consciousness about the impossibility of an objective and neutral account of the reality researchers want to investigate. Every description is necessarily partial, opinionated, and value-driven, and therefore political. We constantly apply filters to make sense of the world: we use a cone of light to illuminate what is relevant to us, through judgments and moral assumptions. From this perspective ethnographies cannot be conceived as the transparent revealing of an ontological reality that existed independently of us. We need to abandon the obsession with a mimetic representation in order to experience a significant metaphorical shift: from discovery and findings to constructing and making. From ontology to epistemology.

Ethnographies have to be built. In this construction process, researchers have a lot of options: they can tell significantly different stories of the same reality. They can tell the same story adopting quite different languages. This process requires self-reflexivity (see Chapter 11).

Ethnographies have to be framed by further narratives aimed at explaining the process through which they are built. This frame has to address specific significant issues: the role of the researcher, the dialogical processes, the research goals, the power relationships, the ethical dilemmas. The frame needs to make those elements explicit (see Chapter 10). Metaphorically, the frame helps the potential spectator in contextualizing the image she/he is observing. It determines the grammar and the pragmatics of the eye which scans the representation. The frame is the compass that can be used to orient the comprehension of a specific narrative; to understand why that specific story and not another one; to avoid the risk of being shipwrecked in the ocean of relativism, in the chaos of different representations/stories that cannot be fully understood if their genesis process is not readable, if their goals are not understandable, if their questions are not examinable. The frame of a research

Fig. 3.5 Self-reflexivity. Graphic elaboration of a painting of M.C. Escher, from the multimedia production "A planning imagination for the 21st century" by Giovanni Attili

product helps the viewer/reader to discern what is beyond the visible part of it: the process and the involved subjectivities. It's the mean through which it is possible to measure the credibility of the research, its situational ethics, and its self-reflexive consciousness.

3.6 Multi-sensory Aesthetics in Digital Ethnographies

As I have argued, ethnographies are self-reflexive analytical practices aimed at portraying lives and stories, at transgressing objectified urban representations, at creatively expressing meaningful narratives. The key word to comprehend the fulcrum of ethnographic analysis is "to evoke": it creates a plausible world taken from everyday life, playing with surprising pieces that combine themselves in transfigured images. Assuming this perspective, ethnography rids itself of the obsession of a mimesis that is rooted in objects, facts, generalization, truth. Rather, it becomes an interconnected patchwork of evocative images that are imbued with ambiguity and indeterminateness. Their comprehension escapes the researcher's intentionality, becoming a field that is open to diverse interpretation and possibilities. This level of interpretative openness transforms ethnographies into possible catalysts for interaction inside planning processes. In other words, they represent a different way of provoking dialogue, suggestions, and inclusiveness in decision-making contexts. It is a way of opening up a public conversation.

In order to be communicated, the analysis of the community *ethos* ("ethno") has to be translated into a *writing* ("graphic"). This is not necessarily a restrictively verbal transcription, rather it can draw from a plurality of different languages. It can be interpreted as a hybrid "text" that makes discourse forms problematic, melting and deconstructing acquired codes. In doing this, postmodern ethnography feeds on the potentialities of new forms of technologies (ICTs). The current technological organization level cannot be thought of as an accidental phenomenon. It represents an influential paradigm that cannot be disregarded: "a new system of restraints and limits, but even of unpredictable and unprecedented possibilities, through which it is possible to undertake new paths of thought, action and behavior" (Gargani, 1999, p. 16).

Fig. 3.6 Video stills from "Where Strangers Become Neighbours" (see Chapter 4). Video stills from "Where Strangers Become Neighbours" (Attili & Sandercock, 2007)

New media have the disruptive and intrinsic capability of contextually using different expressive languages. They seem complex scores of multi-sensory idioms that can be creatively reassembled to express and communicate specific contents. Potentially, new media have as many epistemologies and languages as you can find in the world itself (Levy, 1997). They represent an extremely versatile and dynamic container inside, which it is possible to build complex "images": forests of signs and communicative metaphors which are co-involved and interpenetrated. The creative bricolage of media and diversified messages produce something more than the simple summation of these elements: it is a digital poetics that is germinative of new meanings.

Digital languages strengthen the expressive possibilities of ethnographies, connecting a qualitative study of the city to the potentialities of richer communicative languages. Digital ethnographies expressively narrate stories, whose role is now widely recognized in the planning field (Forester, 1989; Mandelbaum, 1991; Eckstein & Throgmorton, 2003; Sandercock, 2003). In simple terms, they are able to communicate narratives through aesthetic involvements, which are crucial in urban interactions. They can give expression to inspiring stories which are potentially able to trigger further planning processes, showing possibilities and sense worlds.

From this point of view, digital ethnographies are creative and very delicate inventions that reveal meaning without committing the mistake of defining it. They circumscribe, without closing or labeling, leaving imaginative spaces open. "Like a space which contains and opens at the same time, like a spoken word and like a sense intention that is never concluded" (Melucci, 2000, p. 112), digital ethnographies point at opacity, semantic fluidity, ambiguities that could give rise to different possible interpretations. All these characteristics are extremely important in awakening new imageries and in allowing people to creatively think about their own space, moving beyond maps, blueprints, and schematics; moving beyond limited forms of interaction.

New technologies transform ethnographic analysis into a different communicative tool that offers a surplus of meanings and interpretations. It doesn't exhaust itself. It is not univocally determined. It never finds a precise answer. Each view finds another richness. It can be impregnated with what is not verifiable or inferable

Fig. 3.7 Video stills from "Where Strangers Become Neighbours" (see Chapter 4). Video stills from "Where Strangers Become Neighbours" (Attili & Sandercock, 2007)

according to logic and scientific languages. This is an imprecise and arbitrary dimension that is not easy to pin down: the more you try to determine its essence, the more this essence withdraws, offering space for new interpretations.

Digital ethnographies embody the transition from rhetoric to poetics: it is a leap which allows the move from referential and argumentative languages to germinative and constructive ones. The potential result is the transformation of the world into a plot of "living metaphors" (Gargani, 1999) which plays a role in breaking acquired codes and in generating new grammars and meanings. It is not the outcome of aprioristic schemes. Rather it emerges poetically. The expressive and communicative characteristics of digital ethnographies create a space for the potential creation of passionate and pulsating metaphors: a creative filter which allows the cohabitation with what is inexpressible; a communicative act that is able to involve and connect people in a public discourse on the environments in which they live.

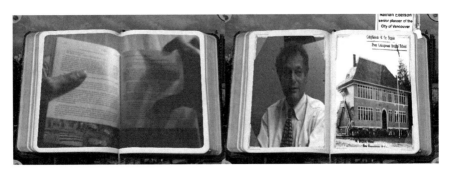

Fig. 3.8 Video stills from "Where Strangers Become Neighbours" (see Chapter 4). Video stills from "Where Strangers Become Neighbours" (Attili & Sandercock, 2007)

3.7 Poetical Gestures and Interactive Astonishment

Like an artistic gesture, digital ethnographies succeed in arousing astonishment: an interrogation state that is suspended between light and shadow, between known things and invisible horizons.

> The amazement in front of the unknown becomes the thought which enlarges the investigated field. From this perspective, astonishment leads to the infinite. The astonishment is the beginning of knowledge and of philosophical thought. It is intended as an emotion which follows something that cannot be totally and integrally absorbed (Gargani, 1999, p. 22).

Paradoxically the pretension of an exhaustive and all-inclusive knowledge is what overwhelms what is investigated, preventing a deeper comprehension. This is the epistemological limit that characterizes the disciplinary specializations when they attempt to exhaustively control their specific object of interest. The disciplinary, formalized, and apparently thorough translation of reality ends up in removing its ambiguity, its depth, its unthinkableness. Astonishment awakens when we abandon the rational and comprehensive control and start exploring the world in questioning terms, putting objectivity into brackets.

Digital ethnographies embody a possible knowledge path that is made of imaginations, poetical gestures, and aesthetic experiences. The astonishment theme, fundamental to a different cognitive approach, is particularly relevant because it is the presupposition for action. Through astonishment it is possible to reinvent the sense frameworks through which people organize their own experience of the world and in the world. Poetical and evocative digital ethnographies offer a space for suggestions and drifting imaginaries. These aesthetic and perceptive drifts are creative actions: they create a space for new possibilities. In opening this space, digital ethnographies represent a field in which acting becomes possible. Just as in the Veda, Vishnu, through his steps, creates a space for the warlike action of Indra (Dumezil, 1969 cit. in De Certeau, 1990, p. 185), so digital ethnographies prefigure possibilities of action, becoming an occasion that could create interactive contexts.

Digital ethnographies act like deforming mirrors that alter events or relations which are not recognizable in the ordinary flows of everyday life. These mirrors are not unidirectional, mechanical, or positive. They don't passively photograph reality. "They act as reflecting consciences and the reflected images are the product of them. These images are modeled in vocabulary and rules, in meta-linguistic grammars through which unprecedented performances can occur" (Turner, 1993, p. 76). In other words, digital ethnographies decline reality in a subjunctive mood, voicing supposition, desire, hypothesis, or possibility. They can be interpreted as active agents of change: a drawing board where it is possible to use the colors that are able to stimulate a social interaction. I'm talking about a strongly involving interaction: one that draws on emotions, aesthetic-perceptive dimensions, and whatever is familiar inside us. This is possible because digital ethnographies transgress technical and specialized languages, which are usually not very involving.

3.8 Digital Ethnographies as Magnets for a Situational Planning

Out of their lives and interests, out of their skill areas, separated one from the other, individuals have nothing to say. The difficulty is to catch them – both in an emotional and topological sense – and to group them together, involving them in an adventure through which they could enjoy imagining, exploring, building together sensitive environments (Levy, 1997, p. 131).

Digital ethnographies aim to reach this goal. They can be used as fulcra of strongly interactive events: these are performatory situations that are able to implicate diverse subjectivities, remembrances, fantasies, and creativities. They are temporary environments of a superior passional quality to be molecularly disseminated in the city, in the wake of the situationist experimentations. In these events, digital ethnographies can be inserted in urban space through psychogeographical projections on the faces of buildings, interactive installations, strongly involving digital games.

The ethnographic event becomes a magnet for interaction:

> after the event there is a multiplication of the narrations that try to explain it, to exalt it, to find the moral from it, to forgive it, to abhor it, to repudiate it, to use it in order to characterize a collective experience and as a model for the future (Turner, 1993, p. 93).

The collective fruition of digital ethnographies in an urban space becomes a playful-constructive moment where propositions, creative listening, metaphors, and symbolic acts interact. The construction of performatory occasions based on the use of digital ethnographies is the "bet of reaching change, pushing the game and multiplying the touching moments" (Debord, 1989). In this way the city could become a net of playful moments, a new theater that could host cultural operations which are concretely and resolutely built through the collective organization of interactive environments. The astonishment and the interactive potential connected with the use of digital ethnographies allow city-building processes to emerge: they are interactive occasions that can collectively define future scenarios and nourish endogenous and creative capabilities in order to produce changes in urban life.

From this point of view, digital ethnographies can be interpreted as *relational and communicative tools* that "help building social bonds through learning and knowledge exchange; communicative tools that are able to listen to, to combine and to give expression to diversity" (Levy, 1997, p. 133). These tools invite people to suggest modifications, further narrations through a dynamic knowledge management to be explored "not only conversationally but even through sensitive modalities according to significant paths and associations" (Levy, 1997, p. 210). Understanding that reason doesn't produce the totality of our actions, to create real communicative space, and induce people to act it is not enough to "tell," rather it is necessary to transfer energies, make sentiments and emotions vibrate, awaken latent aspirations, knowledge, and energies, rediscovering the powerful role of artistic and poetic languages. It is necessary to focus on the cognitive and communicative performance of aesthetic pleasure, a pleasure that is not an accessory but rather a central moment of every communicative process (Gargani, 1999). These tools are the foundations of a different idea of planning: an opportunity for the (possible) construction of common goods and not top-down politics that emerge from interaction. It is a form of planning that is deprived of its argumentative, categorical, and controlling aura. It is the construction of processes rooted in the power of narrative exchange and constructions of endogenous territorial practices.

The assumption of this perspective means abandoning the idea of an intentional, comprehensive, state-controlled, and panoptical planning in favor of the construction of *strong* interactive processes and of the "images," tools, and situations that could potentially catalyze them. This means thinking about a *propulsive* planning that could stimulate sense-making occasions, giving value to socially hidden or inactive potentialities, activating empowerment, multiplying different learning situations. I'm talking about a less normative planning, one that is more inclined to make needs, actions, and politics emerge from inhabitants themselves.

The implications of this perspective are particularly important and can contribute to a cultural re-orientation of territorial politics which are oriented to multiply the occasions of social interaction. This approach is difficult: it requires more and not less intervention. Moreover it requires the public sector workers to have a deep comprehension of the phenomena, a less normative attitude, abandoning the standardization of social behaviors that is traditionally considered the best solution for their control (Tosi, 2000, p. 1218).

The unforeseeable outcomes of the social interactions (produced locally and contextually) become the fulcrum of a different idea of planning. Assuming this perspective, the control anxiety of planning breaks down.

Given the crisis of political representation and of state-controlled planning, it is urgent to creatively imagine other paths such as the multiplication of the collective learning occasions that can produce innovative change grammars. The use of digital ethnographies seems to answer this kind of exigency. They have the potential to catalyze people's interaction, socializing evocative and powerful stories-images of the city, involving inhabitants in creatively discussing the interconnected space dimensionalities in which they live. They are intended to prefigure possible changes. They can do this by creating "sonorous buildings, cities of voices and songs, instantaneous, luminous and moving like flames" (Levy, 1997, p. 134).

Notes

1. See Olivetti (1954), Doglio (1995), and Lanzani (1996).
2. In general: subjects must agree voluntarily to be interviewed as a result of full and open information about the project; the relationship between interviewer and interviewee must be built with no deceptions; confidentiality and privacy of interviewees must be preserved; the interviews must be accurately transcribed without omissions or fraudulent interpretations; particular care must be taken to prevent dangerous consequences for the life of the interviewees.

References

Abbott, A. E. (1993). *Flatlandia. Racconto fantastico a più dimensioni*. Milano: Adelphi Edizioni.
Blanchard, M. A. (2002). *Should all disciplines be subject to common rule? Human subjects of social science research panel*. US Department of Health and Human Services. Retrieved from http://findarticles.com/p/articles/mi_qa3860/is_200205/ai_n9076777/pg_1
Bourdieu, P. (1995). *Ragioni Pratiche*. Bologna: Il Mulino.
Debord, G. (1989). *Rapporto sulla costruzione delle situazioni*. Torino: Nautilus.
de Certeau, M. (1990). *L'invenzione del quotidiano*. Roma: Edizioni Lavoro.
Denzin, N. K. (1997). *Interpretative ethnography: Ethnographic practices for the 21st century*. Thousand Oaks, CA: Sage.
Denzin, N. K. (2003). *Performance ethnography: Critical pedagogy and the politics of culture*. Thousand Oaks, CA: Sage.
Denzin, N. K., & Lincoln, Y. S. (Eds.). (2005). *The sage handbook of qualitative research*. Thousand Oaks, CA: Sage.
Doglio, C., Mazzoleni, C. (Eds.). (1995). *Per prova ed errore*. Genova: Le mani Microart's Edizioni.
Eckstein, B., & Throgmorton, J. (Eds.). (2003). *Story and sustainability: Planning, practice and possibility for American cities*. Cambridge, MA: MIT Press.

Forester, J. (1989). *Planning in the face of power*. Berkley, CA: University of California Press.

Gargani, A. G. (1999). *Il filtro creativo*. Bari: Editori Laterza.

Lanzani, A. (1996). *Immagini del territorio e idee di piano 1943–1963*. Milano: Franco Angeli.

Levy, P. (1997). *L'intelligenza collettiva*. Milano: Feltrinelli.

Mandelbaum, S. (1991). Telling stories. *Journal of Planning Education and Research, 10*(1), 209–214.

Manganelli, G. (1993). Un luogo è un linguaggio. In: A. E. Abbott (Ed.), *Flatlandia. Racconto fantastico a più dimensioni*. Milano: Adelphi Edizioni.

Melucci, A. (2000). *Culture in gioco. Differenza per convivere*. Milano: Il Saggiatore.

Olivetti, A. (1954). Perché si pianifica. *Comunità 27*.

Sandercock, L. (2003). *Cosmopolis II – mongrel cities of the 21st century*. London, New York: Continuum Books.

Tosi, A. (2000). L'inserimento urbano degli immigrati. In AAVV (Eds.), *Migrazioni Scenari per il XXI secolo, Dossier di Ricerca vol II*. Roma: Agenzia Romana per la preparazione del Giubileo.

Turner, V. (1993). *Antropologia della performance*. Bologna: Il Mulino.

Young, I. M. (1997). *Intersecting voices: Dilemmas of gender, political philosophy and policy*. Princeton NJ: Princeton University Press.

Part II
Contemporary Practices

Chapter 4
Mobilizing the Human Spirit: An Experiment in Film as Social Research, Community Engagement and Policy Dialogue

Leonie Sandercock

> *Our hope of social achievement ... lies in a complete mobilisation of the human spirit, using all our unrealized and unevoked capacity*
>
> (Jane Addams, quoted in Knight, 2005, frontispiece)

4.1 Introduction

In 2004 I received a 3-year grant for a project titled 'From the campfire to the computer: an inquiry into the powers and limitations of story and storytelling in planning research and practice'. That same year I was also the recipient of a Canada Foundation for Innovation (CFI) grant to establish the Vancouver Cosmopolis Laboratory,[1] whose goal was to investigate the potential of ICTs (new information and communication technologies) for assisting or enhancing the democratization of planning. The CFI grant paid for the renovation of a physical space ('the Lab') at UBC and enabled us to purchase computers, video and digital cameras, microphones, film editing software and lots of server space. I thought of the Cosmopolis Lab as a multimedia studio in which I could experiment with the uses of film/video in planning research and practice, but I had none of the technical skills of film making (cinematography or editing). The grant enabled me to recruit a brilliant young Italian, Giovanni Attili, who had just graduated with a PhD in Planning from the University of Rome and who was a self-taught film maker who had also spent time in theatre and studying visual anthropology. We have become an inseparable research team over the past four years (see Preface). This chapter discusses our first 'experiment' in/through the Cosmopolis Lab, a 3-year project that started in one neighbourhood in Vancouver, and then went national and international.

L. Sandercock (✉)
School of Community and Regional Planning, The University of British Columbia, Vancouver, BC, Canada
e-mail: leonies@interchange.ubc.ca

L. Sandercock, G. Attili (eds.), *Multimedia Explorations in Urban Policy and Planning*, Urban and Landscape Perspectives 7, DOI 10.1007/978-90-481-3209-6_4, © Springer Science+Business Media B.V. 2010

Fig. 4.1 The Cosmopolis Laboratory (SCARP, UBC, Vancouver). Photos by Giovanni Attili

I begin by locating film as a mode of inquiry which is part of a post-positivist paradigm that draws on the importance and powers of story and storytelling (Banks, 2001). I outline our initial thinking about the potential of film as a mode of inquiry, a form of meaning making, a way of knowing and a way of provoking public dialogue and community engagement around planning and policy issues. I connect our approach, which Attili calls 'digital ethnography' (see Chapter 3), with what Flyvbjerg (2002, p. 3) describes as 'phronetic social science' or value-rational research. I then explain the research question we chose to work on: 'how do strangers become neighbours?' and our research 'site', one of the most culturally diverse neighbourhoods in the City of Vancouver, and a specific local institution, the Collingwood Neighbourhood House (CNH). The next section describes and discusses the three-stage research process, beginning with the making of the film 'Where Strangers Become Neighbours: the story of the Collingwood Neighbourhood House and the integration of immigrants in Vancouver' (Attili and Sandercock, 2007), followed by the development of a manual to accompany the film, for public education purposes, and a series of workshops in four different Canadian cities which used the film as a catalyst for community dialogue. The third stage was the writing and preparation of a book and DVD package which could make the Vancouver story a learning experience for cities and regions beyond Canada. The final section offers reflections on the successes and limitations of this project, specifically what we learned about the potential of film as social research and in community dialogue.

4.2 An Emerging Paradigm

The beginning of an epistemological shift in the field of planning was foreshadowed in the early 1970s in the works of Friedmann (1973) and Churchman (1971). Friedmann outlined a 'crisis of knowing' in which he skewered the limitations of 'expert knowledge' and advocated a new approach which he called 'mutual learning', or 'transactive planning', an approach which could appreciate and draw on local and experiential knowledge in dialogue with expert knowledge. At the same time, Churchman's inquiry into knowing was exploring the value of stories. 'The Hegelian inquirer is a storyteller, and Hegel's Thesis is that the best inquiry is the inquiry that produces stories' (Churchman, 1971, p. 178). Over the next several decades, the termites kept eating away at the Enlightenment foundations of modernist planning, anchored as it was in an epistemology that privileged scientific and technical ways of knowing. Accompanying a broader post-positivist movement in the social sciences (Stretton, 1969; Geertz, 1983; Rabinow & Sullivan, 1987; Bourdieu, 1990; Flyvbjerg, 2002), pushed further along by feminist and post-colonial critiques (Said, 1979; Hooks, 1984; Trinh, 1989; Lerner, 1997; Sandercock, 1998), planning scholars began to see the need both for an expanded language for planning and for ways of expanding the creative capacities of planners (Landry, 2000, 2006; Sandercock, 2004; Sarkissian & Hurford, 2010) by acknowledging and using the many other ways of knowing that exist: experiential, intuitive and somatic knowledges; local knowledges; knowledges based on the practices of talking and listening, seeing, contemplating and sharing; and knowledges expressed in visual, symbolic, ritual and other artistic ways. An 'epistemology of multiplicity' (Sandercock, 1998) would nurture these other ways of knowing, without discarding or dismissing more traditional forms of scientific or technical reasoning.

The 'story turn' in planning has been one response to this epistemological crisis (see Chapter 2). In the past two decades a growing number of planning scholars have been investigating the relationship between story and planning (Forester, 1989; Mandelbaum, 1991; Marris, 1997; Eckstein & Throgmorton, 2003; Sandercock, 2003a; Attili, 2007). These investigations highlight how planning is performed through stories, how rhetoric and poetics are crucial in interactive processes, how the communicative dimension is central to planning practices and how story can awaken energies and imaginations, becoming a catalyst for involving urban conversations, for deep community dialogues.

Today, new information and communication technologies (ICTs) provide the opportunity to explore storytelling through multimedia forms, including film/video, which offer a vast repertoire of analytical as well expressive possibilities. When I began my research collaboration with Giovanni Attili we were attempting to mesh two forms of inquiry, digital ethnography and phronetic social science, which turned out to be extraordinarily compatible. Attili's formulating of a digital ethnography for planning research and practice can be summarized as follows (and see Chapter 3):

> The language of film can give expression to a dense qualitative analysis of social phenomena in a territorial context. It can be used to give thick and complex accounts of the city focused on stories, interviews, and narration. Qualitative analysis succeeds in expressing what lies beyond the surface of maps, physical objects, classifications and aggregate quantitative data. It intentionally focuses on individual lives in urban settings made up of changing densities, memories, perceptions and aesthetics. It is an attentive, extremely focused analysis of urban space, where existence, intersections, languages and interstitial freedoms delineate controversial and palpitating urban landscapes...

> Bypassing the ideology of the Archimedean observer who stands outside the observed, the qualitative approach privileges collaborative contexts to produce a collective invention of interconnected stories. In this perspective, there is no longer a single eye that encompasses "everything" in its vision, but a multiplicity of stories told by the inhabitants of specific neighborhoods who no longer can be thought of as isolated monads (as for example in survey research), and whose stories must be understood as an interconnected web. Through in-depth interviews and the confrontation of diverse visions of the world, this approach becomes a powerful tool for a deeper comprehension of what animates the many souls, conflicts and resources of the city.

> The result is an ethnographic narrative that is built on the intersection of multiple narratives captured by the ethnographer. It is a story that doesn't pretend to represent "the truth;" rather, it is explicitly subjective, even partial. The key word to comprehend the fulcrum of ethnographic analysis is "to evoke," that is, to create a plausible world – one of many such worlds – taken from everyday life. Assuming this perspective, ethnography rids itself of the obsession of a mimesis rooted in objects, facts, empirical generalizations, and ultimately in a single truth. Rather, it becomes an interconnected patchwork of evocative images imbued with ambiguity and indeterminacy. Their full comprehension escapes the researcher's intentionality, as the film creates a dynamic field that is open to diverse interpretations and possibilities. This level of interpretative openness transforms a digital ethnography into a potential catalyst for participatory planning. In other words, digital ethnographies represent a new way of provoking dialogue in decision-making contexts. It is a way of starting a public conversation (Attili, 2009, pp. 260–261).

My own advocacy of the importance of multiple ways of knowing, and particularly of the power of story in planning (Sandercock, 2003b), resonated with the approach that Danish planning scholar Bent Flyvbjerg (2002) was forging into what he calls 'phronetic social science'. This is an approach that, by explicitly focusing on values, could effectively deal with public deliberation and praxis. Using this approach, the point of departure is a series of classic value-rational questions: Where are we going? Is it desirable? What should be done? For anyone in the planning and policy fields, researchers or practitioners, these questions ought to be central to praxis, along with their obvious companions, 'Who gains and who loses, through what kinds of power relations? What possibilities are there for changing existing power relations? And is it desirable to do so?' (Flyvbjerg, 2002, pp. 130–131). Finally, for post-modern, self-reflective researchers, 'Of what kinds of power relations are those asking these questions themselves a part?'(ibid)

Flyvbjerg's mode of inquiry is particularly well suited to investigating contemporary policy or planning issues and evolved through reflection on his own case study of a failed attempt at urban environmental planning reform in the Danish city of Aalborg. It is particularly useful for us as digital ethnographers, committed to immersion in the place and people we are filming, yet also seeking some critical distance. It presents a way of thinking beyond the objectivity/subjectivity divide, recognizing that the researcher becomes part of the phenomenon being studied.

> For contemporary studies, one gets close to the phenomenon or group whom one studies during data collection, and remains close during the phases of data analysis, feedback, and publication. Combined with the focus on relations of values and power, this strategy typically creates an interest by outside parties, and even outside stakeholders, in the research. These parties will test and evaluate the research in various ways. The researchers will consciously expose themselves to reactions from their surroundings – both positive and negative – and may derive benefit from the learning effect which is built into this strategy. In this way, the researcher becomes part of the phenomenon being studied, without necessarily "going native" or the project becoming simple action research (Flyvbjerg, 2002, p. 132).

Fundamental to phronetic research is a focus on thick description (see also Geertz, 1983), generated out of asking 'little questions'. This requires patience and the accumulation of a vast amount of detail. (In the case of our film, perhaps 60 hours of video footage, along with a massive digital archive comprising thousands of photographs, newspaper clippings and so on, all of which had to be edited down to a 30-minutes film.) Also fundamental to such research is the art of narrative. If the question driving the phronetic research process is the 'How' question, then the clearest way to answer such a question is by doing narrative analysis.

> Narrative is our most fundamental form for making sense of experience. Narratives not only give meaningful form to experiences already lived, but also provide a forward glance, helping us anticipate situations before we encounter them, allowing us to envision alternative futures. ... Narrative inquiries develop descriptions and interpretations of the phenomenon, from the perspectives of participants, researchers, and others (Flyvbjerg, 2002, p. 137).

Phronetic research then, along with digital ethnography, is dialogical in the sense that it includes and (if successful) is included in a polyphony of voices, with no one voice, including that of the researcher, claiming final authority. It is also potentially liberatory, in creating the space for people to tell their own stories (Freire, 1970). The goal is to produce an input into the ongoing social dialogue and praxis of a society, rather than to generate ultimate, unequivocally verified knowledge. But, like any good scientific inquiry, storytelling at its best needs to be a blend of careful, cautious, and bold, creative knowing.

Such were our epistemological and methodological starting points. But what was the research question through which we were going to test the potential of multimedia/film as a mode of inquiry, a form of meaning making and an intervention in a public policy dialogue?

4.3 The Research Question

My own research had been focused for a decade or so on the challenges of planning in multicultural cities and regions and in cross-cultural contexts. Moving to Vancouver, on the western edge of Canada, in 2001, I was immediately curious about what made this multicultural city so apparently harmonious. In the City of Vancouver, in particular (population 600.000, one of 22 municipalities in a Metro region with a population of just over 2 million), with 51% of its population from non-English-speaking backgrounds, the level of peaceful co-existence seemed pretty remarkable.[2] I began to wonder what had been done, actively, to encourage this peaceful co-existence over the previous three decades, which had seen immigration from a completely new set of 'source countries', no longer the Anglo-European countries but, since the reform of discriminatory immigration laws in 1967, newcomers from various parts of Asia, Africa and the Middle East as well as Latin America. Well aware of Canada's multicultural philosophy at the national level, I posed a rather large sociological question. Immigration policy is determined at the national level, but its effects are felt most directly at the neighbourhood level, where newcomers and oldtimers meet each other face to face in schools, shops, streets, parks, on public transit and so on. The rate of immigration to some neighbourhoods has been pretty dramatic in the past two or three decades.

Fig. 4.2 Multicultural cityscape. Graphic elaboration by Giovanni Attili

How then does a neighbourhood that was, until the 1970s or the 1980s, predominantly Anglo-European, adapt to the arrival of quite large numbers of newcomers who are from very different and for the most part unfamiliar cultures? How does the process of social integration actually work, on the ground? How do immigrants begin to establish a new life and develop a sense of belonging to a new place? How do the oldtimers facilitate or obstruct this? In short, how do strangers become neighbours?

This then was the big sociological 'How' question. How do strangers become neighbours? Understanding this, in a positive context, could be instructive for other Canadian cities and cities in other countries (in Europe and Asia, for example) that are just beginning to struggle with this issue of acceptance and integration. My new research partner from Rome, Giovanni Attili, had just finished his PhD, which looked at the situation of Afghani refugees in Rome, following a group of them up close and personal and getting to know them well enough that they were prepared to tell their stories. These personal stories were then set against the daily informal and institutionalized treatment of refugees in Rome, a story of policing of certain (refugee) bodies in space. The 2-h CD-ROM that Attili presented as part of his dissertation showed the ways in which the hourly movements of these homeless Afghanis were controlled by various authorities in Rome, on a 24-h basis, being moved from one location to another within a very small radius, close to the main railway station. Attili was as interested as I was in this big 'How' question.

But this was never intended as 'pure' scholarly research. The story that we wanted to tell, of the work of the Collingwood Neighbourhood House (CNH) in creating a gathering place for everyone, was chosen precisely because we saw it as a very positive story of the overcoming of anti-immigrant sentiment that existed in

Fig. 4.3 How do strangers become neighbours? Photos from the Collingwood Neighbourhood House archive

the Collingwood neighbourhood and in the city in the 1980s and the 1990s (and still today). Understanding how this was done, how this change came about, seemed to be a way of informing a broader public dialogue about acceptance as well as inspiring other communities to learn from the CNH achievement. Additionally, there was an action research agenda. I had been helping the CNH in writing their grant proposals during a period of provincial funding cutbacks and had been asked by the Executive Director, Paula Carr, whether there were ways in which the university might be able to be of further assistance to the mission of CNH. Through further discussion, Carr and I developed the idea of a university-community collaboration in which I would use the resources of the Lab to make a film telling their story.

Fig. 4.4 The Collingwood Neighbourhood House. Photos by Giovanni Attili

Our thinking was that a well-crafted story could appeal to funders and government agencies in a more emotionally powerful way than was available by reading the Annual Reports of the CNH, which by definition are rather dry, statistics-based documents whose primary purpose is to report what money was spent on what programmes. Thus, from the very beginning, there was both an advocacy and collaborative dimension of our film/research project. We believed, but had yet to do the research to prove, that the work of the CNH over its almost 20-year life span had resulted in some quite transformational social changes. We needed to find out as much as we could about what they had done and how. We also believed that the best way to do this was to work collaboratively with CNH, developing relations of trust with them, seeking their advice and feedback throughout the research and especially through the film editing process. Paula Carr agreed to assign the Coordinator of Settlement Services at CNH, Val Cavers, as our liaison and through Val we were initially put in touch with potential interviewees and given access to all CNH archives.

A third piece of our agenda as researchers/film makers was to teach the digital ethnographic approach to a class of master's students in the School of Community and Regional Planning at UBC. In January of 2005, 15 students signed up for this one-semester class and while Attili introduced them to the digital ethnographic approach and taught them camera, interviewing and editing skills, I began to organize the research in the neighbourhood. We organized the students into small research teams, each of which would make a 5- to 10-minutes video by the end of semester. I explained the significance of the research question as well as the neighbourhood context; we made an initial visit to the CNH and did walking tours of the neighbourhood; and then we brainstormed research themes for each group, themes that would each contribute to an understanding of the larger research question. We aimed for both breadth and depth in coverage. The themes/topics that we agreed on as a group were as follows: the history of the neighbourhood; the history of the CNH as an organization; the emergence and achievements of the Community Leadership Institute in the 1990s; the youth-oriented Buddy Program; the Arts Pow-Wow, a community cultural planning effort which spanned several years and several 'programmes'; the reclamation and participatory redesign of a neighbourhood park; the annual MultiWeek celebrations; and a theme of leaving, arriving and belonging, which was intended to tell individual stories of emigration and immigration, of loss and change, sadness and growth.

Over the next 3 months, students spent a lot of time interviewing people in the neighbourhood, both oldtimers and newcomers, as well as staff, volunteers, members of the Board that runs the CNH, and residents, city planners and politicians who had been involved in the initial community planning process that had resulted in the residents' desire to create the CNH as a gathering place and a facility that could provide services for families and children.

Over a hundred people were interviewed, using the video camera to collect their voices, unless the interviewees requested the use of audio tape only. Actually, nobody declined to be interviewed on camera, but the camera does sometimes add a further level of difficulty in interviewing, when people become shy, awkward or stiff.[3] We had many discussions in class about the potential distancing effect of the camera, and students were asked to be reflective and sensitive about this issue.

The result of the students' work was a series of digital narratives, mini-films of micro-stories, based on in-depth interviews as well as archival and other research, then combined using specific editing and graphic software. These films were screened at the Annual General Meeting of the CNH in June 2005, and the residents' enthusiastic response was a great reward for the students' hard work. This screening revealed that we were on the right path in making something that touched people, retrieved memories for them and made a larger sense of something that they had been a part of.

Once the work of the students was finished, Attili and I started to work on the next phase: identifying further research, expanding the horizon of the interviews and reflecting on the shape and content of the story we wanted to tell, the story of a neighbourhood that, just 20 years earlier, had been locking its doors, was afraid

Fig. 4.5 CNH's activities in the neighbourhood. Photos from the Collingwood Heighbourhood House archive

of change and telling immigrants to go back where they came from, but that is now a totally welcoming place. We spent 3 more months in the neighbourhood, talking with many people in an ever-widening web of relations and consolidating our relationship with CNH. At a certain point, we realized that people were recognizing us as we walked around the streets with our camera and tripod, were friendly and

Fig. 4.6 Students' discussion at the CNH. Photos by Giovanni Attili

welcoming towards us, and were curious about how our project was coming along. In other words, we were developing a sense of identification with and affection for this neighbourhood and were, on a number of occasions, moved to tears by the stories we were being told, the passionate intensity of the lived experiences of upheaval, arrival, struggle and achieving a new sense of belonging. At the same time, we were also trying to think critically and analytically about what we were absorbing and how to interpret it, always aware that our own voices would ultimately mingle and dialogue with those of our interviewees, both implicitly, in the way that we chose to edit, and explicitly, in the narration that I was beginning to write. We were, always consciously and reflectively, trying to be in and out at the same moment, walking a tightrope between empathic compassion, admiration and distanced observation. Being a film-making team of two was a constructive aspect, as we had long dialogues at the end of each day of the data-gathering phase about the meaning of what we were hearing, filming and experiencing.

4.4 Research Findings

Once we began the editing phase in the Lab we were confronted with some agonizing decisions about what to cut and what to include, especially when this involved sifting through and portraying people's life stories in highly truncated ways, or in many cases, in excluding entire interviews, for reasons of space, relevance or communicative power. The process of constructing the story line and selecting its component parts is similar in most ways to writing a book. There is a long period of sitting with, immersing oneself in the material, listening over and over to interviews, editing each interview and digitally filing the edited pieces into thematic files, making notes about connections and ways of interweaving different stories. It is a creative challenge, exciting and exasperating and agonizing at the same time, demanding continuous analytical, emotional and aesthetic judgements.

Our approach to editing is actually a two-stage process, in the first of which we are asking what is the story we want to tell? What is the answer to our initial question (How do strangers become neighbours?) and how can we best tell that story? So the first challenge is how to tell the story in a powerful way, as narrative, using as much as possible the voices of the actual community. At the end of that stage, we essentially have a 'talking heads' story. The second stage is the visual storytelling, the layering in of all the digital material we had been collecting (photographs, old video footages, newspaper clippings, posters, location footage, statistics and so on) and the creative invention of visually stimulating ways of placing all this on a screen, often telling multiple stories in one frame through the use of multiple images alongside and around a 'talking head' or voice over narration.

The theme that emerged most powerfully from the multiple interviews was how this neighbourhood had been transformed over a 20-year period, from initial fear and anxiety and even hostility towards the new immigrants to eventual acceptance and working together to build a community where none had previously existed: in other words, a community development story. It was clear that the central actor in this story was the Neighbourhood House itself, but the story of the NH was in turn a story about the people who founded it, their vision and mission, and their ongoing efforts at outreach and social inclusion. We also realized that it was important to explain how and why this particular local institution was established in 1985, as

Fig. 4.7 CNH's programmes for children. Photos from the Collingwood Neighbourhood House archive

that story reflected something about the planning culture in the City of Vancouver (in other words, a larger contextual element of explanation). The short answer to the question of how strangers had become neighbours in Collingwood was the community development approach of the CNH (as opposed to being simply a service and programme delivery agency) and the vision of social inclusion. Our challenge was how to explain this community development process and the gradual shift in attitudes it produced.

We decided to construct the narrative both as a 'then and now' story and as a sequence of stories around themes, programmes and events which illustrated the community development approach. Beginning with the 'origins story' of how the NH came into being, we then proceeded to construct sequences focusing on the growth of the CNH, both physical and programmatic; the development of a Community Leadership Institute that helped local residents to acquire leadership skills in order to take on important roles in the community; the development of the Buddy Program which involved matching local youth with newcomers and then developing programmes taught by youth themselves about anti-racism and violence/bullying; the unearthing of local artistic skills through the Arts Pow-Wow, a community cultural development process that began with an inventory of residents' skills and then involved mobilizing those skills in an array of community development activities, led by these local artists (from gardening to music and dance to lantern making, puppetry, storytelling, and so on, all of which are used to enhance local celebrations); the story of the reclamation (from drug dealers and gangs) of a local park and its transformation through a participatory design process led by local residents; and the story of the annual celebration of cultural diversity in 'Multiweek', one week in February during which the many cultures that co-exist in this neighbourhood come together to share traditions and customs.

Fig. 4.8 Video stills from the documentary 'Where strangers become neighbours' (Attili & Sandercock, 2007)

As film makers, we were always conscious of the question of *voice*, of who is telling the story, and we were committed to having the local voices tell the story as much as possible. As we reviewed our digital interviews, we realized that there were five women whose personal stories of leaving, arriving, struggling to find their place and achieving a sense of belonging through the CNH could drive the narrative forward and provide a very involving emotional dimension. We used their voices to convey, through life stories, what the CNH had been able to achieve. Finally we realized that in order to weave some of these sequences together, we needed a voice-over narration, which could also convey some analytical and thematic information such as 'the age of migration' and the global forces operating on a neighbourhood, as well as the national political philosophy of multiculturalism that shaped federal and provincial funding and enabled the CNH to access resources for the kinds of programmes it was inventing. So our own interpretive voice was added to provide these additional contextual dimensions.

As we worked on the film it became more and more evident to us that we were making an advocacy documentary, one that could be used in the policy and funding arenas to raise awareness of the importance of a local, place-based, community development approach to foster the social integration of immigrants, through demonstrating the achievements of the CNH, and specifically help CNH with its funding crisis. In other words, we understood that we were acting politically in making this film, in assuming the responsibility of narrating an inspiring story, showing how a local institution managed to help a neighbourhood to overcome its fear of strangers and in the process to do remarkable community building work.

Every single choice we made during the editing process was connected with these emerging objectives that affected not only the construction of the story itself but also the way it was told visually. From this perspective, what we produced was a multi-stratified visual layout, a complex web of images and information that were interconnected and displayed on the same screen. The documentary was thus not merely talking heads, but an intricate tangle of visions potentially able to allow the spectator to dive into the story's depth. What we pursued was the possibility of creating aesthetic connections intended as different ways of learning through visual, narrative and musical languages (Attili, 2009, p. 250).

We had started the editing process in July 2005 and by September we had a rough cut which was about 65 minutes in length, in spite of the fact that we had set out to make a 30-minutes story. We were working to a deadline of sorts, in that we knew that the CNH folks wanted to show the film at their 20th Anniversary celebrations in late November, if they thought it 'worked'. Ultimately we, as film makers, had the final say about the story form and content, but we had always been committed to a collaborative process. So, at this point, we invited members of the resident-run Board of the CNH as well as the Executive Director and the Coordinator of Settlement Services to watch it with us and give us their feedback. Had we adequately captured their story, we wanted to know? Had we misrepresented anything? Had we left out important elements? Did the film work at an emotional and also at an informational level?

Fig. 4.9 Video stills from the documentary 'Where strangers become neighbours' (Attili & Sandercock, 2007)

The response from this first 'audience' was both exuberantly supportive *and* critical. Overall, the verdict was that the film was emotionally powerful, especially because of the use of the five personal stories. The criticisms and concerns were quite specific. There were small factual errors that were easy to correct. More difficult was a concern over one of the personal narratives, Satinder's story. During the telling, Satinder often broke down in tears as she remembered the pain of arriving in this strange, emotionally cold land and how she would have returned to India after 6 months if her husband had agreed. Then she told of her discovery of CNH and her gradual involvement in its programmes, becoming a volunteer and how through this involvement she had found her place and a sense of belonging in Canada. CNH folks were concerned that Satinder might be upset at seeing herself on screen in tears and they suggested that we cut some of those sections, which we did. (Then, when we talked with Satinder about this, she insisted that it was okay to include these emotions, so we re-inserted some of that material.)

The most significant critical feedback we received about the narrative was that we had not included any First Nations voices or indicated how much outreach work the CNH had done with local Native people (almost a thousand of the 45.000-member neighbourhood). Our 'defense' of this omission was that we had been trying all summer to reach the Elder whose name we had been given as the appropriate person to speak to, but could not make contact. We agreed to try again, but continued to be unsuccessful and we were aware of the importance of the protocol of speaking with Elders and having Elders speak for that community. Our compromise was to construct a sequence which described the proposal to build a Native Housing Coop in the neighbourhood, the initial opposition to that and how that opposition was worked through, and to show the Coop as it exists today, an important and beautiful part of the neighbourhood. Part of this story, too, was how, in the process of working through this conflict, non-Native residents came to appreciate that Native people were bringing assets to this community as well as needs.

Once we made these changes, we invited the CNH folks back for a second screening and at this point we had to start the fine-tuning. One crucial issue was the length of the film. We had intended to make a 30-minutes film, and now had 70 minutes. We had to think a lot about who our target audience was, what length would work for different audiences and how much 'information' we needed to convey, about programmes and services for example, as opposed to the more involving personal stories.

Fig. 4.10 Video stills from the documentary 'Where strangers become neighbours' (Attili & Sandercock, 2007)

It was a delicate balance we were seeking and it was very hard to find this balance. We knew that some viewers would want to know how the CNH was financed, for example, and what kinds of programmes were offered, but conveying that information is hard to do in an interesting way and always tends to stop the narrative and the emotional involvement dead in its tracks. Here we had to acknowledge and accept community priorities as opposed to our artistic instincts about storytelling. (And to this day we are bothered by the 7-minutes 'informational sequence' in the middle of the story!)

We simply could not decide on an 'ideal' length for the film, as this really depended on the different contexts in which it would be shown. For the CNH's use of the film in presentations to funders, a 15- to 20-minutes film would have been the ideal length. For use in classrooms and at conferences, and film festival screenings, we thought probably 40–50 minutes could work. In the month before the November anniversary we worked on cutting and inserting music.

We found ourselves so attached to the different elements of the story, and the CNH to other elements, that we were unable to reduce our story to less than 50 minutes.

Fig. 4.11 Video stills from the documentary 'Where strangers become neighbours' (Attili & Sandercock, 2007)

4.5 Stage Two: Dissemination of the Film/Research

The single most important audience to us, as film makers, was the local community, and they were the first to see the film, at the 20th birthday celebration of the CNH in late November 2005. On that occasion, their gym was converted into a big movie theatre holding 300–400 people. We rented a huge screen and professional sound equipment, there was a reception before the screening, and there was a lot of excitement and anticipation in the air. Giovanni and I stood at the back of the hall in the dark, each of us feeling a little sick with nerves. It was the first official projection of the documentary, and the audience's reaction was incredible. Many people were in tears after the screening, so positively moved by the inspiring story, and many stayed around wanting to talk with us. Most of the people we had interviewed now saw their own story as part of something much larger, as a web of connections and actions that amounted to a heroic story of human achievement. There was incredible pride as people realized what they had done, and understood the bigger picture of a complex story of which they only knew the small segments in which they had personally been involved. The consciousness of being part of a bigger story was both empowering and an important step in a renewed sense of belonging. This was something that we had not fully anticipated as film makers: the way the film could contribute to this ongoing process of creating a sense of community and belonging. For many, it was akin to a ritual passage that enabled them to make sense of the previous 20 years of history of this institution. It was both energizing and an occasion, subsequently, for further reflection by CNH staff and Board, about the future.

For us as film makers, the saddest and most personally difficult aspect of this screening was the evident disappointment of some of our interviewees whose words had not made it into the final cut. The interviews we had conducted (along with the students' interviews) with each person ranged in length from 20 minutes to 2 hours, and it is hard for most people to understand why we used only, say, 20 s of some, several minutes of others or in some cases nothing at all. The editing decisions are hard to explain and some people felt slighted, while others were more understanding. There was de-briefing work that was necessary for some of the disappointed ones, who had seen themselves in the students' short films and expected to be in the final cut. There is no way around this emotionally brutal reality of editing, when working with communities, although we did try to explain at the time we did the interviews that we may use very little, or even none at all.

In addition to the local residents at this screening, there were also some local politicians and some of the city planners who had been involved in the community planning process that resulted in the establishment of CNH, and folks from other Neighbourhood Houses in Vancouver. The screening generated a lot of interest in the film, and shortly after this we began to receive a lot of requests for further screenings. We now had to think about the distribution and dissemination issue: how could we get the film out there, without ourselves travelling with it everywhere. But first we went back to the Lab for some fine-tuning and commissioned a composer to do an original score for the film. Simultaneously we were discussing with CNH how they would like to use the film, and we made copies and gave them to CNH for their own use, while agreeing that we would try to get the film shown as widely as possible because of its educational value and policy relevance, as well as find a professional distributor (ideally, we thought, the National Film Board of Canada).

While Giovanni was working with the composer and completing the final cut, I worked with Paula Carr on a grant application with the idea of producing a Manual to accompany the film and then taking both film and Manual 'on the road' in a series of workshops in different Canadian cities. We got the grant, from the Metropolis research network, and hired Val Cavers, the Settlement Services Coordinator at CNH, to research and write the Manual (Cavers, Carr, & Sandercock, 2007).[4] This became stage two of our project. We agreed that the Manual would try to convey more of the details of the How question: *how* the CNH had done what it had done. We also agreed that the Manual would be written as much as possible through stories. That work proceeded through 2006, with Carr and myself adding and editing, and by early 2007 we were ready to graphically design and print copies of the Manual and organize our 'road trip'. Also in December 2006 the National Film

Fig. 4.12 Video stills from the documentary 'Where strangers become neighbours' (Attili & Sandercock, 2007)

Board of Canada had agreed to become the official distributor of the film, which was finally released for sale through the NFB website in late 2007.

Our Metropolis grant funding enabled us to visit four cities (Edmonton, Halifax, Moncton and Toronto) to run half-day workshops using the film as a catalyst for community dialogue about immigration and integration and leaving participants with copies of the Manual to take back to their organizations. The collaboration with the Metropolis research network was a magical part of this stage of the project. Each of the Metropolis Centres of Excellence advertised our workshops through their local networks, so we were able to reach exactly the audiences we hoped to reach: local organizations involved with immigrants and refugees, non-profits and faith-based organizations as well as municipalities who were becoming increasingly concerned about the challenges of the arrival of significant numbers of newcomers. Provincial and federal policy makers also attended in each city, as well as folks from the arts sector and university researchers. In Toronto, we had an audience of between 70 and 80 people. In the other three cities, attendance was between 30 and 50. We used the same format for each, a brief introduction about why we'd made the film, followed by a screening, followed by 90 minutes or so of facilitated discussion, tailored to the interests and concerns of the specific audience.

These workshops had diverse goals: creating dialogue in each city between different actors in the policy sector concerned with immigration and integration; raising awareness of the importance of a focus on the neighbourhood level as a policy domain; demonstrating the value of a community development approach to active citizenship; understanding what brings about positive changes in attitudes towards immigrants; and empowerment of other communities through the example of this one.

Workshop attendees were given a copy of the manual *How Strangers Become Neighbours: Constructing Citizenship Through Community Development*, which tells how the CNH developed its unique approach of relationship building; what kinds of programmes and services it offers; where it gets its funding; how it trains staff and volunteers; how its outreach programmes work; how the resident-run Board operates; how they develop community leadership; why its approach is inter-cultural rather than multicultural; and above all, the values that have shaped this very special place.

Discussions were extraordinarily animated and the response was extremely positive. In all post-workshop evaluations, 90% of attendees rated the workshops in the top category (on a scale of 1–5) and rated the value of the film at the same level. In addition, an interesting dynamic emerged in the course of these workshops. People working on the same policy issues and in the same city discovered each other for the first time, thus establishing new networks concerned with the social integration of immigrants.

Two other final pieces of the dissemination process are worth mentioning. Attili and I have received many invitations to screen the film and facilitate discussion, from government agencies to community meetings to keynotes at academic conferences,[5] as well as screenings at several international film festivals where the documentary was awarded an Honourable Mention (International Federation of Housing and Planning, International Film and Video Competition, Geneva, 2006) and a Special Mention (Berkeley Video and Film Festival, 2006). Social issues, immigration policies, planning themes, media and communication topics became the subjects of intense discussion wherever we have shown the film. Perhaps most gratifying of all, in terms of awards, was the use of the film as the 'evidence' submitted by CNH in nominating itself for the BMW Award for Intercultural Learning in the 'Practice' category in 2007. CNH was awarded First Prize and the Executive Director and the Chairman of the Board of CNH were flown to Munich to receive the award, with a lot of attendant publicity.[6] It was the first time in the 10 years of this award that an organization outside of Europe had received the prize.

Finally, Attili and I decided that in order for the film to have any significant impact in Europe, we would need to write a book to accompany and contextualize the film for European audiences, setting it in its metropolitan planning context as well as in the national political, legal and philosophical contexts (Sandercock & Attili, 2009). This was stage three of our project. The book was again a collaborative enterprise between the two film makers and two CNH folks (the Executive Director, Paula Carr, and the former Coordinator of Settlement Services, Val Cavers), and the book includes a DVD of the film.

4.6 Critical Reflections

The intent of digital ethnography is both to evoke and to provoke: to evoke the richness and diversity of urban life through a polyphonic multimedia approach and to provoke an urban conversation, a community dialogue about the subject matter.

The intent of phronetic social science is to contribute to public dialogue on critical policy issues. What follows is a self-evaluation, bearing in mind these intentions.

On reflection, there were a number of failures and omissions in the storytelling, some of which we only realized through dialogues with various audiences. Perhaps the most frequently asked question at screenings was the relative absence of conflict in the story, apart from the mention of anti-immigrant sentiment by one or two oldtimers in the second sequence of the film. Our answer to this expressed our own frustration at not succeeding in getting interviewees to tell those stories on camera. We heard a lot more, in informal conversation with residents, about levels and forms of racism and xenophobia, than we were able to capture on camera. Most people were reluctant to dig up these old wounds, especially since they thought these problems had pretty much been overcome in the past two decades, thanks to the work of CNH. The relative absence of conflict is a problem in filmic terms, resulting in less tension and less of a sense of what was at stake here in the past two decades. It is even more of a problem in terms of social learning. Other communities could learn more from the film if they had a better understanding of how great the challenges were, back in the 1980s. As we became aware of this shortcoming, we sought to address it in the Manual, foregrounding stories of specific conflicts and providing a detailed description of how these conflicts were handled by CNH staff.

The second most frequently asked question concerned the apparent dominance of women in CNH activities. As discussed previously (see footnote 3), this was the result of obtaining more lively interviews from the women than from most of the men we interviewed, resulting in an editing/selection process that gives an inaccurate portrayal of the levels of involvement of men in CNH programmes and governance. Reflecting on what we learned from this, for future projects, we would either spend more time preparing, with interviewees who are intimidated by the camera, or record them on audio tape and create audio montages of voices, in order not to exclude people on the grounds of their lack of articulateness or shyness on camera. Interestingly, though, we found that people's level of articulation and animation was not closely related to either class or education. This is a low- to moderate-income neighbourhood in which 73% of the population does not speak English as their first language, yet most people were in fact wonderfully engaging interviewees.

A third omission is the absence of voices from the First Nations residents of the neighbourhood. As already explained, we were unable to contact the Elder who was the appropriate spokesperson for that community, as he was away all summer. We compensated by creating a story sequence about the struggles over the Sinhala (First Nations) Housing Coop project, and we inserted as many images and as much video footage as we could find of First Nations people engaged in CNH activities.

A related shortcoming was that our voice-over narration begins with a brief reference to the theme of migrations in human history and then focuses on late 20th century immigration to Canada, without acknowledging First Nations as the original inhabitants of this land. Because we were worried about the length of the film and felt that a couple of sentences on this topic could easily be regarded as 'tokenism', we chose not to mention it at all, a decision I came very much to regret.

There were two other dilemmas we faced in constructing the narrative. One was length and the other the burden of 'information'. Some audiences have felt that the film is perhaps 15–20 minutes too long, (others, that it's not long enough!). This is partly related to people's interest in the theme itself, but also perhaps to the compromises we had to make in terms of filmic storytelling in order to convey (for CNH purposes) essential information about programmes and services. In retrospect, the solution may have been to make two films, one short advocacy/promotional film which CNH could use to show to funders and potential funders and another film that covered the various achievements in more depth. But we did not have the time or the budget to make two films. More recently, when we were approached by CNH

Fig. 4.13 Video stills from the documentary 'Where strangers become neighbours' (Attili & Sandercock, 2007)

to make a shorter film for their specific fund-raising purposes, our distributor, the National Film Board of Canada, refused permission to use the material to create a short version.[7]

There is no ideal length, of course, and decisions about length are partly pragmatic (related to time, money and audiences) and partly artistic. We used our own judgment about what was important and what was deeply moving, and we had much more material that we thought was emotionally powerful, but we felt strongly the need to keep the film less than 1 hour, in order to be able to use it for educational purposes. Our dilemma with the 'information sequence' (7 minutes of details about the range of programmes and services offered at CNH) slowing the film down was resolved by our acknowledgement that this was a priority to the community and CNH in particular. And that is a very important part of our approach to digital ethnography, which speaks to an ethical and trusting relationship between film makers and the community, and to the collaborative aspect of the work.

If these were some of the weaknesses we have identified, how to gauge the successes of the project? Given the intent expressed earlier, the project could be assessed by the community dialogue it produced; by the range of organizations currently using the film for education and training; by the number of invited screenings and awards; and, in the longer term, by community and government responses. From the point of view of phronetic social science, the research/film-making process and the ideas and values expressed in the work are important in themselves as well as, hopefully, producing desired 'outcomes'. Outcomes are hard to identify and even harder to measure in this kind of research, but here is what we have observed, evaluated and heard, 3 years after the film was finished but just a little more than a year after its official release by the NFB.

4.7 Impact on the Local Community

One more or less immediate impact was the sense of psychological empowerment experienced by local residents and the CNH. Even those interviewees who had been involved with the CNH from its inception, or over many years, had a kind of epiphany about the scope and achievement of the organization and the way it had transformed so many lives. Among those interviewees who were more selective users of programmes or had been volunteers at a certain stage of their lives in the neighbourhood, there was an eye-opening sense of the larger history of which they had been a part. This realization, and the enormous pride it engendered, has been energizing and renewing for staff, volunteers and the Board, as well as local residents. In the fall of 2008 we screened the film at CNH for a class of UBC master's students and we also invited a group of young people (late teens and early twenties) who had grown up in the neighbourhood and been involved in CNH programmes at one time, and they too were deeply impressed at their neighbourhood. (So much so, that one of them applied for a job at CNH the following week, which he got.)

Fig. 4.14 Mural painted by residents to celebrate the opening of CNH's new building in 1996. Video stills from 'where strangers become neighbours' (Attili & Sandercock, 2007)

It was something of a surprise to us, as film makers, that the film to some extent taught the local community (and their politicians) about themselves and helped to further motivate and empower people. The subsequent publicity and attention focused on CNH, both nationally and internationally, especially as a result of the BMW Award for Intercultural Learning, has brought an enormous sense of recognition and generated new opportunities. In late 2008, Paula Carr put forward a proposal to the Board to start a social enterprise within CNH, offering their acquired expertise to other non-profits and government agencies as consultants in 'creating welcoming communities'. In this future work (the proposal is currently being implemented) the film will again be used as a catalyst and training tool.

4.8 Wider Impact

As word has spread about the film, through screenings, conference presentations and keynotes, a number of organizations have purchased the film and are using it in training with their staff. These organizations include the following: the municipalities of Halifax, Nova Scotia, and Richmond and Vancouver, British Columbia; the planning department of the City of Auckland, New Zealand: the City of Oslo and the Police Department of Oslo; the Norwegian National Housing Authority; and the Race Relations Office of the Northern Ireland Housing Executive. This is a random sample, known to us only because these organizations approached us for copies, rather than going directly to the NFB. We have no way of knowing which organizations are purchasing the film directly from the NFB.

Find yourself in
Collingwood
Neighbourhood House

Fig. 4.15 Mural depicting the inclusive intention of the CNH. Photos from the Collingwood Neighbourhood House archive

There has certainly been great interest and lively debate at all of the screenings of the film that we have attended, whether in universities or in communities. Anecdotal evidence from these occasions is that the film works well in sparking dialogue, as an inspiration and as a learning tool that demonstrates the effectiveness of community development approaches to particular issues. But the only systematic evidence that we have is from the aforementioned four workshops organized using our Metropolis research grant. The 90% approval rating for both workshop and film after each of these workshops seems to confirm both the power of the story and the power of film as the storytelling medium.

Beyond these outcomes, there are a few other interesting strands worth a brief mention, suggesting ongoing influence in the policy realm in diverse arenas. In 2008, Paula Carr was seconded part-time to the provincial government of British Columbia as a member of an advisory group on the contributions of non-profits to community well-being and to government policy implementation. At the same time, the province released $750.000 in funding for five Neighbourhood Houses to continue with 'welcoming communities' programmes, suggesting an awareness of the CNH work. And I was invited to Ottawa (Canada's seat of national government) in March 2009 to address and have a dialogue with public servants in a series known as 'The Armchair Discussion', organized by the federal department of Citizenship and Immigration Canada, a discussion which is also webcast. Currently there seems to be a new interest in Ottawa in local, place-based approaches to social policy issues, and the CNH story is feeding into and reinforcing that policy trend.

Perhaps then, this is an as-yet unfinished story, one that has short, medium and longer term outcomes, a story still being written, an experiment still unfolding.

4.9 Epilogue

This chapter has focused on an experiment in using film as social research, as a mode of inquiry, a form of meaning making, a way of knowing and a way of provoking public dialogue around a planning and policy issue. But the last words should surely return to the core story, the transformative work of the CNH over several decades. Neighbourhood Houses are themselves the descendants of an earlier social movement, the Settlement House movement, which emerged in late 19th century London and spread quickly to North America, seeking to address problems of poverty and immigrant integration. The first Settlement House on this continent, Hull House on Chicago's south side, was founded by Jane Addams, who wrote several books reflecting on the experience as she lived it. Her words, from *The Second Twenty Years at Hull House*, seem like a fitting celebration of CNH's achievement as they enter their second 20 years:

> Our hope of social achievement . . . lies in a complete mobilisation of the human spirit, using all our unrealized and unevoked capacity (Addams quoted in Knight 2005, frontispiece).

That is precisely what has happened in the Collingwood neighbourhood, through the social inclusion mission of the CNH, and it explains why the making of the film was such a profound human as well as learning experience for us, as film makers.

Notes

1. The name was taken from the title of my book, *Towards Cosmopolis: Planning for Multicultural Cities* (1998).
2. Which was not to deny the everyday incidents of racism that I occasionally witnessed, waiting in line in the liquor store or supermarket, for example. But these were tones of voice or body language, rather than the refusal to serve someone... I was yet to learn about the various forms of hiring and workplace discrimination.
3. Interestingly, this was the case with quite a few of the men (young and old) we interviewed, but not with the women. As a result, and because we had so much good interview material to choose from, we tended in the editing process to exclude those interviews that were wooden, with the result that the film inaccurately suggests that the CNH is a place where many more women are involved than men. The statistics of use of programmes refute this.
4. Cavers had just resigned from CNH and relocated to Winnipeg with her family, but she clearly had 'insider' status with folks at CNH when it came to ongoing research for the Manual, which was hugely important.
5. All told, we have personally screened the film at 32 venues between November 2005 and January 2009.
6. I shared First Prize with CNH, for my essay on 'Cosmopolitan Urbanism' and for my collaboration with CNH through the film.
7. The NFB holds copyright of the film for 5 years, according to our contractual arrangement with them.

References

Attili, G. (2007). Digital ethnographies in the planning field. *Planning Theory and Practice, 8*(1), 90–98.

Attili, G. (2009). Qualitative inquiries and film languages in the planning field: A Manifesto. In: L. Sandercock & G. Attili (Eds.), *Where strangers become neighbours: The integration of immigrants in Vancouver, Canada*. Dordrecht, The Netherlands: Springer.

Attili, G., & Sandercock, L. (2007). *Where strangers become neighbours: The story of the Collingwood Neighbourhood house and the integration of immigrants in Vancouver* (*50 minute documentary*). Montreal, QC, Canada: National Film Board of Canada.

Banks, M. (2001). *Visual methods in social research*. London: Sage.

Bourdieu, P. (1990). *In other words: Essays towards a reflexive sociology*. Cambridge: Polity Press.

Cavers, V., Carr, P., & Sandercock, L. (2007). *How strangers become neighbours: Constructing citizenship through neighbourhood community development*. Vancouver: School of Community and Regional Planning.

Churchman, C. W. (1971). *The design of inquiring systems*. New York: Basic Books.

Eckstein, B., & Throgmorton, J. (Eds.). (2003). *Story and sustainability*. Cambridge, MA: MIT Press.

Flyvbjerg, B. (2002). *Making social science matter*. Cambridge, UK: Cambridge University Press.

Forester, J. (1989). *Planning in the face of power*. Berkeley, CA: University of California Press.

Freire, P. (1970). *Pedagogy of the oppressed*. New York: Herder and Herder.

Friedmann, J. (1973). *Retracking America*. New York: Doubleday Anchor.

Geertz, C. (1983). *Local knowledge: Further essays in interpretive anthropology*. New York: Basic Books.

Hooks, B. (1984). *Feminist theory: From margin to center*. Boston: South End Press.

Knight, L. W. (2005). *Citizen: Jane Addams and the struggle for democracy*. Chicago: University of Chicago Press.

Landry, C. (2000). *The creative city*. London: Earthscan.

Landry, C. (2006). *The art of city making*. London: Earthscan.

Lerner, G. (1997). *Why history matters*. Oxford: Oxford University Press.

Mandelbaum, S. (1991). Telling stories. *Journal of Planning Education and Research, 10*(1), 209–214.

Marris, P. (1997). *Witnesses, engineers, and storytellers: Using research for social policy and action*. College Park, MD: University of Maryland, Urban Studies and Planning Program.

Rabinow, P., & Sullivan, W. M. (Eds.). (1987). *Interpretive social science: A second look*. Berkeley, CA: University of California Press.

Said, E. (1979). *Orientalism*. New York: Vantage Books.

Sandercock, L. (1998). *Towards cosmopolis: Planning for multicultural cities*. Chichester: Wiley.

Sandercock, L. (2003a). *Cosmopolis 2: Mongrel cities of the 21st century*. London and New York: Continuum.

Sandercock, L. (2003b). Out of the closet: The importance of stories and storytelling in planning practice. *Planning Theory and Practice, 4*(1), 11–28.

Sandercock, L. (2004). Towards a planning imagination for the 21st century. *Journal of the American Planning Association, 70*(2), 133–141.

Sandercock, L., & Attili, G. (2009). *Where strangers become neighbours: the integration of immigrants in Vancouver, Canada*. Dordrecht, The Netherlands: Springer.

Sarkissian, W., Hurford, D., & Wenman, C. (2010). *Creative community planning: Transformative engagement methods for working at the edge*. London: Earthscan.

Stretton, H. (1969). *The political sciences*. London: Routledge and Kegan Paul.

Trinh Minh-ha T. (1989). *Woman native other*. Bloomington, IN:1 Indiana University Press.

Chapter 5
(Re)Presenting the Street: Video and Visual Culture in Planning

Elihu Rubin

The practice of city planning cannot be separated from its visual culture: the images produced by urban professionals to make proposals, advance arguments, and assert expertise. By way of prologue, consider a drawing created by Jules Guérin for the 1909 *Plan of Chicago* (Fig. 5.1). In the blink of an eye, the picture embodies the plan. Reproduced on the paperback cover of Peter Hall's *Cities of Tomorrow* (1988) for nearly every recent student of city planning to see, the image of a new Civic Center for Chicago has come to stand for many of the ideals of city planning: bold physical proposals, a progressive role for government, the enhancement of the public realm.

Consider the picture's point of view. You are raised above the ground and look out across a vast, unfolding landscape. You stand at the very center of a new city that spreads before you along the lines of radiating boulevards, as if the piercing force of your own vision was pushing the city outward. This is no fleeting glance. Guérin's placid illustration does not suggest the jarring, fragmented succession of images and encounters that characterize the lived experience of the modern city. Instead, the viewer sustains a fixed gaze upon the landscape. The colors and light lend the picture a distinct mood. Orderly rows of street lamps have been lighted and human figures shimmer on the surface of the large plaza, punctuated (in the fashion of Baroque urban design) by an obelisk. Here is the city of tomorrow after a light rain. The ills of the old city – social, political, and physical – have been washed away.

The planner's ability to produce compelling images of the city has been tightly bound with the profession's claim to expert knowledge. From Guérin's Beaux-Arts renderings of boulevards to the most sophisticated Geographic Information Systems (GIS) tools for mapping statistical information, the planner employs visual techniques to assert mastery over urban space. Planners cultivate their authority by insisting that "the city" can be analyzed as a definite object and that they are the best suited to conduct this analysis. This claim is fundamentally linked to vision: to regard the city as an object requires that it be perceived as a discrete entity and

E. Rubin (✉)
Yale School of Architecture, 180 York Street, New Haven, CT 06511, USA
e-mail: elihu.rubin@yale.edu

L. Sandercock, G. Attili (eds.), *Multimedia Explorations in Urban Policy and Planning*, Urban and Landscape Perspectives 7, DOI 10.1007/978-90-481-3209-6_5, © Springer Science+Business Media B.V. 2010

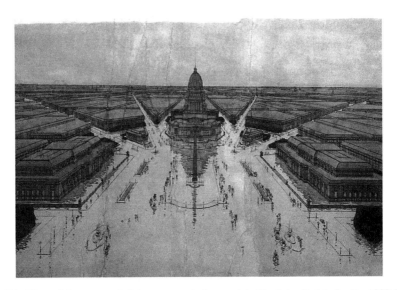

Fig. 5.1 View of the proposed civic center and plaza, painted by Jules Guérin for the 1909 *Plan of Chicago*. Painting by Jules Guérin

represented visually as such. The planner's panoply of visual tools is designed to perceptually stabilize the urban realm, to hold it still long enough for examination and intervention. But consider the countering claim that the city is not stable. It moves unceasingly in an infinite variety of tempos, rhythms, and directions. Urbanism is a plural experience and not a singular event. If this is true, is it possible that stable images actually estrange urban professionals from the unsettled and contested social realities of the city?

Critics of modernist planning practices have challenged the notion that the city can be apprehended as an objective, unified entity (Sandercock, 2003; Scott, 1998). Ascendant paradigms in planning process ask professionals to take a less positivist approach toward their roles as social scientists (Forester, 1989; Innes, 1995). As opposed to immodestly perceiving the city as an object for scientific examination, diagnosis, and curative prescription (complete with medico-biological metaphors like these), the city is instead arrayed as an open field for encounter and engagement. In this model, the city planning process can include self-conscious, even tentative, efforts to mediate between place-bound interests and power brokers who circulate in the realms of politics and capital. The products or forms of knowledge that are today generated in the planning process need not be absolute or unambiguous. Professional representations that stem from urban encounters need not masquerade as objective or factual "data." A compelling alternative is to imagine planning as a collaborative act of listening and storytelling (Eckstein & Throgmorton, 2003). At its best, video-making presents an effective fieldwork method for this mode of planning. In the field of transportation planning – long preoccupied with rendering the street as a functional space of circulation – I propose video as a representational tool that asserts the primacy of the street as a diverse social space.

Video is not immune from a critique of visual methods as positivist or objectifying (Pink, 2007). Like any form of visual ethnography, video practitioners must exercise a reflexive approach that foregrounds questions of patronage, authorship, and audience. The planner-videographer may draw on the medium's representational strengths and the editorial capacity of montage to embrace, and not homogenize, the disjointed and disorienting qualities of the urban experience. In this essay, I first situate video-making in a history of visual methods in planning. Drawing from a case study experience, I propose a model for using video as a form of engagement and documentation with applications for planning practice. This technique emphasizes the role of video-making in fieldwork: the potential of video to record the fragmentary yet richly detailed urban "moment" and to serve as an invitation to urban sociability – a catalyst for otherwise unlikely encounters.

5.1 Picture This: Scenes from the Alley, the Region, and the Street

One branch of planning's expansive genealogy dates back to Victorian urban reform movements. In the United States, Jacob Riis's photographs of slum and tenement districts in New York spurred this movement by showing *how the other half lived*. These were postcards from the edge, and Riis brought them to uptown reformers as evidence of the city's degraded social and physical environments. The images were thus used to support progressive causes like modern housing. Riis, who came from Denmark to New York in 1870 at the age of 21, worked as a police reporter before taking up flash photography and making pictures of people and street scenes in the city's immigrant neighborhoods. Riis used photography to complement his social observations, which were published by Scribner in 1890 as *How the Other Half Lives: Studies Among the Tenements of New York.*[1] But these pictures were more than mere illustrations. They transcended Riis's didactic prose, which talked down to his subjects and tended to treat them like fauna. Some images, like "Bandit's Roost" (Fig. 5.2) or "Mullen's Alley," were luminous alley scenes where sharply defined characters posed and confidently addressed the camera.

The vertical framing of the alley accentuated the intimacy of this vital social space. Riis shot some street scenes from a wider angle. "Mulberry Bend," for example, traced the arc of a lively street, full of people, horses, carriages, and wagons and framed by a jumble of buildings. In a third type of photograph, Riis documented the people of lower Manhattan's slum districts in the fashion of European social surveys like August Sander's study of German social types or Eugène Atget's work in Paris (Becker, 2007, p. 190). Riis could be condescending toward his subjects, but he implicated the upper classes in subjecting the lower classes to an environment that bred bad behavior and distress: "If it shall appear that the sufferings and the sins of the 'other half,' and the evil they breed, are but as a just punishment upon

Fig. 5.2 Jacob Riis's photograph "Bandit's Roost" (1888), part of the journalist's effort to show how the "other half" lived. Photo by Jacob Riis

the community that give it no other choice, it will be because that is the truth" (Riis, 1890, p. 3). With this prompting, I can imagine how Riis's photographs were viewed with trepidation by their bourgeois audience, unsettled by a host of fears relating to social chaos, moral decline, the spread of cholera, and sinking property values.

Jacob Riis used photography to (re)present what he perceived to be a social crisis. When the landscape architect Charles Eliot produced a map of the Boston region in 1893, he took aim at what he saw as a political dilemma of the industrial metropolis. His map of the Metropolitan District characterized the region as an ecological unit that transcended the area's fractured political geography (Fig. 5.3). The District Commission, a new body outlined in an accompanying text coauthored with Sylvester Baxter, was proposed as an umbrella authority charged with

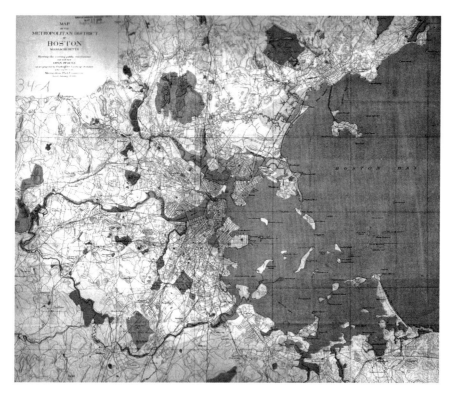

Fig. 5.3   Map of the metropolitan District of Boston (1893) by Charles Eliot, where the shading indicated proposed open spaces. Map by Charles Eliot

procuring a network of waterways, parks, and open spaces to shield the area from overdevelopment (Scott, 1969). Ignoring provincial town boundaries, Eliot demarcated the District's dominion by shading-in the areas on the map that should be preserved for public use.

Eliot's map signified the sweeping act of a planner's comprehensive vision. The top-down view of nineteenth century cartography was akin to seeing the city from the sky, a feat made possible with twentieth century aviation. Aerial photography was used for reconnaissance during World War I and companies like Fairchild made the practice commercially viable in the 1920s by providing aerial surveys to government, industry, and real estate developers (Campanella, 2001). Planners like Robert Whitten, a New York-based consultant, were quick to realize the potential of this technology.

In 1930 Whitten prepared a "Thoroughfare Plan for Metropolitan Boston" for local officials. The bound report's frontispiece featured an aerial photograph that looked directly down on Boston (Fig. 5.4). It served as a kind of surgical diagram that crisply rendered the city's system of streets. In the plan, Whitten proposed a set of limited-access "expressways," including a Central Artery through the core of the city. Using a low-angle aerial shot of the business district, Whitten charted the

Fig. 5.4 A photograph of downtown Boston taken by the Fairchild aerial survey and used to introduce the 1930 *Thoroughfare Plan for Metropolitan Boston*. Photo by Fairchild Aerial Survey

course of the Central Artery by painting its route into the photograph (Fig. 5.5). The elevated highway would follow Atlantic Avenue, a broad street that marked an edge between the wharves and the business district.

Whitten was an early adopter of another tool of positivist urban knowledge: traffic statistics. His firm conducted extensive origin and destination studies with area

Fig. 5.5 Robert Whitten's proposed route of the central artery in Boston, painted into an aerial photograph, from the 1930 *Thoroughfare Plan*. Robert Whitten's painting on aerial photograph

motorists and generated traffic volume data. Traffic counts on the street were translated into charts, graphs, and diagrams by intersection. These statistics were then
mapped onto a line image of the city, where streets were thickened to indicate traffic
demand. In one of Whitten's maps, the entire peninsular center of Boston appeared
to be choked by thick lines that represented "congestion" (Fig. 5.6).

Whitten's congestion maps were arguments for the construction of new thorough-
fares. The planner illustrated these proposed new roads for his readers to scrutinize
and rendered street designs in plan, sectional, and perspective views. The images of
plan and section were more technically descriptive and showed the dimensions of
a street that resembled City Beautiful-era boulevards enhanced by overpasses and
underpasses. But a three-dimensional, perspective rendering struck a different tone:
it allowed lay audiences to see what the road would look like, albeit from a bird's
eye view rarely obtainable in daily life. Whitten's perspective drawing of the Central
Artery diminished the impact of the road on the overall streetscape (Fig. 5.7).

From this view the elevated highway appeared as a light, urbane embellish-
ment to the street, with ornamental lighting standards punctuating the roadside
balustrades. After countless charts, graphs, maps, and aerial photographs, Whitten's
most persuasive image was this drawing: automobiles streamed down the sparsely
trafficked thoroughfare and trucks sidled to the street's edge while groups of unhur-
ried pedestrians ranged across wide sidewalks lined with the clean, flat façades of
large office buildings.

5.2 The Street on Film: That "Glistening Wheel of Life"

It is no small irony that late nineteenth century pioneers of filmmaking were fas-
cinated by precisely the congested thoroughfare that planners like Robert Whitten
and modernist intellectuals like Le Corbusier wanted to replace with a strictly functional street. The Lumière Brothers in France were content to capture ordinary
street scenes with their film camera, which was light enough to carry into the field
(Kracauer, 1960, pp. 30–33). These early experimenters in the art and technology
of film created moving (in a physical, not specifically emotional sense) portraits
of modern urban phenomena. The camera served as an invisible spectator, rarely
acknowledged in the faces of the people who walked before its lens.[2] The earliest
films produced by Louis Lumière and his brother, Auguste, from around 1895, portrayed a suite of ordinary activities: a family eating lunch, a gardener watering his
plants, a group of women exiting the Lumière factory (which produced film and
camera equipment), and, famously, the arrival and emptying of a train. In 1896, the
Lumières stationed a camera at the intersection of Broadway and Union Square in
New York City. Trolleys, horse-drawn carriages, and pedestrians flow across the
screen. A police officer stands in the street, waving pedestrians across and occasionally taking the arm of a woman to guide her through the messy scene. The
architecture of Union Square – including the steel frame of an unfinished new building – composed the static background of this busy urban setting. The subjects of

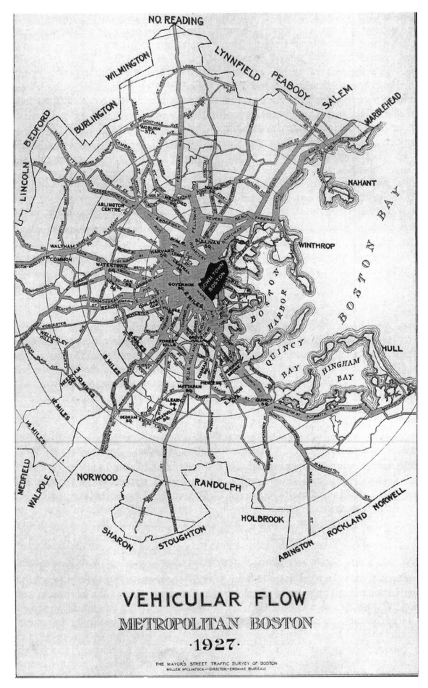

Fig. 5.6 Map of vehicular flow in metropolitan Boston from the 1930 *Thoroughfare Plan*. Map from the 1930 *Thoroughfare Plan*

Fig. 5.7 Robert Whitten's vision of the Central Artery in Boston. Painting by Robert Whitten

Lumière films seemed simple enough. And yet they made a big impact on contemporary audiences: "The familiar, seen anew in this way, brought astonishment" (Barnouw, 1993, p. 7).

The first experimenters in film were intrigued by the medium's descriptive powers more than its potential as a narrative vehicle. Thomas Edison's earliest films – recorded in his West Orange, New Jersey, studio with a large, unwieldy, electrically driven kinetoscope of his own invention – captured the physical dexterity of vaudeville entertainers performing their routines, like a dancer twirling her cloaks in "Serpentine Dances." Edison's short portraits echoed Eadweard Muybridge's studies of animal locomotion from the 1880s, produced by reeling a succession of photographs snapped at set intervals and triggered by a galloping horse, for example, or a leaping cat (Barnouw, 1993, p. 3; Solnit, 2003). Documentary film historian Eric Barnouw writes that Muybridge's experiments hit upon the fundamental capacity of film to "open our eyes to worlds available to us but, for one reason or another, not perceived" (Barnouw, 1993, p. 3).

Siegfried Kracauer emphasized the same quality of filmic representation in his brilliant work, *Theory of Film: The Redemption of Physical Reality* (1960). Kracauer pointed out that everyday places and happenings – familiar streets and buildings, ordinary social exchanges – existed beneath the active threshold of our perceptual environment. But film could reveal the "material phenomena which elude observation under normal circumstances" (Kracauer, 1960, p. 46). A filmmaker forces the audience to confront the banal and see it anew by capturing the commonplace on camera and projecting it on a screen. Film, Kracauer argued, has the capacity to "alienate our environment in exposing it" (Kracauer, 1960, p. 55). By virtue of filmic estrangement, the mundane becomes poignant and full of new meanings.

Certain cinematic techniques, such as irregular camera angles or "close-up" shots, further accentuate the strange in the ordinary.

Kracauer saw a direct relationship between the representational capacities of film and the jocular, unpredictable, and seemingly disorganized world of the public realm as embodied by the street:

> The affinity of film for haphazard contingencies is most strikingly demonstrated by its unwavering susceptibility to the "street"—a term designed to cover not only the street, particularly the city street, in the literal sense, but also its various extensions, such as railway stations, dance and assembly halls, bars, hotel lobbies, airports, etc. (Kracauer, 1960, p. 62)

Kracauer believed that film had an inherent affinity for the "unstaged reality" of the street, where "the accidental prevails over the providential" (Kracauer, 1960, p. 62). "The street in the extended sense of the word is not only the arena of fleeting impressions and chance encounters but a place where the flow of life is bound to assert itself" (Kracauer, 1960, p. 72). More so than photography, film embraces this "continuum" or "flow of life" as it streams across time. An audience's delight in film spectatorship derived from the isolated individual's ability to partake in the street's "fragmentary happenings" as a voyeur – a seated incarnation of the strolling *flâneur*. Film gratified the viewer's thirst for life – "glittering, allusive, infinite life" – by capturing and rendering it on the screen (Kracauer, 1960, p. 170).

In his 1929 filmic portrait of Berlin, Walter Ruttman represented the roving eye of the *flâneur* in his portrayal of the everyday workings of the modern metropolis. In "Berlin: Symphony of a Great City," Ruttman focused on both the smallest details – a cat prowling the streets at dawn, for example – and the overriding rhythms that coursed through the day: the productive forces of the factory, the equally mechanistic operations of the business office, the gendered division of domestic work, the evening's leisure activities. Ruttman established intense rhythms and organized his urban symphony – a silent film accompanied by a symphonic score – through the essential act of film editing: montage, the art of juxtaposing one image with another. In portraying the morning rush hour, a homogenous throng of office workers scurry across the street, an image that Ruttman quickly followed with a pack of trundling swine, presumably herded to slaughter. Ruttman's clips acquire meaning, and express a social commentary, by virtue of their filmic proximity.

At the same time Ruttman was working in capitalist Berlin, Dziga Vertov documented Soviet cities in his 1929 film *Man With a Movie Camera*. If Ruttman's camera eye represented the effortless drifting of the *flâneur*, Vertov broke the voyeuristic spell of the "glistening wheel of life," as Kracauer called it, by exposing the means of the film's production. Vertov never allowed his audience to luxuriate completely in the "being there" quality of spectatorship. Vertov's technique was to film, with a second camera, the act of filming itself. On the screen, we frequently see the filmmaker trudging along with a bulky (by today's standards) hand-crank camera affixed to a heavy wooden tripod. Where Ruttman showed a train roaring across the tracks, Vertov showed how you might acquire such a shot: by digging a hole between the tracks and burying there an up-tilted camera. Vertov also exposed the production of montage by including scenes of a female film editor examining and splicing reels of film negatives. In Vertov's world, the filmmaker was as much a member of the proletariat as the working people documented in the film.

More than 50 years after Ruttman and Vertov, the urban critic William H. Whyte turned to filmmaking with a specific planning-related agenda. City planners in New York had granted floor bonuses to developers in exchange for the provision of "public" plazas on the ground (Kayden, 2000). Some of these plazas were useful and vibrant social spaces while others were dreary and abandoned. What elements made some places successful while others languished? Whyte assembled a team and launched a social research project to find out.[3] He began with direct observation of the "social life of small urban spaces," but eventually turned to time-lapse photography and "candid camera" style filmmaking to more closely observe the city's behavioral landscape.[4] Despite his policy-driven research question and the concrete suggestions he eventually made for effective plaza design, Whyte admitted that much of the research produced by the Street Life Project was "fundamental – that is, I can't now think of any especial applicability for it" (Whyte, 1980, p. 8). In his voice-over for the film, Whyte adopted the witty, urbane style of the *flâneur* who took a connoisseur's interest in the behavioral arcana of urbanites in public space. Like a mid-twentieth century anthropologist narrating an ethnographic film, Whyte remarked on the patterns and quirks of indigenous New Yorkers mingling in and around the corporate plazas of Park Avenue.

5.3 Video and the Production of Social Space

Whyte's voyeuristic style cast him as an outsider analyzing local culture. This approach adhered to the social scientific standard of professional detachment that has been the stock and trade of city planners.[5] Critics of modernist planning practices have impugned the model of planner as *flâneur*, the strolling urban dilettante who visually consumed "the fragmented aspects of street life that appealed to him" (Wilson, 1991, p. 5). The *flâneur* was tolerant, cosmopolitan, and unmotivated to intervene. But when adopted by a city planner, the *flâneur's* gaze projected a desire for order and clarity across the disorganized, mysterious, and feminized urban landscape (Wilson, 1991). A progressive, if not radical, model for fieldwork in city planning must transcend the model of the detached *flâneur* and strive for a more reflexive, engaged, and participatory ideal. Perhaps ironically, a video camera can aid this process. As the filmmaker Dziga Vertov illustrated, the camera is not a transparent mode of capturing and representing urban scenes. In "the field," the act of filmmaking is also an active tool for producing social space. Photographer and urban planner Helen Liggett has noted this phenomenon: "Take the camera out into the street, and the potential for unpredictable encounters with the city is built in" (Liggett, 2003, p. 120).

Take an example from the production of a narrative film. When shooting "on location," a large film crew can commandeer an entire city block, clear it of the people who would normally be there, and re-people it with actors to stage a scene.

Smaller, independent crews might film more surreptitiously, allowing the rhythms of daily life to continue around them. Both situations create a buzz of activity, not unlike a crime scene or the site of a car collision. People stop to look, mill around, and ask aloud what the fuss is all about. They engage with each other through a process that William H. Whyte called "triangulation," when an outside event brings together two otherwise unacquainted people (Whyte, 1980). Spectacles of this kind – small disruptions in the ordinary flow of daily life – can break through the urban social norm of "civil inattention," which specifies that for the most part city people will tolerate one another in public space but tend to keep to themselves (Goffman, 1966).

On a much smaller scale, even a single videomaker, balancing a camera on a tripod or monopod (a retractable peg used to stabilize the camera), can create a bit of street-spectacle. By virtue of this self-conscious activity, the video-maker emerges as a public figure – a type of "public character" evoked by Jane Jacobs in her description of Greenwich Village street life (Jacobs, 1961; Duneier, 1999). In this scenario, the camera itself becomes a prop that invites "face engagement" between the videographer and another person. The sociologist Erving Goffman observed that encounters between people required an "opening move," a social overture of some kind to break the ice (Goffman, 1966, pp. 89–90). The presence of a video camera can serve as the "opening move" that invites social overtures from others. For this reason, it is important *not to hide* the video camera in "the field" because it is the prop that initiates conversations.

This has been true in my experience as a videographer in the street. I use a mid-sized camera (a Sony PD-150 that records on MiniDV tapes) affixed to a monopod, which I rest on my shoulder while walking. Admittedly, the process of filming begins with a bit of *flânerie* as I stroll, eyes up, until spotting a scene that interests me – a busy street corner, people waiting to board a bus, a unique neon sign. I place the foot of the monopod on the ground to balance the camera and focus on my subject, choosing scale and composition based on instinct. My aim is to record not only the street's physical conditions but also to show how it is used and occupied by people. The rhythm of human activity against the backdrop of the built environment produces a sense of atmosphere, for lack of a better term, that marks the representational strength of video-making.[6] The act of video-taping often draws some notice: *What is he looking at? Is something "newsworthy" happening that I should know about? Why would someone film an ordinary street like this one?* The video camera represents – it caricatures, in a sense – the act of looking. This sign of purposeful observation is itself an irruption in the flow of ordinary life. It is the "opening move".

What happens next is never the same. Not everyone will want to appear in a stranger's video and these people seek to protect their privacy. They will shy away, avoid eye contact, even actively cross the street to avoid a meeting. But just as frequently, I am approached: "Say, what are you shooting?" Young people and children have asked if I am taking video for television, if so which station, and could they be interviewed on camera so as to appear on TV that night. If I pass someone who I sense might be happy to speak with me, I will reach out: "Excuse me, Ma'am? Let me ask you – how long have you been waiting for the bus?"[7] Once an invitation has been extended and accepted, the permutations of this interaction and the nature of the conversations that follow are endless. At some point in this exchange, I ask permission to turn the camera on my partner and to record them as they speak.[8] As a rule, I explain what I am doing: "I'm making a video about San Pablo Avenue." This sometimes allows my conversation partner to speak as a local expert, pleased to have an opportunity to share a story. They might say something like this: "Oh, I know all about San Pablo. I've lived around here for more than 15 years". Thus video-making in the street is a tool not only for representing the urban scene, but also for initiating conversations that tap into a wealth of local knowledge.

5.4 San Pablo Avenue: (Re)Presenting the Street

The footage recorded with a video camera is of course only a tiny sample of the sum of activities and interactions that occur in urban space. From this sample, the film-maker further reduces the material in the process of editing. Like the composition of an individual photograph, the linear composition of a video implies an author's set of choices. What image comes first? What next? For how long? How will I edit and thus distill this rambling monologue to make it more accessible? Will there be music to score the video? What should it sound like? Will there be voice-over narration? What will it say? Video is among the most expressive forms of representation because of its facility to capture sound, movement, and atmosphere. But video cannot be regarded as an objective or accurate rendering of social facts. Like Ruttman's montage of Berlin, the act of film production is necessarily editorial. It reduces the urban environment to a series of scenes.[9] The issue of subjectivity in video production is especially salient in the realm of city planning, where the planner-videomaker may enter "the field" with an agenda. Acknowledging the patronage and intended audience of a city planning video is the first step in adopting the reflexive approach I advocate.

Some videomakers go into a project with an already defined goal or with the intention to advocate a position: to show that bike lanes are a good thing, for example, or to celebrate a "Critical Mass" event where bike riders take to the streets at the expense of car traffic. There is a place for this type of filmmaking, just as there is a role for video to play in documenting the proceedings of public meetings so that they may be shared with those who could not attend in person. But a different approach asks the planner-videomaker to engage with the city without a preconceived agenda, regardless of the expectations of the film's patron. My 4.5-minutes video about San Pablo Avenue is an imperfect example made in a short period of time, but it distills many of my basic ideas about the role of video in city planning while pointing to the challenges of this method.

In 2004, California State Assembly Member Loni Hancock asked the University of California Transportation Center at Berkeley (UCTC) to reconsider the development and planning of San Pablo Avenue. The state's Department of Transportation (Caltrans) was planning to repave San Pablo and there was a question if certain design improvements could be included in that plan. In terms of social and physical geography, San Pablo Avenue was a diverse street. Before Interstate Highways 80 and 580 were built in the 1960s, San Pablo Avenue (called U.S. 40 in 1927 and now also known as California 123) was the most important automotive thorough-fare in the East Bay, running from Oakland to Richmond and passing through a handful of other independent towns in between. In some parts, nearer to Berkeley, small boutiques and coffee shops had opened in the 1920s-era commercial strips and tree-lined sidewalks were alive with activity. In other parts, closer to downtown Oakland, the street showed signs of physical deterioration and disinvestment. There were many "greyfield" sites – abandoned gas stations, for example – that required large investments to detoxify in order to redeem for future development. These parts of San Pablo had fewer trees and, at first glance, a sparser street life than the more socially and physically lush areas of the street in Berkeley or further north in Albany. In a meeting with U.C. Berkeley planners, Assembly Member Hancock asked if the entire avenue couldn't become a "world class boulevard" – she evoked the Champs Élysées – a vibrant place that attracted people.

Planners who had begun to conduct survey research of San Pablo's market catch-ment had a ready answer for Assembly Member Hancock: there was not enough population density near San Pablo to support a consistently high level of commer-cial activity across the length of the boulevard. Planners had to address a central paradox of the road: it was both a highly trafficked regional artery that served daily commuters, service vehicles, and freight-carrying trucks and a local commercial street in some places serving a wide variety of shopping functions for both local and visiting people. The regional public transportation authority, the Alameda-Contra Costa Transit District (AC Transit), had recently inaugurated a "Bus Rapid Transit" line on San Pablo, establishing several new bus shelters, some of which included a light-emitting diode (LED) screen that predicted when the next bus would arrive. The new bus infrastructure, combined with Caltrans' repaving plans, provided an opportunity to rethink the social and physical qualities of the street.

The immediate purpose for the video was to kick off a presentation that UCTC planners prepared for Loni Hancock along with local planners, academics, and students. I followed the fieldwork method outlined above, which generated several conversations that I recorded on camera. The result is what I think of as a subjective "sense of place" video that visually represented the street from a variety of perspec-tives – on foot, from a car, through the window of a moving bus. I used music and montage to intensify these rhythms and scored the video with Afro-Cuban-inspired jazz by Cal Tjader, the vibraphone player (I used tracks from his 1966 album "Soul Burst").[10] My intention was to use Tjader's music to imbue San Pablo with a feeling of hybrid cosmopolitanism that reflected my sense of the place. I had no predeter-mined script planned for the video. Yet the finished product advanced an attitude toward the street that emerged over the course of making the video – a view that was shared, I think, by my cohort of UCTC planners – that stressed two aspects of San Pablo Avenue: it contained a set of neighborhood nodes distributed (albeit unevenly) across the street and it also acted as a busy street for carrying traffic. I interspersed my own voice as a loose narration to emphasize, even advocate, this mixed-use vision of the street. The film begins with a selection from an interview I had with a man on San Pablo Avenue just north of downtown Oakland (Fig. 5.8).

Fig. 5.8 Video-stills from "Introducing San Pablo: Signs of a Great Street" produced by the author in 2004

Fig. 5.9 Video-stills from "Introducing San Pablo: Signs of a Great Street" produced by the author in 2004

Fig. 5.10 Video-stills from "Introducing San Pablo: Signs of a Great Street" produced by the author in 2004

I have transcribed the voices of the short video below, with brief descriptions of the speakers:

Older African-American man wearing a purple beret:
See, San Pablo is legendary to me because, and to many people, because it was open all night long – the buses. And if you had to go from Richmond through here, you come through San Pablo. You come through there, and like, you catch that 72 bus. All the other buses stopped at midnight or one o'clock, San Pablo's still going on.

Older White man wearing a fishing vest and cap:
San Pablo I can see is starting to go through some changes. It was sort of a long New Jersey of chop shops, that kind of thing.

Group of three, multi-ethnic school-age kids wearing backpacks:
We should be able to run through and have fun out here.

Elihu's Question:
You don't think it's safe for kids to walk around San Pablo?

The kids continue, speaking hurriedly and on top of one another:
No, not at night. Nope, Nope, Nope, Nope. I mean, unless you with somebody. There's really no place safe for you to walk around at night, I'm not saying day.

Elihu's Narration:
San Pablo has for a long time been a garrulous strip. A place for gambling, gaming, carousing, and so much more. Recent investments in transit present an opportunity to rethink the nodes of activity on San Pablo and to build on their strengths.

Older African-American Woman:
It does so much for us. You know, it's a thoroughfare. It goes between so many different cities, and we have all kind of businesses up and down it. So it's really great. I love it here. My son picks me up a lot, and I take the bus. And then we have the "Go Round."

Elihu's Narration:
There are many interesting places on San Pablo, and there are many opportunities to create more of them. Well, it may not be the Champs-Élysées. But the signs are clear. San Pablo Avenue could be a world class boulevard.

Between the short moments that (re)present selections from my conversations on the street, there is a dense succession of video images of San Pablo (again, from a moving vehicle or a stationary position on the street). The result can be disorienting. The viewer is not told where on San Pablo each shot has been taken. In one "scene," a man struggles to cross the street – despite a crosswalk and landscaped median – in the face of fast-moving traffic. In another, a group of teenage girls leans out into the street from a "Rapid" bus stop that possessed neither a shelter nor a "Next Stop" LED screen. The camera-eye is consistently drawn to the street's signage and commercial architecture, which evoke many layers of development over time in various states of upkeep. My minimal narration is somewhat bullish on San Pablo, while acknowledging its legacy as a linear honky-tonk district, and I entitled the piece to reflect that tone: "Introducing San Pablo: Signs of a Great Street." The last lines of narration were intended as both a nod to Loni Hancock's aspirations for the street and a wry acknowledgment that San Pablo Avenue, which received national attention as a locus of prostitution (Marshall, 2004), does not always adhere to the Assembly Member's ideal despite its diversity and vitality.

The video was shown in conjunction with other papers produced by U.C. Berkeley planners at the 2006 Transportation Research Board conference in Washington, DC (Cherry et. al., 2006). I have used the video in my teaching to illustrate issues in planning method and practice. But "Introducing San Pablo" was never properly reintroduced to the street itself. It was my failing that I did not pursue local screenings of the video, nor was I able to share the film with those who had participated in it. In my videographic drift across San Pablo, I neglected to take down the names or phone numbers of the people I met. This points to a challenge posed by this approach. My encounters were inspired by the disruptive presence of the video camera, yet they were passing and essentially anonymous encounters nonetheless. This limitation diminished the interactive possibilities of the video project. In the future, I think it is important to take down those names and to make an effort to return the video to participants and interested communities as a way to stimulate additional conversations about the future of streets, neighborhoods, and cities.[11] Like my encounters with people on San Pablo Avenue, my role as an outsider and planner was fleeting.

5.5 Return to the Street

For many planners, designers, and engineers, it is easier to see the street as a piece of urban technology instead of a social space where people acknowledge one another as citizens with mutual interests. Planners have made a habit of pathologizing urban space and seeing the street as an artery that may have hardened or become clogged. From this perspective, streets are part of a circulatory system that organizes movement through the city – a mobile space for traffic – and not a local social space or a meaningful extension of the public realm. Video-making is a way to see the street as a place for events and encounters as well as to stimulate them. Where planning has sought to be objective and comprehensive, video can be personal, impressionistic, and spontaneous. Where aerial photography or cartography has promised totality and mastery, video is selective and disorienting. Planners have a tough time with disorientation because it goes against their instinct to want to fix problems. But there is utility in disorientation, which – like the medium of film itself – makes strange the familiar and thus destabilizes dominant visions and accepted ideas about places. We take a positive step forward by acknowledging the complexity of the street as a social space instead of replacing it with a visual abstraction. This method does not always yield ready solutions; but by reasserting the primacy of the street itself, video-making is one way to start the conversation.

Acknowledgments The University of California Transportation Center at Berkeley sponsored the research for this project, and I thank Betty Deakin for her support of video as a form of planning research and practice. I am indebted to Leonie Sandercock and Giovanni Attili for their incisive editorial observations and encouragement to pursue a self-reflexive voice.

Notes

1. Just a portion of Riis's halftone photographs were included in Scribner's first printing of the book in 1890, which also included illustrations by Riis based on other photographs.
2. By contrast, consider the film work of Lumière's contemporaries in Britain, Sagar Mitchell and James Kenyon, who produced short films for exhibition at fairgrounds. During the day, Mitchell and Kenyon would shoot footage of everyday settings and ordinary people. The subjects – often directed to wave their hats or parade slowly in front of the camera – would pack the cinema later that evening to enjoy the thrill of seeing a motion-picture portrait of themselves and their community on the screen (Toulmin, 2008).
3. Whyte produced a 55-minutes film, "The Social Life of Small Urban Spaces" distributed by the Municipal Art Society of New York as well as a companion manual with the same name.
4. The term "behavioral landscape" is drawn from James Borchert's study of alley life in Washington, DC (Borchert, 1980, p. 291).
5. It should be said that William H. Whyte's compelling observations ring true. However, I would argue that the fascinating quality of Whyte's film accentuates a sense of detachment.
6. For a perspective on "rhythms" as a mode of urban analysis, see Lefebvre (2004).
7. There is no substitute for instinct and no precise set of rules that govern how street encounters evolve. The presence of the camera changes the social environment in which these encounters take place, and I argue that it creates a relatively nonintimidating excuse for reaching out to people – an act that might otherwise seem strange or eccentric.
8. The act of pressing "record" to begin taping is itself a slippery moment. I may be in the midst of filming a bus shelter when an encounter begins and I turn the camera, mounted on the monopod at my side, toward my conversation partner. In this case, permission to record is granted implicitly or retroactively. I try to maintain eye contact and treat the camera as a third party, like a friend who is listening in. Sometimes the framing of the person is a bit off until I can take a moment to look through the viewfinder and adjust focus.
9. There are rare exceptions to the practice of edited film and most have come from the realm of art film. See, for example, Andy Warhol's "Empire State," which comprises one continuous shot of the Empire State Building in New York for a full 8 hours and 5 minutes. Another example is Fernand Léger's unrealized dream of a 24-hours film representing the life of a man and a woman during 24 consecutive hours (Kracauer, 1960, p. 64).
10. For many videomakers, including myself, music is helpful in the act of editing. Once I have chosen music that reflects the suite of moods I would like to project, I frequently "cut" footage to the music. The rhythm of the music creates a template for editing.
11. A group of Berkeley planners went on to conduct focus group interviews with residents from neighborhoods bordering San Pablo (McAndrews, Flórey, & Deakin, 2006). The video might have been used as part of those focus group discussions or in other forums to create a space for productive dialogue.

References

Barnouw, E. (1993). *Documentary: A history of the non-fiction film.* New York: Oxford University Press.

Becker, H. S. (2007). *Telling about society.* Chicago: University of Chicago Press.

Borchert, J. (1980). *Alley life in Washington: Family, community, religion, and folklife in the City, 1850–1970.* Champaign, IL: University of Illinois Press.

Campanella, T. J. (2001). *Cities from the Sky: An aerial portrait of America.* New York: Princeton Architectural Press.

Cherry, C. R., Deakin, E., Higgins, N., & Huey, S. B. (2006). Systems-level approach to sustainable urban arterial revitalization: Case study of San Pablo avenue. *Transportation record, Journal of the Transportation Research Board, No. 1977.*

Duneier, M. (1999). *Sidewalk.* New York: Farrar, Straus & Giroux.

Eckstein, B., & Throgmorton, A. (Eds.). (2003). *Story and sustainability: Planning, practice, and possibility for American cities.* Cambridge, MA: MIT Press.

Forester, J. (1989). *Planning in the face of power.* Berkeley: University of California Press.

Goffman, E. (1966). *Behavior in public places: Notes on the social organization of gatherings.* New York: The Free Press.

Hall, P. (1988). *Cities of tomorrow: An intellectual history of urban planning and design in the twentieth century.* Malden, MA: Blackwell.

Innes, J. (1995). Planning theory's emerging paradigm: Communicative action and interactive practice. *Journal of Planning Education and Research, 14*(3), 183–190.

Jacobs, J. (1961). *The death and life of great American cities.* New York: Random House.

Kayden, J. S. (2000). *Privately owned public space: The New York city experience.* New York: John Wiley & Sons, Inc.

Kracauer, S. (1960) *Theory of film: The redemption of physical reality.* New York: Oxford University Press.

Lefebvre, H. (2004). *Rhythmanalysis: Space, time, and everyday life.* New York: Continuum.

Liggett, H. (2003). *Urban encounters.* Minneapolis, MN: University of Minnesota Press.

Marshall, C. (2004, September 14). Bid to decriminalize prostitution in Berkeley. *New York Times.*

McAndrews, C., Flórez, J., & Deakin, E. (2006). *Views of the street: Using community surveys and focus groups to inform context-sensitive design.* Transportation record: Journal of the Transportation Research Board, No. 1981.

Pink, S. (2007). *Doing visual ethnography.* London: Sage.

Riis, J. (1890). *How the other half lives: Studies among the tenements of New York.* New York: Scribner.

Sandercock, L. (2003). *Cosmopolis II: Mongrel cities of the 21st Century.* New York and London: Continuum.

Scott, J. C. (1998). *Seeing like a state: How certain schemes to improve the human condition have failed.* New Haven, CT: Yale University Press.

Scott, M. (1969). *American city planning since 1890.* Berkeley: University of California Press.

Solnit, R. (2003). *River of shadows: Eadweard Muybridge and the technological wild West.* New York: Penguin Putnam.

Toulmin, V. (2008). *Electric Edwardians: The films of Mitchell and Kenyon.* London: British Film Institute.

Whyte W. H. (1980). *The social life of small urban spaces.* New York: Conservation Foundation.

Wilson, E. (1991). *The Sphinx in the city: Urban life, the control of disorder, and women.* Berkeley, CA: University of California Press.

Chapter 6
Digital Media and the Politics of Disaster Recovery in New Orleans

Jacob A. Wagner

> *What kind of America would we have if New Orleans never*
> *existed? Certainly not one that was beloved for two centuries*
> *around the world for the daring of its music, the inventiveness of*
> *its culture, the epic sweep of its writers. Certainly not an*
> *America whose cities are now waking from ages-long slumber*
> *to find their night, their youth, their creative energies.*
> (Andrei Codrescu, 2006, p. 36)

6.1 Introduction[1]

In the wake of Hurricane Katrina and the failure of the federal hurricane protection system, residents of New Orleans have struggled to rebuild their city in a context of uncertainty, contested leadership, and a highly politicized planning process. In the absence of a well-organized process, people have turned to other modes of planning action to address the problems of communication and information experienced during the recovery. In this chaotic context, digital communication tools served as an indispensible medium for disaster recovery by providing a forum for the critique of planning, which reflects a significant process of social learning and socio-political empowerment (Rocha, 1997; Friedmann, 1987).

In contrast to existing research on New Orleans recovery planning that emphasizes government-led planning (Nelson, Ehrenfeucht, & Laska, 2007; Olshansky, Johnson, Horne, & Nee, 2008), I find that the most significant aspect of the New Orleans experience has been the recovery activism and unofficial planning led by citizens. In particular, this chapter explores the political dimensions of digital media[2] and their use in the official and unofficial planning processes following Hurricane

J.A. Wagner (✉)
Department of Architecture, Urban Planning and Design, University of Missouri-Kansas City, Kansas City, MO, USA
e-mail: wagnerjaco@umkc.edu

L. Sandercock, G. Attili (eds.), *Multimedia Explorations in Urban Policy and Planning*, Urban and Landscape Perspectives 7, DOI 10.1007/978-90-481-3209-6_6,
© Springer Science+Business Media B.V. 2010

Katrina. I focus on the tensions between competing planning processes and the different approaches to digital media use. Because the recovery process in New Orleans has been the most digitally mediated planning process to date, it is critical to analyze the use and the impact of these tools (see Ritchin, 2009) to determine what this means for urban planning in the age of the Digital City and the Network Society.

Given the proliferation of planning action in post-disaster New Orleans, this case study provides a critical opportunity to analyze practice in the context of existing scholarship. In particular, this case study considers New Orleans planning processes in light of recent debates in planning theory about critical pragmatism, communicative action and social learning (Beauregard, 2000; Lauria & Wagner, 2006; Friedmann, 2003; Collins & Ison, 2006), the use of digital media in planning (Drummond & French, 2008; Klosterman, 2008; Krieger, 2004; Campbell, 1996; Batty, 2001; Craglia, 2004), participation and the right to the city (Campbell & Marshall, 2000; Sandercock, 2000; Lefebvre, 1996), and the structural context for urban planning in the Network Society (Castells, 1996, 1997).

In New Orleans, grassroots innovation stands in stark contrast to the processes sponsored by elected officials and government agencies. Unofficial planning processes have often been a form of advocacy planning in response to the official processes (Culley & Hughey, 2008, p. 102) that occurred between the fall of 2005 and the spring of 2007. While many of these unofficial plans were produced by neighborhood organizations, it is important to point out that the unofficial planning has not been limited to neighborhood planning (Checkoway, 1984) and that citizen activism has often focused on issues of citywide or regional significance, such as levees, wetland ecology, or affordable housing. As explained in the analysis that follows, unofficial planning processes unfolded in a highly politicized environment in which competing factions sought to control the official recovery processes, public participation, and the financial resources attached to recovery plans.

The unofficial processes include the plans developed by neighborhood associations, local community development corporations (CDCs), nonprofit organizations, and private individuals. These include plans developed by the Mid City Neighborhood Organization Plan, Mary Queen of Vietnam CDC, Broadmoor Improvement Association, Holy Cross Neighborhood, and the Friends of Lafitte Corridor, as well as the advocacy-oriented meetings run by Neighborhood Planning Network.[3] I find that important social learning and empowerment processes (Friedmann, 1996, 2003; Rocha, 1997) have developed in New Orleans in which digital media use enhanced the development of planning knowledge and action. Neighborhood and nonprofit organizations, artists, activists, independent journalists, university faculty and students, and local advocacy planners have employed digital media to bridge new geographic and information divides between returned and displaced residents of New Orleans, volunteers, and public officials. Digital tools have provided a flexible and adaptable means of communication, representation, and critique of planning processes, as well as a venue in which the politics of recovery were debated.

While neighborhoods and nonprofit organizations mobilized through electronic communications, the official plans lagged behind the processes led by citizens in terms of social learning, empowerment, and the use of digital media. The official processes include the plans sponsored by elected officials or government agencies and managed by teams of private consultants. In New Orleans this includes (in chronological order) the following: the Federal Emergency Management Agency's ESF-14 Plan, the Mayor's Bring New Orleans Back Commission (BNOB), the City Council's New Orleans Neighborhoods Rebuilding Plan (NONRP, also known as the "Lambert Plan" after the lead consultant – Paul Lambert), and the Unified New Orleans Plan (UNOP) – which is the main focus of this chapter.[4]

Since its rocky start in late July 2006, the UNOP process was staged as a high-stakes recovery plan that developed in a media-saturated context (see Fig. 6.1), which raises significant questions about the balance between the need for documentation and publicity versus the saturation of planning by media spectacle. Despite heightened public awareness of planning and increased expectations about recovery information and communication, the UNOP plan neither emerged from civic activism nor captured public approval, despite the claims of its champions (Olshansky, 2006; Williamson, 2007; Wilson, 2008). To further complicate the process, this chapter makes the case that public officials and their consultants failed to recognize and build upon the social learning occurring outside of their official plan-making efforts.

While on the surface the UNOP plan appears to be the result of a process enhanced by the use of the latest digital technology, underlying aspects of the UNOP process, including its governing structure, and Community Congress II "town hall"

Fig. 6.1 "How much media is too much?" Photographer uses digital technology to document visual and audio components of the July 30, 2006 meeting of the Unified Plan of New Orleans (UNOP). Photo by Jacob A. Wagner

meeting suggest a need to analyze how the use of digital media impacts planning processes, the content of plans, and outcomes. Although digital media provide new opportunities for the enhancement of participatory processes, the evidence from post-Katrina New Orleans indicates that the use of digital technologies in planning does not necessarily result in a more democratic process and that the use of digital media can increase rather than diminish the systematic distortion of information in planning.

I find that the shortcomings of the "final" recovery planning process – the Unified New Orleans Plan (UNOP) – are symptomatic of a crisis of democratic governance that has prevented a more equitable recovery from occurring. The management structure created to facilitate the UNOP process and the public meetings, including Community Congress II, are analyzed below.

I argue that the UNOP plan presents a troubling case of privatized planning, planning as media spectacle, and conflict avoidance that exposes both the strengths and weaknesses of digital media use in urban planning.

6.1.1 Disaster Recovery and the Digital City

Viewed from the perspective of planning theory, the flurry of planning and design activity in New Orleans represents a confluence of trends in participation, communication, and digital technology that heralds the arrival of a new era of practice in which digital media and communications are ubiquitous – yet deeply political and contested. Whether or not this new era represents the triumph of the visual image in urban planning (Neuman, 2000, p. 348) or a "second revolution" in the use of technology in planning (Klosterman, 2008) is less important than our understanding of the impacts that digital technology can have on democratic planning. In particular, as some have suggested (Castells, 1997), the use of digital technology can affect the democratization of planning by leveling the playing field in terms of access to information and increasing the ability of multiple publics to participate in and shape planning decisions. At the same time, Graham (2002) finds that the use of information and communications technology (ICT) on a global scale is occurring in a way that maintains or increases social polarization.

So, while the current planning moment in New Orleans may be "new" in this sense, perennial issues within planning ethics and theory are heightened rather than resolved by this emergent context for practice. These key concerns include the following:

1. citizen influence and empowerment in local governance and spatial decision-making,
2. elite and expert control of planning processes versus planning based on collaboration and mutual understanding, and
3. the communicative politics of planning information, including the production, use, and control of digital media, ICT, and urban data (see Bates & Green, 2007).

Table 6.1 Digital city matrix

	"Raw data" of the city	Methods and ways of thinking
Non-digital ("traditional"; analog; tangible)	**A:** the physical city and its artifacts, goods and services, people interacting in physical, urban space...	**B:** Traditional forms of analysis in urban planning, sociology, architecture...
Digital	**C:** Data and communication flows, electronic services, digital models of the city...	**D:** Computer-based methods for representing, self-representation, and analyzing the city...

Source: Craglia (2004) and Batty (2001).

From the perspective of Digital City scholarship, Batty (2001) and Craglia (2004) offer a heuristic device to explore the complex and sometimes contradictory relationships between the digital and the physical city. Table 6.1 provides a framework for analyzing the digital and the physical city, and research methods and theories developed to conceptualize and explain the urban experience.

Applying this framework to New Orleans, we can explore the complex mediations between the digital city and the physical city, digital modes of representing the physical city, and how traditional practices of planning and design have been altered or expanded by digital methods of representing and understanding the city. Table 6.2 applies this matrix to the conditions in post-disaster New Orleans.

This matrix suggests additional questions. Are the digital modes of representing and thinking about cities simply a reinvention of "traditional" approaches? Have digital modes of urban representation fundamentally altered planning practice and our ways of representing the urban experience? Have digital representations of New Orleans following the catastrophe created a new understanding of the city, a new legibility of its creole urbanism (Wagner, 2008) or its planning apparatus? Finally – how has the use of digital media altered the reconstruction of everyday life in a city devastated by catastrophe (see Fig. 6.2)?

While New Orleans may provide an extreme case of planning under the pressure of disaster recovery, the ubiquity of digital means of understanding and representing the physical city, its people, and places suggests the significance of the New Orleans experience for urban planning practice. This case study demonstrates that rather than simply facilitating participation, citizen, and professional use of digital media in planning creates new challenges and dilemmas for practitioners who seek to develop plans and spatial policies that are equitable, collaborative, and democratic (Campbell, 1996). Further, many of the digitally mediated planning scenarios suggested by Drummond and French (2008, p. 172) have already occurred in New Orleans – although the realities

Table 6.2 New Orleans digital city matrix (Application of Craglia, 2004; Batty, 2001)

	"Raw data" of the city	Methods and ways of thinking
Non-digital ("traditional"; analog; tangible)	**A:** Housing units flooded and damaged; People displaced; temporary housing and "FEMAvilles"; public and historic housing demolition; impacts to local culture; failed levees...	**B:** Field surveys of neighborhoods; structural assessments of homes; interviews and oral histories; planning meetings; published books and journal articles...
Digital (electronic communications; computer software; binary data systems)	**C:** GIS; GPS; the Internet; Websites and blogs; digital audio and podcasts; digital photography; digital data; on-line archives; web-published plans; web-based public notification; email, listserves...	**D:** Online forums of debate; digital visualization of the disaster; digital maps; geospatial analysis of human and environmental aspects of the disaster and its aftermath; online artistic exhibits...

Fig. 6.2 "GPS in Lower Ninth Ward". Evidence of the digital city methods of marking and mapping the analog city in the midst of disaster, December 2005. Photo by Jacob A. Wagner

on the ground are far more complex than those suggested by these authors.[5] As demonstrated in this chapter, the use of digital media in the official and unofficial arenas of recovery planning has complicated planning practice and theory with challenging questions and ethical dilemmas arising from the combination of online tools with more traditional planning processes (cf. Graham, 2002, p. 35).

6.2 Overview of Urban Planning in New Orleans

Urban planning in New Orleans prior to the disaster included numerous public, semipublic, and private organizations. The city's strong mayor form of government provides a political structure in which the executive branch has considerable influence over planning through mayoral divisions, policy agendas, and appointments of staff that focus on economic development and policy at a citywide level. The City Council includes five officials elected to represent specific council districts and two at-large members. The de facto politicization of land-use planning before the storm was characterized as a system based on "unbridled discretion" and "deference" in which City Council members defer to the wishes of the district council member on the land use and planning decisions based within their district (Bureau of Governmental Research, 2003).

The City Planning Commission's authority over planning is weakened by this de facto system of deference and by the fact that the City's charter does not require the City Council and Mayor to adopt the Comprehensive Plan into law (Mandelker, 2002). Despite these challenges, the City Planning Commission completed a recent update of the Master Plan in 1999 and was in the midst of a revision of the city's comprehensive zoning ordinance when the disaster struck. In addition to the City Planning Commission and its staff, there are other agencies that play an important role in the spatial regulation of the built environment. These include the Historic Districts Landmarks Commission (HDLC) and the Vieux Carré Commission (VCC), which are responsible for the regulation of the city's local historic districts and the historic French Quarter, respectively.

Outside of city government, the Regional Planning Commission (RPC) serves as the metropolitan planning organization for the five parish areas centered around Orleans Parish and the City of New Orleans. The RPC has considerable influence locally in terms of transportation, environmental, and economic development planning – each of which provides considerable sources of funding that are used to shape the built environment and infrastructure of the city and its metropolitan region. Nongovernmental organizations involved in planning include the Bureau of Governmental Research (BGR), which often serves as a forum for the public discussion and critique of planning, public policy, and government practice within the metro area (Reichard, 2006). The Committee for a Better New Orleans and the Metropolitan Area Committee (CBNO/MAC) includes two reform groups that merged around 2000 to create a Blueprint for a Better New Orleans focused on governance and citizen participation. This group includes many of the city's elites involved in economic development, real estate, education, and public affairs. For example, both Joseph Canizaro and Norman Francis were named chairs of CBNO when it was established. After the disaster, Canizaro served as the controversial chair of the Bring New Orleans Back Commission while Dr. Francis, president of Xavier University, served as chair of the Louisiana Recovery Authority (LRA) of the State, appointed by Governor Kathleen Blanco.

6.2.1 Post-disaster Planning Processes, 2005–2007

While existing planning organizations have not disappeared, new organizations have been created in the wake of the disaster as municipal and state governments were thrown into a crisis that included a significant restructuring of the planning function. Both New Orleans Mayor C. Ray Nagin and Louisiana Governor Kathleen Blanco appointed recovery commissions within about 1 month following the catastrophe. Mayor Nagin called on business elites to lead the Bring New Orleans Back Commission (BNOB). This process included several subcommittees including urban planning (led by Canizaro and the private planning firm of Wallace, Roberts, and Todd) and urban design (led by the politically connected architect Ray Manning and Reed Kroloff, Dean of the School of Architecture at Tulane at the time). A small army of professional and community volunteers served on the various subcommittees and through this participation the BNOB process benefitted from a wide range of expertise. However, in terms of citizen participation, the BNOB process was limited to a few town hall meetings in New Orleans and in the cities with the largest concentrations of displaced residents.

A report produced by the Urban Land Institute (ULI, 2005) and the plan developed by Wallace, Roberts, and Todd for the BNOB urban planning committee in January 2006 recommended a phased approach to rebuilding that ranked areas of the city by their elevation and vulnerability to future flooding. This initial plan, which included turning many low-lying neighborhoods into "green space," created a firestorm of political activity within the City Council and among neighborhood organizations (Reichard, 2006; Wagner, 2006). In response to the backlash against his plan, Mayor Nagin retreated from a citywide, planned response to a "you can rebuild, but you are on your own" message (Donze, 2006). Since this initial foray into citywide planning backfired, Nagin has been a reluctant participant in subsequent planning processes despite the State requirements to have a "unified" plan to gain federal funding (see below).

Following the marginalization of the City Council from the BNOB process and FEMA's failure to fund implementation of the next phase of the BNOB plan, the City Council extended a contract with consultant Paul Lambert to lead a process known as the New Orleans Neighborhoods Rebuilding Plan (NONRP). This "Lambert Plan" was more participatory than the BNOB as it involved extensive meetings with neighborhood organizations in the city's 13 planning districts.[6]

At the end of the Lambert process in September 2006, many people involved in the process felt that the plans were sufficient to allow the city to move forward with implementation. There was also a general concern about spending more of the city's limited financial resources on another planning process. The City Council's plan, however, did not include all 78 neighborhoods in New Orleans, but rather focused on the 49 "most devastated" neighborhoods. Ultimately, the omission of powerful Uptown and French Quarter neighborhoods became a point of contention and a justification for a third, "unified" planning process known as the Unified New Orleans Plan (UNOP).

The State of Louisiana through its Louisiana Recovery Authority (LRA) with financial backing from the local Greater New Orleans Foundation (GNOF) and the national Rockefeller Foundation initiated a "unified" plan in which the warring factions had to work together to access federal funds for rebuilding by creating a plan for all of the neighborhoods in New Orleans. With the initiation of this third planning process, the "official" process became muddled and then embroiled in a battle of control fueled by competing political bases. A memo of understanding signed 1 year after the disaster was the outward symbol of this agreement and signaled the beginning of the Unified New Orleans Plan (UNOP), which is analyzed in more detail below.

While the political competition between the various official plans reasserted the importance of neighborhood planning and leadership, citizen fatigue increased as an unintended consequence of the multiple processes and many people active in the earlier plans opted out of the UNOP process.[7] Lingering uncertainties about rebuilding radically altered expectations about public information and leadership. Thus, when the actions of elected officials did not meet their needs, citizens responded with multiple and diverse forms of political action, including unofficial planning processes and the use of digital media for recovery activism. I now turn to an explanation of digital media use within the unofficial planning processes that arose as a response to the official recovery planning processes.

6.3   Citizen Activism, Neighborhood Planning, and Digital Tools for Disaster Recovery

In the spring of 2006, several neighborhood organizations took Mayor Nagin's statements about the need to prove their viability to heart and began planning processes. These unofficial plans were often enhanced by the use of online tools, web-based communications, neighborhood surveys and mapping, and through partnerships with local and nonlocal universities. At the neighborhood level, both the process and the product of neighborhood activism are important in terms of the politics of communication and the social learning that developed.

By engaging in various planning processes, residents took the recovery into their own hands in a proactive manner that resulted in the production of new, citizen-created information, new literacy about planning, government regulation, and other key issues. Producing a neighborhood plan also gave residents a bargaining tool to use while working with planning consultants, outside foundations, developers, the city, and state agencies. The Mid-City Neighborhood Organization (MCNO), for example, developed its own plan, wrote, revised, and published the plan online, and submitted the final version as part of the recovery plan adopted by the City Council. MCNO has used this document in its negotiations with the City, ORM, and real estate developers.[8]

Citizen engagement in recovery planning after a disaster is far more than an exercise in public involvement between elections. Citizen engagement in this situation expresses a deeply held belief in a "right of return" to New Orleans – an expression that eloquently captures what urban scholars refer to as the "right to the city" (Lefebvre, 1996). As Sandercock (2000, p. 10) expresses: "Above all, the right to the city meant the rights not to be excluded from centrality, and to participate in decision-making." Because citizens carry the burden of recovery and reconstruction as they work with government planners, politicians, and hired consultants, a process of problem solving occurs, which defines the social learning mode of planning practice (Collins & Ison, 2006).

In this context, access to digital media is no longer simply a matter of convenience but rather a necessary political strategy for the restoration of urban systems. As one participant in the process reported:

> Personal blogs became more than just diaries; they became tools of civic activism. In perhaps an unprecedented manner, the Internet has become for New Orleanians, an essential tool for reestablishing personal connections, for sharing stories, for communicating the will of residents, and for fighting for desperately needed answers and resources from every level of government (Denzer, 2007).

In New Orleans, the politics of planning communication are front and center in the everyday process of recovery. The digital innovations of citizens provide an important but underappreciated aspect of the recovery. Although there has been some attention to digital activism in the mainstream journalism (Greene, 2006; Tisserand, 2006), there has been very little critical reflection from the professional planning community on the fact that digital media have provided a basic infrastructure for citizen-based action that has helped to improve the official efforts of municipal, state, and federal governments.

As such, the emphasis placed on digital communication in the official and unofficial arenas of planning action has been strikingly different. For neighborhood activists and citizen-planners, the Internet has been a crucial medium for communication about planning, critiques of plans and public meetings, publication of neighborhood plans, and a vehicle for citizen-driven policy analysis. In post-disaster New Orleans, innovations in the use of digital media have occurred as a result of citizen education, experimentation, and participation – not through a process led by planners, as Drummond and French (2008) theorize.

Usage of web-based communications has been uneven and issues of equity and public access to technology have impacted recovery planning. Some people who returned to the city had Internet access first through their place of employment –

if they weren't laid off – or through the wireless services provided by local businesses. The Mid-City neighborhood put considerable effort into opening a new library branch that provided public Internet access and computers once it opened. Public access to computers, use of computer technology, and digital literacy are complex matters that are not simply reduced to issues of race and class. As one observer suggested, while there has been a diffusion of digital technology across the city, the technology available is not as important as the "constellation of skills" that individuals and organizations use to shape the political process of recovery (Coats, 2008). In this context, web-based communication provided an important counterbalance to the preexisting "urban digital divide" (Graham, 2002) in New Orleans, although it is likely that social polarization in the city has generally increased as a result of the disaster.[9]

6.4 Social Learning and Disaster Recovery Planning

The catastrophe in New Orleans created a massive interruption of the systems that make up the human and built environments of the physical and the Digital City, including information and communication technologies. Given the diversity of challenges faced by the average citizen, this recovery effort has been no small task. Government and corporate bureaucracies, battles over insurance and city hall permits, FEMA base flood elevations, levees, pumps, and hurricane protection systems, wetlands ecology, multiple and competing urban planning processes, mold remediation, soil contamination and sunflowers – the list of issues to grapple with has been overwhelming. In this situation, some citizens became leaders of the recovery through their struggle to comprehend the disaster and to rebuild their city and their lives.

The social learning mode of planning theory (Friedmann, 1996) emphasizes the relationships between experience and knowledge as well as the dynamic interaction between multiple sources of information to produce mutual understanding among planners, public officials, and citizens. From this perspective, planning practice should be shaped by expert and local knowledge situated in a context that is geographically and culturally specific. This approach is critical in the context of the aftermath of disaster in which the process of rebuilding is uncertain, complex, and requires widespread participation and a commitment to rebuilding trust as well as infrastructure (see Umemoto & Suryanata, 2006). Because the disaster exposed design flaws in systems of democratic governance – as well as flood protection and the regional political economy – social learning was a necessary aspect of the restoration of the city (see Fig. 6.3).

Furthermore, the use of digital media made the recovery process more accessible because citizens with varying degrees of digital literacy were able to explain and share their knowledge with others through the Internet.

Neighborhood and nonprofit organizations have shown significant innovation and creativity in the use of digital technologies to communicate about their recovery processes and to share these experiences with others. This section details

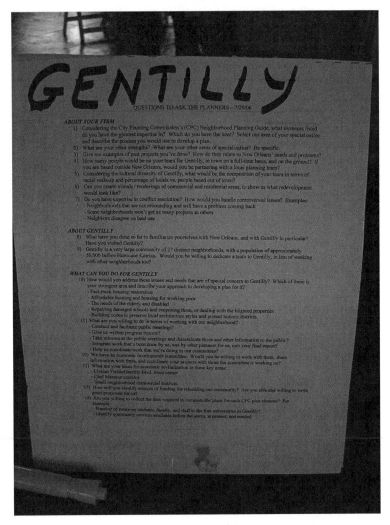

Fig. 6.3 "Questions to Ask the Planners, Gentilly". Social learning processes at the neighborhood level altered how participants engaged with planners from the beginning of the UNOP process. Photo by Jacob A. Wagner

some examples of how this process has worked from the perspective of residents rebuilding in Orleans Parish.[10]

In the early phase of recovery, the Internet and digital media have been used as communication tools for displaced people wishing to return to the city. Once people returned, the Internet has been employed to ask and answer everything from the most basic questions ("How can I find a reliable contractor?") to questions that facilitated communication and social learning about local governance and planning ("What neighborhood do I live in? Who do I contact to attend a meeting?"). In this sense, digital forums provided a context for sharing information that facilitated greater awareness and involvement in recovery efforts by providing avenues for citizen engagement.

Websites, blogs, and listserves provided a venue for citizens to communicate about planning and recovery. This included communication about the official, government-led processes as well as the neighborhood plans independent of municipal or state government. In this sense, the Internet provided a venue for innovations in planning communication through citizen-led, self-organizing, and improvised responses based on self-motivation, mutual understanding, or collaboration. The Mid-City Neighborhood Organization used their website, a Wiki site, several online surveys, and a Yahoo group to support their neighborhood recovery and planning. The website provides a message board for meetings and announcements related to both neighborhood-led and government-sponsored plans. The combination of face-to-face meetings with digital communications provided an ability to respond quickly to the challenges of land-use politics and other recovery issues.[11]

Various bloggers have tracked the recovery planning process through online analyses and reports that provide a public record and independent sources of critical planning feedback.[12] Nonprofits across the city used the Internet as a forum for organizing around particular recovery plans, policies, or strategies. The Preservation Resource Center used an online discussion group to help residents rebuild and preserve their historic homes and the city's historic neighborhoods, as well as discussion about particular contractors and rebuilding materials.[13] The Urban Conservancy through its Stay Local! program has established an online database and mapping program for locally owned businesses. This effort provided early visibility for local firms as they reopened and an organizing tool for community economic development aimed at greater sustainability and local self-sufficiency.[14]

Individuals and groups used the Internet to publicize and visualize recovery information that might otherwise have remained invisible without a representation online. In some cases the gathering and web-based publication of data facilitated political action around the built environment and residential recovery. Karen Gadbois' digital activism with the website Squandered Heritage provides digital photographs and maps of homes and buildings slated for demolition. Gadbois has continued her activism and was the person who helped to expose fraudulent use of federal funds within the city's affordable housing program.[15] The Hurricane Digital Memory Bank provides a database for urban memory related to the disaster experience. The project's goal is to "preserve the record of these storms by collecting first-hand accounts, on-scene images, blog postings, and podcasts."[16] Neighborhood groups and advocacy organizations used the Internet and digital media to bring the issues of New Orleans to a new audience and to seek supporters beyond the city. Neighborhood organizations and public interest architects collaborated on multiple projects in the Lower Ninth Ward, including a webcast to publicize the plans of the Holy Cross neighborhood to become a "carbon neutral" neighborhood.[17]

The Internet has provided a medium for the sharing of oral histories, interviews, music, and other sound recordings of significance to the recovery process. Community Gumbo provides a local, online radio show focused on the recovery process – including analysis of planning processes and discussions with activists involved in the recovery.[18] Data and file sharing for recovery planning has have been accomplished through digital networks. This included tasks as simple as emailing, ftp, and other tools for data sharing – or something as complex as creating databases of public information, including geo-coded data sets produced and distributed via Google and other websites. Activists have developed new information and data through action research, independent journalism, and publication of ongoing research findings via the Internet. One example of online action research was a project developed by Matt McBride called "Fix the Pumps." McBride conducted a long-term and independent investigation of the Army Corps of Engineers and their work on the City's hurricane protection system, including the pumping system.[19]

The Neighborhood Planning Network provided weekly meetings as a regular organizing forum for neighborhood groups, nonprofit organizations, and other advocacy groups to increase their influence in the recovery planning process. The group used the Internet to publicize their meetings and agendas.[20] Independent planners and architects have used the web to publish recovery plans or to advocate for a particular normative framework to guide post-disaster planning. Public artists have used websites to assemble and publicize works of art and to provide a space for reflection on the trauma of the disaster experience. New Orleans artists Rondell Crier and Jana Napoli, for example, have used their website to publicize digital art focusing on the trauma of personal displacement from homes and the tragic loss of personal possessions.[21]

These examples show that people make meaning from the overwhelming experience of urban disaster through conversation, visualization, inquiry, and self-representation. In this sense, these uses of digital media illustrate the framework outlined in Table 6.2 of this chapter. Residents employed digital media to communicate, critique, participate in, and literally invent the disaster recovery process in the absence of adequate government or private sector responses. Digital media provided a medium in which these diverse experiences and projects were shared in the absence of other public spaces. Considered in isolation, each use of digital media may seem insignificant, yet as a whole they comprise an indispensible component of the recovery process and a venue for the development of knowledge that is connected to the official plan-making processes. Furthermore, if we consider these innovations in light of the politics of the Unified New Orleans Plan, we begin to see two very different approaches to the use of digital media in the disaster recovery process. The use of digital media in the Unified New Orleans Plan and the strategies employed by America Speaks, a Washington, DC-based, nonprofit organization at the Community Congress II in December 2006, are analyzed next.[22]

6.5 UNOP and the Communicative Politics of Recovery Planning

The Unified New Orleans Plan (UNOP) is significant among the official recovery plans for several reasons. First, UNOP exhibited a high degree of sophistication in terms of the use of digital and non-digital tools to engage citizens. The UNOP team made a concerted effort to engage a large and representative population of New Orleans residents, including many still displaced in cities across the United States.[23] Furthermore, the plan was the product of an important alignment of local, state, and national leadership. If there was any moment during which the governing regimes across multiple geographies had finally come together, UNOP was it. With funding from the Rockefeller Foundation, the Bush/Clinton Katrina Fund, and the Greater New Orleans Foundation (GNOF) and driven by state and local governing elites, UNOP was as much a response to a post-disaster crisis of urban governance as it was a physical rebuilding plan.

Given these characteristics, this section explains how the plan-making process of UNOP used multimedia and digital technologies, and asks the use of these tools enhanced the democratic qualities of the plan. The UNOP process was initiated in June 2006 with the putative goal of "unifying" political factions to produce a plan that included all neighborhoods within Orleans Parish – including those that did not flood. From the beginning there was conflict between the City Council's process and the UNOP plan. In August 2006, the City Council's lead planner, Paul Lambert, lambasted UNOP in a full-page ad in the local newspaper and several members of the City Council never truly recognized UNOP as a legitimate process.[24]

Nonetheless, according to GNOF, "The Unified New Orleans Plan is the *single*, comprehensive recovery and rebuilding plan for the City of New Orleans. . .".[25] Contrary to this claim, recovery planning in New Orleans was never "singular." It would more accurately be described as a pluralistic and competitive process of multiple and competing plans developed in a politicized and sometimes racially polarized environment (Warner, 2006). This difficult environment was exacerbated by the structure created to manage the UNOP process. While GNOF was the fiscal agent, the decision-making for planning was entrusted to a group called the "Community Support Organization" (CSO). How exactly the CSO was formed and how it could be held accountable were never clear. The CSO was further removed from decision-making by serving as an advisor to the Community Support Foundation of the Greater New Orleans Foundation. This group – composed of trustees of the GNOF board – was even more insulated from public review. This confusing governance structure is one indicator of a problematic and privatized planning process.

Unfortunately, the confusion about the control of UNOP was not overcome by the planning process. From the beginning, the lead consultant, architect Steve Bingler, and his firm, Concordia, created a discordant process. Bingler's speech kicking off the UNOP process in July 2006, for example, was one of the most revealing moments of the arduous recovery process. In this short speech, the architect managed to obscure the underlying political conflict between the City Council's Lambert Plan and UNOP and, by doing so, set the tone for the UNOP process as conflict avoidance (see Baum, 1994). In fact much of what Bingler claimed as fact was contested and his presentation smoothed over the rough edges by ignoring the politicization of the very process he was attempting to manage (participant observation, July 2006; see also Wagner, 2006).[26]

Despite this rocky start, UNOP involved two innovations intended to increase citizen participation and thus to establish the democratic legitimacy of this process. These included (1) the use of online voting to select planning consultant firms for each Planning District and (2) an elaborate Community Congress II orchestrated by America Speaks, a nonprofit organization that facilitates large-scale public participation processes – including webcasts to create simultaneous participation across multiple cities, audience participation via electronic voting, and live artistic performances. Each of these innovations and the results are analyzed below.

6.5.1 UNOP Online Voting for the "Selection" of Planning Teams

During the launch of the UNOP process in July 2006, participants were asked to select teams of consultants to complete their neighborhood and district plans.[27] Teams of consultants auditioned for the job at a follow-up meeting and digital videos of these presentations were made available online through the UNOP website. Unfortunately, this initial component was a misleading exercise that failed to recognize the increased knowledge and experience in planning by citizens, activists, and neighborhood organizations across the city. In a piercing essay entitled "Outsourcing Democracy," local blogger Alan Gutierrez outlined how the voting process could be easily subject to manipulation:

> The citizens of New Orleans have been asked to choose the planners that will guide them through the process of developing a city wide plan for rebuilding. The method to record the response of the neighborhoods is an online poll. The online poll is open to fraud (Gutierrez, 2006).

By suggesting that residents would choose their planning teams, the UNOP team failed to manage expectations and opened themselves to distrust. While the degree to which the neighborhoods and individual residents had influence over the selection of their planning consultant team was exaggerated and clouded by the possibility of voting fraud, the reality of organizing teams for 13 planning districts made a voting process untenable. Other political considerations were also at play in this selection process.

The firing of the ACORN planning team for Planning Districts 7 and 8 (see Reardon, Green, Bates, & Kiely, 2009.) suggests that the selection process was masked by the appearance of democracy via online voting while the ultimate authority of selection remained in the hands of a small group led by Steve Bingler and the CSO. According to Reardon et al. (2009, p. 394), the ACORN planning team was fired from the UNOP process because of a "conflict of interest" between ACORN's housing development arm and their planning team. Whether this incident reflects a political decision to remove ACORN from the plan-making process is unknown. However, it should be noted that other conflicts of interest were evident that did not stop other actors from participating in the UNOP planning process. For example, Jeanne Nathan, a local media consultant, actively participated in the July 2006 UNOP meeting for Planning District 4, which began the selection process for consultant teams. Nathan was ultimately hired to participate as a consultant on several planning teams. Furthermore, architect Steve Bingler, the lead consultant in charge of running the UNOP process, has also participated in the development of several houses in the Lower Ninth Ward as part of the "Make it Right" initiative.

These contradictions suggest that what constituted a "conflict of interest" in the UNOP process was selectively applied and thus open to political bias. This problem is a symptom of the weakness of public sector planning in New Orleans and the degree to which the privatization of recovery planning has created significant problems with its administration. By failing to rebuild the capacity of the City Planning Commission and through their choice to create a competing and privatized planning organization (in the form of the CSO and the UNOP process), the State of Louisiana and its national foundation partners have undermined local governance and failed to build on the social learning occurring in the neighborhoods.

6.5.2 UNOP Community Congress II: Participatory Planning or High-Tech Therapy?

In contrast to the July 2006 UNOP launch, the Community Congress II facilitated in December 2006 was a well-organized production that employed diverse methods of participation including webcasts, electronic voting, televised coverage, and participation across multiple cities. The event was orchestrated by America Speaks in collaboration with the citywide UNOP team led by local planner Stephen Villavaso. According to the final report of the UNOP citywide plan:

> 2,500 participants gathered for Community Congress II, which took place simultaneously in 21 cities, including New Orleans, Atlanta, Baton Rouge, Dallas, and Houston. In the five largest cities... participants were part of an interactive meeting made possible through satellite technology (UNOP, 2007, p. 17).

While the UNOP team suggested that "participants were given the opportunity to suggest and prioritize action-based solutions in various areas" (UNOP, 2007, p. 17), the simplification of complex recovery decisions into options with three categories undermined the usefulness of this process. The framing of the questions posed to the participants by the America Speaks team and the categorization of the "options" resulted in strange choices between ideological views of the rebuilding process. For example, the choices presented about the "level of government intervention" only encouraged respondents to "vote" their ideological values rather than to consider the complexities of the recovery decisions at hand. As Campbell and Marshall (2000, p. 338) have pointed out: "To simplify planning problems down to a choice between a set of predefined options, as often occurs in participation exercises, is to diminish the essence of the activity."

While the electronic voting at the Community Congress II allowed for direct responses to specific questions, both the survey design process and the tabulation of data remain a critical and yet unexamined component of the process. Planners who participated in the UNOP team were skeptical of how the results of the "voting" process would later be used by elected officials.[28] Unfortunately, the use of an elaborate system for real-time participation did not improve the end result because the analysis of data was often limited and important cross-tabulations were not made publicly available during or after the meeting. For example, although the America Speaks team could have presented important differences of opinion by planning district or other important characteristics (age of respondent, tenant status, ethnicity, etc.); these important differences were ignored.

The demands of the American Speaks "town hall" voting process created a counter-productive burden on the planners engaged in processing the comments of thousands of citizen participants, which ultimately limited the sharing of information. During the meeting, teams of planners, called the "theme team," were responsible for summarizing thousands of comments provided to them through a complex system of computer networks that allowed an aggregation of public comments. Facilitators at each table processed comments made by participants and sent those comments on to the theme team via computer. These comments were then processed and edited by the theme team before they were displayed later to the entire meeting (see Fig. 6.4). This process of electronic voting and editing of citizen comments raises significant questions about the digital mediation of planning information and highlights the more fundamental issue for planning theory and ethics of how digital media are employed and to what ends.

At other moments, the meeting devolved from citizen engagement to a strange form of televised group therapy. Throughout the day, the process was augmented

Fig. 6.4 America Speaks or "Speaks for America"? Use of digital media saturated communication and distorted information in the Community Congress II, December 2006. Photo by Jacob A. Wagner

by interludes that seemed to be provided to make participants feel good about their city and their involvement in the Community Congress. One segment, for example, included a feature on the participation of youth at a previous meeting. Two contributions by poets seemed to provide inspiration, evoke community identity and melancholy, and even generate confusion. On the sidelines, a painter created a visual response to the meeting that was later displayed across several large video screens in the convention hall.

As a whole, the America Speaks approach shifted participant attention away from the primary focus – making the hard, public decisions about how the city should be rebuilt and where limited public resources should be spent. By "filling the time" between the voting processes with televised entertainment, the America Speaks process reduced opportunities for citizen interaction. Instead of allowing participants to engage in deliberative discussions, the process substituted real interaction with a mass experience of televised self-expression. As Arnstein long ago pointed out – this type of "group therapy, masked as citizen participation," is one of the most troubling forms of public involvement (Arnstein, 1969, p. 218).

According to one source, the Community Congress did successfully convince some New Orleans elites of the value of the UNOP plan. This finding is revealing because it indicates that one underlying goal of the process was to convince key elites in the city's governing regime that citizen participation could be a valuable part of the recovery process. Yet the study is even more revealing when it finds that these same elites were "less clear about the role that public input played in influencing the substance of the plan" (Williamson, 2007, p. 2). Despite the intense media strategy of the America Speaks process, the UNOP team failed to develop a process that built upon the increased planning literacy and social learning among New Orleans residents. This situation seems to reflect the political origins of the plan, its underlying structural organization, and competing visions of the purpose for participation.

6.6 Conclusion: The Recovery Will Not Be Televised... (But It Has Been Digitized)

Nearly a decade ago, Michael Neuman (2000, p. 350) asked planning theorists to take into consideration the role of the image in communicative planning theory: "Yet if communicative planning theory is to reflect the full range of modes and media of communication in planning and society, then shouldn't it incorporate images as well as words?" As this case study reveals, in New Orleans the use of digital images and media has not replaced the traditional practices of planning and design, but rather supplemented, augmented, and sometimes contradicted the more traditional methods employed. In particular, web-based tools have provided important venues for the development of counter-narratives to the "official" voices of the recovery process. These counter-narratives in turn have facilitated social learning processes that enhanced the socio-political empowerment of the city's residents.

What has occurred among citizens in New Orleans has been a profound process of social learning leading to changes in both individual and organizational behavior (Collins & Ison, 2006). Citizen use of digital media and online tools has played a significant role in the disaster recovery process, informing, and facilitating official planning processes as well as counter-planning efforts by activists and other groups. Yet digital and multimedia technologies, while creating new opportunities for expression and new modes of planning practice, cannot resolve the deeply challenging democratic issues of our time. In the absence of a responsive planning process and open public dialogue with elected officials, citizens may produce their own critical feedback mechanisms but the recovery process overall continues to suffer.

Recovery planning in New Orleans could not have functioned without citizen participation and leadership. Neither the few city planning employees who survived the massive job cuts nor the hired consultants could have done the job without participation because they lacked capacity, data, expertise, or local knowledge. As Friedmann (2003, pp. 78–79) reminds us, the key to successful planning is the *combination* of professional expertise and the experiential knowledge of local residents. In New Orleans, local citizens provided something much more profound than simply "public input." They provided local expertise, detailed knowledge of their neighborhoods and the city, a skilled understanding of local politics, a good sense of humor, and a deep passion for their city and its restoration. Most of all, citizen activism provided continuity in the face of a recovery process that has been rapid, disjointed, contested, and fraught with a scarcity of resources relative to the magnitude of the catastrophe. If planning is to be successful in the aftermath of a major disaster, an engaged citizenry is absolutely critical, but public and private leadership must expand their view of participation to recognize the social learning framework.

Professionals and elected officials continue to take for granted the experiential knowledge and sweat equity of residents who have carried the burdens of recovery and who have worked for free despite the substantial costs of participation. The true test of successful planning in New Orleans will be the degree to which we have cultivated local capacity to solve problems and work toward mutual understanding without sacrificing the city's diverse culture (Wagner, 2008). This will require active partnerships between planners, elected officials and citizens, neighborhood organizations, and nonprofits in which new modes of planning practice emerge from open communication and greater power sharing (Holden, 2000; Wagner, Frisch, & Fields, 2008).

At the local level, digital media and forms of interaction are important because they foster critical feedback and provide a venue for public, as well as institutional, memory that are essential for a social learning model of planning (Friedmann, 2003, p. 79). The Internet has provided a venue in which residents can formulate and revise strategies that later impact public policy. While digital communications tools have not replaced the streets, the council chambers, or Capitol Hill as venues for political action, they have contributed to the empowerment of local citizens as they developed collective responses to the disaster and its mediation by local, state, and federal governments. Marches on City Hall still matter and the politics of recovery are unfolding on every block in the city. In this sense, the digital city cannot replace the physical city. Instead, digital technology has provided a critical forum for the creation of a meaningful and hopeful recovery process in the face of great disaster and uncertainty.

Notes

1. The author would like to thank Leonie Sandercock, Geoff Coats, and Joe Hughey for their constructive reviews of earlier drafts of this chapter. All culpability for critical omissions and communicative distortions lies solely with the author.
2. By "digital media" I mean the use of communication tools including computers, websites, digital audio and video to create, manipulate, and distribute information. While digital media generally are associated with the use of computers, cell phones and compact discs are also tools of digital communication. Another term used in the paper is "multimedia," which is employed to suggest the use of a combination of different forms of information, such as video, audio, still images, photographs, or maps, and text to communicate information – which may or may not include digital media or communications.
3. Additional plans and policy studies have been developed by numerous advocacy groups outside of New Orleans, including OXFAM and the US Green Building Council. A number of university planning and architecture departments have also developed plans and planning studies. These types of plans, while important to the recovery process, are not the focus of this chapter.
4. These official planning processes also include ongoing planning conducted by the City of New Orleans Planning Commission and its staff, the Office of Recovery Management (ORM, led by Ed Blakely), the Regional Planning Commission (New Orleans's Metropolitan Planning Organization), and the plans developed by the State of Louisiana and its agencies, including the Office of Culture, Recreation and Tourism (run by Lieutenant Governor Mitch Landrieu), and the Louisiana Recovery Authority (LRA).
5. Drummond and French (2008) suggest that Internet-based GIS could be combined with citizen input to produce "unprecedented levels of citizen participation." Further they suggest that GIS and other software could be used to produce "alternate plans" that would be published on the Internet. These uses are already evident in New Orleans.
6. See http://www.nolanrp.com/index.php.
7. Personal observation, see also the "Planning Presentation Marathon" blog by Laureen Lentz, which captures this sentiment among people involved in the Lambert/City Council process: http://neworleans.metblogs.com/2006/09/23/planning-presentation-marathon.
8. For more detail, see www.mcno.org and http://mcno.org/plan.
9. Certainly there is evidence to this effect. However, the situation is far from resolved and it may be too early to tell. Loss of affordable housing and federal policies are certainly a key aspect of this equation.
10. I do not cover how the Internet has been used by nonlocal volunteers, design professionals, or academics working on the recovery, although this is certainly significant. Sources include participant observation, informal interviews, and review of secondary data.
11. See http://www.mcno.org.
12. See http://neworleans.metblogs.com and http://thinknola.com.
13. See http://groups.yahoo.com/group/preserveneworleans.
14. See http://www.staylocal.org.
15. See http://www.squanderedheritage.com.
16. See http://www.hurricanearchive.org/about.
17. See http://www.zerocarbonnola.org/index.html.
18. See http://communitygumbo.blogspot.com.

19. See http://fixthepumps.blogspot.com.
20. See http://thinknola.com/wiki/Neighborhoods_Planning_Network.
21. See http://www.floodwall.org.
22. America Speaks is a nonprofit organization that facilitates large-scale public participation processes, which it has branded the "21st Century Town Hall" meeting. The organization claims to be on the cutting edge of deliberative democracy in the United States and uses the latest technology available such as keypad voting by participants and on-site analysis of voting data through the use of laptop computers.
23. It should be noted that the effort to involve a representative group of citizens at Community Congress II occurred only after several embarrassingly unrepresentative meetings.
24. Personal observation. See also http://www.nolaplans.com/unop_analysis.
25. See http://www.gnof.org, accessed 7 November 2006 (emphasis added).
26. A video of Bingler's speech is available on YouTube at: http://www.youtube.com/user/UnifiedNewOrleans.
27. New Orleans includes 78 neighborhoods recognized by the City of New Orleans. These neighborhoods are aggregated into 14 planning districts. During the July 2006 meeting of the UNOP process residents of two planning districts in New Orleans East joined together, which resulted in 13 planning districts.
28. Interviews and participant observation, December 2006.

References

Arnstein, S. (1969, July). The ladder of participation. *Journal of the American Institute of Planners, 35*(4), 216–224.

Bates, L., & Green, R. (2007). *(Mis)uses of data: What counts as damage in Post-Katrina New Orleans recovery planning.* Retrieved from http://www.urban.illinois.edu/research/NOLA/MisUses%20of%20Data_working.pdf

Batty, M. (2001). Contradictions and conceptions of the digital city. *Environment and Planning B: Planning and Design, 28*(4), 479–480.

Baum, H. S. (1994). Community and consensus: Reality and fantasy in planning. *Journal of Planning Education and Research, 13*(4), 251–262.

Beauregard, R. (2000). Neither embedded nor embodied: Critical pragmatism and identity politics. In: M. Burayidi (Ed.), *Urban planning in a multicultural society.* Westport, CT: Praeger.

Bring New Orleans Back Commission. Accessed June 23, 2009, from http://www.bringneworleansback.org/

Bureau of Governmental Research. (2003). *Runaway discretion: Land use decision making in New Orleans.* New Orleans, LA: Bureau of Governmental Research.

Campbell, H. J. (1996). A social interactionist perspective on computer implementation in planning. *Journal of the American Planning Association, 62*(1), 99–107.

Campbell, H. J., & Marshall, R. (2000). Public involvement and planning: Looking beyond the one to the many. *International Planning Studies, 5*(3), 321–343.

Castells, M. (1996). *The rise of the network society: The information age: Economy, society and culture* (Vol. 1). Oxford, UK: Blackwell.

Castells, M. (1997). *The rise of the network society: The power of identity* (Vol. 1). Oxford, UK: Blackwell.

Checkoway, B. (1984). Two types of planning in neighborhoods. *Journal of Planning Education and Research, 3*(2), 102–109.

Coats, G. (2008). Personal Interview.

Codrescu, A. (2006, September–October). The (unreasonable) argument for our existence. *World Watch Institute, 19*(5), 36–37.

Collins, K., & Ison, R. (2006). *Dare we jump off Arnstein's Ladder? Social Learning as a new policy paradigm.* Walton Hall: Open Systems Research Group, Systems Department, Faculty of Technology, Open University. Available from http://oro.open.ac.uk/8589

Community Gumbo. Accessed June 23, 2009, from http://communitygumbo.blogspot.com

Craglia, M. (2004). Cogito ergo sum or non-cogito ergo digito? The digital city revisited. *Environment and Planning B: Planning and Design, 31*(1), 3–4.

Culley, M. R., & Hughey, J. (2008). Power and participation in a hazardous waste dispute: A community case study. *American Journal of Community Psychology, 41*(1–2), 99–114.

Denzer, B. (2007). *Civic Activism, Blogging, and Media Democracy in the Rebuilding in New Orleans*. Accessed June 23, 2009, from Pt. 1 http://communitygumbo.blogspot.com/

Donze, F. (2006, March 20). Rebuild, but at your own risk, Nagin says; Recommendations from BNOB come with warnings and worries. *Times-Picayune*.

Drummond, W. J., & French, S. P. (2008). The future of GIS in planning: Converging technologies and diverging interests. *Journal of American Planning Association, 74*(2), 161–174.

Fix the Pumps. Accessed June 23, 2009, from http://fixthepumps.blogspot.com. The Floodwall Project. Accessed June 23, 2009, from http://www.floodwall.org

Friedmann, J. (1987). *Planning in the public domain: From knowledge to action*. Princeton, NJ: Princeton University Press.

Friedmann, J. (1996). Reviewing two centuries of planning. In S. Mandelbaum et al. (Eds.), *Planning Theory in the 1990s*. Brunswick, NJ: Center for Urban Policy Research.

Friedmann, J. (2003). Toward a Non-Euclidian mode of planning. In S. Fainstein & S. Campbell (Eds.), *Readings in Planning Theory*. New York: Wiley-Blackwell.

Graham, S. (2002). Bridging urban digital divides? Urban polarisation and Information and Communication Technologies (ICT). *Urban Studies, 39*(1), 33–56.

Greater New Orleans Foundation. Accessed November 7, 2006. from http://www.gnof.org

Greene, T. (2006, August 21). Eye of the hurricane: New Orleans prepares; Disaster-recovery plan following Katrina based on Wi-Fi, VoIP. Network World.

Gutierrez, A. (2006, August 4). Outsourcing democracy, ThinkNOLA blog. Accessed June 23, 2009, from http://thinknola.com/post/outsourcing-democracy/

Holden, M. (2000). GIS in land use planning: Lessons from critical theory and the Gulf Islands. *Journal of Planning Education and Research, 19*(3), 287–296.

Hurricane Digital Memory Bank. Accessed June 23, 2009, from http://www.hurricanearchive.org

Klosterman, R. (2008). Comment on Drummond and French: Another view of the future of GIS. *Journal of American Planning Association, 74*(2), 174–176.

Krieger, M. (2004). Taking pictures in the city. *Journal of Planning Education and Research, 24*(2), 213–215.

Lauria, M., & Wagner, J. A. (2006). What can we learn from empirical studies of planning theory? A comparative case analysis of extant literature. *Journal of Planning Education and Research, 25*(4), 364–381.

Lefebvre, H. (1996). The right to the city. In E. Kofman & E. Lebas (Eds.), *Writings on cities*. New York: Blackwell.

Mandelker, D. R. (2002). *A report on planning in New Orleans: For the master plan coalition*. Accessed June 23, 2009, from http://www.wulaw.wustl.edu/landuselaw/neworl.htm

Mid-City Neighborhood Organization. Accessed June 23, 2009, from www.mcno.org

Neighborhood Planning Network. Accessed June 23, 2009, from http://thinknola.com/wiki/Neighborhoods_Planning_Network

Nelson, M., Ehrenfeucht, R., & Laska, S. (2007). Planning, plans and people: Professional expertise, local knowledge, and governmental action in Post-Hurricane Katrina New Orleans. *Cityscape, 9*(3), 23–53.

Neuman, M. (2000). Communicate this! Does consensus lead to advocacy and pluralism? *Journal of Planning Education and Research, 19*(4), 343–350.

New Orleans MetBlogs. Accessed June 23, 2009, from http://neworleans.metblogs.com

New Orleans Neighborhood Rebuilding Plan. Accessed June 23, 2009 from http://nolanrp.com/index.php

Olshansky, R. (2006). Planning after Hurricane Katrina. *Journal of the American Planning Association, 72*(2), 147–153.

Olshansky, R., Johnson, L. A., Horne. J., & Nee, B. (2008). Planning for the rebuilding of New Orleans. *Journal of the American Planning Association, 74*(3), 273–287.

Preserve New Orleans. Accessed June 23, 2009, from http://groups.yahoo.com/group/preserveneworleans

Reardon, K., Green, R., Bates, L., & Kiely, R. C. (2009). Overcoming the challenges of post-disaster planning in New Orleans: Lessons from the ACORN housing/university collaborative. *Journal of Planning Education and Research, 28*(3), 391–400.

Reichard, P. (2006, August/September 6–11). Curves Ahead, Planning.

Ritchin, F. (2009). *After photography.* New York: W.W. Norton & Company.

Rocha, E. M. (1997). A ladder of empowerment. *Journal of Planning Education and Research, 17*(1), 31–44.

Sandercock, L. (2000). Cities of (In)Difference and the challenge of planning. *DISP, 140,* 7–15.

Squandered Heritage. Accessed June 23, 2009, from http://squanderedheritage.com

Stay Local! Accessed June 23, 2009, from www.staylocal.org

ThinkNOLA. Accessed June 23, 2009, from http://thinknola.com

Tisserand, M. (2006, September 18). Don't mourn, link. *The Nation.*

Umemoto, K., & Suryanata, K. (2006). Technology, culture and environmental uncertainty. *Journal of Planning Education and Research, 25*(3), 264–274.

Unified New Orleans Plan. (2007). Citywide Strategic Recovery and Rebuilding Plan. New Orleans, LA. Accessed June 23, 2009, from http://www.unifiedneworleansplan.com/home3/section/136/city-wide-plan

The Urban Conservancy. Accessed June 23, 2009, from www.urbanconservancy.org

Urban Land Institute. (2005) *A strategy for rebuilding New Orleans, Louisiana.* Washington, DC: ULI.

Wagner, J. (2006). *The privatization of urban planning and public space in New Orleans in the Wake of Hurricane Katrina.* Paper presented at the Association of the Collegiate Schools of Planning Conference, Fort Worth, TX.

Wagner, J. (2008). Understanding New Orleans: Creole Urbanism. In: R. Shields & P. Steinberg (Eds.), *What is a city? Rethinking the Urban after Hurricane Katrina.* Athens: University of Georgia Press.

Wagner, J., Frisch, M., & Fields, B. (2008). Building local capacity: Planning for local culture and neighborhood recovery in New Orleans. *Cityscape: A Journal of Policy Development and Research, 10*(3), 39–56.

Warner, C. (2006, August 31). N.O. planning process puts residents on edge. *Times-Picayune.*

Williamson, A. (2007). Citizen Participation in the Unified New Orleans Plan. Kennedy School of Government, Harvard. Accessed June 23, 2009, from http://www.rockfound.org/library/032807no_harvard.pdf

Wilson, P. (2008). *Deliberative planning in disaster recovery: Re-membering New Orleans.* Chicago: Presentation at the ACSP/AESOP Joint Congress IV.

ZeroCarbon NOLA. Accessed June 23, 2009, from http://www.zerocarbonnola.org/index.html

Chapter 7
Social Justice and Video: *Imagining* as a Right in Vancouver's Downtown Eastside

Jessica Hallenbeck

7.1 Introduction

In this chapter I want to examine the relationship between the right to the city, social justice and video, using as an example a short film *Wishlist* which I co-produced in Vancouver, Canada, in 2006. *Wishlist* was one of a trio of short films made in the Spring of 2006, originally conceived as a participatory video project that focused on a particular street in the Downtown Eastside (DTES) of Vancouver. Carrall Street was at that time the subject of a design project by the City of Vancouver and it was the film-makers' collective intention to experiment with the use of video as a way of eliciting residents' desires for this pivotal street which connects different parts of the downtown area (see Maps 7.1 and 7.2). The purpose of *Wishlist* was twofold. First, we wanted to engage people in a dialogue about how they see themselves and their neighbourhood. Second, we wanted to be able to convey this vision to City of Vancouver planners, in the hope of affecting decisions made about the street. So *Wishlist* was intended both as an action research project and as a vehicle for reflecting on the potential of video in contributing to social justice in the planning of the city.

The right to the city has attracted considerable attention in recent academic literature,[1] but the concept has remained theoretically amorphous, rarely grounded in practical application. My project sought to examine the ways that video can advance claims to the city, drawing on theories of social justice put forth by Iris Marion Young and Henri Lefebvre. *Wishlist* provides a unique opportunity to ground social justice theories in a video case study, thereby expanding the range of tools available in the community's struggle for social justice. The study of *Wishlist* also has important implications for the role of video in planning, a topic that will be explored later in the chapter. My argument is that the right to the city starts with an

J. Hallenbeck (✉)
Ear to the Ground Planning, Vancouver, BC, Canada
e-mail: jessica@eartotheground.ca

This chapter is best read after viewing *Wishlist*, which is available online at http://www.eartotheground.ca/wishlist.php

L. Sandercock, G. Attili (eds.), *Multimedia Explorations in Urban Policy and Planning*, Urban and Landscape Perspectives 7, DOI 10.1007/978-90-481-3209-6_7,
© Springer Science+Business Media B.V. 2010

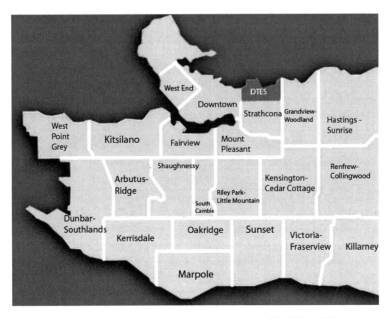

Map 7.1 The Downtown Eastside in relation to the rest of the City of Vancouver

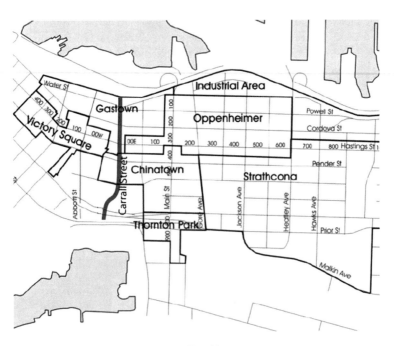

Map 7.2 Street map of the Downtown Eastside

imagining of our city as being different from its present state. Video, by engaging people in a dialogue over their rights to participation and appropriation, fosters this essential act of imagining, thereby contributing to the struggle for social justice.

Wishlist was part of a larger action research project that began with three questions.[2]

1. *What role do rights play in our understanding of social justice and the city?* In answering this question, I explore certain theories of social justice, arguing that the rights to participation and appropriation are crucial to the active inhabitation of the city.
2. *Can video promote dialogue?* In addressing this question, I examine the importance of dialogue in affirming our right to participation. *Wishlist* is used as an example of an inclusive process that deploys utopian thinking to encourage new understandings of city rights.
3. *What role does video play in encouraging urban imagination and appropriation?* I explore how, in affirming our right to participation, we come to claim our right to appropriation. I look at how *Wishlist*'s visuals, vision and politics serve to empower people to imagine how they could appropriate the city.

In the first section of this chapter I begin my exploration of the relationship between social justice and video by establishing *Wishlist*'s context in Vancouver's political geography and planning history. I then lay the theoretical framework for the study, exploring the question of how we define the city. The next section establishes the geographical, institutional, and production context of *Wishlist*. Turning to the question "what is the city"? I explore the idea that the city is a site of dialogue and appropriation, and that we claim our rights to dialogue and appropriation through engaging in utopian thinking. I then expand on this argument by looking at how *Wishlist*, through an inclusive interviewing and production process, facilitates dialogue. By analyzing *Wishlist*'s visuals, vision and politics, I suggest how we can move from dialogue to appropriation. The chapter concludes by evaluating *Wishlist*'s applicability, reception and institutional integration, and argues that many of *Wishlist*'s dissemination problems are common impediments in the use of video as a planning tool.

7.2 Contextualizing

It is essential to note from the outset that this chapter focuses on video and not participatory video. Participatory video is defined in various ways and its methodology is derived from participatory action research. Johannsen, in "Questions and Answers about Participatory Video", defines participatory video as "a scriptless video process, directed by a group of grassroots people, moving forward in often iterative cycles of shooting and reviewing. The aim is to create video narratives that communicate what those who participate in the process really want to communicate, in a way they think is appropriate. Participants take part in some or all of: shooting, scriptwriting, determining content" (2000, p. 3). In order to avoid getting into a discussion of how participatory the project was, and because this chapter is more concerned with product than with process, the scope has been narrowed to examine social justice and video through the lens of *Wishlist* as simply a video.

But before discussing the links between social justice and video, it is necessary to situate *Wishlist* geographically, institutionally and methodologically.

7.2.1 *Situating* Wishlist *Geographically*

Wishlist, as part of the Carrall Street Participatory Video Project, is a video focused on a single Vancouver street, Carrall Street, located in the Downtown Eastside. The street runs north/south in downtown Vancouver, beginning at Water Street, and ending at Pacific Boulevard (see Map 7.2). Importantly, it connects the communities of Gastown, the Downtown Eastside (DTES) and Chinatown. The DTES[3] is an inner city neighbourhood that occupies 113 hectares (DTES community Webpage) and has been the site of contested definitions, naming and categorizing. It is not within the scope of this paper to give a detailed, discursive account of the socio-economic evolution of downtown eastside. PIVOT Legal society defines it as follows:

> The DTES is found in the downtown core of Vancouver. It is one of the city's oldest neighbourhoods. Although it is relatively small geographically, its population is very diverse. Forty-eight percent of its population consists of members of ethnic minorities, and men and seniors are overrepresented in the population compared with other areas of Vancouver. The neighbourhood consists of five distinct areas: Chinatown, Gastown, Victory Square, Strathcona and Oppenheimer. In 2006, there were 18025 people living within these five areas (Wesley, 2009, pers. comm., 10 June) It has long been a community with a high concentration of social problems, including poverty, mental illness, drug use, crime, survival sex work, high HIV/Hepatitis infection rates, unemployment and violence (Eby, 2006, p. 5).

The DTES is infamous for being Canada's poorest postal code. According to Statistics Canada, in 2006 the average household income in the DTES was $ 25.132. While the DTES has a high proportion of intravenous drug users in its population, the area is also home to a vibrant, artistic community with many diverse social groups, including a high percentage of First Nations Peoples. Exact percentages vary. PIVOT Legal Society estimates that 30 percent of DTES residents are intravenous drug users, amounting to 5,000 users in approximately 10 city blocks (PIVOT website). According to PIVOT legal society, Aboriginal Peoples constitute 8.4 percent of the DTES population, compared with 4.4 percent in the province of British Columbia (Eby, 2006, p. 8). As a low-income inner city neighbourhood, it is the focus of ongoing contestations over the nature and scale of gentrification.

7.2.2 *Situating* Wishlist *Institutionally*

In an always politically charged and antagonistic atmosphere, the City of Vancouver is making a concerted effort to economically revitalize the DTES.[4] The redesign of Carrall Street into a greenway is intended to play an integral role in this venture. [5]

The City of Vancouver approved five million dollars for the Greenway in its 2006–2008 capital budget plan (City of Vancouver, 2007b). Additionally, the Carrall Street project is receiving funding from the private sector (City of Vancouver, 2007b). According to the City of Vancouver's Carrall Street Greenway Webpage, the purpose of the Greenway is to foster community building and encourage economic revitalization. The redesign of Carrall Street "incorporates green infrastructure, facilitates private investments, and provides opportunities for social services, arts and culture programming to help achieve environmental, economic, social and cultural sustainability for the area" (City of Vancouver, 2007d). The City of Vancouver has held a number of charrettes and meetings surrounding the redesign of Carrall Street.

The Carrall Street Participatory Video Project (CSPVP) was in part created to articulate DTES residents' visions on how Carrall Street might be used as a public space.[6] The intention at the outset was to use the videos to inform the City of Vancouver's redesign of Carrall Street. *Wishlist* was one of three video productions resulting from the project.

The CSPVP was a joint venture among three groups: Projections, Ear to the Ground Planning and the University of British Columbia's School of Community and Regional Planning.[7] A portion of the funding for the videos came from the City of Vancouver's Planning Department. The participants in the CSPVP included five youth with "limited access to resources", six planning students and five mentors. My role in the project was as a planning student participant. Working in the Spring and Summer of 2006 we completed three separate, but thematically connected video productions: *Wishlist*, *The Spinning Image* and *Stories from Carrall Street*. The whole group discussed broad themes, and then individual videos were collaboratively written, filmed and edited by groups of three to five participants. *Wishlist* is the result of collaboration among three planning students and one youth with limited access to resources.

The conceptual framework for *Wishlist* was developed over the course of a weekend and shooting and editing took just over 3 weeks to complete. During production, the *Wishlist* team worked closely together on the vision and argument of the film, decided how interviews would be conducted and who would be interviewed. The specific aesthetic and narrative decisions addressed later in the chapter were made collectively by the four participants and sometimes a resolution was arrived at only after heated debate.

Our group determined that *Wishlist* would have several purposes. The first was simply to get DTES residents thinking and talking about the Carrall Street redesign. The second purpose was to honour people's ideas for the space, by incorporating them into the film. The third purpose was to communicate the ideas expressed in the video to several different parties: the general Vancouver public, officials at the City of Vancouver responsible for the Carrall Street redesign and DTES residents.

7.2.3 A Note on Methodology

Planning theorist John Friedmann asks "Aren't we all social actors?" (Friedmann, 2000, p. 461).[8] This question guided my action research project. My intention at the CSPVP's outset was to explore the ways in which *participatory video* could contribute to the struggle for social justice in the city. However, due to time restrictions in making the film, my initial plan to focus on understanding the relationships among participation, video and social justice shifted to examining *Wishlist* in the context of social justice theory. Therefore *Wishlist*, as a video, became my data set.

Using *Wishlist* as a data set for the project provided a unique opportunity to integrate the two components of reflective practice: reflecting *in* action and reflecting *on* action (Schön, 1983). In what follows, *Wishlist* is primarily utilized as a discursive device, grounding social justice theory in a video case study. As such, it serves as a reflection on action, and later, is used as a reflexive device.[9] In addition to reflecting on action, I kept a journal of the video-making process, including personal experiences, meeting agendas and audience reactions to *Wishlist*. My experience as a participant provided additional insights into specific stylistic and ethical choices made during the course of the project. In turn, these experiences facilitated an analysis of reflecting *in* practice.[10] The next sections examine *Wishlist* through the methodological approach of a reflective practitioner.

7.3 Living: The City and Habitation

> The city writes and assigns, that is, it signifies, orders, stipulates. What? That is to be discovered by reflection (Lefebvre, 1996, p. 102).

Cities are an assemblage of differences: places of overlapping dialogues, narratives and identities. As such, people can only engage in the city if they are able to exercise their rights to participation and appropriation.

7.3.1 Cities as Sites of Dialogue and Appropriation

Cities are sites of difference, where the "being together as strangers" is constitutive of city life (Young, 1990, p. 237). This being together is often fraught with challenges, as different lifeways bump up against each other, taken-for-granted ways of doing and being are called into question, and we struggle to find ways of peacefully coexisting. In spite of the aversion of most people to such discomfort, these challenges are often useful, as they force us to question our own epistemologies, meanings and narratives (Lefebvre, 1996). The result is that we are constantly re-interpreting, re-imagining and re-making the city. The city is therefore both the *site* and the *product* of the evolving engagement of its inhabitants.

Participation in city life can change our sense of meaning and belonging, our sense of place and our understanding of our right to the city. When this happens, the city becomes the site of appropriations intended to enact new meanings (Lefebvre, 1996). Through our interaction with others, we adopt aspects of their perspectives that then inform our own narratives. These moments of appropriation are unpredictable, ambiguous and playful and, for Young and Lefebvre, it's important to embrace them as being at the heart of city life (Young, 1990; Lefebvre, 1996).

7.3.2 The Right to Participation and Imagination

For cross-cultural dialogue and appropriation to occur, we first need to claim our right to participate in the city. We must know that we have a right to *inhabit* the city before we can be empowered to change it (Lefebvre, 1996). Inhabiting the city means recognizing that we have the right to shape our living conditions through active engagement in the city (Young, 1990). This involves the ability to see our current environments and circumstances as aspects of our lives that we can change. Thus, the right to participation is crucial to the active inhabitation of the city.

7.3.3 Participation, Imagination and Utopia

If participation is a critical component of city life, how then do we come to claim this right? Lefebvre (1996) argues that acts of imagination allow us to come together, despite our differences. It is through imagining things as being different from their present state that we begin to participate in the creation of the city. The right to the city therefore originates with the right to imagine participating in its creation.

Because utopias are stories that critique the present in order to construct a better future, they are powerful devices for initiating this process of imagining (Friedmann, 2000). For Iris Marion Young, this type of thinking is the first step towards social justice. In expressing our desire for change, we claim our right to imagine things differently (Young, 1990; Mitchell, 2003). Utopias are useful tools for fostering dialogue because they allow people to articulate their visions for their future without having to make direct reference to their (often painful) present.

This detachment can be liberating because it enables people to move from their present context of fear, or feelings of powerlessness, to a future context of hope. Instead of evaluating the present for what it lacks, utopian thinking insists that people imagine the future for what it holds. In this way, people are able to engage with their right to inhabit the city.

7.4 Dialoguing and Representing

The preceding section has argued that one way that we claim our right to inhabit the city is through utopian dialogue. Films can engage people in dialogue and are therefore an important tool for stimulating multiple understandings of the city. Through a close reading of *Wishlist*'s aesthetic, stylistic and procedural choices, this section reveals the important role that video can play in fostering utopian dialogue through an inclusive process.

Wishlist is divided into three parts: "Basic Needs", "Pigeon Park" and "Community Space" (Fig. 7.1). Pigeon Park is a park located on the northwest corner of Hastings Street and Carrall Street (see Map 7.2). It is Vancouver's smallest official park and a place where many residents congregate throughout the day. Pigeon Park is often described as being the heart of the DTES community and (as a

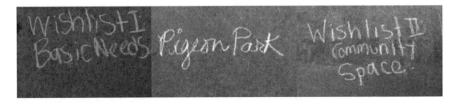

Fig. 7.1 Screenshots of *Wishlist*'s three sections, video stills from "Wishlist" (2006)

Fig. 7.2 *Wishlist*'s Screenshots of Carrall Street pan and of Pigeon Park, video stills from "Wishlist" (2006)

Fig. 7.3 Screenshot of *Wishlist*'s first animation sequence, video stills from "Wishlist" (2006)

recently painted graffiti tag in the park reads) it is "the people's park". *Wishlist* contains three main visual devices: a long pan of Vancouver's Carrall Street (Fig. 7.2), three still images taken along the street (Fig. 7.2) and two 1-minute segments of stop-motion animation (Fig. 7.3).

The visuals are driven by the film's soundtrack, which contains a mix of music, poetry and dialogue. Thirteen unidentified Downtown Eastside (DTES) residents drive the narration, which focuses on re-envisioning Carrall Street. Why did we make these structural and aesthetic choices?

7.4.1 Video and Dialogue

Neil Leach, a British architect and cultural studies theorist, argues that our identities are constructed around place-specific performances (Leach, 2005). Like place-specific performances, film viewing changes our individual identities and alters our perceptions of place. When we "read" a film, we make sense of the on-screen world by projecting parts of ourselves into the story. However, this is not a one-way exercise; because we have projected ourselves onto the film, we are also affected by it (Leach, 2005). Films make us cry or laugh because we have invested parts of ourselves into them. Film, through its very medium, facilitates a process of self-reflexive dialogue.

7.4.2 Dialogue, Style and Voice in Wishlist

If dialogue is central to asserting citizens' rights to the city, how can certain stylistic choices in filming influence the nature of the conversation? The *Wishlist* production team struggled over this question and made several stylistic and narrative choices in order to address issues around the stereotyping of DTES residents and the neighbourhood, as well as the question of representation.

The first and most divisive consideration for our group was whether to show people's faces in the film. Given the dream-like tone that we envisioned for *Wishlist*, it made sense on a narrative level to avoid a talking-head montage. However, we also wanted to valorize people's opinions and worried that not showing their faces would be disempowering, especially considering that DTES residents are usually portrayed as being part of a homogeneously dysfunctional community. After many animated discussions, we finally decided that the sets of assumptions that outsiders might carry could eclipse what the speakers were saying: people would see class, addiction, or physical trauma instead of actually listening and thereby might be prevented from entering into a dialogue with what was being expressed. As one of the main goals of the film was to address non-DTES residents' stereotypes of the area, we felt that this decision not to show interviewees' faces was crucial to the success of *Wishlist* as a dialoguing tool.

The second concern involved deciding which members of the DTES to interview. This was a highly charged issue because the people chosen would define the content and dialogue of our film. Making interview decisions directly engages with issues of representation, voice and censorship.

One of the drawbacks of *Wishlist* is that, given the time constraints of the project, we were unable to make new connections in the DTES. As trust and rapport are crucial to the success of any interview, it was decided that the people with whom we already had an established relationship would be willing to share their utopian visions with us and a larger audience.[11] This decision meant that DTES residents who were less visible, vocal and politically engaged were unable to participate in the formal, sit-down interviews that we conducted.

In an attempt to mitigate this issue of voice, we also conducted informal street interviews in the neighbourhood. Given that video crews and television newscasters have repeatedly exploited DTES residents, we decided that it was best to only use an audio-recorder.[12] This decision also made it easier in post-production to integrate the informal and formal interviews. Unlike the formal interviews, the street interviews consisted of asking people one succinct question: "If you could put anything on Carrall Street, what would it be?" This question was designed to be as open as possible, while still adhering to the geographic constraints of the video project.[13]

In addition to recorded interviews, we employed a third strategy to include as many visions as possible. Because the DTES is an artistic community and also one with a large percentage of English as second language residents as well as high illiteracy rates, we felt that it was necessary to include non-verbal forms of expression in the film.[14] We asked some of the people who felt uncomfortable being audio-taped, if we could write down a few of their ideas, and incorporated these visions

Fig. 7.4 Screenshot of *Wishlist*'s second animation sequence, video stills from "Wishlist" (2006)

into the animation.[15] We also asked people to contribute music, poetry, and art to *Wishlist*. The result was a montage of visions for Carrall Street, based on both verbal and non-verbal ways of dialoguing.

This montage of visions (as seen in Fig. 7.4) was made possible by our decision to use animation as the primary visual device for *Wishlist*. Our reliance on animation circumvented one of the main drawbacks of video, in which all too often inarticulate or camera-shy people are edited out of the final product.

While using animation certainly resolved some issues of representation, we were still left with the difficult task of editing interviews. This process involved listening, (re)interpreting and deciding which portions of people's interviews to use in the final video. In most cases, this meant that a 20-minute interview was reduced to a few words, which were then loosely categorized into either the "basic needs" or "community space" sections.[16] Once again, we tried to mitigate this by writing down the ideas that were cut from the audio track and incorporating these concepts in the final animation. This ensured that every person interviewed was represented in the film and guarded against potential feelings of disempowerment or disappointment.

7.5 *Wishlist's* Production: Process, Politics and Product

I have referred to the stylistic and aesthetic decisions made by the *Wishlist* production team as decisions that "we" collectively made. While it is essential to acknowledge that *Wishlist* potentially empowers its viewers, it is equally crucial that the film-making process be equitable and just, serving to empower those involved in the film's production. Any analysis of social justice in relation to video needs to include a discussion about how group dynamics influenced the film-making process, politics and the final product.[17]

7.5.1 Process

As previously mentioned, the *Wishlist* production team consisted of three planning students (myself, Ian Marcuse and Elana Cossever) and one youth with limited access to resources (April Curry). The production teams were formed after an early morning brainstorming session, where group facilitators asked us to stand by our favourite brainstorming words and concepts. I and two other planning students gravitated towards a poem that April (after some encouragement from me and another student) had written. Her poem was about a city emerging from a forest, and had prompted a lot of discussion about what an alternative greenway might look like. Once the groups were formed, we were asked to brainstorm further and present our ideas to the wider group. We were then given until our next meeting to develop a treatment for our film.

The treatment process was interesting because two of the planning student group members were absent. April and I were therefore responsible for co-developing the initial concept for the film. Upon the return of the other two planning students, we quickly set up a production plan and then met regularly for at least 4 days each week, until the completion of the project, 2 months later.

7.5.2 Politics

Group politics and decision-making strategies invariably affect any final video product. In the case of *Wishlist*, group politics played a critical role in both directing the film's content and empowering the film-makers.

Wishlist's early group politics were affected by the over-representation of planning students in the production team. Being acutely conscious of issues of voice, the planning students were frequently deferential to April during the first 2 weeks of concept development. This deference was exacerbated by our film being inspired by a poem that April had written. Additionally, one of the planning students in our group had worked as a social worker in the DTES for many years and felt it was their role to teach and support the group's youth representative. While continual deference is rarely beneficial, I feel that this initial deference helped to give April a sense of confidence in her own decisions. In fact, April in later conversations told me that she was frightened at first to voice her opinion because she thought that we were so highly educated, but then she realized that she was just as intelligent as the rest of us![18]

This initial deference abated as soon as we began to understand the talents each of us brought to the project. April and myself, as the only group members with previous video experience, became the creative and technical side of the team, while Ian and Elana naturally fell into the process side of the production. Additionally, because Ian (40) and Elana (32) were both considerably older than April (21) and myself (22), April and I often found ourselves relating better to each other than to the older members of the group. This also helped to overcome the "planning student" and "youth with limited access to resources" categories within which we were initially operating.

Despite this division of talents, tasks and ages, the *Wishlist* team used consensus-based decision-making for all production issues, including editing. This model meant that everyone in the group needed to understand, and agree with, what was being proposed. On several occasions, this led to very lengthy discussions that always involved trade-offs and compromises among the group members. One such debate was about the overall tone of the film. One planning student felt that we were making an overly optimistic piece and that we needed to be more critical of the city's plans for the Greenway. The result was that we typed up and then printed off all of the recorded interviews. Together, the team spent 2 days cutting and categorizing people's quotations, before agreeing, based on the transcripts, that we really didn't have enough overt critique in the interviews to make them an integral part of the film's narrative. While lengthy, this process allowed us all to step back from our own positions on the Greenway, and consider what our actual content looked like, before making any decisions.

7.5.3 Product

While consensus-based decision-making helped us to overcome the experience/inexperience divide with regard to video skills, we also made one significant decision to mitigate this problem. Because we were operating within a very short time frame, it was clear that I would have to do most of the editing. This posed a problem because part of the film's purpose was to train those involved in video-making skills. While we had collaboratively shot the interviews and edited together on paper, the three other group members would be missing out on the opportunity to acquire video-editing skills. To compensate, we agreed to use stop-motion animation, rather than Flash animation (a process that allows you to digitally animate a film). While I edited the film from Projection's office, April, Ian and Elana, in a time-consuming process, manually altered each animated frame for the film's two sequences. The result, I would argue, is an aesthetic that is much more in tune with the film's tone: rather than appearing overly technical, *Wishlist* appears to be driven by collaboration.

In spite of initial power imbalances, *Wishlist*'s process was overwhelmingly collaborative, based on the consensus decision-making model. It was my impression that every group member felt empowered to speak their own mind, as we openly (and sometimes painstakingly) discussed every issue. Additionally, because fundamental decisions around the skills-building component to the project were made early on, each group member walked away with a broader film-making skill set.

Clearly, while video can be a powerful tool for fostering dialogue, issues of accessibility, representation and censorship need to be carefully considered at a project's outset. *Wishlist* has shown that in order to make an inclusive film that fosters dialogue, a film's style and aesthetics need to be driven by the multiple ways of knowing that exist in the community(ies).

7.6 From Dialoguing to Appropriating

What do you see? Does it always have to be that way?

As a utopian film, *Wishlist* urges people to claim their rights to participation and appropriation through engaging them in a dialogue based on imaginatively reinterpreting the present.

7.6.1 Wishlist *as Utopia*

Wishlist opens up a space for dialogue by confronting feelings of powerlessness and invisibility often expressed by DTES residents. *Wishlist* demands the impossible as a way of realizing all that might be, creating a space for new possibilities while urging the viewer to add her own voice to the assemblage of voices (Attili, 2007). In asking the latent question, "What would *you* put on Carrall Street?", *Wishlist* confronts people's fears of powerlessness (Lefebvre, 1996). This confrontation is crucial to claiming the right to participate in and to appropriate the city; we can only truly inhabit the city once we are able to believe that things can change. Hope means believing that the impossible is possible, despite all evidence to the contrary, and this very act makes the evidence change, as Loeb (2004) has demonstrated, historically. *Wishlist* fosters this hope through using animation to imagine what an appropriated Carrall Street would look like.

7.6.2 Wishlist: Imagining Spatial Appropriation

Through its imagined street appropriations, *Wishlist* establishes a dialogue based on the right to actively inhabit the city. We are alienated from our urban environments when we cannot see ourselves reflected in them. The movement from fear to hope therefore begins with imagining that we have the right to physically alter the spaces of the city so that they respond to our needs, desires, and identities (Young, 1990).

Wishlist transforms Carrall Street into a place where people's meanings are validated, projected and transmitted to others (Leach, 2005). For DTES residents viewing the film, they may hear (through the sound of a shopping cart on the street) or see (through their art appearing in an animation sequence) aspects of their lives reflected in the space. These validations and transformations are critical to initiating a dialogue over who has the right to appropriate space. For Marxist cultural critic Walter Benjamin, appropriation occurs both through use and by perception (Benjamin, 1968). *Wishlist* engages overtly in appropriation by perception; when people view the film, they enter into a dialogue with others over the multitude of possible uses (and users) of the street. For DTES residents, the establishment of this dialogue is crucial for changing how the DTES is perceived. As one resident states in the film, "the frustrating part for me is that the DTES is not recognized for what it is, a vibrant, artistic community". *Wishlist* therefore plays an important role in empowering residents, while simultaneously transforming people's narratives to include a broader understanding of the interplay among space, place and identity (Harvey, 1973). This comprehension is crucial for advancing the right to the city, as it opens up a forum for discussions based on the rights to participation and appropriation (Dikec, 2001).

7.6.3 Wishlist's Vision for Inhabiting the City

Wishlist grounds spatial appropriation in a vision of inhabiting the city based on a politics of multiplicity. This framing is crucial to the film, as insights and revelations come not from recording and transmitting stories but from weaving them together (Gurstein, 2007). On *Wishlist*'s Carrall Street, social groups intermingle while resisting homogenization, embracing the differences of opinion and understanding that are constitutive of city life (Young, 1990). On this imagined street, ideas for change ("I think there should be an area for play, where children and adults can interact, like a fair that's always happening, where the multicultural, multiinterests can be expressed") are juxtaposed with demands for leaving things as is ("Honestly, I'd just leave it the way it is. I like it. It's real"). Because *Wishlist* is a compilation of overlapping images, ideas and soundscapes, it demands that the viewer engage with the film as an active listener and mediator. The result is that *Wishlist* allows the viewer to move from an individual analysis of place to a collective, politically charged critique of space, thereby rendering the act of viewing a highly political one (Harvey, 1973).

7.6.4 Wishlist's Politics

> There are no inevitabilities in this world...
> there are always responses, resistances,
> attempts at shaping and reshaping
> the historical forces that impinge on our lives
> (Friedmann, 2000, p. 461)

When we use our imaginations, we are playfully engaging in appropriations that are often deeply political. In creating *Wishlist*, the production team was keenly aware that direct action could be one of the film's outcomes. Because the Carrall Street redesign process was already well underway by the time we were editing, we decided that *Wishlist*'s potential was in asserting a vision that did not so much depend on mobilizing to address or respond to the current political regime, but rather depended on individuals and social groups mobilizing for their right to appropriate space *in spite of* political power. As one resident in the film argues: "Using that space in a productive way, socializing there, we can take something that we didn't really ask for and turn it into a community building tool". In other words, the Carrall Street redesign process could act as a catalyst for multiple forms of (re)appropriation. By spatially appropriating Carrall Street through perception, *Wishlist* establishes the context in which such a physical (re)appropriation could occur. *Wishlist* is therefore less of a "Wish List" for City of Vancouver planners and more of a do-it-yourself (DIY) "Wish List" for current and future users of Carrall Street.[19]

Conceivably then, *Wishlist*, as a utopian film, empowers DTES residents to imagine how their acts of participation and appropriation might affect Carrall Street. Relying on animation, *Wishlist* challenges both DTES residents' and non-residents' perceptions of Carrall Street, thereby initiating a dialogue over who has rights to the city. This dialogue describes the possibilities for the creation of a more diverse Carrall Street based on the principles of DIY or (in Lefebvre's language) *appropriation*.

7.7 Conclusions: Imagining as a Right

We've seen how *Wishlist* fosters the right to inhabit the city by engaging people in a dialogue over their rights to participation and appropriation. This last section moves away from this discussion to evaluate *Wishlist* for its applicability, reception, institutional integration and relevance as a planning tool.

7.7.1 Applicability

When I have had the opportunity to screen *Wishlist* to city planners and community organizers, the question I am asked first concerns the film's applicability to wider social and geographical contexts. My first instinct is to answer that it does not matter, that broader applicability was not the purpose of the film. After further consideration, I usually explain that because the film is relatively short (just over 5 minute in length: an imposed project constraint), it does not contain the necessary space to frame Carrall Street's social, geographic or political context. For example, the film does not even mention that Carrall Street is located in Vancouver. The reason for this is because *Wishlist* was never intended to be screened separately from the other Participatory Video project films and that "package" of films includes a 10-minute process piece that contextualizes all three films. This is a point which was much debated amongst the participatory video group: some of us felt that it was important to be able to screen the films separately, but organizers emphasized that this would undermine the collaborative nature of the project. If *Wishlist* were to be screened separately, it would be quite easy to put some text at the beginning of the film to explain the overall context in which the film is set. Without establishing the relevant context, it has been difficult for some people to see how they could use a similar film in their work. However, others have suggested that the film's aesthetic and narrative characteristics could be applied to different planning contexts.

I have two main comments regarding applicability. First, I would argue that many of the ideas expressed by DTES residents are relevant to communities in other cities: the desire for safe drinking water, emergency pay phones and even farmers markets are all items that most people would want to have access to in their neighbourhoods, although, of course, each neighbourhood has its unique and context-specific needs. The second and more important question is whether *Wishlist*'s approach, its aesthetic and narrative choices, are artistic and political strategies with wider applicability. The two preceding sections suggest that they are. The real challenge, however, is related to scale. For a large neighbourhood, or city, can such video-making principles be applied? And what would be the cost implications of such an expanded scale of engagement? I would suggest that a large-scale video-making process would need to be carefully evaluated and planned before being undertaken. Examples, such as Igloolik Isuma Productions,[20] suggest that video can be a valuable tool for ensuring cultural survival and community cohesiveness.

7.7.2 Reception

One measure of the success of a film is the audience's reaction. For films like *Wishlist*, intended to promote dialogue, people's responses are crucial to evaluating effectiveness. Due to circumstances described later in this section, *Wishlist* has been screened only on a few occasions and only twice in the DTES. The Participatory Video group screened preliminary versions of all three films at the Interurban Gallery, located at the intersection of Carrall Street and Hastings Street in the DTES. Participants from all three films were invited to attend and were asked for their feedback. *Wishlist* was shown last and, unlike the other two films, was met with some degree of apprehension. A few residents expressed concern that this video, unlike its predecessors, was uncritical of the Carrall Street Greenway redesign and seemed to accept gentrification as a *fait accompli*.[21]

What this reaction underscored for us was that *Wishlist* successfully challenged residents' narratives of place, power and agency. Instead of "preaching to the converted" by focusing on the negative actions of city planners and developers, *Wishlist* seriously challenged residents to move beyond their anger and to imagine that they had the power to affect the street. Essentially, I would argue that *Wishlist* caused such a stir because it had successfully urged people to move away from their fear of displacement towards the hope that they could change Carrall Street.

Wishlist has also been screened to non-DTES residents.[22] The first reaction amongst non-residents is to ask about the logistics of undertaking animation; most people are curious about the process and often express the belief that animation could be used in their own projects. At one screening, audience members began to brainstorm about the different spaces in Vancouver that could be used for a sequel (they finally settled on the Vancouver Art Gallery steps).[23] This reaction shows that the film is successful in getting people to imagine how they can appropriate their own spaces. Non-DTES residents also commonly express surprise when they find out that the articulate, educated voices in the film belong to DTES residents.

This reaction usually instigates a conversation over people's misconceptions and stereotyping of the DTES. This reaction is another indication that *Wishlist* is a successful dialoguing tool.

7.7.3 Institutional Integration

Patsy Healey argues that imagination needs to be coupled with proper institutional analysis in order to bring about change in the public realm (Healey, 2001). In the case of *Wishlist*, several problems occurred with the video's dissemination that significantly hampered its ability to be used as a wider dialoguing tool. It is important to underscore that many of the problems pertaining to *Wishlist*'s dissemination are problems frequently experienced when people attempt to use video as a planning tool.

The first issue for us was one of project timing. The CSPVP began when the City of Vancouver was wrapping up the public outreach component of the Carrall Street redesign. In a meeting with a senior planner at the City of Vancouver, we were informed that the physical design of the street had already been decided and therefore, our videos could only have a minimal impact on the street's design. While it was suggested during this meeting that the videos could potentially contribute to the programming of the space, there was no formal agreement between the City of Vancouver and the Carrall Street Participatory Video group. Consequently, there was no structured venue in which to screen *Wishlist*.

The second problem was one of flawed communication between the Carrall Street Participatory Video group and the City of Vancouver. As already mentioned, *Wishlist* was one of three films produced about the Greenway. Upon project completion, some of the staff of the Planning Department within the City of Vancouver deemed one of the other films to be controversial and inappropriate. In response to their concern, the School of Community and Regional Planning, Projections, Ear to the Ground Planning and staff of the Planning Department of the City of Vancouver agreed that none of the films would be publicly screened or distributed until the controversy was resolved. Unfortunately, this decision meant that *Wishlist* could not be used to inform the last part of the Greenway planning process.

Patsy Healey explains that when we critically imagine, we enter into new dialogues about governance and decision-making (Healey, 2001). The *Wishlist* story told here has shown that without proper institutional buy-in, this dialogue can never get started. An important lesson, therefore, is that future video projects negotiate opportunities for engagement with planning and governance institutions at the outset of the project.

7.7.4 Relevance

The experience of *Wishlist* suggests that, in the proper context, video can serve as a powerful tool for stimulating conversation over people's rights to inhabit the city. DTES residents are often unable (or unwilling) to engage with institutionally driven public meetings, workshops, design charrettes and council reports. Video, as a visual medium, offered them a different way to engage in an inclusive and locally based discussion over their rights to the city.

Community-based videos such as *Wishlist* have the potential to serve as an *a priori* policy document, in which discussions about changes to public space can occur in the public domain, without people having to form interest groups.[24] To this end, community control over the medium and its dissemination is crucial in ensuring its legitimacy and applicability (Gurstein, 2007). Issues of representation and censorship need to be carefully considered in a project's scoping and venues for dissemination need to be confirmed at the project's outset.

While there is great potential for multimedia to influence policy and promote community development, video is only one of the many tools at the disposal of city planners, community organizers and residents (Sandercock, 2007). Because video has come into fashion as a way of disseminating information and ideas, there is a tendency for it to be seen as a brave new way forward in difficult planning contexts. Our experience with the CSPVP suggests that video be approached from a critical standpoint and, like other planning tools, be tailored to different community contexts.

This chapter has argued that the right to the city originates with the right to imagine participating in its creation. Video, as demonstrated by *Wishlist*, has the potential to catalyze this right to participation. *Wishlist* establishes a dialogue based on utopian imagining and visual appropriation, thereby contributing to the struggle for social justice.

But even though video has the potential to foster innovative modes of participation, relationship building and decision-making, it is clear that institutions and communities need to develop their capacity to incorporate video into their governance structures. More theoretical and practical research is needed in order to encourage governments and institutions to take risks in incorporating video into their governance processes.

Notes

1. For a detailed account of why there has been renewed interest in the right to the city and in the thinking of Henri Lefebvre, see Purcell (2002).
2. These questions were derived from the author's own initial questions as part of a larger action research project.
3. For a history of the Downtown Eastside, see Sommers (2001). For a critical look at social movements and space in the Downtown Eastside, see Blomley (2004).
4. For more information on the economic revitalization plan for the DTES, please see City of Vancouver (2007b).
5. The City of Vancouver has a greenways plan for the city. Their greenways website explains: "Greenways in Vancouver are linear public corridors for pedestrians and cyclists that connect parks, nature reserves, cultural features, historic sites, neighbourhoods and retail areas" (City of Vancouver, 2007c).
6. Because this video project was a participatory video project, the intent was never clearly delineated. Furthermore, due to time constraints, the actual ability of the City of Vancouver to use the videos to inform the public design process was limited. For an extended discussion of this, see Vallillee (2007).
7. Projections provide skill building and video mentorship opportunities to "youth with limited access to resources", mainly from Vancouver's Downtown Eastside. The term "youth with limited access to resources" is used by Projections, who developed the term in partnership with the youth involved in their video projects. Ear to the Ground Planning is a planning consulting company that uses video as part of the planning process.
8. John Friedmann has written extensively on the role of utopian thinking and insurgency in planning. Particularly relevant to this thesis is *The Prospect of Cities* (2002), in which Friedmann discusses the usefulness of utopian thinking.
9. I am relying on the following definition of reflexivity: Reflexivity involves applying our critical thinking to practice, therefore changing contexts, projects and people: "examining critically the assumptions underlying our actions, the impact of those actions" (Cunliffe, 2004, p. 410).
10. Schön (1983) describes reflecting in practice as a reflecting in action that is about the thinking involved in doing.
11. It is important to note in this regard that having a youth who worked and sometimes lived in the community was essential to building trust and setting up interviews.
12. While using an audio recorder made some people more willing to be interviewed, there was still significant reluctance from people to be recorded. Consequently, a large proportion of the voices in *Wishlist* come from the formal interviews that we conducted.
13. In the formal interviews, we chose not to start with a set list of questions: we began each interview by asking what the interviewee would put on Carrall Street, but the follow-up questions were based on our knowledge of the person. For the informal interviews, we only asked one

question: "If you could put anything on Carrall Street, what would it be?" In conducting informal interviews, the device of making a film allowed us to discuss openly the Carrall Street Greenway in a non-institutional environment. It raised awareness of the changes occurring on the street and consequently encouraged people to reflect on how they have used the space in the past and would want to use the space in the future.

14. According to a report released by the University of British Columbia's Learning Exchange, the DTES has a higher number of people who have less than a Grade 9 education when compared to the rest of Vancouver (Newman, 2005).

15. We would write down peoples' ideas and then read them back to them, to ensure accuracy. Editing requires the selection of specific ideas that work with the narrative coherence of the piece. As such, while we tried to incorporate either visually or audibly something from everyone with whom we spoke, that was not always possible.

16. It is also important to note that these categories were developed by the *Wishlist* team and that interviewees did not describe which categories they thought their ideas fitted into.

17. Please note that the following discussion about group dynamics stems only from my own observations and is therefore a highly subjective account of the film-making process.

18. What is interesting about this conversation is that at the end of the project, many of the youth with limited access to resources expressed a strong desire to return to school, and April was determined to become a midwife. For more evaluation of the project's benefits, please see Hunt (2006) and Marcuse et al. (2006).

19. The idea for the title of the film came from one group member, who liked the idea of naming the film *Wishlist* because the film, unlike so many planning processes, demands that residents see themselves (rather than the State) as agents of change.

20. Igloolik Isuma Productions describes their company as follows: "Our name Isuma means 'to think'," as in Thinking Productions. Our building in the centre of Igloolik has a big sign on the front that says Isuma. Think. Young and old work together to keep our ancestors' knowledge alive. We create traditional artefacts, digital multimedia and desperately needed jobs in the same activity. Our productions give an artist's view for all to see where we came from: what Inuit were able to do then and what we are able to do now.

21. While this was the sentiment expressed by three vocal residents, it is unclear whether everyone who attended the screening shared their opinion. Several other members of the audience approached me afterwards and expressed their happiness with the piece. Clearly, screenings in the future need to be facilitated in order to generate a variety of responses.

22. The film has been screened at the World Urban Forum, the World Planners Congress, Planners for Tomorrow, DOXA (a curated and juried festival comprising public screenings, workshops, panel discussions and public forums) and at community consultations.

23. This comment is interesting because the Art Gallery used to be Vancouver's courthouse and was traditionally the place for political protests.

24. Young (1990, p. 73) explains how the formation of interest groups depoliticizes public debate.

References

Attili, G. (2007, March). Digital ethnographies in the planning field. *Planning Theory and Practice, 8*(1), 89–114.

Benjamin, W. (1968). *Illuminations*. London: Harcourt Brace Jovanovich Inc.

Blomley, N. (2004). *Unsettling the city: Urban land and the politics of property*. New York: Routledge.

City of Vancouver. (2007b). *The carrall street greenway*. Accessed June 4, 2007, from http://www.city.vancouver.bc.ca/engsvcs/streets/break greenways/city/carrall/index.htm

City of Vancouver (2007c). *Greenways plan*. Accessed June 4, 2007, from http://www.city. vancouver.bc.ca/engsvcs/streets/greenways

City of Vancouver (2007d). *Explore the greenway.* Accessed June 6, 2007, from http://city. vancouver.bc.ca/engsvcs/streets/greenways/city/carrall/greenway.htm

Cunliffe, A. (2004, June). On becoming a critically reflexive practitioner. *Journal of Management Education, 28*(4), 407–426.

Dikec, M. (2001, August). Justice and the spatial imagination. *Environment and Planning A, 33*(10), 1785–1805.

Eby, D., & Masura, C. (2006). *Cracks in the foundation: Solving the housing crisis in Canada's poorest neighborhood.* Vancouver: Pivot Legal Society.

Friedmann, J. (2000, June). The good city: In Defense of utopian thinking. *International Journal of Urban and Regional Research, 24*(2), 460–472.

Friedmann, J. (2002). *The prospect of cities.* Minneapolis: University Of Minnesota Press.

Gurstein, P. (2007, March). Multimedia and planning: *Commentary, Planning Theory and Practice, 8*(1), 112–114.

Harvey, D. (1973). *Social justice and the city.* London: Johns Hopkins University Press.

Healey, P. (Ed). (2001). *The governance of place: Space and planning processes.* Sydney: Ashgate.

Hunt, A. (2006). *How participatory, how productive? A reflective evaluation of the Carrall street participatory video project.* MAP project, University of British Columbia, Vancouver.

Leach, N. (2005). Belonging: Towards a Theory of identification with space. In J. Hillier, E. Rooksby (eds) *Habitus: A sense of place.* Burlington: Ashgate.

Lefebvre, H. (1996). *Writings on cities.* (E. Kofman & E. Lebas, Trans. from French). Oxford: Blackwell Publishing.

Loeb, P. (Ed.). (2004). *The impossible will take a little while: A citizen's guide to hope in a time of fear.* New York: Basic Books.

Marcuse et al. (2006). *Wishlist: Meaningful participation in the Carrall street greenway plan through participatory video.* Vancouver: Masters Project, University of British Columbia.

Mitchell, D. (2003). *The right to the city: Social justice and the fight for public space.* New York: Guilford Press.

Newman, J. (2005). An overview of Vancouver's downtown Eastside for the UBC learning exchange TREK program participants. Research Report. University of British Columbia, Learning Exchange, Vancouver.

PIVOT Legal Society. (2007). PIVOT Legal Society Website. Accessed June 4, 2007, from http://www.pivotlegal.org/Issues/addictions.htm

Purcell, M. (2002, October). Excavating Lefebvre: The right to the city and its urban politics of the inhabitant. *GeoJournal, 58*(2), 99–108.

Sandercock, L. (2007, March). Multimedia and planning: Introduction. *Planning Theory and Practice, 8*(1), 89–90.

Schön, D. (1983). *The reflective practitioner: How professionals think in action.* New York: Basic Books.

Sommers, J. (2001). *The place of the poor: Poverty, space and the politics of representation in downtown Vancouver, 1950–1997.* Ph.D. thesis, Simon Fraser University, Burnaby.

Vallilee, A. (2007). *What's video got to do with it?* MAP thesis, University of British Columbia, Vancouver.

Wishlist. (2006). Directed by April Curry, Elana Cossever, Jessica Hallenbeck, Ian Marcuse. Vancouver, Projections and Ear to the Ground Planning [DVD: mini DV].

Young, I. M. (1990). *Justice and the politics of difference.* Princeton: Princeton University Press.

Chapter 8
"The Beginning of Something": Using Video as a Tool in Community Engagement

Wendy Sarkissian

8.1 First Attempts

I've been working as a social planning consultant since 1981. Back in 1990, working in Melbourne, I found myself with the perfect client with the perfect project that allowed my firm and professional colleagues to explore the potential of video in community engagement. On a windswept site in suburban Melbourne called Timbarra, we designed and managed a workshop for new residents of a private housing development. The client was the Urban Land Authority (ULA), the State land developer in Victoria. The project manager was community artist and activist, Graeme Dunstan.[1] We called our workshop "A Welcome Home" – a conscious play on words. This participatory design workshop was intended to assist participants in making decisions about their house design and siting, in consultation with their neighbours and expert advisers. A complementary aim was to introduce them to local community services and facilities and to plant the seeds of the community development process for the new housing estate. We were welcoming people who had recently purchased a residential lot and we wanted them to feel at home, as they negotiated with their neighbours to make decisions about siting their houses on their lots.

The workshop was attended by a small group of new land buyers, many of whom were moving from inner city locations to experience what they saw as the benefits of living on the urban fringe.

The workshop was very ambitious in its objectives. We aimed to showcase local community services and facilities, to introduce new residents to their immediate neighbours, to pilot test an innovative participatory design model and to trial some innovative approaches to community engagement with children. While the corporate culture of the ULA generally supported a "marketing" approach to community engagement, this was not an explicit focus of this workshop, as all participants had already purchased their house lots.

W. Sarkissian (✉)
Sarkissian Associates Planners P/L, Nimbin, New South Wales, Australia
e-mail: wendy@sarkissian.com.au

L. Sandercock, G. Attili (eds.), *Multimedia Explorations in Urban Policy and Planning*, Urban and Landscape Perspectives 7, DOI 10.1007/978-90-481-3209-6_8,
© Springer Science+Business Media B.V. 2010

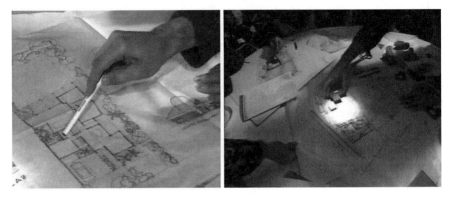

Fig. 8.1 Lot buyers at the Timbarra Welcome Home. Video stills from "The Smart Blocks of Timbarra" (Dunstan & Sarkissian, 1990a)

One of the features of the programme was the use of a professional video team (Lemac Film and Video, Melbourne) to produce a short edited videotape of the children's participatory activities to be shown to the adults at the conclusion of the half-day workshop. To achieve this, an editing suite was set up in the primary school's nurse's office and arrangements were made to videotape both the children's activities and the adults' workshop.

The adults' workshop was set up in a dramatic and eye-catching manner. From the ceiling of the brand new Berwick Park Primary School gymnasium, we hung a peach-coloured marquee liner. This simple touch transformed the gymnasium into a soft womb-like space, which drew an immediate comment from participants as they entered the room. All participants, who had been interviewed by telephone before they arrived, were allocated to tables shared with their immediate neighbours. Mock street signs showed the location of each resident group. Welcoming them at each table was a trained facilitator and recorder, as well as a professional architect to assist with house-siting decisions.

Created for the participatory design exercise and built at great expense by a model maker was a lamp that exactly simulated the sunlight at the solstices and equinoxes for that Melbourne location, enabling participants to see movements of the sun on their house lots and even into their dwellings, represented by small timber models.

In the children's workshop, facilitated by planner Kelvin Walsh, we used two methods. In the face-painting exercise, the facilitator asked the children to describe features of their ideal neighbourhood and then painted the child's face with a representation of these qualities. For example, one child who especially appreciated "wildness" received a wild animal face and long paper claws on his fingers. A tape recorder at the facilitator's elbow recorded children's responses to predetermined questions, as did the video crew.

The second children's exercise was the edible or food model, where Timbarra children designed their ideal community and neighbourhoods using food. Video cameras captured huge smiles and microphones captured squeals of delight as

Fig. 8.2 Wildness in my neighbourhood. Photo by Kelvin Walsh

"taboo" materials like liquorice and Smarties were used in the collaborative design process. (And eagerly devoured when the project was complete.)

The adults responded to the 2-minute video of the children's work with surprise, delight and appreciation. The video revealed a great deal of wisdom in the children's recommendations. However, in common with many adults with whom we have worked, the Timbarra residents appeared surprised by their children's ideas. This is a common experience for people using engagement processes with children. In another project, we heard the primary school principal remark,

> I was surprised how much the kids came up with which was the same as what was being put forward by the [adult] community. . . . I was a bit unsure what the finished product would be like. . . But when I saw the pictures and what the kids had actually said about them, that made it meaningful.[2]

In the Timbarra case, the video provided a kinaesthetic and dramatic representation of the *materiality* of the children's work. What the parents *saw* and *heard* were their children's stories about the community they dreamed, the qualities they hoped would be embodied in the place and the life they dreamed for themselves in that place. The sight of their children working diligently to create their ideal community drew a respectful response from the adults: they could clearly see that this was not play. It was what others have called "the work of childhood"[3]: a most diligent application of their skills and intentions to the question at hand: *How could Timbarra be designed to meet the needs of young children?*

Not everything went smoothly in the first *Welcome Home* Workshop. Consistent with our commitment to *welcoming*, a bush band and a gracious lunch greeted participants. When the members of the School's Parents and Friends Association arrived to prepare lunch, their first act of turning on every pie warmer in the kitchen, coupled with the power drain from the lights required by the video crew, blew every fuse in the building. The School's Principal, who (in my recollection), had a commonplace Anglo name like Smith or Jones, had only just left for home with the keys to the fuse box in his pocket. This was before the days of cellphones and he lived in a distant suburb. I stood staring at the fuse box with visions of my entire professional life evaporating when I was nudged aside by the video technician. Unfolding a paper clip, he quietly picked the lock, the pie warmers were then turned on one by one and the workshop proceeded without incident.

I learned from this inaugural experience that there is no substitute for video in capturing squeals of delight, a toe-tapping bush band, the energy of children working collaboratively and the industrious focus of their parents working in a hands-on way to negotiate with their neighbours so they could site their houses on their lots. The act of producing a professional video in 1 week to meet a competition deadline for an award (which we won) convinced me of what was possible with professional assistance. The visceral quality of our video captured impromptu interviews, with one man whose house was poorly sited by his builder candidly admitting, "We never planned the sunlight". The participants' and facilitators' tone of voice as they reported back to the whole group reflected both enthusiasm and exasperation. All was not perfect in this suburban estate-in-the-making. Some participants, like my videotaped interviewee, had bought house-and-land packages, only to realise that their houses were sited inappropriately to achieve solar passive benefits. Some houses were clearly sited backwards but could not be turned around because contracts had been signed!

I've used photographs for decades for training and in professional reports. Video offers more, I discovered. Humour, for example: a quality that video captures that photographs cannot. We designed an elaborate role-play training session for all the *Welcome Home* workers, who played the roles of invited participants (based on our careful pre-workshop research). A somewhat nervous crew collapsed in howls of laughter when the expensive prototype of the solar lamp fell apart in the hands of landscape architect Kevin Taylor as he was demonstrating its finer points.

Most of these hilarious moments were ultimately edited out by our somewhat humourless client, but the original training videotape remains a cherished archive. As John Forester sagely notes:

> Humor can give us the gift, even if momentarily, of recognizing that something links and connects us as adversaries in the room. We now see something that we mutually share: a need to learn to understand the situation in which we actually find ourselves interdependently connected and that gift of humor then can contribute in a small but perhaps still important way to creating a "we" of nevertheless distrusting and skeptical parties... (Forester, 2005).

Embodiment shows up in video in ways that other media cannot display. Only with video can we demonstrate exactly how participatory design exercises work and then refine our approaches. After a few minutes, despite intrusive cameras, microphones and hot lights, both adults and children ignored the video crew. These were the days before privacy legislation and signed permissions were not required, but even today we find that video is not as intrusive as some might expect.[4]

8.2 Further Experimentation

In the 1980s and the 1990s, Graeme Dunstan and I were regular participants in workshops by Jean Houston, a frequent visitor to Australia (see Houston, 1982, 1987). We dreamed of ways to modify her ritual approaches in less metaphysical contexts. We loved Houston's use of heroic language that acknowledged her debt to Joseph Campbell (see Campbell, 1949). And we found resonances with our own approaches in "the pattern that connects", scientist and philosopher Gregory Bateson's holistic perspective of how the world works and the universe holds together (see Bateson,

Fig. 8.3 Kevin Taylor and the solar lamp. Photo by Wendy Sarkissian

Fig. 8.4 The major gods: Zeus, Gaia and Arteriosclerosis. Photo by Wendy Sarkissian

1979). Sharing a Melbourne office and apartment, we spent many hours dreaming of ways to use Bateson's and Houston's approaches in our own work to raise an issue above the "everyday" to the archetypal or heroic so we could see more easily the relationships and the patterns that connect people and positions. In the early 1990s, we experimented with our new ideas in two workshops for different clients in which video played a major part. We called these "The Gods Must be Crazy" and "The Conference of the Birds", a workshop for home builders and developers in Melbourne.[5]

In the first of these, an ambitious project in Melbourne in 1990 (the year that came to be known in our small firm as "the year of living dangerously"), Graeme pushed a cooperative client (the Victorian Roads Authority, VicRoads) almost to the edge with a wild workshop called "The Gods Must be Crazy". In a 20-minute role-play scenario inserted into a day-long stakeholders' workshop, the gods of

Melbourne's arterial roads were convened by the supremo, Zeus, assisted by two major gods: Gaia (mother of all life on Earth) and the God of Ageing Road Infrastructure, Arteriosclerosis. A highly ineffectual Hermes attempted to negotiate the conflicting needs of Melbourne's arterial road users with little success, as he was yelled at by a gang of uncooperative and territorial minor gods.

These truculent characters, played by some of Melbourne's prominent planners, included a particularly argumentative and domineering *Taxidermus* (God of Taxis), *Bicyclops* (God of Bicyclists), *Pantechnicon* (God of Truckies), a rational and unbending *Statuometheos* (God of Statutory Planning), *Roadeometheos* (God of Road Planning), *Bureaucratus* (God of Economic Rationalism) and other minor gods. A burly police officer embodied a fierce and demanding *Hestia* (Goddess of Children and the Hearth).

The video revealed the strong conflicts between representatives of arterial road user groups and the humour generated by this archetypal role play took our respectful gesture towards the work of Gregory Bateson and Jean Houston to another level. The sound and visual effects we used (particularly Zeus's control of thunder and lightning) highlighted the authority of the supremo. The loud squabbling, emphatic gestures and other body language of the truculent gods came to life in the video. When the older male *Taxidermus* turns and screams at the younger female *Bicyclops*, "Keep your bike off the footpath!" the video reminds us of power relations in planning issues. Similarly, *Autolycus*, God of the Automobile, was particularly impressive as he ingratiatingly described how his devotees worship him in huge, cavernous underground temples. Language, gestures and sound effects (as well as robes and laurel wreaths) combined to make a dramatic point in the video.

In another project, Kevin Taylor and I used video to record proposed changes to the foyer of the State Library of South Australia, using 100 percent mock-up techniques and a highly structured role play to test the effectiveness of the proposed changes for different user groups. The "new" foyer featured a full-scale desk constructed of cardboard and extensive signage indicating the new location of key features (the Newspaper Reading Room, photocopiers, the Foyer Manager's Office).

Aspects of the old foyer that would not be part of the proposed new design were hidden from view. Black and clear plastic indicated where new walls would go, the locations of skylights and hanging plants. Cardboard representations were made of new equipment. An important feature was the props made by staff out of paper to represent the vast array of items typically stored as "bags": backpacks, umbrellas, bouquets of flowers, briefcases, shopping bags...all in paper!

The video crew captured arguments and conversations among library staff and team members preparing props to transform the library foyer according to the new design. They captured debates about the design of specific props needed to test the simulated environment. The focus of this videoing was on the staff in Preservation Services, who spent their days in a windowless room repairing historic books and documents. They were an ingenious group, very much like industrial engineers in their approaches. The challenge of the props was clearly within their abilities and a welcome change (they said) from their more mundane tasks. With much laughter, they set about making oversized cardboard suitcases, paper backpacks, umbrellas, paper bouquets of flowers and shopping bags to be used by other staff playing the roles of encumbered shoppers whose "packages" placed a huge strain on library storage resources. Other roles included an elderly woman, a professional researcher, a foreign student, a hard-working staff member and an overladen staff member in a hurry.

To our delight and considerable surprise (we thought the new design would work better), the video captured the prop-production process with all its detail and flamboyance. It also captured the process of testing to see if the new design (and especially a huge cardboard desk to replace the existing front desk in the foyer) would actually work for hypothetical library users. The video captured the noise, confusion, paralinguistics and bodies in conflict, blocked sightlines from the reception desk to the Reference Department and severe congestion caused by those embodying the roles of staff with library trolleys, wheelchair users and encumbered shoppers. Body language and gestures were particularly clear as bewildered first-time library users wandered off into the reference area with no idea where to go,

Fig. 8.5 The *Talk Any Kine* SpeakOut, 2006. Photos by Noel Mau

clearly demonstrating the weaknesses of the design as a "communicating medium". Combined with a very systematic (and videotaped) scoring system whereby staff assessed the mocked-up foyer's suitability for different user groups, the video provided a clear example of changes necessary to support the predicted uses. The desk in the foyer had to be redesigned and relocated. Again, the video captured many humorous interchanges.[6]

In a participatory design exercise in South Australia in late 1990, we used a role-play video to train facilitators and recorders (and to explain to the funding municipality how we were spending their money). Again, we encountered moments of group hilarity as I played a truculent child who interrupted the adults' process. Our videotape session allowed us to fine-tune the model, even though this was the first time we had used it. The reality turned out to be much easier than the role play.[7]

Continuing the use of video as a training tool, we videotaped the set-up and operation of a community SpeakOut in the Brisbane suburb of Bracken Ridge in 2003. Here the videotape captured the frenetic activity and effort required to prepare individual issue stalls and mount interpretive materials. Made by Chris Fuller, a high school student volunteering in our office, this silent videotape became a helpful training tool. A SpeakOut is an innovative, interactive drop-in event that can be used in a variety of community engagement contexts. The model is used widely in Australia and has taken off in places such as Hawai'i and Thunder Bay, Ontario. We have used video extensively in training facilitators and recorders for SpeakOut processes. Wiwik Bunjamin-Mau, Indonesian-born and now resident in Honolulu, made a video of her Honolulu SpeakOut, in 2006: *Talk Any Kine*, designed to elicit feedback from the Chinatown community as part of a community planning process initiated by the City and County of Honolulu.[8]

In another project managed by Graeme Dunstan, a professional videographer, Abraham Zuniga, was hired to document a 3-month community cultural development project at Eagleby, a low-income suburb on Queensland's Gold Coast. This project is described in an interview with me by John Forester reported in 2005 (see Sarkissian, 2005). This complex project, entitled "Stories in a Park", saw Abraham training Year 10 high school students in the use of video for interviewing their neighbours about park planning and design. On this project we encountered a common but very disturbing problem. While our government client had provided ample resources for Abraham to record every aspect of the project, no budget was allocated for the production of the final video. This was seen as a major betrayal by the community and the consultants alike. In the end, the consultants, assisted by some community members, worked as volunteers to prepare a summary videotape.

Stories in a Park honoured the WSI tradition with its many theatrical components. A dramatic and touching feature of the celebrations was a children's lantern parade, winding through the Park with 400 lanterns, which included a storytelling session for the children by lantern light. Approximately 1.500 people (about 450 children and over 1.000 adults) participated in the lantern parade. Captured on the videotape were the words and emotions of Bob Engwicht, a community activist and former Christian minister. Bob and I stood on a hill overlooking the park in Eagleby when the children's lantern parade wound through the park. Both of us were crying. Later, reflecting on the whole experience, Bob said this:

> I felt community happening. . .. That night something changed. People used to be ashamed and now they are proud to be Eagleby residents. Something lifted that night. There was a change in the people. You could almost feel it, especially in the young people. There was a cleansing where they (residents) could discard the negative things they were hanging onto – they put them in and watched them burn. Positive changes. It was an event where people could stop and think.

The final event, a very powerful process, was the burning of a huge painted cardboard effigy of the Stigma of Eagleby (an eagle held down by a thumb, in all over 5 m long and 3.5 m tall). The bad stories of Eagleby were burned and new stories were created, reaffirming the community's desire to people and use their public spaces free from stigma, fear and intimidation.

Captured on Abraham's video was the chanting of a crowd of 3,000 local people as flames engulfed the stigma: "Burn the stigma! Burn the stigma!" Only the videotaped record was able to convey that powerful moment when something lifted, something changed forever in Eagleby.

Abraham Zuniga also videotaped the team development workshop in 2001 for Melbourne's Urban and Regional Land Authority.[9] Here, in an exercise in "giving voice to non-human Nature", I worked with a team of planning and development consultants who constructed a beautiful representation of non-human Nature to participate as a member of their team for the next 10 years as they planned a suburban housing development for 25.000 residents. The video documented the design and construction of the non-human Being and the team members' self-conscious

Fig. 8.6 The Eagleby Stigma. Photo by Wendy Sarkissian

Fig. 8.7 Making the Nonhuman Being. Photo by Wendy Sarkissian

Fig. 8.8 Deferring to the Nonhuman Being. Photo by Wendy Sarkissian

but touching ceremony designed to welcome the Being into the team. It revealed participants' unabashed enthusiasm and their unquestioning commitment to incorporating principles of environmental ethics and sustainability into the planning process. The video showed something that photographs could not: the absolute enthusiasm of the team members as they threw themselves into what would have been seen (in 2001) as a pretty unusual task. Again, personal interactions, body language and gestures confirmed that participants were not simply "playing along" but were wholeheartedly engaged in the process of creating the Nonhuman Being.[10]

8.3 Final Reflections: Why Use Video in Community Engagement?

My brief review of the use of video in my practice over the past 20 years brings back vivid memories of the value of immediate and authentic feedback which video can provide in community engagement contexts. It's an invaluable tool for showing spaces and places and people moving around in them. It conveys emotions, body language and relationships in a way that photographs simply cannot. It shows and gives permission for humour. Because participants in community workshops and role-play exercises quickly come to ignore the camera, microphone and even the lights, video communicates a sense of verisimilitude that cannot be conveyed by any other medium. For practitioners who seek to be engrossed in the subject matter of our work, video communicates a felt sense of the experience that we cannot otherwise communicate. It's great for communicating off-the-cuff and impromptu interviews and for demonstrating exactly how to set up an activity and how the process looks when it's happening. Diversity, congestion, conflicts and spatial relations are all easier to see than in still photographs.

Another invaluable aspect of video is its repeatability: a video of a process can be shown repeatedly as an instructional tool. One does not have to keep repeating the process and reconstructing similar events, thank heavens, because we have found that "perfect clients" (cashed-up and open to innovation) are few and far between. Our humble homemade training video, *Listening to all the Voices*, now out of print, contained clips of some of our innovative projects. It had a loyal following among students and teachers of planning and design (Sarkissian, Walsh, and Gherardi, 1994).

For those of us who sometimes find that we are working at the edge, video reminds us of what is possible and brings us back to the laughter of the moment. We remember what worked and what didn't work. And we can see why.

Importantly, video helps us remember what really happened. We hear the gossip that the display villages manager reported to his boss that the role-play simulation in which he played a kookaburra was "a waste of time". Concerned, we review the video of the 1990 "Conference of the Birds" segment in a workshop for developers on segmentation in Melbourne's housing market. We see the manager wearing an elegant painted cardboard mask, enthusiastically embodying a laughing kookaburra. And we hear him demanding (in a shrill kookaburra's voice) that builders must acknowledge his family's unique nesting needs.

What other evidence would we need?

Notes

1. Graeme Dunstan is Australia's pre-eminent lantern maker and community artist, trained by the renowned British artist collective, Welfare State International (WSI), a collective of radical artists and thinkers who explored ideas of celebratory art and spectacle between 1968 and 2006. I thank him for his generous and passionate collaborations over 20 years. Graeme's

comments on this article are also gratefully acknowledged. A deep bow of gratitude acknowledges the creativity, bravery and expertise of landscape architect Kevin Taylor, planner-urban designer Kelvin Walsh and artist Edward Car. Many of the processes described in this article are chronicled in the suite of five books, Community Participation in Practice (especially the Casebook), written and edited by staff and former staff of Sarkissian Associates Planners and published by Murdoch University. They are listed in the references. The approaches used in this article are also explained in three new books for Sarkissian, Hofer, Shore, Vajda, and Wilkinson (2008), Sarkissian and Bunjamin-Mau (2009), and Sarkissian and Hurford (2010).

2. See Chapter 11 of: Sarkissian and Hurford (2010).
3. Berliner and Casanova (1989).
4. While our developer client was slightly bemused by the process, the 13-minute videotape earned us many professional accolades, boosted our confidence and helped enormously in training. It received two Australian professional awards and the project, video and the resulting *Welcome Home* manual were shortlisted for the UN World Habitat Award in 1992 and 1993. For several years, the Urban Land Authority continued to use a somewhat less ambitious version of the workshop model with new land purchases in Timbarra and other estates with the videotape, *The Beginning of Something*, used as a training tool for the workshops.
5. In Sarkissian and Walsh (1994a) see: Sarkissian and Walsh (1994b) and Sarkissian and Dunstan (1994) The Conference of the Birds. See also: Dunstan and Sarkissian (1990b). Andrew O'Brien and Associates, Transportation Planners, Melbourne. [Produced by Tony Nicholson]. (Contains full "Gods Must be Crazy" role play shown in shorter version in the Listening to All the Voices Videotape, 1994.)
6. See Williams (1994). John Forester explores the role of humour in planning (Forester, 2005).
7. See Stewart (1994).
8. See http://www.speakoutplanning.com/resources/talk-any-kine.
9. The URLC was the ULA with a new name. It has now morphed into a different organization, VicUrban. From a distance, it appears that archetypal psychology and myth no longer play a conscious role in their planning processes.
10. For more about this process see Chapter 6 of Sarkissian and Hurford (2010).

References

Bateson, G. (1979). *Mind and nature: A necessary unity*. Toronto: Bantam Books.

Berliner, D., & Casanova, U. (1989, March). Play is the work of childhood. *Instructor, 98*(7), 22–23.

Campbell, J. (1949). *The hero with a thousand faces*. Princeton, NJ: Princeton University Press.

Dunstan, G., & Sarkissian, W. (Producers). (1990a). *"The Smart Blocks of Timbarra" and "The Beginning of Something": Two videotapes documenting the Timbarra "Welcome Home" workshop and the workshop process*. Urban Land Authority and Lemac Film and Video, Melbourne.

Dunstan, G., & Sarkissian, W. (Producers). (1990b). *Whose roads? Videotape of the Victorian Roads Corporation Search Conference on the Future of Melbourne's Arterial Roads*. Andrew O'Brien and Associates, Transportation Planners, Melbourne. Produced by Tony Nicholson. (Containsfull "Gods Must be Crazy" role play shown in shorter version in the Listening to All the Voices Videotape, 1994).

Forester, J. (2005). Irony and critical moments in negotiations: On humor and irony, recognition and hope. In J. Ulla & J. Woodilla (Eds.), *Organizations: Epistemological claims and supporting field stories*. Copenhagen: Copenhagen Business School Press.

Houston, J. (1982). *The possible human*. Los Angeles: Tarcher.

Houston, J. (1987). *The search for the beloved: Journeys in sacred psychology*. Los Angeles: Tarcher.

Sarkissian, W. (2005, March). Stories in a park: Giving voice to the voiceless in Eagleby, Australia (from an interview by John Forester). *Planning Theory and Practice, 6*(1), 103–117.

Sarkissian, W., Bunjamin-MauWwith Cook, A.,Walsh, K., & Vajda, S. (2009). *SpeakOut: A step-by-step guide to speakouts and community workshops*. London: Earthscan.

Sarkissian, W., Cross, A., & Dunstan, G. (1994). The conference of the birds: A role play within a workshop. In W. Sarkissian & K. Walsh (Eds.), *Community Participation in Practice: Casebook*. Perth: Murdoch University, Institute for Sustainability and Technology Policy.

Sarkissian, W., Hofer, N., Shore, Y., Vajda, S., & Wilkinson, C. (2008). *Kitchen table sustainability: Practical recipes for community engagement with sustainability*. London: Earthscan.

Sarkissian, W., Hurford, D., & Wenman, C. (2010). *Creative community engagement: Transformative engagement methods for working at the edge*. London: Earthscan.

Sarkissian, W., Dunstan, G., & Walsh, K. (1994b). "The Gods Must Be Crazy": A role play simulation within a Search conference. In W. Sarkissian & K. Walsh (Eds.), *Community participation in practice: Casebook*. Perth: Murdoch University, Institute for Sustainability and Technology Policy.

Sarkissian, W., & Walsh, K. (Eds.). (1994a). *Community participation in practice: Casebook*. Perth: Murdoch University, Institute for Sustainability and Technology Policy.

Sarkissian, W., Walsh, K. (Producers), Gherardi, J. (Director). (1994). *Community Participation in Practice: Listening to All the Voices*. 28-Minute Videotape. Murdoch University, Institute for Sustainability and Technology Policy, Perth.

Stewart, K. (1994). Speaking out for a suburban town centre: The salisbury experience. In W. Sarkissian & K. Walsh (Eds.), *Community participation in practice: Casebook*. Perth: Murdoch University, Institute for Sustainability and Technology Policy.

Williams, M. (1994). The foyer experience: Worker participation in the redevelopment of the state library of South Australia, Adelaide. In W. Sarkissian & K. Walsh (Eds.), *Community participation in practice: Casebook*. Perth: Murdoch University, Institute for Sustainability and Technology Policy.

Chapter 9
"La Campagna che si fa Metropoli": Film as Discovery

Leonardo Ciacci

"La campagna che si fa metropoli"[1] is a short film that was commissioned by the Italian Association of Planners (INU) to be screened during the 23rd INU conference and used in public meetings of planning technicians and researchers. Conceived and made in a couple of months in autumn 2000, its purpose was to visually describe the most significant of the local components that in the previous decade had changed the landscape of the Veneto region in north-east Italy. The description, however, had a dual aim: on the one hand to show how wrong it was to exclude town planners, who were considered relevant only to the debate on architecture, from the larger regional canvas; on the other, to shift current thinking on the future of the city and focus attention on the future importance of what was happening outside the city in its traditional sense.

The title originally chosen for the film, on the basis of these motivations, was "The country that becomes city", a title that immediately proved wrong. This was the first sign of the film's potential capacity for revealing a different, more complex and in many ways more surprising reality than that apparently known. The countryside was changing, but not to become a city, as had been the trend for well over a century of industrial society. The meaning and regional organisation of the countryside was actually changing from the inside, on the basis of a new process made evident by the adoption of new urban structures, but that, nevertheless, was confirming most of the old values and traditional settlement structures. Paradoxically, this process seemed destined to produce a reversal of the familiar understanding of urbanisation, a flow from countryside to city. The significance of the countryside's success, with its proposed new meanings of habitation, seemed directed toward the old urban areas, accentuating their limits as the now obsolete structures of post-industrial cities.

The preconceived desire to use the film to show the spreading[2] of the city toward the countryside then immediately appeared to be an unsuitable choice, influenced by American models noted since the 1950s, and it was natural to abandon it right

L. Ciacci (✉)
Department of Town Planning, University IUAV of Venice, Venice, Italy
e-mail: ciacci@iuav.it

L. Sandercock, G. Attili (eds.), *Multimedia Explorations in Urban Policy and Planning*, Urban and Landscape Perspectives 7, DOI 10.1007/978-90-481-3209-6_9,
© Springer Science+Business Media B.V. 2010

from the stage of organising the takes. The visits made to choose the situations and buildings to be filmed immediately showed the sense of familiarity with which the old and new inhabitants of the countryside seemed to have already accepted the most important innovations in their daily habits (for example long journeys by car to the various places of their daytime activities) and the ease with which all the generations seemed to have adopted new "urban habits" (for example, a Sunday stroll along the banks of the river, now seen as an urban park). This required a new consideration and guided the construction of a film that thus seemed more a suitable means of revealing than a technique for describing. "Revealing" in this case is meant as the action of constructing a story, that in establishing new connections between objects, sense and meanings, makes practices (individual projects) already under way comprehensible (revealing), but perceived individually and by fragments in their dimension of a diffuse system (collective project). So "revealing", in other words, over the course of the filmed representation, is the same as making explicit the implicit project that contains the diffuse practices in a given time and a geographically defined space, projecting them not onto their past, as a cognitive quantitative study would do, but onto the planning perspective of their possible future uses.

The Veneto countryside, despite the transformations made by importing elements and characteristics of urban life, such as the organisation of the 24-hours day, the planning of daily and periodic engagements, the specialisation of roles, the externalisation of services, individual isolation and the reduction of social rites, does not appear likely to become a city, not even in the ambiguous definition of a "sprawling city". Translated into the reality of daily actions, the new metropolitan organisation of the countryside is an endogenous product; it is an internal adaptation to a situation of new use, of a reality that remains in many ways close to tradition.

It is now well known how this came about: an entrepreneurial class of rural origin, capable of adroitly operating in its own sphere, within its own system of values and relationships and according to its own specific behavioural models, produced its own transformation from within. The move from cultural model of self-sufficiency to that of consumerism, now in its post-industrial stage, was as rapid as it was evolutionary, and without evident breaches. The family nuclei, remaining isolated, prolonged the traditional fragmentation of rural families, even though the adult members of these were now employed solely in the production of industrial goods and services. The social identity of the Veneto people was profoundly changed by this, as was the countryside, especially the more extensively inhabited parts. But despite what seems most obvious, the new model has confirmed the traditional settlement system. The overall structure that kept urban centres of different size and different regional role and the scattered settlement of the countryside together was reinforced; it is the old system of hierarchies that, faced with shopping centres, light industrial estates and places of entertainment, seems completely upset and stripped of meaning. In short, in the arc of a little less than 30 years the Veneto seems to have made the move from rural to post-industrial society, almost entirely avoiding the stage of urban concentration, both of industry and of population.

Fig. 9.1 Video stills from "La campagna che si fa metropoli" (Ciacci, 2000, 2005)

As will be guessed from reading these considerations, images had a considerable weight in this phenomenon and were often a driving force for change, through the spread of easily adopted commonplaces. In a spontaneously produced process of overlaying interests and practices, imitation becomes the most direct means of acquiring the tools made necessary by the speed of change. That which my neighbour, competing business or neighbouring administration does becomes the guide towards establishing customs that make the action of individuals fast and effective, without any specific planning process. Images fed the identity of this renewed Italian region that is now a synonym of a new "economic miracle". It is based on the unfettered spread of factories, light industrial estates, gaudy shopping centres, technological architecture for multi-screen cinema complexes (more than 12 screens operating at the same time), highly coloured venues for sport and entertainment, sometimes located in old industrial areas, carefully restored villas and historic buildings turned into service or research centres, old farm buildings converted into prestigious offices, primary industrialisation in which to concentrate related professional activities and, finally, parks created out of marginal areas no longer used for economic ends or transport, like river banks and areas less suited to farming.

There is a significant recurring aspect in the choice of locating the metropolitan apparatus that has changed the appearance of the Veneto countryside. The places initially chosen are capable of generating a local and urban feeling, but seem a long way from the desire to generate urbanisation as it was traditionally intended, in the form of the progressive, wildfire expansion of the city from the centre toward its outer border. Business activities favour rather the relationship with the road network and have given rise to islands of activity in which service, entertainment and new production activities were systematically added to the initial business functions. Families, on the contrary, at first favoured locations that allowed them to remain within known spatial confines, within which to reproduce family relations and the solidarity of the village street. Subsequently, they opted for new locations that seemed more knowingly conceived as imitations of "neighbourhood unity":

groups of small buildings sited around green areas that are nominally public but actually used as residents' areas. The preferred location for these new residences is in any case far from the city and mainly in villages and small communities scattered around the country. The high mobility that typifies the occupants' personal experience in Veneto, the need to rely on the family of origin for the care of the children, the need to keep the channel of established relations that ensure social participation, all impel families to see the house as the only fixed point. The car and mobile phone together allow all members of the family to organise the needs of daily life in circumstances in which distances and individual engagements would seem to have favoured the choice of relocating.

9.1 Different Realities Seen from Different Points of View

If one persists in observing what is outlined above with the aim of reaching a synthetic, rational description, it is unlikely that an explanation of how such a system operates will be achieved. An area like that described above is inevitably the result of a multiplicity of individual actions, not planned on the basis of a single rationale or a knowingly shared logic, nor of actions assessed in the light of the effects they produce overall within the socially shared space. Despite this, the combination of those actions has rapidly caused a profound reinterpretation of daily reality to the point of quickly becoming widespread, shared (albeit unconscious) custom. The success of many of the innovations introduced to the countryside has depended on their capacity to capture and reinvigorate the old customs of country life. Every small centre in the region keeps the tradition of the weekly market alive, even if diminished. Traditionally, families isolated in the country used the weekly appointment in town as an opportunity for shopping and also for seeing to administrative matters, doctor's visits and, in general, all that could be gained from both the concentration of services and urban functions and the meeting opportunities. The present shopping centres, though very different from the traditional places – a conglomeration of enclosed spaces, with no seasonal character, homogenised by the same invasive music – nevertheless propose a similar situation: along with the variety of retail offerings, they also contain various kinds of consultancies and services, constantly and easily accessible by car and adaptable to very different needs.

The rationale behind individual behaviours is difficult to relate to generalising syntheses. Their tracks may be followed by measuring the effects of behaviours by means of their success that seem repeated and preferred, but the thing that counts most is to take note of the fact that spontaneous individual practices can become a genuine way of knowing a region. A social system that quickly adopts innovative customs cannot count on the sharing of old codes of evaluation and parameters of judgement handed down by tradition. A language is nevertheless necessary for relationship exchanges; the success of some of the individually adopted practices ensures that these become the elements of a new collectively shared language and therefore also the parameters of shared evaluation. The car, along with the mobile phone, as mentioned above, changes the cost in time and money of daily commuting

Fig. 9.2 Video stills from "La campagna che si fa metropoli" (Ciacci, 2000, 2005)

from a negative condition of urban life to flexibility and strengthening of the individual capacity to be in different places, reached very quickly, in which to engage in different activities. The area in which this takes place loses its hierarchical rigidity and becomes a map on which to compose one's own personal menu. This very soon becomes an acquired, shared fact and does not involve or refer any longer to a personal, subjective judgement: the urbanised countryside takes on the form of a place without distances, whose points, though illogically far from one another, can all in the same way be easily reached.

9.2 From Local Phenomenon to Model

The plain, that of the Veneto primarily, and also those of Apulia and the central Adriatic coast, favours individual mobility over considerable distances in times compatible with the organisation of everyday activities. This overturns the more familiar trend for the residential growth of the main urban centres, those in which the system of social amenities has been concentrated over time, with schools, public offices and public transport networks. The explosion in property prices has further amplified an "anti-urban" migratory trend, already strong at the time the film was made. The average age of the people who migrate from the city to provincial towns and villages is shown by statistical surveys to be around 30 years; hence, the move presumably coincides with the formation of the family, the purchase of a house and the birth of children. According to Guido Martinotti,[3] one of the more meticulous urban sociologists, changes of residence in Italy are based on environmental conditions, but are particularly linked to the historic settlement characteristics of towns and traditional villages, which accept those flows with growing frequency. Torres (2004), the town planning scholar who has most often gone back to the nature of the Veneto urban dispersal, citing Hilman and Truppi (2004), summarises the reasons as the need to "... live in a place that is suited to your spirit and that ties you to it with duties and habits".

When observation is made of a "spontaneous" phenomenon, as the growth of residential and entrepreneurial settlement in central Veneto has certainly been, adopting a scientific approach to refer the empirical data to a "logical" model does not assist comprehension. The behaviour of individuals, on a par with that of the community, does not follow logical evaluations, if by logical we mean an analogous evaluation, proposed every time one is confronted with analogous conditions. Deep-rooted convictions and ancient behaviours are mixed with imported behaviours, generating practices and logics that are difficult to relate to knowingly rational schema. Flexibility – of work, production, family organisation and access to services – is undoubtedly the main reason for the success of this spontaneous model. However, the "opportunist" nature of the "exploitation" of already available resources is equally indubitable. The rhetorical image that best expresses the sum of "these flexibilities and these exploitations" is that which "tells" of the gradual erosion of the rural spaces and discloses its economic and cultural seriousness. The loss of the traditional landscape's historic identity, and the growing congestion of a region whose ability to function seems destined to rapid collapse, is recurrently and commonly associated with the constant removal of areas of rural cultivation and organisation. Nevertheless, this conviction, experienced as a genuine emergency, is not met by an equally mature and heartfelt need for control, for the adoption of a practice of strategic planning that is able to mobilise and guide actions.

Fig. 9.3 Video stills from "La campagna che si fa metropoli" (Ciacci, 2000, 2005)

9.3 The Film and Its Ability to Interpret

The film, as noted, was intended for screening in Naples (which it was), during the days of the main meeting held in Italy every 4 years of town planners belonging to the INU (Istituto Nazionale di Urbanistica), to shift technicians' attention onto these contradictions, indicating subjects considered of little importance by a discipline too greatly influenced by the administrative aspects of the town plan, while paying little attention to the physical, visible aspects of the new regional infrastructure. The "objects" to be shown were known and easily identifiable; it was a question of connecting them in a narrative order that was not didactic or tediously educational. The only representational choice that did not change during the making of the film right from the start was the idea that the sections of the film showing places of work, residence, services and leisure would be interspersed with the repeated refrain of a blurred image of the side of the road seen from a moving car that would give the idea of continuous movement and of the traveller's indifference to the places passed by. We thought this could be done by accelerating the images of the takes from the car window, using a wide-angle lens, capable of blurring the close-up shots, and alternating these with rapid sharp images when the roadside opened up to the country behind. The initial idea (which remained in the final version of the film) was to illustrate the isolation and distance of the new places shown. From one move to another, between "geographical islands", the new buildings in the countryside would be seen in all their extraneous newness, paradoxically capable of establishing a new, yet already established landscape. Both representational choices were influenced by the chosen language. The move from one place to another, if resolved objectively, was cinematographically unsustainable, given the length of the journeys, during which the spectator would be lost looking for something in the images that could not actually be found: 5 minutes of driving is no more than five boring minutes of driving. In the same way, the places chosen to represent a local structure that should have been perceived as integrated, starting from the quality of their architectural appearance, were at times located in geographical areas too far from one another to be shown in an "objective" narrative way. So it was necessary to give the idea of a unity of space and time with the images, basing this not on the reality of the places but on the significant coincidence of the practices: every time someone individually gets into his car to reach different, separated places, he repeats the same banal, indifferent, subjective operation, but in doing so he produces a system of values and choices with a high transformational impact on the "inhabited" places.

Only at an advanced stage of the work was a proper screenplay built up to tie the different places and themes together into a single day of a family presented as an average family; this was then definitively adopted as a narrative strategy during editing. The dialogues with which the two characters – two professionals, mother and father – communicate their movements to each other, coming to different agreements over the course of the day with regard to their working conditions, the management of their children or entertainment activities, were only added after editing, simulating repeated phone calls from mobile to mobile. This way of organising the day, now ubiquitous but then already widespread, was added to the film only for narrative purposes. Only later, when viewing the film, did it prove to be a discovery that was almost the desired result of a conscious thought. The same may be said of the sound track that accompanies the car journeys in the film. During filming, with a video camera (a Sony Betacam) held outside on the roof of the car, the car radio had been left on. When the film was edited, the voice and music seemed a natural choice that was perfect for emphasising the long time spent in the car.

Similar anecdotes could be added, but without adding much to what is now obvious: in making a film, a narrative is established to represent places objectively separated from one another and you end up discovering that precisely this makes them appear as factors or guiding elements in the organisation of an average family's day, spontaneously and solidly constructed on the basis of the opportunities offered by the organisation of the inhabited space. In its radical visual simplification in sequences of the daily behaviours of individuals and families, the film proved capable of presenting a new scenario and providing a vital interpretation of that scenario, showing a complex, not ritual, not only negative picture of a model of regional change in its formative stage through the account of individual actions. What the film showed was already there for everyone to see, but no one seemed to have perceived it as a system, as an already widespread practice: condemned in words as regressive, adopted in daily practice as advantageous.

This point is worth clarifying. A good measure of cultural perversity seems necessary to condemn practices with effects such as the waste of precious agricultural land, housing dispersal, landscape deterioration, traffic congestion, environmental pollution, waste of resources, deviant behaviours, poor social integration, etc., and at the same time individually make all those choices that together inevitably produce these effects: favouring the isolation of the individual house, spending a significant portion of one's income on the car, compelling young people to earn an income as soon as possible (to the detriment of investment in education) and seeking identity values in the nostalgic glorification of the past, with the result of distancing reality from its perception rather than obtaining awareness of one's own social role. In reality, the adoption of this double standard – negative judgement of the collective action, justified individual action – corresponds to the desire to reject the idea that any form of planning and restriction of individual action is necessary. The apparent (or short term) success of flexibility seems to have made the value of the individual action unquestionable and the logic of contrast between this and a not easily measurable "collective interest" unacceptable. The numerous times the two versions of the film[4] have been screened in various places, years apart, have shown that one of its purposes finds increasingly positive confirmation: the precise conviction that by showing the audience themselves, as if in a mirror, it would be possible to obtain their knowing recognition of their own personal contribution to the transformation of the inhabited environment, and an equally knowing acceptance of the idea that an implicit plan must necessarily be followed by an explicit one. A guide to individual actions is made necessary both in view of the reinforcement of their individual effect and as a defence against practices that together produce a negative outcome both on the social level and on the individual one, above all, traffic.

The language of film, which can be generalised, simplified, evocative and emotive, rather than didactic, is perhaps the most effective way to obtain the necessary result of awareness. When the film was first made, in 2000, only a 100 copies were produced and distributed after the screening at the INU conference. In 2004, the administrative planning office of the regional government of the Veneto commissioned a new edition of the film, with a new introduction, with the intention of distributing the film among local politicians and the general public. This time, 5,000 DVD copies were made, a statement in itself of the perceived communicative power of the film, in the eyes of the regional government.

9.4 Images and Communication

The filmed representation of actions and, especially, the circulation of those images that, once transferred onto DVD, can be seen again and again on different occasions and in different ways, allows the construction of shared "visual" scenarios within which individual stories, partial individual interests (interpretations perceived as individual) find their necessary composition at the start of planning actions. The non-demonised depiction of individual actions ends up showing the inevitable conflicts between different though equally legitimate interests. Recognition of the cumulative effect of individual actions can produce an opening in the usual reserve with which it is thought that ostensibly private decisions must be handled. Clarification of the inconsistency between declarations and actions may finally induce different relationships between institutions and the public. All this depends on a new attitude being adopted by the public administration and its technicians who interpret the conditions and tools for the planning of regional controls. Representation/communication of the directions (institutional or spontaneous, public or private) of regional change must be given the necessary statutory power as a tool to be added to the traditional ones of planning and town planning.

This experiment in capturing on film an apparently spontaneous regional change process that is producing harmful consequences suggests that there is considerable potential for using film to generate from the beginning of such processes a better understanding and public dialogue in situations where individual and collective interests appear to be in conflict. The inclusion of *La campagna che si fa metropoli* in the preparatory programme of the Piano Territoriale Regionale di Coordinamento della Regione del Veneto (Veneto Regional Coordination Plan), in 2004, 4 years after it was made, shows that the time is ripe. It is time to film a new version of *La campagna che si fa metropoli*.

Notes

1. "The countryside that becomes metropolis".
2. The definition of the "widespread city" is usually traced back to the book by Indovina (ed) (1990), La città diffusa. Daest, Venice.
3. See *Il Corriere della Sera-Lombardia* of 31 October 2005.
4. The video was produced in VHS in 2000 by INU (Istituto Nazionale di Urbanistica) and by Università IUAV di Venezia. Its first public projection was 30 November 2000, during the XXIII INU Congress. In 2005, it was republished in DVD as contribution to the PTRC (Piano Territoriale Regionale di Coordinamento) of the Regione del Veneto. It is now presented in http://www.planum.net/archive/movies-08.htm.

References

Ciacci, L. (2000). *La campagna che si fa metropoli* film-vhs produced by Istituto Nazionale di Urbanistica and Istituto Universitario Architettura di Venezia.

Ciacci, L. (2005). *La campagna che si fa metropoli. La trasformazione del territorio veneto* (DVD + book) with texts by R. Toffano, C. Magnani, L. Ciacci, B. Dolcetta, P.L. Crosta, & G. Caudo. Venezia: Regione del Veneto.

Hilman, J., & Truppi, C. (2004). *L'anima dei luoghi. Conversazione con Carlo Truppi.* Milano: Rizzoli.

Indovina, F. (Ed). (1990) *La città diffusa.* Venezia: Daest.

Torres, M. (2004). *Nuovi modelli di città. Agglomerazioni, infrastrutture, luoghi centrali e pinificazione urbanistica.* Milano: Franco Angeli.

Chapter 10
Representations of an Unsettled City: Hypermedial Landscapes in Rome

Giovanni Attili

10.1 Un-settling the Scene

Globalisation represents the empirical condition of the contemporary world, probably the most meaningful sign of an epoch facing a deep transition phase: it is a condition of complex connectivity, which is characterised by an intensification of interconnections and of global interdependence (Tomlinson, 1999). The increasing migratory phenomena are surely one of the most visible aspects of this new post-modern condition: these phenomena are significantly changing places, experiences, our way of being in the world. Western societies are intersected by the presence of ethnic subjectivities and are becoming more and more fragmented and complex. Cities are changing into a mixture of differences, contradictions and conflicts. The multiplication of spatial signification processes, the new temporariness of individual lives, the new way of living and interacting with the territory, testify to a deep change.

The Esquilino district, situated on the edge of the historical city centre and near the Termini railway station, is widely recognized as the most culturally diverse area of Rome. In recent years, it has been increasingly characterised by a complex stratification of cultural, religious, linguistic and ethnic minorities, levels of income, life styles and knowledges.

The district is characterised by a significant presence of immigrants (newcomers who plan to permanently settle down in this part of the city) and transitory migrants: people who don't intend to settle and who live in the neighbourhood on a temporary basis.

The research I developed focuses its attention on these transitory migrants who have progressively transformed the Esquilino into a "caravanserai": a place where emigrants stop before heading somewhere else; the crossroads of different migratory

G. Attili (✉)
Dipartimento di Architettura e Urbanistica per l'Ingegneria, Università "La Sapienza" di Roma, Roma, Italy
e-mail: giovanni.attili@gmail.com

L. Sandercock, G. Attili (eds.), *Multimedia Explorations in Urban Policy and Planning*, Urban and Landscape Perspectives 7, DOI 10.1007/978-90-481-3209-6_10,
© Springer Science+Business Media B.V. 2010

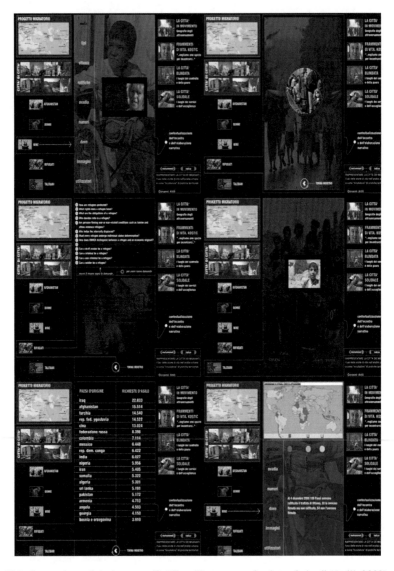

Fig. 10.1 Screenshots of the hypermedia "Esquilino: space of points of view" (Attili, 2003)

projects, people and life stories; the crucial junction of an intricate nomadic geography that connects diverse places and spatial scales; the stratification of various "circulatory territories" produced by the collective memory and the social exchange practices of migrant populations (Tarrius, 1992).

This threshold area and its nomadic inhabitants transgress what Callari Galli, Ceruti, and Pievani (1998) call "the metaphysics of sedentariness": the conviction and the prejudice of considering being settled as the living condition which

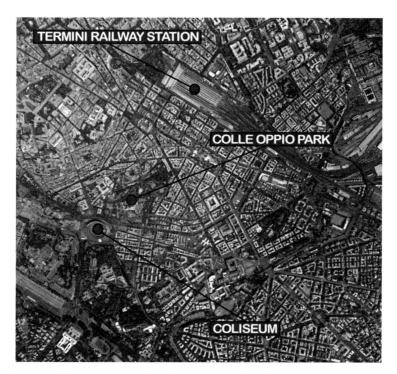

Fig. 10.2   Aerial Photo of the Esquilino Neighbourhood. Graphic elaboration on aerial photo by Giovanni Attili

is universally accepted and desired by mankind. The fluid subjectivities who live across the Esquilino district are testament to a different way of inhabiting the city, which cannot be confined to the ownership of a house. These populations live in the city in temporary ways through relational processes which are characterised by multi-belongings to different places, by a complex relationship with the environment they temporarily live in, by nomadic rhythms made of movements and pauses. It is a way of living the existential oxymoron of a dynamic rootedness. With regard to this, Maffesoli (2000) suggests the powerful image of a "hermetic" inhabiting process, evoking the iconographical representation of the god Hermes: a winged foot which recalls the movement of one who skims over the ground without adhering to it.

The residential settlement explodes into a plurality of temporarily occupied spaces: a multiplication of living flows which reinvent the concept of urbanity. If it is true that cities change with their inhabitants even if their walls remain the same, the contemporary multiplicity recalls a different interpretation of the relationship between people and territory: a relationship which is no longer linear or natural (a specific community "naturally" linked to a specific space) rather it is unstable, diachronic, intermittent and able to produce always changing identities.

10.2 Representing Transient Humanities

This fluctuating world crossed by a kaleidoscope of individuals in transit is not traditionally considered in the urban planning field: our discipline has always focused its attention on permanencies, persistency and fixity of contexts, adopting representational languages that are not able to get in touch with these pulsating cityscapes. Urban planning, in fact, has always described the city through zenithal

Fig. 10.3 Migrants in Colle Oppio Park. Photos by Giovanni Attili

and panoptical visions, which freeze urban flows and movements into abstract cartographies. This is a kind of description which has always privileged the physical space of the city, not considering that the morphological structure of the city is the product of circumstances, social relations, paths and conflicts. Not considering that urban space is a complex superimposition of physical and social dimensions which are deeply interpenetrated.

> Like someone from a plane looking at the sea foam and seeing it motionless, without understanding that close up it is instinct and movement, the modern planner doesn't realise that behind the silence of forms blows the burst of life (Merleau Ponty cit. in Decandia, 2001, p. 39)

He doesn't realise that the morphological urban structure is the expression of a relational space, of a *relative* territory (Maffesoli, 2000) which means nothing in itself but only if it creates relations. The heterogeneous space in which we live is not only buildings: it is made of internal moving densities and relational networks which require more sensitive analytical tools. It is necessary to build representational devices that are capable of accounting for individual existences and collective memories; naming differences, fathoming rooted and transient relationships, mapping mental spaces, feelings and expectations; and connecting local and global networks.

The study of the Esquilino district, with its plurality of populations in transit, was an occasion to experiment with such an analytical path. It suggested taking an upside-down perspective that would build a complex urban portrait of its changing inhabitants, especially those who are traditionally invisible and silenced. The goal was primarily to get in touch with those human beings who, for too long, have been invisible in modern urban planning representations. To abandon a bird's eye view perspective. To leave that isolated perspective at the top of a tower from where we mistakenly believed that we had an all-embracing view of the city. To go beyond plans, cartographies, pre-codified maps and comfortable old analytical containers. To immerse ourselves, as much as possible, in the living body of the city, through the rich texture of sensemaking processes, lives and stories.

10.3 Biographical Mapping

I chose to adopt a primarily biographical approach to get in touch with the variety and the uniqueness of stories that significantly marked the area I was about to study.[1] To undertake this path was not easy. It required the effort of meeting the "other" and the "unexpected". In depth. It implied listening capability and interpretative skills. It asked for an *empathetic distance*. Haraway (1995) would call it a *passionate detachment*, that is the ability of establishing a deep and close relationship with the interviewee and, at the same time, the capacity of putting a distance which allows a self-reflection on the dialogical process, the role we play in it, the context which shapes it, the non-verbal communication, the implicitness and the ethical traps.

The biographical approach requires both rigour and reflexivity to overcome the limits of a possible superficial use (Attili, 2008). It is a complex approach which is basically rooted in two hermeneutical activities: the first is the one performed by the interviewee who tells his own story, making sense of his life; the second one is the interpretive activity of the researcher who tries to make sense of the sense-making process of the interviewee. As a result, collecting and interpreting a life story is quite a complex activity but it has great potential in representing a city crossed and lived by a myriad of irreducible inhabitants.

Life stories pluralise urban horizons that are imbued with subjectivity. This approach was particularly significant in addressing the study of the Esquilino district. In this case it was necessary to deconstruct the abstract idea of "immigration": a dangerous and homogenising analytical container which doesn't account for differences. Urban planning needs to transgress the obsolescence of certain analytical approaches. The increased variability and complexity of emerging problematic figures characterised by uncertain and temporary connotations doesn't find a proper setting in traditional morphological urban planning schemes.

Sensitive policies can be built only through the recognition of innumerable differentiations: origins, models, migratory routes, stories, expectations, hopes and needs. From this perspective, life stories are potentially able to offer a thicker and more articulated knowledge of these phenomena. The abstract "immigrant" category is not able to capture a plurality of original and singular subjectivities who produce transversal and unforeseeable requests, who have different territorial appropriation rhythms and embody irreducible life projects.

Moreover, life stories have the potentiality to make the invisible visible: they give legitimacy to people who otherwise are condemned to invisibility. Nancy (1992, p. 172) argues that the undisplayable is the nonexistent. "To exist means to expose oneself in a plural scene where everybody shows his uniqueness [. . .]. To appear is the only principle of reality" (Cavarero, 1997, pp. 32–33). Life stories show subjectivities, memories, projects and meanings. Life stories allow people to appear and therefore to exist in a public scene. Arendt defines *politics* as this scene where people actively show themselves. "The active process of revealing oneself to others, with acts and words, offers a plural space and therefore a political space to identity, confirming its exhibitive, relational and contextual nature" (Cavarero, 1997, pp. 33–34). From this point of view, the life story analytical approach I chose for this study is a political act in itself: the attempt to give visibility to invisible migrants who temporarily live in the city and the promotion of the resources and capabilities of people who can envisage themselves as individuals engaged in a meaningful project, the project of their lives.

Finally, the biographical approach constitutes a form of *ordinary knowledge*: a knowledge which is produced through the interaction of diverse people. It springs from the occasion of a narration. It transgresses academic, pseudo-scientific or pre-codified languages, rooting itself in people's everyday life. Everyone has a story to tell. This means that *ordinary knowledge* is a form of diffused awareness, part of everyone's experience. It is contextualised because it is built here and now in the course of a specific interaction between embodied, gendered and cultured subjects.

Fig. 10.4 Migrants in Colle Oppio Park. Photos by Giovanni Attili

It is produced in a more responsive way because it doesn't rely on the supposed objectivity of scientific knowledges. It is more complex because it intertwines
different cognitive approaches and rationalities. "The technical path to follow
is approximately to take back scientific languages and practices to their origin:
the everyday life. This return, nowadays more and more insistent, is paradoxical

Fig. 10.5 Migrants in Colle Oppio Park. Photos by Giovanni Attili

because it implies an exile from the disciplines whose rigour is measured by the definition of their limits" (de Certeau, 2001).

The biographical approach doesn't seem to be part of the analytical tools of the urban planning discipline. It evolved in the anthropological and sociological fields. But if we carefully look back at some historical experiences which took place in the 1950s (around the "community movement" in Italy, for example),[2] we can find some interesting experiments which tried to create horizontal connections among different knowledges. The goal was to give voice to a plurality of human beings and to transform them into the creators of their own environment. It was necessary to focus on the social nucleus of the territory, connecting *urbs* and *civitas*.

According to this conviction, planners adopted more sophisticated analytical lenses which were able to catch the specific connotations of the local communities: they involved geographers, sociologists, anthropologists and social psychologists, creating interdisciplinary groups working and exchanging skills and capabilities. In that historical period, qualitative approaches were deeply integrated in the analysis/planning of territories. Later, our discipline progressively chose to abandon those methods in favour of more quantitative approaches made of numbers, weights, matrixes, classifications, measures and objective cartographies. Today, it is time to bring qualitative inquires up to date, especially if what we are researching requires new tools that can capture and give expression to the human worlds which pulsate in our cities.

Bourdieu (1994) argues that disciplines are not natural, rather they are historical products which are characterised by acts of institutionalization. In this historical path, disciplines leave other possibilities of knowledge articulation unexplored. Maybe it is time to go back to those crossroads and set out on uncontemplated paths.

10.4 Space of Points of View

The analytical approach previously outlined was the main tool through which the exploration of the Esquilino district took place. It implied the effort to immerse myself in the stories of the people I met. A world of different stories. Different points of view. If it is true that cities are crossed by multitudes of urban subjectivities, it is necessary to account for their different representations. The creation of a space of points of view where diverse perspectives are juxtaposed and overlapped is the analytical vehicle through which it is possible to make sense of the complex urbanity we live in: a cosmopolis (Sandercock, 1998) made of men and women who interact and compare their own worlds; a mongrel city (Sandercock, 2003) made of conflicting aspirations, changing stories and insurgent perspectives. Life stories, and their capability of pluralising the world, helped me in accomplishing this task. Points of view are not disjointed nomads. Rather they are connected and need to be examined in relation to the diversity that springs from a comparison of non-homogeneous visions of reality. Bourdieu would say that:

> in order to understand what happens in places like cities and *grands ensembles* that bring people together, forcing them to live together, both in ignorance or in mutual incomprehension, both in latent or declared conflict, with all the suffering that arises from it, it is not enough to separately consider each point of view. These points of view also need to be compared as they are in reality, not to make them look relative, letting the game of intersected images play *ad infinitum* but, on the contrary, to reveal, through the simple effect of juxtaposition, whatever comes from the clash of different and antagonistic visions of the world, or rather, in certain cases, the tragedy that comes from the clash of incompatible points of view: a clash without concessions or compromises because each point of view is equally rooted to social reasons (Bourdieu, 1993, p. 13)

What I tried to accomplish is a multi-focal vision of the neighbourhood, capturing the sum of relationships that embrace public and private life, institutional and everyday life, the stories of individuals as well as of collective experiences. To create a space of multiple points of view means to widen the spectrum of the voices involved and to reveal the fragility of the traditional descriptive structure, which is severely prescriptive, falsely homogenous, compact and *true*. What needs to be methodologically introduced in the analysis of the city is the *epochè*: a suspension of judgement, embedded in Husserl's thought, through which it is possible to introduce doubts and destabilise prejudices and universalisms. When we start raising doubts about what we believe, when we open ourselves to other points of view, trying to understand the social reasons which sustain them, we don't risk falling into a relativism. Rather we put ourselves in the position of renegotiating our point of view. We put ourselves in a learning process which is nurtured by the possibility of listening to other perspectives.

In the Esquilino case, an operation of this type was sustained even, and above all, by the attempt of granting visibility to those eloquent, yet invisible, figures that can tell us something about the new territorialisation-de/territorialisation processes that characterise the contemporary city (Tarrius, 1992). Their conflicting relationships (sometimes latent sometimes explicit) with the historical inhabitants of the neighbourhood give rise to new questions, with the awareness that new questions are always the first step for responding to problems in new ways (Melucci, 2000). The result of all of this is "perhaps the same as Brechtian alienation, namely managing to see something that has become too familiar with new eyes, and in this case, the city itself" (Pala, 2000, p. 87).

10.5 Deconstructing Pre-constituted Images: Medea

The Medea narrated by Wolf (1996) is a significant example of how a pluri-vocal portrait has the capacity to deconstruct/reconstruct consolidated images. Medea is a myth: she is the woman who murdered her own son. Christa Wolf is not happy with this depiction. In her book she juxtaposes the voices of six characters: a narrative structure which reveals the difficulty for a discursive rationality to move across different conceptions of the world. Only a multiplication of the gazes succeeds in portraying a dense image of Medea. It is a vision that undermines the myth itself in favour of a more articulated image: the image of a strong and generous woman who is a repository of an archaic knowledge. A woman who is violently marginalised by an intolerant society and who ends up in killing her son. Only the intersection of those voices helps to go beyond what has been already told about Medea. To go beyond that prison where the myth confined her. Christa Wolf talks about misunderstanding. We misunderstood Medea. The only path we can follow is listening to other voices. And *voices* is the subtitle of the same novel.

Like Medea, the Esquilino district had to be investigated according to a plurality of superimposed and conflicting voices. It was necessary to hear the crash of pre-constituted images collapsing. It was crucial to escape those closed and auto-referential representational systems in which the right to speak becomes an exclusionary weapon. Voices are sense-making perspectives which cannot be reduced to just one vision. They portray the ambiguousness of the city: a space which condenses a *pluriverse* of meanings; a space which is constantly changing according to its different inhabitants. It is time to abandon the obsolescence of solipsistic and zenithal representations elaborated by a restricted group of experts, in favour of a real and constructive interaction with the variety of worlds and representations that inhabits the city.

The process of truly listening to voices allows us to avoid the prejudice of one who thinks she/he has understood the other before having met him/her. The prejudice is the short cut that anticipates the encounter. The short cuts are easy to undertake. But the result is catastrophic and mutilating. To express a plurality of points of view is not an obstacle to comprehension, rather it constitutes a richness to work with, favouring sustainable learning processes and a complex knowledge to be used as a guide to actions.

In the Esquilino district different perspectives were gathered: the voices of many migrants living and sleeping in the Colle Oppio Park, with their embodied stories; the mixed perceptions of different historical residents facing these unpredictable flows of migrants and their changing worlds; the diverse attitudes of the old settled

Fig. 10.6 Migrants in Colle Oppio Park. Photos by Giovanni Attili

immigrants; the initiatives of some policy-makers trying to deal with security issues in the district; the positions of several representatives of neighbourhood committees, churches and groups of people working in solidarity associations. The image that comes out of the juxtaposition of these diverse voices and opinions delineates a controversial neighbourhood.

An urban space crossed by diversified subjectivities in transit which recalls: racist attitudes in some historical residents and in some old settled immigrants; populist security policies especially during electoral periods; tacit agreements between local institutions and clandestine migrants about their temporary location/presence in the neighbourhood; and even compassion and understanding in a wide range of people of diverse social and working backgrounds. What seems to be interesting is the quite transversal and common perception that there is something in the neighbourhood which is problematic and is not addressed with adequate initiatives and policies. A well-defined geography of power is the frame in which these diverse voices ask to be listened to and somehow, in some cases, offer synergistic visions for possible actions. This is the reason why the construction of a space of points of view is strategic, in planning terms. Because it depicts a diffused knowledge (shared but sometimes significantly conflicted) and guides possible initiatives which can be built in more sensitive ways through the deep interaction with the diverse people living through and working in the neighbourhood.

10.6 A Narrative Hypermedial Structure

All the voices, biographies and fragments of life stories I gathered during my immersion in the neighbourhood needed to be expressed in significant ways. What kind of representation could I build in order to emphasise the potentiality of the chosen analytical approach?

Narration seemed to be the most appropriate response. Traditional urban planning representations have always played on the description of single, isolated and uncommunicating parts of the territorial system (thematic maps, classifications, layers). They were not capable of reconnecting them, in the desperate attempt to sum up self-referenced components sets. Compared to this additive representational approach, narrations appeared to be a valid alternative. In actual fact, narratives have the potentiality to respond "concisely" and directly to complexity, overcoming the simple summary of descriptive, piecemeal information. Narratives have the ability to circumscribe without closing off or labelling, creating a space open to interpretations, imaginaries, comparisons and possibilities. "Narrative as space that contains and opens up at the same time, as spoken word and as a sensemaking intention that is never completely settled, seems to be a response to the difficult task of holding together the multiplicity and incompleteness of the contemporary I" (Melucci, 2000, pp. 112–113). When it is not limited to being presented as private experience, but as "a public space where the differences of the words may be contained and heard without violence" (Melucci, 2000, p. 118), it offers the possibility of constructing a representational structure based on points of view, stories open to discussion and to planning.

Therefore, narratives. But again I was looking for something more expressive, interactive and potentially interconnected than the simple text form. Digital languages and their potentiality in creating an interactive and expressive space of points of view represented the route to follow. The idea was to create a hypermedia which was able to juxtapose those different voices and perspectives in a way that each user could be able to see and explore their connections.

The hypermedia is an interactive device that multiplies the communicative potentialities of a hypertext. In this tool, textual language is substituted for, integrated with and expanded by a variety of other languages and expressive codes: texts, films, graphic animations, numbers, sounds, photographs.

The mingling of these various languages is potentially able to account for the complexity of our cities where the centrality of private memories, the emotional dimensions, the meshing of crossed spaces and lived times require a plurality of representational grammars.

The hypermedia transgresses narrative linearity, creating interactive spaces and multiple access possibilities: these are instruments which grant the user flexible manoeuvring spaces; the user is thus transformed into an explorer, a navigator who can choose, in each instant, the route to follow. In other words, the open structure of the hypermedia creates a sensemaking field that is qualitatively superior to a printed book because the user has to perform an active role, making decisions, choosing paths, associating diverse informational sources.

Fig. 10.7 Screenshot of the hypermedia "Esquilino: space of points of view" (Attili, 2003)

The interactivity is the means through which a message becomes bi-directional, allowing the intervention of the user in the communication. In the non-interactive media, the only possible intervention of the user is to interrupt the communication: cinema is not interactive; television is not interactive because changing channels is more the interruption of a contact than a real intervention in the message.

Interactivity is peculiar to computer-based communications. Hypermedia is intrinsically interactive because it invites the user to weave paths and nodes, to surf through different representational layers, to rearrange knowledges and visions. In the hypermedia I created for the research project, the user can explore branched analytical channels according to his or her own cognitive intentionality: she/he can build his/her own images and representations of the neighbourhood, selecting mosaic pieces, embracing specific inquiries and narratives.

Through the life stories of some migrants and the connected further interactive sections, the potential user can have access to multiple readings of the city, listening to different voices and intercepting a variety of images and perspectives. He can potentially connect a desperate sea voyage from Turkey to the conditions of women

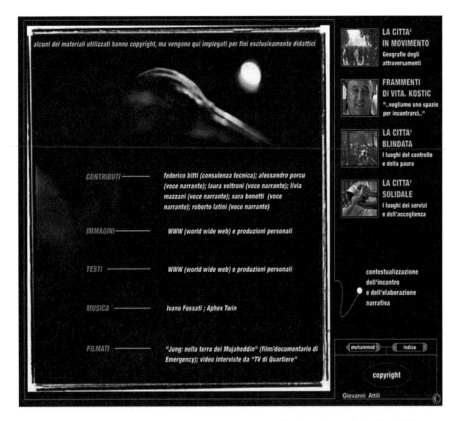

Fig. 10.8 Screenshot of the hypermedia "Esquilino: space of points of view" (Attili, 2003)

in Afghanistan, to the story of a child in wartime, to the racist attitudes of old historical residents of the Esquilino district, to the analysis of some Italian security policies, to the description of geographies of movements and so on. He can create connections and build sensemaking associative processes.

Hypermedia has the potentiality to be configured as an *eclectic atlas*: urban accounts that are able to create a space of points of view, connecting physical and mental spaces, inquiring into forms of spatialities embedded in relational networks. These multiform atlases produce maps with multiple accesses and multidimensional configurations which assemble different representational perspectives: qualitative and quantitative, top-down and bottom-up. In order to reach this goal it is necessary to abandon the utopian belief of a privileged and comfortable observational point of view: *to see more it is better to see small*. It is necessary to adopt a versatile and mobile point of view that is able to redefine itself according to the specificity of the observed object. It is a point of view that is always able to trace and capture meaningful sense signs in the urban world: signs which move across space and society, following principles that are not the ones of the geometrical bi-dimensionality.

The hypermedia "Esquilino: space of points of view" tried to perform this analytical approach drawing different geographies of the district: bottom-up geographies built from the perspective of those who live the contradictions of the contemporary city; pulsating geographies which transgress the functional notion of space in favour of a spatial image crossed by relational networks; strategic geographies that are able to build new images suggesting possible urban changes; plural geographies which are developed through a wide range of diversified idioms and different points of view; distorted geographies that are partial, subjective and far removed from any neutral or objective representational claim.

10.7 Mohammed

The structure of the hypermedia is rooted in the story of Mohammed, an Afghan migrant who chose the Colle Oppio Park as his temporary space to live. In the central part of the screen we can see a film of Mohammed during his interview: a long dialogical interactive process that took months to be accomplished. In this film clip, Mohammed speaks. In the background, we can see the park where he slept, the courtyard of a church where the police forced him to move, the Roman ruins where he occasionally had to sleep, the streets of the neighbourhood where he lived. His eyes tell the story even before he utters a word. The kinetic and paralinguistic code of his facial expression and his gestures offer a non-verbal communication that goes beyond mere words.

A voice-over condenses the story he has been telling me. The voice is a re-elaboration of his life fragments I've been collecting during our long interaction. It is the I-narrator but it is not his original voice. The problematic choice of substituting his own voice for that of an Italian actor had three main reasons: to be easily understood by an Italian audience; to assemble together life and story pieces which were collected in too many fragmented occasions; and to emphasise the communicative dimension of the story itself rather than its literal accuracy.

Mohammed talks about his migratory project, about the reasons that have led him to leave his homeland, the exhausting and seemingly never-ending trip that brought him to Italy, the incurable wounds of loss and abandonment that fill his thoughts daily, the alienating conditions of survival in which he is forced to live and the way in which he inhabits the spaces of the area where he has found himself in transit. It is a highly charged story, an anthology of significant intensity that is represented by more than the film clips and the voice narrating it.

Further expressive codes were contextually used on the screen, during the development of the story itself. As in the case when Mohammed recounts the conditions of his family living in Afghanistan, the wars and his sisters' suffering. To support and expressively enrich this part of the narrative, some drawings of Afghan children, some expressive images of the Afghan-Russia war and its devastation, diverse pictures of the Taliban regime and several film clips portraying the conditions of Afghani women appear on some other parts of the screen. And again when Mohammed dwells on the trips he made, a map in motion appears with his migratory route. This route is traced in real time, synchronised with the progressive story of that difficult journey and the description of main cities and places he passed through. The images of these cities/places are portrayed one attached to the other, building a sort of continuous mental map that connects the place of origin to the temporary destination – Kabul to Rome, city to city.

Or again when Mohammed speaks about the places in the Esquilino where he lives, the problems and the relationships he has with the institutions, the other migrant groups and the permanent residents of the area, some other images and

Fig. 10.9 Screenshots of the hypermedia "Esquilino: space of points of view" (Attili, 2003)

Fig. 10.10 Screenshots of the hypermedia "Esquilino: space of points of view" (Attili, 2003)

film clips appear: other foreigners with whom he shares the space in the park where he is forced to sleep at night; the geography of movements he has to make due to police harassment; maps of the city are sketched out when such movements are narrated. And so on, filling the screen with further representational elements. All of this happens while the main interview film clip and the voice-over continue to recall Mohammed's life story. At the same time, the written transcription of the story progressively appears, as the voice-over goes on, on the part of the screen surrounding the film clip. A white text on a black screen. But the transcription is not neutral.

Some of the text's words accompanying the film suddenly change colour, emerge and become detached from the background. Some yellow and bold-type keywords. They are graphically emphasised. The attention of the user is driven towards them. These words recall some dimensions I consider to be crucial in the analysis of Mohammed's life story. But it's my intervention: the partiality and the subjectivity I put into the construction of the representation. I chose some words, not others. I chose to underline some aspects, not others. As these keywords become underlined and emphasised on the screen, some interactive buttons appear. These buttons are connected to the concepts expressed in those words now modified. The progressive emerging of those buttons creates an interactive multi-dimensional menu, whose access allows the user to immerse himself/herself in further representational levels that were recalled by Mohammed's words.

These further accessible dimensions of the hypermedia, the interactive buttons that appear as Mohammed's story goes on, are divided into two sub-menus. The first, on the left side of the screen, is connected to his origins and to the reasons why he had to leave Afghanistan. The second refers to the Esquilino district and to the ways it is experienced by Mohammed: his perceptions, his sensemaking process,

Fig. 10.11 Screenshots of the hypermedia "Esquilino: space of points of view" (Attili, 2003)

his territorial appropriation. His life story bridges these two menu-dimensions: his homeland and the temporary space in which he lives, Kabul and Rome.

The interactive sections that characterise this first sub-menu are "Afghanistan", "Women", "Mines", "Refugees" and "Taliban". Each of these sections can be further explored. The hypermedia provides the possibility of an indefinite number of ramifications. In our case each interactive button allows the user to surf through diverse representational layers that portray the geographical, social and cultural background of Mohammed. In order to depict this, many coexisting expressive languages have been used: statistical data offering a quantitative image of the Afghan country (population, ethnic groups, area, cities, etc.); a voice-over and diverse pictures that tell the story of Afghanistan; historical images which portray the Soviet invasion; schemes, maps and photos of the main cities, with particular attention to Kabul; a voice-over, a text and historical images taken from the notebook of Bruce Chatwin; voice-overs, texts, documentary pieces, film clips and performed poems that narrate all the prohibitions imposed on women, their fears, the suicide plague, the widows' life conditions; a film clip taken from a documentary, a filmed theatre piece, statistics, images and maps which recount the devastation of land mines and the policies to fight this inhuman scourge; statistics, matrixes, images, music, maps and texts depicting the refugee conditions; documentary pieces, texts and voices to portray the effects of the Taliban regime, its origin and its religious and cultural background.

10.8 Esquilino's Interactive and Pulsating Geographies

The second sub-menu opens up a representational space on the Esquilino district. The story of Mohammed invites the user/viewer to stop and consider several significant analytical layers: a series of interactive buttons for different and interconnected urban geographies. Mohammed's narrative focuses on a particular aspect of his temporary belonging to the neighbourhood. He tells us: "they obliged us to move as tourists". Let's try to understand how and why and what is "they".

The Colle Oppio Park is usually crowded with hundreds of migrants who adopt the park as their temporary domicile. The presence of migrants in the park has different rhythms: seasonal, daily and induced by particular events which gather a large number of persons in the area.[3] In particular periods (for instance electoral times) the local political institutions embrace populist security approaches towards this variegated presence of people and control the park in a very harsh way. Policemen recurrently garrison the park. Their presence is experienced as a dangerous threat: many of these migrants are clandestine. They could ask for the recognition of their refugee status but they don't want to do it in Italy because they don't feel comfortable with what this State could offer them in terms of assistance. Most of them are moving to other countries where every refugee is given significant economic and social support. Meanwhile they transitorily and illegally survive in a limbo condition, waiting for the next phase of their migratory projects.

In the neighbourhood, when the presence of the State becomes more visible, groups of migrants feel menaced and start moving around, looking for other places to stay. For instance, when Rome Municipality decided to gate the park and to close it at night, migrant communities were obliged to select other urban places to sleep. After that, a strange daily urban diaspora took place: in the daytime, migrants are allowed to stay in the park. At night, some police cars come: policemen begin moving among groups of migrants, forcing them to move and dispersing them into the surrounding areas. It is not important where these people are going to stay: the only important thing is that they don't have to be irritatingly visible.

Fig. 10.12 Screenshots of the hypermedia "Esquilino: space of points of view" (Attili, 2003)

Fig. 10.13 Screenshots of the hypermedia "Esquilino: space of points of view" (Attili, 2003)

Obliged to abandon the park, many migrants seek shelter among the Roman ruins of the Palatino Hill. When it rains, the only place they can go is under the arcades of Vittorio Emanuele Square. This refuge is allowed by the police only after 11.30 p.m., when their presence does not disturb the quiet living of the neighbourhood. Wake up time is at 6.00 a.m.: the order is to vanish again. The result of these movements is an erratic geography in which gathering places vanish and reappear elsewhere.

These places are like TAZ, temporary autonomous zones,[4] which have to preserve their autonomous extra-territorial dimension and therefore are obliged to eclipse themselves flowing elsewhere, just like a dense fluid facing some coercive obstacles. The gathering place, initially rooted in the Colle Oppio park, moves: Palatino, Vittorio Square and then Colle Oppio Park again. It is an operation of appropriation and progressive liberation, which attributes temporary sense to specific urban places and to the communities that live through them.[5] TAZ has a temporary but real location in time; TAZ has a temporary but real location in space. It is sucked into "strange attractors" (chaos science helps us in understanding these phenomena) made of forces connected to different levels: city, stories, projects, relationships. "Then it fades to rebuild itself in other places, before State could crush it" (Bey, 1998, p. 14). This is the reason why TAZ rejects any kind of mapping. "Map is an abstract political grid, a gigantic cheat [...]. Immensities are hidden among creases which cannot be appreciated by the ruler. Map is not precise; it cannot be precise. Map is closed while temporary autonomous zones are open. Metaphorically TAZ unfolds inside the fractal dimensions which are invisible to the control cartography" (Bey, 1998, pp. 17–18).

So the question was: how to map these phenomena? Once again the stories told by Mohammed needed to be analytically and expressively deepened. The digital

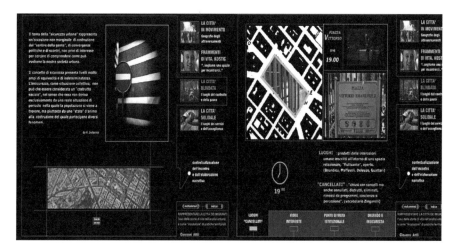

Fig. 10.14 Screenshots of the hypermedia "Esquilino: space of points of view" (Attili, 2003)

potentiality of the hypermedia allowed me to introduce a crucial representational variable: time.

A variable which is traditionally excluded by cartographies, which end up freezing urban movements and flows. Through this variable I succeeded in mapping a mutable and human landscape in motion. It is the representational experiment of a chrono-geography that is capable of connecting space and time. In China, people would say: *yu* (all the different places) and *zhou* (all the different times): *yu-zhou*.

The clock strikes 7 p.m.: on the screen a map zooms on the Colle Oppio Park; a film shows a man closing the gates; the mapped area of the park is filled with the iconic image of a gate. Time goes on. The clock strikes 9 p.m.: the map zooms on the Piazza Vittorio Square; a film shows a man closing the gates; the mapped area of the gardens is filled with the iconic image of a gate. Time goes on. The clock strikes 10 p.m.: the map zooms on the Piazza Dante; a film shows a man closing the gates; the mapped area of the square is filled with the iconic image of a gate. Time goes on. The clock strikes 1 a.m.: the map zooms on the Termini Railway Station; a film shows the Station automatic gates closing the space; the mapped area of the Railway Station is filled with the iconic image of a gate. Time goes on. A metallic music emphasises this process in which more and more spaces of the city become inaccessible. The clock's hands reach 6 a.m., then 7 a.m.: a film shows the opening of all those gates and the return of those places to urban fruition. The images of the gates disappear from the moving cartography.

An interactive space of points of view appears on the screen: the user can click on different buttons, listening to a wide range of different voices talking about the closing of these urban spaces. Some people agree with the necessity of preserving some places from the presence of migrants and homeless. Some other people find this measure quite inappropriate: in their perspective the closing of these public spaces doesn't really solve the problem, rather it simply moves it somewhere else.

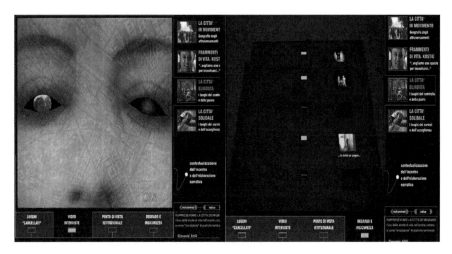

Fig. 10.15 Screenshots of the hypermedia "Esquilino: space of points of view" (Attili, 2003)

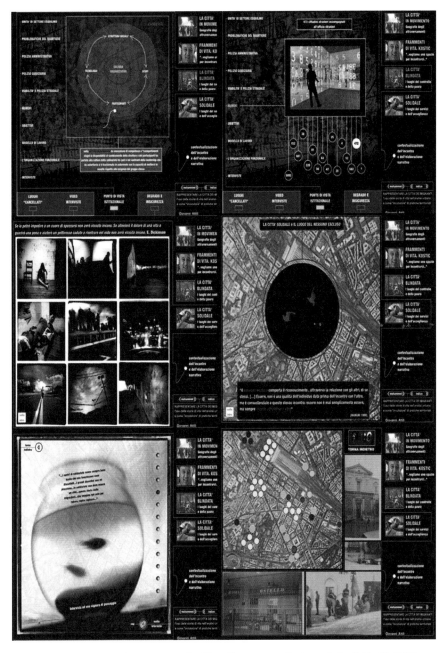

Fig. 10.16 Screenshots of the hypermedia "Esquilino: space of points of view" (Attili, 2003)

The security issues require further voices and representations: historical residents shouting against the presence of these illegal people; some others explicating a connection between lack of security and environmental deterioration; yet others showing empathetic attitudes towards these suffering worlds; the representative of the local Neighbourhood Committee provoking and waiting for answers from the mayor through a local television inquiry. These voices are collected through video interviews and accompanied by symbolic images and neighbourhood pictures. The institutional point of view is represented as well: the analysis of security policies, the organisational structure of the municipal offices, the tasks and the different roles of the different subjects who are involved are portrayed through text, interviews and graphics.

Again time and space. A cartography crossed by hundreds of red spots which move along the streets of the neighbourhood: the multitudes of migrants inhabiting the city. These red spots move and stop: they cover spaces and sometime concentrate themselves in particular sites of the district. As an effect of these movements the cartography underneath begins squirming around emerging meeting places.

The geometrical and measurable space disappears in favour of a relational and inhabited space crossed by moving subjectivities. The places where people gather become interactive doors: the user can surf through them and access further representations: films, images, statistics portraying urban fragments and its inhabitants.

Other geographies are placed one upon another. As we saw, urban movements of migrants are partially interpretable as flight trajectories due to the presence of institutional forces that are perceived as threats. There are other elements that draw and influence these movements: the presence of social exchange practices[6] and the presence of solidarity services that stimulate aggregations of migrants in specific places. A map shows these sites: Caritas refectories, little churches and charity organisations, NGO locations and the so-called "street unities" that offer concrete help to these people by going directly to the places where migrants meet, giving them support and food. Again a space of points of view has been built in order to portray different opinions about this complex world. The hypermedia reports the results of a questionnaire given to people working in these solidarity services, to migrants/users of these services and to historical residents of the neighbourhood. This questionnaire is interwoven with some video and audio interviews of a wide range of individuals. The image that comes out of this multilayered representation outlines the resentfulness of most of the residents with regard to what is perceived as an "incredible concentration of charity organizations" in the area. In their eyes, this concentration (more than five refectories in a few blocks) attracts too many migrants into the area and is responsible for the deterioration of the district. The suggested relocation of these services to wider and more peripheral areas strangely meets the exigencies of a consistent number of migrants. The ones who don't live in the park but in other parts of the city, in fact, feel that it could be more useful for them to have these services close to where they live instead of having one big concentration in the Esquilino district. Different reasons for a shared approach.

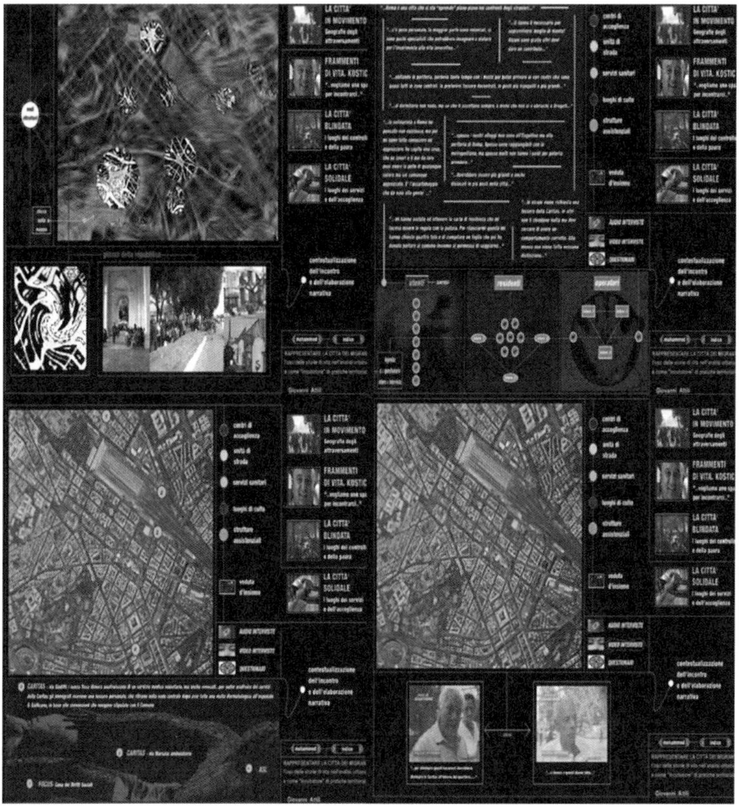

Fig. 10.17   Screenshots of the hypermedia "Esquilino: space of points of view" (Attili, 2003)

Other voices narrate the difficulties of these organisations, the needs of these illegal populations, the conflicts which inevitably characterise this territory.

10.9 Framing the Hypermedia

This whole hypermedia is biased, subjective and distorted. To frame the hypermedia means to make these distortions and this subjectivity visible, to make every representational choice explicit and transform them into objects of reflection. It means to incorporate the subject in the representation she/he produces. Those who observe reality cannot be considered detached or neutral in relation to the world they seek to describe. The self is not independent of the social context that surrounds it; rather it is an indissoluble part of it. In this way, representation can be read as the formalisation of this interdependence – a vision situated in a reality that is characterised by a subject–object circular relationship. Hypermedia incarnates this awareness and goes even further. The user can surf through a special interactive section, which was created to explain the partiality of the cognitive and representational route I chose. In Mohammed's case, for example, there is an attempt to declare in-depth what might be defined as the contextualisation of the encounter: the how, when, where and why that characterised that meeting; the surrounding conditions (the roles, the unspoken questions, the prejudices, the relationship with the surrounding space, the ways of relating); the changes in the subject encountered and in the same observer over the course of time. To explain these elements means to narrate the story of these encounters, to provide a basis for understanding the reasons why some visions of the city have taken a certain direction rather than another, to comprehend how the proposed portrayals do not come to light by accident but are the result of paths of knowledges and of encounters which are rooted in the interaction between two gendered, culturally and socially defined subjects.

In the same interactive section the user can have access to another interpretative layer connected with the choices that have informed the representational choices in the hypermedia. Each representation, in fact, involves a filtering operation which selects and highlights some facts and circumstances, specific contents and perspectives; moreover, it chooses a specific language to express the selected elements. To make this operation explicit means to make the illusion of a narration "that mirrors reality in a transparent way" crumble. Narrative (and representations are always narratives) circumscribes reality and "it is by definition always selective" (Melucci, 2000, p. 117). In each narrative, in fact, even before "we talk about the others", and before "we talk to others", we "talk to ourselves" and "we talk about ourselves" (Melucci, 2000, p. 114), revealing an invisible thread, "a rebus that conceals a desire, or else its flip side, a fear" (Calvino, 1993, p. 44). This rebus has to be solved: the I-narrator has to be readable.

It is necessary to clarify the cognitive and narrative mechanisms of the stories developed for the hypermedia and provide the keys for identifying and understanding the different depictions and the different routes/developments that structure it. Such operations clearly require the user to perform "a different type of interpretation not only regarding what is narrated, but also how it is narrated" (Pala, 2000, p. 80).

The self-reflection embedded in the attempt of framing the hypermedia recalls another important ethical dimension of planning: the necessity of taking responsibility for the representations planners produce. These representations will affect and guide actions. They are crucial in every planning process. To build adequate and sensitive representations is not easy and is always partial and subjective. It is time to assume the risk and disclose what is beyond the representation itself. It is time to add a frame to the representation itself. Metaphorically, the frame helps the potential spectator in contextualising the image she/he is observing. It determines the grammar and the pragmatics of the eye which scans the representation. Just like the frame of a painting, it shows, indicates, exhibits. A sign which separates the painting from the world. A sign which directs the vision of the spectator, transforming the painting into an object which can be envisioned and interpreted. To frame a representation means to enact a significant shift: from the vision of the "aspect" to the interpretation of the "prospect" (Poussin, 1995, pp. 30–31), from the eyesight to the deeper understanding.

In the Esquilino case, building the frame (or context) of the hypermedia meant creating an interactive section and writing a book (Attili, 2008). In this book I set out my position and outlined as transparently as I could the process of building the research itself. I portrayed a sense-making narrative of the path I followed: an inside view of the different stages, the challenges and the goals which constantly accompanied and shaped my inquiry. The book and the self-reflective interactive sections reveal the *hows* and the *whys* that made me choose to narrate the Esquilino district in that specific way: the language I used, the ethical dilemmas, the contents I tried to portray. The frame (both digital and textual) is a fundamental interpretative tool which potentially helps the spectator to contextualise the hypermedia, situating the multilayered representation of the Esquilino and its genesis, adding informative layers and analytical suggestions.

Marin (2001) suggests that each representation is characterised by two basic and interconnected dimensions: transparency and opacity. The first dimension is a transitive one: the act of representing something. The second dimension is reflexive: the act of presenting one's self in the process of representing something. In other words, each representation is not only the attempt to more or less mimetically describe something but it is also the result of a situated subject, of an embodied view that makes the representation itself more opaque, or perhaps, densely layered. Bateson (1997) would say that the map is not the territory: the map is not the passive and accurate photograph of the world, rather the reinterpretation of it. This assumption reveals an important shift: from the world as it is to the world as we know it. In this process there are no veils to tear in order to get in touch with a noumenal or objective reality which would exist outside ourselves. Representing something means being part of a process that connects subject and object through an aesthetic relationship, an allusive transposition, a redundant translation. Framing a representation means

Fig. 10.18 Screenshots of the hypermedia "Esquilino: space of points of view" (Attili, 2003)

creating a space to make sense of this process, transforming its opacity into an object of interpretation.

In the Esquilino case, framing the hypermedia meant making my analytical and representational project explicit. A way to ethically address the potential confusion connected with the concept of storytelling itself. I told a story (polyphonic, multi-stratified and pluri-codified): one among the many others that could have been told. The frame is the compass that can be used to orient the comprehension of it; to understand why that specific story and not another one; to avoid the risk of being shipwrecked in the ocean of relativism, in the chaos of different representations-stories that cannot be fully understood if their genesis process is not readable, if their goals are not understandable, if their questions are not examinable.

10.10 Planning Potentialities

The hypermedia described here has many potentialities. It is a very significant analytical tool. It depicts the city in an eclectic but rigorous way. It gives space to life stories as narratives that are able to portray urbanities in movement. It can be used in two different ways: analytically or interactively.

First of all, it can be used in the traditional "analytical problem solving" approach to planning. It is an approach which follows the well-known stages: knowledge–decision–action. According to this approach, in order to have a considered and rational decision, a planner should first develop a deep knowledge of the situation in which she/he operates. It is necessary to know the problems that need to be solved, appreciating the difference between the current situation and the desired one. The decision then is the necessary antecedent to action. The three phases are temporally distinct. First, knowledge and the acquisition of information. Second, the decision that is connected to what the information communicates. Third, rational and responsible action according to what has been decided. Planners, as experts and powerful decision-makers, are the ones who elaborate representations, make decisions and guide actions. In this traditional approach, the hypermedia "Esquilino: space of points of view" could represent the knowledge phase: a deep and complex analytical tool which can be used to define decisions and determine actions. From this perspective, this digital tool can potentially provide an articulated envisioning of the neighbourhood that is based on the many voices which cross it.

A second possible way the hypermedia could be used is in an "interactive problem solving" approach. This approach deconstructs the linear mechanism of knowledge–decision–action, favouring the relational nature of the interaction among diverse actors. The expert urban planner is no longer the repository of a knowledge process which guides decisions and then actions. Planning as social interaction is based on the involvement of the society and its capabilities and skills. The professional model, which creates a dichotomy between planners and planned, falls apart. It is a deconstruction which debates the two main accepted versions of the same model: in the reformist version, society (guided by experts) is reduced to social needs; in the participatory version, planners invite people to dialogue but in asymmetrical ways. Planning as social interaction is built through multiple interactions among different forms of knowledge and actions, individuals and interest groups, professional practices and ordinary ones.

The hypermedia can potentially be used to solicit such interactions. It can be thought of as a catalyst and incubator of social interaction: a tool capable of producing "images", raising some resonance, generating emotions and launching some "innovative metaphors" by means of which further imaginative processes can be activated. The hypermedia uses an ordinary, accessible language made up of stories and narratives. It can be accessed by both experts and non-experts. It plays with multiple expressive codes: symbolic and ambiguous images and narratives which require discussion. This hypermedia can be thought of as a tool capable of provoking interaction and sensemaking, focusing on a complex idea of "aesthetic rationality" in which all senses are involved. This dimension is central for every communication and interactive process. To create real communication spaces it's not enough "to say something"; it's necessary to transfer energies, awakening aspirations, knowledges and dormant creativity. The hypermedia aims at reaching this goal, emphasising its communicative and expressive dimensions, creating a potential and involving space for a "strong interaction": it is an interaction which doesn't seek the confirmation of a pre-constituted system of *roles/functions*. Rather, it is based on a deep learning process in which roles and functions are disarranged in productive ways. It is an unpredictable and potentially conflicting interaction in which diverse actors, knowledges and skills are indeterminately at play.

The hypermedia can be thought of as the fulcrum of this interactive approach. Its configuration potentially provides aesthetic resonances and deep involvement. Its contents raise questions, outline conflicting perspectives and unfold invisible stories. But the hypermedia "Esquilino: space of points of view" cannot accomplish its potentialities without the creation of a space in which it could be open to the involvement of a wide interactive audience. To achieve that, it would have been necessary to develop a second stage of the research project in which the potentialities of the hypermedia could be tested, bringing this digital tool back into the neighbourhood and opening up an urban conversation: a real dialogue catalysed by the variety of contents displayed by the hypermedia itself. For various reasons, this second phase never came to life. And this is the most significant limit of the project itself.

Finally, an anecdote. After I completed the research on the Esquilino district, the City Council member in charge of "jobs and sustainable development" at that time was shown the hypermedia. He was really impressed. He had been responsible for those security policies I'd been criticising in my representation of the neighbourhood. He was just not aware of the many migrants inhabiting the Colle Oppio Park. He was not conscious of that reality because of the forced invisibility that characterises the lives of these clandestine subjectivities. His knowledge stopped just where the hypermedia started. The vision of the multi-layered representation of the Esquilino neighbourhood allowed him to perceive that, in that park, there was a heterogeneous world crossed by irreducible stories. It was a world that needed to be understood and managed with appropriate and sensitive policies. The council member agreed that closing the park didn't solve the problem or the conflicts within the district. This action only deferred, temporally and spatially, a possible and shared initiative able to meet the exigencies of both migrants and residents. He thought that the hypermedia was a very powerful tool which could potentially create a deeper consciousness in the neighbourhood with regard to people whose lives and stories are unknown to almost everyone. He proposed to permanently install in the park little digital screens in which people could see and interact with the hypermedia. It was, in a small way, a revolutionary proposal because those screens would not have shown the traditional history of the park, its archeological ruins and its reclamation projects. They would have shown the lives of people temporarily inhabiting the park: their stories, their struggles and their dreams. It was a way to open people's eyes and find a way to deal with the numerous problems the hypermedia focused on.

Despite the good intentions, this idea was never realised: partly because the municipal council was not re-elected and partly because the hypermedia had an intrinsic problem. It mostly portrayed illegal individuals who agreed to be filmed only if the hypermedia would be circulated within restricted academic environments. It was an ethical issue I needed to respect in order to protect the lives of these people who had trusted me with their stories.

This anecdote shows a way: the upsetting of the perspective of a policy-maker. A learning process activated by a multi-linguistic digital analytical tool which was able to transgress flatlands representations in favour of a more complex depiction of the city as a living and relational space.

Notes

1. As a result of a close research exchange with the Anthropology Department of the Bologna University, I gradually realised that the analytical tools of my discipline were not enough to reach the goals I established and to portray the complexity of my case study.
2. This movement historically refers to a planning path whose roots can be found in the participative/anarchical approach of Kropotkin, Reclus, Le Play and Geddes.
3. When Ocalan, the leader of the PKK political Kurdish party, was forced temporarily to live in Rome (1999), thousands of Kurds stayed in the Park, creating a real city made out of cardboard: there were tea spaces, barbers, rooms to sleep in, places to meet and discuss. Everything was precisely organised and established in the park. When Ocalan left Rome, that temporary city vanished.
4. The temporary co-habitation of these not institutionally recognised people transforms the park into a sort of enclave which survives beyond the State itself. In order to describe poetically–politically these kind of realities, Bey (1998) proposes the evocative metaphor of TAZ, in other words: Temporary Autonomous Zone. Like the pirates of the seventeenth century who pressured some islands to share the spoils and to stock up on water and food, our contemporary migrants intensively take shelter in some urban places, exchanging information and weaving relationships with the city and with their origin communities. We are talking about some "freed places", TAZ where transient inhabitants organise themselves, elaborating new forms of living together. We are talking about extra-territorial places where State authority has difficulty to enter. These places are not rooted in the city; they move, disappearing and appearing in different space-time dimensions, according to the presence of law and institutions.

5. These temporary autonomous zones give hospitality to different and not easily describable communities: complex networks which are able to renew the social fabric of the cities and interpersonal relationships in a deep way. These are networks of delocalised communities; they stem from social exchange practices and from the construction of support networks to various migratory projects. They are permeable, changing, unstable, transitory and multi-scaled, where relationships and interactions are not deterministically related to the territorial dimension. TAZ is deeply connected to an idea of community which cannot be seen as a systemic, closed, consolidated and unchangeable structure. The moving and uprooted communities which characterize places like Colle Oppio park could be interpreted as gangs: "the gang is open, not to everybody – naturally, but to affinity groups. The gang is not part of a wider hierarchy rather it is part of an horizontal model of habits, extended relationships, contracts and alliances" (Bey, 1998, p. 18).

6. These social exchange practices are mainly connected to the necessity of finding a place to stay, somewhere to eat, sites to gather. These practices are historically stratified as testified by an Afghan migrant who refers to being shown a picture of Colle Oppio Park when he was in Turkey. He was advised to go there to find other countrymen who could help him.

References

Attili, G. (2003). *Hypermedia "Esquilino: Space of points of view" in PhD Thesis "Rappresentare la città dei migranti. L'uso delle storie di vita nell' analasi urbana e come incubatore di pratiche territorial"*, unpublished.

Attili, G. (2008). *Rappresentare la città dei migranti. Storie di vita e pianificazione urbana*. Milano: Jaca Book.

Bateson, G. (1997). *Una sacra unità. Altri passi verso un'ecologia della mente*. Milano: Adelphi.

Bey, H. (1998). *TAZ. Zone Temporaneamente Autonome*. Milano: Shake Edizioni Underground.

Bourdieu, P. (1993). *La misère du monde*. Paris: Editions du Seuil.

Bourdieu, P. (1994). *Raison pratiques. Sur la théorie de l'action*. Paris: Edtion du Seuil.

Callari Galli, M., Ceruti, M., & Pievani, T. (1998). *Pensare la diversità. Per un'educazione alla complessità umana*. Roma: Meltemi.

Calvino, I. (1993). *Le città invisibili. Palomar S.r.l. e*. Milano: Arnoldo Mondadori Editore.

Cavarero, A. (1997). *Tu che mi guardi, tu che mi racconti. Filosofia della narrazione*. Milano: Feltrinelli Editore.

de Certeau, M. (2001). *L'invenzione del quotidiano*. Roma: Edizioni Lavoro.

Decandia, L. (2001). Il tempo e l'invisibile. Dalla città moderna alla città contemporanea. In E. Scandurra, C. Cellamare, & P. Bottaro (Eds.), *Labirinti della città contemporanea*. Roma: Meltemi.

Haraway, D. (1995). *Manifesto Cyborg. Donne, tecnologie e biopolitiche del corpo*. Milano: Feltrinelli.

Maffesoli, M. (2000). *Del Nomadismo. Per una sociologia dell'erranza*. Milano: Franco Angeli.

Marin, L. (2001). Della rappresentazione. Roma: Meltemi.

Melucci, A. (2000). *Culture in gioco. Differenza per convivere*. Milano: Il Saggiatore.

Nancy, J. L. (1992). *La comunità inoperosa*. Napoli: Cronopio.

Pala, M. (2000). Città di carta: analogie tra analisi letteraria e urbanistica nella condizione post-moderna. In G. Maciocco, G. Deplano, & G. Marchi (Eds.) (2000), *Etica e pianificazione spaziale*. Milano: Franco Angeli.

Poussin, N. (1995). Lettere sull'arte ed. by D.Carrier (Hestia Edizioni, Cernusco) & L. Sandercock (Eds.) (1998) *Making the invisible visible: A multicultural history of planning*. Berkley: University of California Press.

Sandercock, L. (2003). *Cosmopolis 2: Mongrel cities of the 21st century*. London: Continuum.

Tarrius, A. (1992). Les Fourmis d'Europe. Paris: LHarmattan.

Tomlinson, J. (1999). Sentirsi a casa nel mondo. La cultura come bene globale. Milano: Feltrinelli.

Wolf, C. (1996). *Medea*. Roma Edizioni e/o.

Chapter 11
Seeing and Being Seen: The Potential of Multimedia as a Reflexive Planning Methodology

Penny Gurstein

11.1 Introduction

To understand increasingly complex planning issues, methodologies are needed that make knowledge and values explicit and communicable in a language that can be shared by diverse stakeholders and can address multiple points of view. Communication is a dialogical process oriented toward developing a shared understanding of the meaning of events and experiences. Effective communication recognizes differences and builds trust. Planners, engaged in interactions of diverse perspectives, necessarily need tools that allow for "active listening" (and seeing) to build that trust. Stakeholders need to be engaged in a social learning process of sharing experiences, learning together, and contributing to decisions within their communities.

Multimedia, with its combination of different content forms such as text, audio, still images, animation, and video, is a communication mode that has great potential to provide a point of entry into understanding the dynamics of community formation. With the convergence of media through the computer, television, and telephone there is a proliferation of technologies and tools that can be used in planning processes.

Combined with the recent development in accessible technology for digital media production and dissemination through computer applications and the Internet, these tools could be used to draw attention to critical and interpretive forms of policy analysis by combining, in creative ways, empirical qualitative and quantitative data with normative concerns. In addition to technologies such as video cameras, communication devices such as cell phones with cameras and audio recording can now record events, edit and download them to the Internet for wide consumption. Digital technologies create a new immersive environment for public communication, which is interactive, relatively inexpensive, and unconstrained by time or distance.

P. Gurstein (✉)
School of Community and Regional Planning, University of British Columbia,
Vancouver, BC, Canada
e-mail: gurstein@interchange.ubc.ca

L. Sandercock, G. Attili (eds.), *Multimedia Explorations in Urban Policy and
Planning*, Urban and Landscape Perspectives 7, DOI 10.1007/978-90-481-3209-6_11,
© Springer Science+Business Media B.V. 2010

Myths and preconceptions often govern public policy formation, limiting its ability to respond effectively. While it is difficult to counteract dominant beliefs and ideologies, the power of multimedia is in its ability to uncover countervailing stories that challenge the dominant discourses and tap into more intuitive and other forms of knowledge. Multimedia can contribute to community development and planning through the creation of new modes of knowledge; opportunities for social learning and community empowerment; and an enhanced understanding of place.

However, there are tensions between the aims and the outcomes of multimedia. How might the power dynamics embedded in the processes and technologies of multimedia be considered in any initiatives intended to foster communication and mobilization? Who has control of the tools and the information generated (i.e., who sends information to whom?) and who is served by the technologies? Who can and does participate in generating, analyzing and interpreting the output from multimedia, how is it used to engage stakeholders, and what legitimacy does that output have in generating policies? The challenge for planning practitioners using multimedia is to foster reflexivity in examining underlying assumptions and narratives, which necessitates rethinking of planning processes, ethical standards, and protocols. Tools and approaches are needed that can allow for genuine public dialogue.

The intent of this chapter is to explore, through reflection on multimedia processes, the role of multimedia in fostering community-building dialogue. Starting with a contextual overview that positions the use of multimedia as a change agent, an analysis is then made of the attributes of multimedia processes that contribute to empowerment of individuals and communities, as well as the limitations of multimedia in generating change. Recognizing the power of multimedia to shape the communication of ideas and visions, reflexivity in its use is introduced as key to developing a dialogical process. Examples of how multimedia can encourage reflexivity in planning processes and in what ways multimedia may impede these processes are identified and embedded within an analysis of power relations that impact the production and use of multimedia. The chapter concludes with a discussion of how and when multimedia can be most effective in planning processes and what is required for their inclusion to occur. I argue that if multimedia is to be effective as a change agent, its use must be integrated within agreed-upon protocols and processes that allow opportunity for mutual trust, collaboration and a commitment from the stakeholders to not only engage in meaningful dialogue, but also act upon its outcome.

11.2 Media for Change

For community development processes to effect change in communities, a range of skills and tools are needed to engage citizens and build political power. Multimedia is one such tool. The use of multimedia to further community development was pioneered by the Challenge for Change Program of the National Film Board of Canada in the 1970s (Wiesner, 1992; Williams, 1988). This program sought to use the process of production as a form of social change by empowering politically and socially disenfranchised people in the course of film production and distribution. There has been a long tradition of documentary filmmakers such as Frederick Wiseman, Errol Morris, and Michael Moore critiquing societal institutions through their productions. Yet the Challenge for Change Program was innovative in facilitating a dialogue between the disenfranchised and the government. To do this, collaboration based on mutual trust and ethical conduct between filmmakers and communities was essential. Equally important was a commitment by decision-makers to engage in this dialogue. In this process, the creative license of film-makers was tempered by community priorities, and community developers who could work with all of the stakeholders became an important part of the process.

The Challenge for Change Program lasted until 1980 and its most active years were between 1967 and 1975, paralleling the period when federal spending in Canada on social services and cultural production (particularly Canadian culture) was at its zenith. Challenge for Change was funded by eight different departments of the federal government and had an operating budget for both English- and French-language programming. This dedicated funding was a tangible demonstration of the commitment that the government had to the aims of the program. The output was conceived as data gathering to understand communities so that the government could address their concerns, and the success of the program was assessed by the community dialogue it produced and the timely government responses to the issues raised in the films. In this way, the process and the ideas generated took precedence over the actual quality of the output. Initially film-makers entered communities and documented the everyday realities of community members; as the program developed, film production was given to community members, who were trained to film events and engage in editing.[1]

While this program was one of the first government-sponsored experiments in the use of film and video to further social change, concerns have been raised about its effectiveness. The difficulty of trying to be both an agent and catalyst for change within a community, and at the same time serve as a means of communication with government, can be problematic. Marchessault (1995, p. 140) argues that the program delivered "access without agency." Power relations were not challenged by the program and the dialogical process that Challenge for Change claimed to initiate was rarely found. Most of the films instead represent a "social reproduction" of "difference" for an audience outside of the community (Marchessault, 1995, pp. 140–142).

The invention of low-cost portable programming technologies such as the Sony "portapak" in 1967 created the opportunity for these community-based experimentations. Despite the many shortcomings of this technology, the portapak was a tool of production and allowed the dissemination of low-budget productions suitable for television broadcast. The portapak used half-inch videotape that could be transferred to a one-inch format compatible with the television format. Concurrently, cable television became widely introduced, and in Canada it was legislated that cable owners must ensure a channel for community programming.

A number of community-based organizations and collectives in North America formed with the mandate to communicate community issues, using these new technologies as community development tools. This, however, was short-lived. As the expectations of broadcast quality rose with the introduction of more sophisticated technologies, the low-budget productions of these groups became marginalized. It has only been in the last decade since the introduction of low-cost digital technologies that link to computers and provide both high-quality production standards and wide dissemination through the Internet that the possibilities for multimedia as a community development tool have been revisited.

Currently, communication and multimedia technologies are effectively being used for community development and mobilization in North America and internationally. There are numerous organizations and institutions that use discussion–Chat Groups to further their democratic ideals. From the Zapatista rebels in Chiapas, Mexico, who use the Internet to communicate their struggle throughout Mexico and internationally, to MoveOn.org, which attempted to mobilize disenfranchised voters for the 2004 and 2008 US Presidential election, to citizen journalists who are reporting and disseminating important stories globally, such as the people in Burma who broadcast videos from mobile phones to circumvent the media blackout and reveal human rights abuses, these tools are used to disseminate information and keep people in constant contact on emerging issues.

Now that communication tools such as the cellular phone are converging in their ability to receive and transmit information wirelessly (i.e., text messaging, digital photography, and video) new forms of instantaneous mobilization are occurring. While the fax machine in 1990 was indispensable to disseminating information and mobilizing dissent during the Tiananmen Square Demonstrations in Beijing, China, text messaging and video feeds off cell phones in 2005 were the preferred communication during the riots in the suburbs of Paris and other French cities. The speed with which information can be disseminated and the innovative uses of the technologies for activist purposes are making them essential tools.

Stories are now being recognized as an effective tool in community development by drawing on local knowledge, through personal reflections of community members, and attempting to find common threads that will help develop community priorities (Sandercock, 2003; Forester, 1999). Recognizing the potential of stories as the memory of a community, online community stories projects and audio archives are being done through community networks. Personal storytelling has exploded with the advent of "weblogs" or "blogs," personal websites updated with links, commentary and other images. Blogs are distinctive for each creator, showcasing their personal reflections and opinions. Attesting to their popularity, an Internet search of the term "blog" yielded 3.33 billion sites.[2] While this form of community process is not always effective in resolving issues, it can become a useful starting point for further community dialogue.

Multimedia is a valuable technology for community development because of its ability to disseminate information quickly and relatively cheaply. The power of multimedia is also in the messages it conveys that can be used to empower individuals and communities to effect change. This will be further explored in the next section.

While the potential of multimedia as a tool for dialogue between stakeholders is considerable, without the necessary buy-in from stakeholders with decision-making powers to respond to the community concerns exposed by multimedia productions, it is limited as a change catalyst. The concluding sections will revisit this issue.

11.3 Empowerment Through Visioning

As defined by the World Bank, empowerment is "the process of increasing the assets and capabilities of individuals or groups to make purposive choices and to transform those choices into desired actions and outcomes."[3] Fundamental to this process are actions which both foster individual and community resources, and advance efficiency and equity within the governing context through access to information, inclusion and participation, accountability and local organizational capacity. Corbett and Kelly (2004) in research on the empowerment potential of Participatory Geographic Information and Multimedia Systems (PGIMSs) have constructed an analytical framework that explores the phenomenon of empowerment at the social scales of the individual and community, in relation to four empowerment catalysts: information, process, skills, and tools.

This framework recognizes that empowerment may occur at one social level but not the others and that increasing empowerment capacity needs to be differentiated from increasing empowerment itself. Empowerment capacity might be long lasting when there is a deep process of change in the internal conditions of an individual or community that influences their empowerment. On the other hand, empowerment may seem more visible when there is a corresponding tangible increase in political power or influence, and yet may be less likely to be sustained.

Within this context, where is multimedia positioned? To foster civil societies and recognize the diversity within them, Throgmorton (1996) and Sandercock (2003) have advanced storytelling as a method to democratize planning, and identify common planning priorities, as well as to disseminate successes and work through conflicts.

Beyond telling success stories, storytelling may act as a catalyst for change by empowering the storytellers themselves to push for change. Clover (2005, p. 631) chronicles how workers who are becoming increasingly marginalized in the face of neo-liberalism are telling their stories of collective action through various media in order to "educate, empower and demand visibility and justice." Frantz (2007) provides an important example of empowerment through skills development, working with street-involved youth in creating a video montage of their ideas and thoughts surrounding a proposed greenway in a socially-challenged inner-city neighborhood. The project was primarily designed to leave a legacy of skills for participants, who gained training in video production as well as insights into the political and technical aspects of urban planning. And Wagner's essay in this volume provides ample evidence of citizen empowerment through digital media that enabled them to produce oppositional plans.

Multimedia production can also enhance community empowerment in a broader sense. Recent literature has pointed to the potential for empowerment through the actual process of participatory video development by enabling participants to gain a clearer understanding of their own needs. In workshops for future residents of a private housing development in Melbourne, the residents' children were filmed describing their ideal communities. This footage provided their parents with a unique point of departure for further explorations of their own desires and aspirations (Sarkissian, 2007, and Chapter 8).

Hallenbeck (2007, and Chapter 7), a participant in Frantz's project, presents another dimension to empowerment – imagining. Multimedia, as a tool that engages people in a dialogue over their rights to participation and appropriation, fosters the essential act of imagining, thereby contributing to the struggle for social justice. Attili (2007), in his analysis of how new knowledge production occurs in the context of digital ethnographies, argues that such immersive exposure creates astonishment, which in turn allows those experiencing it "to reinvent the sense frameworks through which [they] organize their own experience of the world and in the world" (Attili, 2007, p. 95). It is this state of astonishment which may enable participants and viewers to eventually take new forms of action not previously envisioned. Storytelling through multimedia can convey the visceral experiential environment. The astonishment, and sometimes indignation and anger, can lead to imagining a better future and acting on that vision. Visioning focuses and drives the creative energy necessary for action.

The power of the medium is evident in its ability not only to tell a story but to shape it. The sequencing, rhythm, contrast and flow of images, the subjects chosen, and the sound and text background can impart a compelling narrative for viewers. That is why documentary films can be so effective at propaganda, as strikingly evident in the classic, *Triumph of the Will*, Leni Riefenstahl's documentary on the 1934 Nazi Party Convention. Chapter 1 in Part I, argues that town planning films have been equally capable of fulfilling this propaganda role.

Bearing in mind the influence of multimedia in manipulating and controlling the message, just how effective can it be in generating dialogue? A recent example of a documentary that was designed as a platform for dialogue was "Wal-Mart: The High Cost of Low Price" (2005), which chronicles the stories and everyday lives of families and communities affected by Wal-Mart.[4] The film was released simultaneously in theaters and on DVD, allowing it to be shown in various venues. Many showings were followed by discussion group sessions to further cultivate the questions created by the film. The film has not only raised awareness but helped to galvanize citizen concerns that are forcing companies to act responsibly.

Even more effective has been the multimedia presentation on climate change, "An Inconvenient Truth."[5] Initially a PowerPoint presentation by Al Gore, the former US Vice-President and crusader for climate change awareness, illustrating the deleterious impacts of climate change, it was subsequently turned into a documentary (that won an Academy Award) with supplementary educational material downloadable free on the web. Community leaders from around the world are selected to go for a training workshop where they are taught how to introduce climate change issues into their communities through the use of the documentary. The strategies employed recognize the power of the documentary's message to stimulate support for measures needed to offset climate change.

While these two documentaries offer examples of how multimedia may contribute to capacity building, how valuable can multimedia be in planning processes where, in addition to dialogue, decision-making is required? How could multimedia help shape desired futures in a purposive manner? Multimedia tools and techniques are embedded in, and created by, a social milieu. Multimedia can contribute to turning ideas and visions into action but it may also create new inequities in access and power distribution.

Multimedia can be useful in enhancing empowerment capacity at the individual level but may not be as effective in developing sustained empowerment and change at the community level. Multimedia tools can also be disempowering at both the individual and community levels due to the cost and complexity of the technologies that impedes their widespread use and restricts who has access to production and dissemination.

Critical and participatory approaches to planning involve "restructuring strategies" (Forester, 1989) that address dynamics of power and powerlessness and combine practical action with political vision. To enhance community building and the dialogue between the state and civil society we require community-based approaches which expand the language of planning to include multiple publics in decision-making. Recognizing the structural impediments posed by hierarchical institutions, the introduction of tools that foster communication to and from governing institutions may become important conduits to further participation and dialogue in decision-making.

Multimedia tools, because of their ability to create interactivity, could be a significant part of fostering that dialogue. However, it is still not clear whether these tools can enhance the "bourgeois public sphere" (Habermas, 1991), and in so doing, assist in enhancing dialogue between the state and civil society and redressing the dynamics of power and powerlessness. For this to occur in planning processes requires reflexivity at a number of levels – the governing organization, the planners, the multimedia producers, and the community members.

11.4 Reflexivity in Practice

Reflexivity refers to an ongoing examination of the underlying assumptions and narratives that drive a practice. Harries-Jones (1991) explains it as "a capacity to act by linking the possibilities of present social action to an alternative epistemology" (156). A reflexive relationship is a dialectic in which it is recognized that both the cause and effect of an action affect each other. Personal reflexivity involves reflecting on the ways in which values, beliefs, and social identities shape our approaches. It also involves reflecting on how our experiences affect and possibly change us. For multimedia producers, reflexivity involves more than knowing who their audience is. It is recognizing their role in both shaping a message and being shaped by it. It is recognizing the unintended consequences of their actions.

For planning professionals, reflexivity refers to examining assumptions that inform their practice and basing future actions on this re-examination. Assumptions are questioned based on facts and experience, and if proved wrong, they are adjusted. Reflexivity is only possible if there is organizational reflexivity – if the system in which the assumptions are embedded encourage this examination. Few organizations are flexible enough to accommodate this self-examination. Rather, the prevalent ideologies become embedded and inscribed in our social spaces and are used as a way to control, dominate, and regulate social practices (Lefebvre, 1991).

The project described by Frantz (2007) illustrates how multimedia can create opportunities for reflexivity in planning processes and can also be stymied by the lack of reflexivity. The project sought to explore the application of Participatory Video as a planning tool. Three teams, each consisting of street-involved youth and graduate planning students,[6] produced three short videos that conveyed their collective perceptions and ideas on the design and installation of a proposed urban greenway in the City of Vancouver's lowest income neighborhood (see also Chapter 7). In the course of doing these videos, the three groups engaged in an iterative process aimed at establishing a dialogue between the youth and the students, and in incorporating ideas from the wider community into their videos. Both the planning students and the youth learned from each other, and from marginalized community members through the collection of rich qualitative data, which was reflected in their three videos.

An unintended consequence of one of the videos, however, resulted in the videos being shown only in a few venues, initially, and now, not at all. This particular video, through its use of certain editing techniques, portrayed a number of local politicians and planners in a manner that was not deemed respectful by a senior planner involved with the greenway project. While these politicians and planners agreed to be interviewed for the video, this portrayal was done without their consent. The reflexivity that had been intrinsic to the process of engagement between the youth and planning students, and to their engagement with marginalized community members, had not carried over to their engagement with the City's professional staff. The project was successful in capacity building of the youth and planning students, and to a certain extent in empowerment and artistic self-expression of the community members to whom the videos gave voice, but it did not enhance trust or relationship building with City planners.

In turn, the planners' reaction to this portrayal puts into question their commitment to the process under which these videos were produced. The marginalized community in which they are working is very distrustful of authority figures and is quick to assume that any interventions will likely have dire consequences for their community. Given this micro-political climate, the greenway process was seen as an attempt at gentrification. Portraying the politicians and planners in an unfavorable light reflected the views of many in the community. Could this video have been used by these authority figures as a point of departure for beginning a dialogue with the community rather than what they did, which is suppressing the message? The opportunity to build better relations between the community and the state was lost.

Perhaps one lesson from this experiment is that clearer ethical protocols that can inform complicated practical, safety and ethical concerns need to be put in place at the outset of such a process, as well as a clear commitment from the planning agency as to how the videos will be used in, or contribute to, decision-making.

Recognizing and portraying multiple points of views can foster reflexivity but in the course of doing this, the message can get diluted. A multimedia production by Gurstein[7] Johnson, Schatz, Tate, and Hallenbeck (2007) was designed as a vehicle for public outreach and dialogue to get beneath the hyperbole surrounding the outsourcing of work, to examine what this means in terms of quality of working life and impact on workers and communities.[8] To further this, the video is part of a public outreach and participation effort that includes viewings for key stakeholders and the public, and an interactive website. The use of multimedia provides a platform for enhancing public participation by providing a venue for citizens to tell their stories and for public feedback and input on policy issues via public forums linked to viewing of multimedia productions.

To counter the myths surrounding outsourcing, the production sought to present the key issues, facts and views in a dispassionate manner. Not all participants in the forums appreciated this balance. One workshop participant who viewed our film called it "academic" because it was developed to make the viewer question the issues, not to convince of one particular viewpoint. Nonetheless, in light of the complexity of outsourcing's impacts and our desire to fuel further dialogue as part of the policy development process, an impassioned, more advocacy-oriented end product was not considered appropriate.

Multimedia can encourage the practice of reflexivity in communities through the dialogue it generates as has been demonstrated in the power of the production, "An Inconvenient Truth," to create awareness of climate change. Multimedia can discourage reflexivity if the product reinforces polarized narratives. There are a number of sites in the process of multimedia production and dissemination where reflexivity is required if multimedia is to be used as a change agent in communities.

Producers of multimedia need to be reflective in their assumptions about which community members should be involved in production and dissemination, and how or if there even needs to be a distinction between multimedia experts and others. They need to examine and reflect on their underlying values, beliefs, and experiences that shape their narrative/interpretations. In turn, for the narratives to inform community building, organizational reflexivity is required that will allow an examination of assumptions that inform practice. A clear commitment is needed by government agencies and other decision-makers, as was found in the National Film Board, Challenge for Change program to a limited degree, that the output from multimedia will be used not only to generate dialogue but as data gathering for issues that need to be addressed.

11.5 Multimedia in Planning Practice and Policy-Making

For multimedia to influence policy and to be a tool for community development, we need to think critically about how and when it can be the most effective and who are the appropriate stakeholders in its production and analysis. As with any other planning methodology, the process is as important as the output, and that means being clear about the context and inherent biases. What multimedia offers is the opportunity for social learning and an open process, as defined by Friedmann (1987), that provides critical feedback and reflection and a strong institutional memory. To further the development of innovative solutions to complex societal problems, diverse stakeholders need to share experiences, learn together, and contribute to decisions. How people, aided by multimedia tools, negotiate through the multiple agendas of the various stakeholders is a critical component of the social learning process.

Multimedia can raise awareness of community members', planners', and policy-makers' appreciation of place and people's connections to place. One way in which multimedia can provide this grounding is through new metaphors for repairing urban places. Ingersoll (2006) claims that our understanding of the city has already become cinematic and that we need to engage with this cinematic understanding in order to enhance our sense of place. He describes the relationship between forms of storytelling and the way people perceive their surroundings – arguing that the concurrent advent of film-making and mass automobile production and distribution radically changed our perspective of the city. These two intertwined developments have yielded a sprawling urban form of multiple, shifting vanishing points, which he labels *jump-cut urbanism*. Tewdwr-Jones (2007) further highlights the value of film in conveying the character and socioeconomic attributes in scenes of urban decay. He calls on planners to reflectively consume film as a means of enhancing their own literacies regarding how place is presented (see also Chapter 14).

Multimedia does more in planning processes than simply allow for active seeing and listening. Multimedia can make technical information related to planning accessible to urban residents and can make the experiences, hopes, and aspirations of urban residents more accessible to professional planners. Multimedia is effectively being used as a vehicle for visioning and to add depth and understanding to the complex array of issues surrounding urban design, and in particular housing density (Levy, 2006). Video-based communication can be a more immediate and accessible medium for the communication of facts and figures. There is a long tradition of multimedia gaming simulation (e.g. Simcity) to understand urban politics and development. Planners effectively use Geographic Information Systems, a tool to collect, store, manipulate, retrieve, and analyze spatially linked data, including audio-visual data, and Google Streetscape.[9]

Participatory video can be a potent vehicle to promote changes in attitudes and social behavior and help communities identify development solutions and convey their message to decision-makers (White, 2003). Text messaging from cell phones and social networking sites (see http://www.facebook.com) have become essential conduits for mobilization. Blogs and virtual realities (see http://secondlife.com) are also being tested for their application as immersive environments for community formation and socio-spatial analysis.

While the tools are there, it is not yet clear just how receptive the planning community is to multimedia planning tools. Most planners lack this literacy. Moreover, they may be uncomfortable with using the technology due to perceived conflicts with their roles, as they currently understand them. The use of multimedia may be perceived as furthering an advocacy agenda, outside of the purview of the detached, unbiased professional planner. However, if others are using this medium to reach the politicians these planners serve, such planners may find it increasingly difficult to provide meaningful and accessible advice to decision-makers without better understanding the medium.

Access to the technologies affects its use and is impeded by the digital divide (Norris, 2001). Those who have control of information and communication technologies are the "haves" and those who don't, or must rely on those who do to provide access, are the "have nots." While the gap in access to some of these tools, such as cellular telephones, is narrowing between rich and poor nations (and the rich and poor within nations), it still remains wide for high-speed Internet connectivity, which is needed for participation in information-rich activities. Mitchell (1999) and others contend that to engage communities in digital communication and exchange, community members need to have training and the technologies must be widely available in community settings.

The costs of multimedia production have decreased in recent years, and the proliferation of websites like YouTube reflects phenomenal growth in the numbers of individuals and groups who have gained access to production technology. To ensure that access to digital communications does not perpetuate existing social inequalities, community access networks, such as Vancouver Community Network[10] and others, provide training and access to low-income communities. Yet it remains inaccessible for large segments of the population. Moreover, even with access to technology, there is still a distinct skill set required to be able to tell stories in ways that can engender social change – a skill set that remains with a relatively smaller segment of the population. As a result, the number and range of stories that may be told with this tool still remain limited.

It is also not easy to evaluate the effectiveness of these tools as it is difficult to measure the changes in empowerment resulting from their use. Multimedia can just as likely be a tool for scrutiny as for empowerment. The output from multimedia can be used as a means to monitor community activities and gather data on particular community members. The proliferation of video surveillance cameras throughout our cities, and our increasing reliance on the Internet for information, entertainment, and commercial transactions, means that we are vulnerable to public scrutiny and surveillance in the most private aspects of our lives.

Multimedia provides both an immersive environment for communities, planners, and policy-makers to experience their communities and a cogent milieu that is a point of departure for further investigation. Its usefulness for planning practice depends on its ability to incorporate and reflect back diverse ideologies, values, and beliefs in a manner that can be understood by all participants.

11.6 Conclusion

To expand the language of planning to include multiple publics in decision-making requires community building and enhancing the dialogue between the state and civil society. Multimedia is an important tool that can be integrated with other planning initiatives to interpret the environments we inhabit, and engage and teach communities and their planners about themselves and their needs. To motivate and empower people to take action to change their lives, however, require a range of process-based communication and mobilization initiatives that can build trust, promote community formation, and facilitate dialogue.

Multimedia tools are constructed within societal processes and as such are entwined with dynamics of power and control within those cultures. Some of the modes of communication generated by information and communication technologies promote decentralized community-based information gathering and decision-making, while others reinforce centralized and hierarchical structures. Before multimedia is introduced into a planning process, questions need to be asked about the accessibility of these tools to various segments of the society (particularly the disenfranchised) and the level of prioritization that multimedia initiatives should receive, relative to other social goals. In addition, planners' receptivity to these tools, particularly in terms of their implications for planners' roles, needs to be considered.

While there are countless new multimedia tools being developed and connectivity is ever increasing, the actual impact in communities, especially low-income and marginalized communities, is still negligible. The potential of these tools must be tempered by the needs and limitations of its users and how fully those users take ownership and control. The same lack of distrust and apathy evident in existing mechanisms for public engagement could also be transferred to these tools, if the process is not designed to be genuinely inclusive. Mere *access* to technology may result in citizens being passive consumers of information created by others.

Effective community building and capacity for action will require users with the power to control the production and dissemination of content. Equally important, planning agencies adopting multimedia technologies in planning processes need to clarify, through negotiation with participants, exactly how the output would be integrated in policy- and decision-making. Reflexivity needs to be incorporated into the processes of multimedia production and dissemination. To ensure that the output informs practice, organizational reflexivity is required. To be effective as a change agent, its use must be integrated within processes that create opportunities for trust-building and collaboration.

Notes

1. For further details see: http://fcis.oise.utoronto.ca/~daniel_sc/assignment1/1966cfc.html
2. The search was conducted on May 19, 2008
3. See the World Bank website: http://web.worldbank.org/WBSITE/EXTERNAL/TOPICS/EXTPOVERTY/EXTEMPOWERMENT/0,,contentMDK:20244572~isCURL:Y~pagePK:210058~piPK:210062~theSitePK:486411,00.html
4. For further details see the Walmart Movie website: http://www.walmartmovie.com/
5. For further details see An Inconvenient Truth website: http://www.climatecrisis.net/
6. This project generated a number of planning theses, for two of which I was the second reader and examiner for one.

7. I was the executive producer of this project.
8. See the EMERGENCE Canada website for more details: http://www.chs.ubc.ca/emergence/details.html
9. See http://earth.google.com/
10. See http://www2.vcn.bc.ca/

References

Attili, G. (2007). Digital ethnographies in the planning field. *Planning Theory and Practice, 8*(1), 90–97.

Clover, D. (2005). Sewing stories and acting activism: Women's leadership and learning through drama and craft. *Ephemera, 5*(4), 629–642.

Corbett, J., & Keller, C. (2004). Empowerment and participatory geographic information and multimedia systems: Observations from two communities in Indonesia. *Information Technologies and International Development, 5*(2), 25–44.

Forester, J. (1989). *Planning in the face of power.* Berkeley, CA: University of California Press.

Forester, J. (1999). *The deliberative practitioner: Encouraging participatory planning processes.* Cambridge, MA: MIT Press.

Frantz, J. (2007). *Using participatory video to enrich planning processes. Planning Theory and Practice, 8*(1), 103–107.

Friedmann, J. (1987). *Planning in the public domain: From knowledge to action.* Princeton, NJ: Princeton University Press.

Gurstein, P., Johnson, L., Schatz, L., Tate, L., & Hallenbeck, J. (2007). *Global work/local lives: Multimedia in creating public dialogue.* Paper presented at 48th Annual ACSP Conference, Milwaukee, WI.

Habermas, J. (1991). *The structural transformation of the public sphere: An inquiry into a category of Bourgeois Society* (T. McCarthy, Trans). Cambridge, MA: MIT Press.

Hallenbeck, J. (2007). *Video and social justice: Reimagining the city.* Unpublished Thesis, School of Community and Regional Planning, UBC, Vancouver.

Harries-Jones, P. (1991). From advocacy to social movements. In P. Harries-Jones (Ed.), *Making knowledge count: Advocacy and social science.* Montréal, QC: McGill-Queen's University Press.

Ingersoll, R. (2006). *Sprawltown: Looking for the city on its edges.* New York: Princeton Architectural Press.

Lefebvre, H. (1991). *The production of space* (D. Nicholson-Smith, Trans.). Oxford: Blackwell.

Levy, R. M. (2006). Urban design and computer visualization: Applications in community planning. In S. Tsenkova (Ed.), *Places and people: Planning new communities.* Calgary: University of Calgary Printing Services.

Marchessault, J. (1995). Reflections on the dispossessed: Video and the "Challenge for Change" experiment. *Screen, 36*(2), 131–146.

Mitchell, W. (1999). Equitable access to the online world. In D. Schon, B. Sanyal, & W. Mitchell (Eds.), *High technology and low income communities: Prospects for the positive use of advanced information technology.* Cambridge: MIT Press.

Norris, P. (2001). *Digital divide: Civic engagement, information poverty, and the internet worldwide.* New York: Cambridge University Press.

Sandercock, L. (2003). Out of the closet: The importance of stories and storytelling in planning practice. *Planning Theory and Practice, 4*(1), 11–28.

Sarkissian, W. (2007). Video as a tool in community engagement, *Planning Theory and Practice, 8*(1), 98–102.

Tewdwr-Jones, M. (2007). Film, space and place identity: Reflections on Urban planning. *Planning Theory and Practice, 8*(1), 108–112.

Throgmorton, J. (1996). *Planning as persuasive storytelling: The rhetorical construction of Chicago's electric future*. Chicago: University of Chicago Press.

White, S. A. (Ed.). (2003). *Participatory video: Images that transform and empower*. New Delhi: Sage Publications.

Wiesner, P. (1992). Media for the people: The Canadian experiments with film and video in community development. *American Review of Canadian Studies, 2*(1), 65–75.

Williams, T. (1988). The fogo process. St. John's, NF: Memorial University Snowden Centre for Development Support Communications.

Part III
Teaching with/Through Multimedia in Planning and Design

Chapter 12
Participatory Design and Howard Roark: The Story of the Detroit Collaborative Design Center

Sheri Blake

12.1 Introduction

Planners have often been criticized for expert-driven practice. "Professional planners, with their urgent need to act, move too quickly to models and inventories" and "tend to screen out the connections between the physical environment and its social meaning" (Tuan, 1977 and Appleyard 1979 in Mehrhoff, 1999, p. 61). Yet citizens perceive their communities as natural, economic and social entities, as well as spatial environments that are sources of delight, displeasure or despair (Mehrhoff, 1999). When processes of change are driven by experts, planning focuses too much on issues of land use and public finance, often ignoring environmental and design issues because they are difficult to quantify. When citizens are given an opportunity to engage in participatory planning and design, expert-driven planners are often at a loss as to how to proceed.

Expert-driven designers are also at a loss as to how to proceed, lacking knowledge about participatory process. In her book *Architecture: The Story of Practice*, Dana Cuff described a typical story of practice, a case study about a stakeholder group of Muslim families in Texas (Cuff, 1991, pp. 173–185). They hired an architect to design a community centre, 30 housing units and several other cultural facilities including a mosque. The architect made building and site design decisions without any significant participation, according to conventional architectural practice. As a result, despite working hard to study Muslim culture and historical precedents in mosque design, the architect did not understand anything about the stakeholders' desires and attitudes about design. The stakeholders gave the architect examples of poorly designed contemporary mosques they admired. They eventually forced a decision on a compromise site plan by combining components from different site designs that were not necessarily complementary. During the decision-making process, the architect was shut out by a lack of cultural understanding and language. It was clear from reading the description by Cuff that the architect also

S. Blake (✉)
University of Manitoba, Winnipeg, MB, Canada
e-mail: blakes@cc.umanitoba.ca

L. Sandercock, G. Attili (eds.), *Multimedia Explorations in Urban Policy and Planning*, Urban and Landscape Perspectives 7, DOI 10.1007/978-90-481-3209-6_12,

knew nothing about participatory design process. This is not unusual. Although theories of participation are sometimes given lip service in schools of planning and design, the tools and techniques are rarely taught and applied in projects. More importantly, the range of communication skills so critical to good process is almost never addressed (Blake, 2006b).

12.2 Why Participation?

The underlying principle of participation is that people have a universal right to participate in development that will impact their lives now and in the future. Participatory planning and design

> ...is based on the recognition that professional technical knowledge is often inadequate in the resolution of societal problems and it represents the addition of a moral and political content to professional practice, it grew from a belief that all citizens had a right to be represented in decisions about the environment and that planning [and design] would benefit from the maximum public input (Comerio, 1984, pp. 227–228).

In 1969, Sherry Arnstein published an influential paper, "A ladder of citizen participation", in which she explored eight levels, from non-participation (therapy and manipulation), to tokenism (informing, consultation, placation), to citizen power (partnership, delegated power, citizen control) (Arnstein, 1969). Deshler and Sock (1985, in Sanoff, 2000) collapsed Arnstein's ladder into four levels of participation: pseudo-participation or planning for (domestication, assistencialism) and genuine participation or planning with (cooperation, citizen control). Participation, as a new form of practice, has provided an opportunity for greater dialogue and direct involvement of local stakeholders. However, planners and designers continue to debate ethical questions related to who should participate, what process is appropriate contextually and when does a process become manipulative or begin to exclude others (Comerio, 1984; Mehrhoff, 1999; Sanoff, 2000).

The goal of participation is to encourage and enable people to build capacity and provide local stakeholders with the tools and techniques to effect change, but the extent to which this is successful depends on the design of the process. If a process is inclusive, it takes into account different world-views and values. It focuses on developing healthy communities, rather than on encouraging growth (Hochachka, 2005; Mehrhoff, 1999). When done poorly, participation is uncritical, protective of the values of the state, and/or conducted to get the citizen users to support actions pre-determined by professionals, including planners and designers (Till, 2005).

12.3 Why or How?...That Is the Question

Introducing the theories of participation to designers is not enough. It is critical to demonstrate good practice. To provide professionals and students of planning and design with an example of quality participatory design practice, I made the film, *Detroit Collaborative Design Center...amplifying the diminished voice* (Blake, 2006a). The film focuses on the participatory design practice of Detroit Collaborative Design Center (DCDC), a non-profit architecture firm and the engagement arm of the University of Detroit Mercy School of Architecture. They are working with Detroit Hispanic Development Corporation (DHDC), a non-profit community-based development organization, in the redesign of DHDC's 28,000 square foot facility. The facility will house administrative offices, a day care, youth programming including a multimedia facility, café and classrooms. DCDC engaged DHDC stakeholders in a series of design programming workshops, each one approximately 3 hour long, once a month over several months. The workshop series is adapted contextually for each project. In this case, workshops included the development of a project statement, a site walk-through, a variety of design programming extending beyond conventional practice, an introduction to architectural language and its meaning, site tours of similar projects, literacy about how to read floor plans, spatial allocation modelling, digital mapping of the building and site, budget negotiations, design feedback sessions and a presentation of the final work and package for capital fundraising purposes. A range of stakeholders, primarily building users, staff and board members, participated in the workshop series. Other representatives who may be involved in workshop processes include contractors, the architect of record, funders (bankers and/or foundations), technical assistance providers and local residents who may be impacted by a development.

An early rough cut of the film took the approach of critiquing expert-driven practice with the intention of introducing alternative participatory design practice and its intent. A portion of the rough cut included footage of stakeholders, technical assistance providers, architects and contractors who critiqued conventional planning and design practice. One stakeholder from DHDC voiced the opinion that designers impose their ideas on clients and then make the client pay. Another stakeholder described how he had talked to a couple of architects in advance of hiring DCDC, but they were not willing to conduct a participatory process. A technical assistance (TA) provider, who had worked with a range of designers over several decades, concurred. He described how many designers respond, when asked to collaborate: "No, I will not take advice. However, I will guarantee you a prize-winning project." As the TA provider explained, "that becomes problematic when that prize-winning project isn't one that people can work in, pray in, or serve in" (In Blake, 2006a).

Another TA provider, who provided community-based development organizations with a range of development skills in advance of design and construction, described the impact of poor design:

> I've seen some firms who come in with their tag line, like we are the New Urbanism firm. And they come in to the room before they enter the room. Their presence is there because of that tag line and who they are and what they want to do. You buy that firm because that is what you want, that tag line. I have seen some really bad designs come out of that type of planning. One non-profit, I won't mention names, I have tried to help them understand that the design is getting out of control on them. Their 6 million dollar project is now a 15 million dollar project, totally unnecessary. Building components they don't need. The design just keeps going. You have to stop it somewhere along the line (in Blake, 2006a).

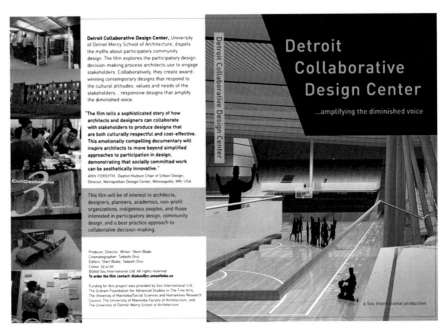

Fig. 12.1 Detroit Collaborative Design Center. . .*amplifying the diminished voice* (Blake, 2006a). DVD Trapsheet designed by Public Image Company, Winnipeg. Graphics and photographs provided by Detroit Collaborative Design Center and Tadashi Orui

An architect described a project he was hired to work on for post-occupancy upgrades. He discovered that a school, recently designed and built by another architecture firm, needed over $ 100.000 in upgrades as soon as the design and construction were complete. The architect hired to work on these upgrades believes the money could have been saved if the original designer of the building had spent time talking to the stakeholders, primarily the users of the building, during the design programming phase. During the process of filming, many architects told similar stories. They described how designers often respond negatively when confronted with the concept of engaging stakeholders in design. One designer described another architect's response when told about the participatory design process they had learned from DCDC and applied in practice:

> Why would you do that? Why would you sit around the table with people who aren't experts? Why would you open yourself up like that? He was actually quite appalled that we were going through the process (Blake, 2006a).

An architect and educator described it as a fundamental problem with architectural education focusing on the heroic architect who builds the Howard Roark object. Howard Roark, the main character in the novel, *The Fountainhead* (Rand, 1943), is an architect who dynamites a housing project he designed, because it was not built to his specifications.

During post-production screenings, architects in particular, when viewing the critiques that were sprinkled throughout the first half of the rough cut, misinterpreted their intent, expressed offense or literally shut themselves down to learning more. When testing the film on a range of planning and design professionals, one architect began talking part way through the film and would not cease talking, making it difficult for others to view the film. This professional demanded that critiques of the profession be removed from the film. After screening excerpts from the film to a large audience of about 100 designers, planners and engineers, a discussion ensued. One architect stood up at the end and boldly stated that even using the alternative practice I was presenting, it would not work unless the architect was like Howard Roark!

Roark, although a fictional character, must be addressed. He looms large in the minds of students and professionals in the field of architecture. He is the heroic architect who individually designs "signature" buildings. More importantly, the intent of Roark's creator, Ayn Rand, in writing this book must be explored.

12.3.1 Design by Committee or Collaboration?

Ayn Rand, the author, began writing *The Fountainhead* in 1935 and finished it in 1938, although it was not published until 1943. The dates are important in the context of the background of the author and her philosophy. In her personal journals, she continually critiqued and analyzed her work in progress. After writing Part 1 of the novel, Rand did an analysis and summarized key points to emphasize:

> Stress the second-handedness whenever possible. . .Cut out episodes that do not bear on that theme. The book is not about architecture, it's about Roark against the world. . .Give only enough pure architecture to make the background real. But only as a background... (Rand in Peikoff, 1993, p. 701).

In Rand's mind, the book is not about architecture but about collectivism (second-handedness) or practice based on a mob mentality, versus individualism (first-handedness) or expert-driven practice.

The focus on second-handedness is particularly emphasized when Rand developed her sketch of Ellsworth Toohey, the ultimate second-hander and Roark's main antagonist:

> Communism, the Soviet variety particularly, is not merely an economic theory. It does not demand economic equality and security in order to set each individual free to rise as he chooses. Communism is, above all, a spiritual theory which denies the individual, *not merely as an economic power*, but in all and every respect. It demands spiritual subordination to the mass in every way conceivable, economic, intellectual, artistic; it allows individuals to rise only as *servants of the masses*, only as mouthpieces for the great average. It places, among single individuals, Ellsworth Monkton Toohey at the top of the human pyramid. . . (Rand in Peikoff, 1993, p. 700).

Rand was born in Russia and lived through the Bolshevik Revolution. She arrived in the United States in 1926 to visit relatives, and stayed. She was very much opposed to collectivism and in particular to the disintegration of free inquiry that was occurring at the time she left (Peikoff, 1993, p. 707). She began writing the book in 1935, during "The Red Decade," a period of US history that was the most sympathetic to communism. Rand's treatise, using the fictional heroic architect Roark, was to emphasize above all else the value of individualism. Roark is portrayed as competent and honest, a man of integrity and, above all, a superb designer. Roark is the classic example of the individual as expert. In her journals, to provide a contrast to Roark's practice, Rand uses a real-life example of collective design practice. The example is an extremely poor one, yet likely representative at a time when the tools and techniques of participation were not understood. She uses the example to paint all collective practice with one brush, denigrating it as a form of mob spirit, "an average on an average" (Rand in Peikoff, 1993, p. 703).

Since the book's primary purpose was to denigrate communism and celebrate individualism, the architecture profession was not described in detail. The reader is left to wonder how Roark develops the building programme from which to design; how he knows so much about structure, materials and all the other trades so necessary to consult as part of the design process. Instead, the term collectivism is lumped together with the terms cooperation and collaboration, implying that asking anyone about anything during the process of design is a crime. So the image of Roark is of someone who simply knows what his clients need, intuitively. Somehow he knows everything there is to know about structure, material and other technical aspects of the profession and can deliver the best piece of work every time, his way.

> The only thing that matters, my goal, my reward, my beginning, my end is the work itself. My work done my way. Peter, there's nothing in the world that you can offer me, except this. Offer me this and you can have anything I've got to give. My work done my way. A private, personal, selfish, egotistical motivation. That's the only way I function. That's all I am (Rand, 1943, pp. 579–580).

This heroic individualist image continues to permeate the design profession, more than 60 years after *The Fountainhead* was first published.

Roark objected to "design by committee" and held to a belief that the project must be completed exactly as he envisioned it. Interestingly, the staff of the Detroit Collaborative Design Center also object to "design by committee". They believe in "design by collaboration". This is not simply a play on words. In the case of design by committee, architects usually defend their design to a client or committee who proffer their opinions after the design is completed. Alternatively, the architect consults with a committee during the design process, without building any design or development literacy. Rand describes this practice throughout *The Fountainhead* and refers to it as second-handedness (Rand, 1943). Cuff (1991) describes similar case studies in her book.

In both cases, working with a committee during or after the process, the participants, user, committee members or client who pays the bill have little to no understanding of the design decision-making process. The staff of DCDC believes that mutual knowledge sharing is core to good collaborative practice in the initial programming stage of design. The designers share professional knowledge while drawing on stakeholder experiential knowledge. The result, Dan Pitera, the director of DCDC, explained during filming is a richer programme from which to design.

I realized, after testing the film with a range of audiences, that architects in particular were not interested in listening to critiques of their profession. They have always been more interested in the question of "how" rather than the more critical question of "why" (De Carlo, 2005; Till, 2005). Giancarlo De Carlo, an architect, describes how the profession restricts itself to

> ...relations between clients and entrepreneurs, land owners, critics, connoisseurs, and architects; a field built on a network of economic and social class interests and held together by the mysterious tension of a cultural and aesthetic class code. This was a field that excluded everything in economic, social, cultural and aesthetic terms that was not shared by the class in power (De Carlo, 2005, p. 5).

He explains that when neighbourhoods and buildings designed "for" people are neglected and deteriorate, it is the users themselves who are blamed, labelled as immature or unable to understand the intent of the designer. However, the reality is that since the users did not participate in the design of their environments, they "are unable to appropriate them and therefore have no reason to defend them" (De Carlo, 2005, p. 16).

Public participation in planning and design continues to face resistance from professionals and design educators. In order to reach the target audience of architects, the critiques of conventional practice were removed from the film and the visual storytelling shifted to changing the perceptions of participatory practice. The focus shifted to "how" DCDC practiced participatory design, rather than the "why" of alternative practice. At the same time, a subtext was applied, based on common perceptions about participatory design. The common perception is that participation compromises design quality. Design is compromised because the public cannot participate effectively in the planning and design process. They cannot participate effectively because they lack expert technical and design knowledge. If those arguments do not work, then planners and designers will state that participation costs too much (Sanoff, 2000; Towers, 1995; Wates & Knevitt, 1987; Francis, 1983; Hester, 1983). Three questions guided the work of the visual storytelling: Is design quality compromised? Can lay people participate effectively? Does participation really cost more?

12.4 Is Design Quality Compromised?

The first two perceptions about participation in design are interrelated. Design quality is thought to be compromised because the public does not have the expert technical planning and design knowledge necessary to participate. Without this knowledge, they cannot possibly know what they want and are indifferent to good design. However, the expert planner/designer intrinsically knows what the public wants and needs. The expert's aesthetic standards far exceed those of the majority and are coded in a specialized language (De Carlo, 2005; Till, 2005). These beliefs were immortalized by Roark in *The Fountainhead* (Rand, 1943).

By selecting Detroit Collaborative Design Center (DCDC) to highlight in the film, the perception that design quality is compromised by participation was addressed in advance of making the film. Basing the core of their practice on participatory design, DCDC has won numerous local, state, national and international design awards since being established in 1995. DCDC won the 2002 Dedalo Minosse International Prize for their project Homeboy Industries in San Francisco. The University of Detroit Mercy's School of Architecture won the Grand Award 2002 National Council of Architectural Registration Board's (NCARB) Prize for successful integration of education and practice, in large part based on the work of the Design Center. The first Director of DCDC, Terrence Curry, won the National Young Architect Award (1999) from the American Institute of Architects (AIA). Dan Pitera, the current Director of DCDC, won the AIA Michigan President's Award (2005). Both directors were Harvard University Loeb Fellows, selected for their fellowship based on their design excellence. DCDC has twice been invited to participate in ArchiLab (2001 and 2004) in Orleans, France. In addition to receiving other design awards, the work of the Design Center has been published and exhibited in numerous countries. Clearly, participatory design has not compromised design quality.

Fig. 12.2 Section through the DHDC's café and multimedia facility, designed by DCDC. Graphics by Detroit Collaborative Design Center

I believed it was important to select an award-winning design practice. This way, the concept that "design matters" would be reinforced and architects would likely be more willing to explore the processes presented in the film. For this purpose, the first 10 minutes of the film introduces the Design Center, describes some of their awards, defines the principles that guide their participatory design practice and introduces some high-quality and award-winning design work.

12.5 Can Lay People Participate Effectively?

The second perception, that the public lacks expert technical and design knowledge, is addressed by DCDC in the way they design and implement their participatory design process. They recognize that no one process can ever be truly inclusive and that everyone expresses themselves in different ways. For that purpose, DCDC has developed or adapted a range of tools and techniques to allow stakeholders to participate in different ways and to limit dominant voices. They apply visual, tactile, written and oral communication techniques within and across workshops. Also recognizing that understanding and education are at least as important as physical design, their focus is on mutual knowledge sharing in the early stages of design programming. Participation should be used not only to draw out local knowledge, which they do throughout the workshop series, but also to assist stakeholders in understanding design and development processes and engaging in significant portions of the design decision-making process.

> Effective participation starts with a recognition that people with no experience of building design need to understand something of the process, and that design needs to be demystified through better communication, so that users have some appreciation of the choices that are available (Towers, 1995, p. 157).

During the production of the film, research methods included participant observation over a period of 8 months combined with site visits to built projects, interviews and focus groups with current and former stakeholders, building occupants, architects, contractors, related technical assistance providers and current and former staff of DCDC. It was obvious during focus group sessions that stakeholders who had participated in DCDC's workshops, during the film and in past projects, had acquired an extensive amount of design literacy. Reviewing the footage during post-production, several aspects of DCDC's literacy building process became more evident. They provided stakeholders with an understanding of how designers think, the language they use and how it is applied in design decision-making. One stakeholder, stimulated by the images presented and gaining a grasp of design decision-making, commented during one workshop that it began to "help my wheels turn...How is it going to relate and how are we going to help create what relates to us" (In Blake, 2006a).

DCDC explained how design and programming decisions made by stakeholders impacted budgets, both during workshops and on-site visits to built projects. Stakeholders learned how to read floor plans in order to critique the designs presented and to pay more attention to detail in their environment. DCDC engaged stakeholders in three-dimensional modelling and mapping exercises to collaboratively explore programme adjacencies, alternative footprints and design opportunities. The budget process was designed to encourage stakeholders to prioritize design expectations and to negotiate among themselves the difficult decisions about what to cut out of the building to reduce the overall budget and to fit the required footprint. Throughout the process, the designers make explicit the relationship between good, fast and cheap: that you can only have two of the three. You can have good and fast, but not cheap. You can have fast and cheap, but not good. Alternatively, you can have good and cheap, but it will not be fast. During a range of workshops and site visits, they continually explore this relationship between design decision-making and budget. They described, for example, how a project that was done fast and cheap, compromised design quality to a certain degree. However, the stakeholders of the project made their decisions based on the fact they only expected to occupy the space for 5 years. The stakeholders are constantly encouraged to make difficult decisions that they ultimately would have to live with, in advance of the design being finalized.

As a result, stakeholders acquired a better understanding of what influenced the decision-making process and where compromises were required and why. At the same time, because the decisions were made in advance of the design being finalized, design quality was not compromised. During the process, DCDC also explored the opportunities and limitations of donated services and self-build in the context of the mandate of the community-based organization. Most importantly, they did not shy away from exploring the attitudes of the stakeholders towards design. They encouraged stakeholders to bring examples of designs they like. Applying the five senses, they tried to draw out an individual's emotional attachment to a design – colour, light, materiality, a reminiscence about a favourite hang-out, cultural symbolism, etc. By exploring the senses and the emotional relationship to design, designers develop a better understanding of the likes and dislikes of stakeholders.

Fig. 12.3 DCDC runs multiple workshops with stakeholders. In this workshop, DHDC staff explores alternate spatial allocations for administration, daycare, multimedia labs, classrooms and other building functions. Photograph by Detroit Collaborative Design Center

DCDC believes it is better to discover this early in the design programming stage than in a confrontational battle when the final design is presented, or in a lack of user appropriation of the space when the project is built and occupied.

12.5.1 Communicating Effectively

> Sense making is not simply a matter of instrumental problem-solving, it is a matter of altering, respecting, acknowledging, and shaping people's lived worlds (Forester in Till, 2005, p. 36).

DCDC demonstrated a focus on designers as guides rather than experts. They helped organize research and workshop tasks, posed meaningful questions, documented dialogues between stakeholders in detail, researched hypotheses, challenged and mediated among differing perspectives, summarized research and workshop findings and took the time to establish relationships. They effectively combined academic and professional knowledge with the experiential knowledge of the community (Mehrhoff, 1999), collaboratively making sense and achieving mutual understanding through the negotiation of values, attitudes and varying world-views.

More importantly, they communicate in a way that stakeholders can understand. Graham Towers describes the problems of professional architecture communication, citing a journal publication:

> . . .the recurring motifs of Hertzberger's architecture that can be formulated in various ways: e.g. polyvalent form and individual interpretation, structure and infill, warp and weft, order and chaos, competence and performance, labyrinthine clarity, casbah organisae, langue et parole. . .Here one sees an example of user orientated architecture conducive to participation (Towers, 1995, p. 162).

Towers continues in his own words, "Perhaps. Certainly not an example of user-oriented language conducive to communication."

Jeremy Till explains that the dilemma lies in the architect's belief that their knowledge is special, a common perspective in expert-driven practices:

> There is a nagging doubt that in dealing with the normal language, one might be seen as normal. Participation thus presents architects with a double bind – the need to reassess what constitutes their knowledge but also the worry that in so doing one may no longer be seen as an architect. Best therefore to avoid the problem altogether. . .Architects thus tend to cling to the certainty of what they know, rather than expose themselves to the uncertainty of what others may know (Till, 2005, p. 32).

DCDC was careful to communicate in plain language, yet shared the language architects used in design decision-making so that stakeholders could engage more effectively. As they shared this knowledge, they frequently used everyday examples, associating architectural language with surroundings common to the stakeholders. They cut a donut in half to demonstrate how to read the basic section of a building (apples and green peppers work well too). A scavenger hunt helped stakeholders understand how to read floor plans and pay more attention to detail in their environment. The architects described the concept of "turning up architecture" to the feeling

Fig. 12.4 DHDC recognizes the importance of hip-hop culture when engaging local youth. Painting, dance and multimedia programming is popular, so related themes have been incorporated into the master plan design for the building by DCDC. Photograph by Tadashi Orui

you get when you hear a good song on the radio. In order to feel the music, you want to turn it up. They explained the relationship between good, fast and cheap on a site visit, explaining how certain decisions were made by the stakeholders to focus on fast and cheap, influenced by the short period of time, 5 years, they expected to occupy that space. By exploring the design limitations that resulted, the architects used the site to demonstrate how different decisions (a different combination of good, fast and cheap) would result in variations in design quality and cost.

12.5.2 Drawing Out Local Knowledge

While it may appear from the description above that the process was one-sided, this was not the case. Each process was designed to draw out extensive amounts of local knowledge. As well, by taking the time to build a relationship of trust with the stakeholders, indigenous philosophy was shared by the stakeholders with the architects late in the programming stage. This knowledge significantly affected the final design.

Discussions expanded far beyond the basic needs assessment interviews architects have with their clients in conventional practice, primarily focused on the programmes of the organization, spatial allocation, hierarchies, room occupancy and related technical data. Extensive dialogues occurred between the stakeholders during the various workshops and were documented in detail by the designers. As Dan Pitera of DCDC emphasizes in the film, planners and designers cannot give someone a voice. Stakeholders already have a voice. "But in our society, some voices are more amplified than others" (In Blake, 2006a). The Design Center believes that collaborative action can help people amplify their voices. The dialogues revealed the workplace culture and the indigenous values that guided the work of DHDC. The architects learned the value of hip-hop culture; the intent to have children fully engaged in the building, not limited to one part of it, while controlling the movements of youth to a certain degree; the importance of the café and media centre as an "electronic basketball hoop"; the goals of programme staff to maximize the privacy of people just informed of positive HIV/AIDS status; and the need to protect the abused from those who abuse them.

As trust between the architects and stakeholders increased, indigenous values that shaped the staff training and community programmes run by DHDC began to permeate design discussions. As a result, the conceptual framework that guided the design decisions was based on the medicine wheel, core to the principles and practice of DHDC. By the end, the stakeholders felt their voices, including minority opinions, had been heard and respected; that their socio-cultural values had been incorporated into the design; and that they had taught the architects something they would be able to use in future design practice.

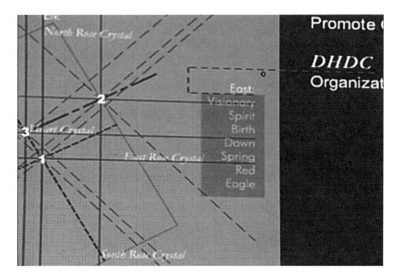

Fig. 12.5 The traditional Aboriginal medicine wheel provided the guiding framework for the master plan design of DHDC's building. Graphic by Detroit Collaborative Design Center. Photograph by Tadashi Orui

12.5.3 Avoiding Organizational Collapse

Equally important to the process is DCDC's caution about not taking on a new project unless they are sure the non-profit organization or community group has the organizational capacity to develop it. In most cases, they will refer the organization to the Nonprofit Facilities Center before beginning the conceptual design workshop series. This centre was jointly established by the United Way for Southeastern Michigan and the Non-profit Finance Fund of New York to provide support to Detroit non-profit organizations to plan, finance, develop and manage facilities. A large part of their programme is technical assistance and they work with about 200 organizations. A programme director from the Nonprofit Facilities Center described their experience with non-profits:

> I get phone calls regularly. I need money. I don't need all the other stuff. Can you help me out? It's not about the money. It's about the commitment, the community, who is involved, how committed is the whole community to the process... We take organizations through a think cycle to measure and assess whether they are in a position to develop the project they propose to do. If the Board is saying we are going to build a new building, it's going to be a $5 million building, let's go. We take them back and say where is your market, where's your demand, where's your Board capacity. Are you able to raise this amount of money? Where's the commitment. What kind of study have you done? Some say wow I had no idea that it was this involved. I thought you just went out and started writing grant proposals. These organizations are feeding people; they are providing community services, health care. None of them went to school to be a developer. We work through funding, financing, real estate issues, design issues, readiness issues, managing the team, so they are ready to hire the right professionals to help them through the process (Blake, 2006a).

An economic development technical assistance provider who has collaborated with non-profit organizations for over 20 years concurs:

> There are a lot of non-profits. There is not a lot of development competency. There are a lot of organizations stuck in the advocacy mode of getting a street light turned on, protesting the city, getting a building demolished. If they are not serious about being proactive in their community, I don't deal with them. If I sense they have a good project, a good team. I will work with them. They need to understand they are part of a team. They are not the team. They are part of a larger team made up of consultants, other non-profits, for-profits, whatever is necessary. Some of them never get to that point. They just want "all by myself, I'm going to do it all by myself, just give me the money" (Blake, 2006a).

Even the designer with the best intentions can walk a non-profit in over their heads in a participatory design process. Detroit Collaborative Design Center has learned from experience how to avoid the pitfalls. Organizations may want to take on more than they can handle financially or may not be ready to do facility management on top of programme management. By helping them achieve their facility, a designer may be leading them to collapse or at the very least instability. It is necessary to understand the mandate of an organization and design the process accordingly. Sanoff concurs (2006):

> Part of a failure is due to the fact that it is not clear from the people who organized it at what stage is participation appropriate, who should be involved, what are the objectives, why do we want people to participate.

During filming, the Design Center explored a different building at the request of the stakeholders. The designers became really excited about the possibilities for great design in the new space. However, instead of encouraging the stakeholders to take on the new building, they had to warn them against taking on so much space. They also referred them to technical assistance providers who could conduct an analysis of the potential for recapturing their investment if they purchased the new building. The rental market in Detroit is very soft and the possibility of renting out the additional space to make some money to run the facility was limited. DCDC designers encouraged DHDC stakeholders instead to explore what they could manage in their existing building and how programmes could share space. This was achieved through several strategies, including, for example, the conceptual arrangement of spaces workshop and the budget workshop. In this case, the process not only saves the stakeholders money in the development phase but may also save them from financial collapse.

Other issues come up frequently throughout the workshop process and designers need to know how to bring issues forward gently, so stakeholders do not become defensive. During the budget workshop, a stakeholder questioned the cost of construction based on $100 per square feet, the average cost for building rehab in Detroit. The stakeholder thought DHDC could do it cheaper if they contributed sweat equity. Dan Pitera explained that sweat equity is fine when you are doing one room, but not necessarily a 28.000-square foot building. When preparing a budget it is best to know the total budget from the beginning. If you are able to do some sweat equity, in the demolition phase for example, that is fine. However, it should not take time away from the core work of a non-profit organization, such as DHDC's work in delivering social and educational programmes. He encouraged them to prioritize the mandate of the organization so that the programmes would not suffer. He also cautioned against in-kind donations of labour. Perhaps an electrician or drywaller may offer in-kind services. The problem will be that they do it on their schedule, which may not fit into the construction schedule at the appropriate time. The biggest issue becomes schedule. Donations rarely line up, resulting in cost over-runs when the project is delayed. DCDC encourages organizations to be realistic about the overall budget from the beginning.

12.6 Does Participation Really Cost More?

Does it really cost more? In fact, participation may save money. When I began making the film, my expectation was that the cost savings in participatory design were in the legal fees saved when new construction, a conversion or demolition is held up due to public outcry or NIMBYism (Not In My Back Yard). As a result, a protracted legal battle and the resultant additional costs in development due to delays could have been saved if the initial process had included public participation.

However, I discovered that the cost savings extend throughout the design and development phases. The Design Center does spend more money up front in the

Fig. 12.6 In the design of Mercy Education Project's (MEP) tutoring support facility for girls and women, DCDC explored, with stakeholders, the concept of "wall". The wall acts as a room for reading, climbing, socializing and hiding. MEP chose fast and cheap as their criteria because they only expected to use the space for about 5 years. DCDC was still able to create interesting and interactive spaces despite the low project budget. Photograph by Glen Moon

design programming stage, due to the extensive workshop process. However, they save money at the back-end due to a reduction of time spent troubleshooting during construction. The on-going discussions about good, fast and cheap keep the relationship between decision-making, cost and design quality forefront and centre. During the budget workshop, $1.3 million dollars was cut from the project, through negotiation between stakeholders. The building finally fit the desired footprint without compromising the desires of the various stakeholders and design quality. By the end of the process, the buy-in of expectations, budget and programme are complete. By shifting the costs to the front-end, DCDC can focus primarily on design rather than on troubleshooting, something all design firms would prefer to do. At the same time, DCDC has discovered that the client saves money once a project goes to bid, because changes are rarely made in the construction phase. It is generally understood that once a project goes to bid and the contract is signed, if you take anything out of a project you lose about half its value. If anything is added into a project, the cost doubles. At the very least, if changes are made after bid, cost over-runs occur. As well, when participation is not part of the process, changes often have to be made in post-occupancy upgrades, resulting in further costs. Again, Sanoff (2006) concurs:

It costs too much!? That is really absurd because it only means that people who have tried it and failed never had a clear sense of purpose, what the expected outcomes were. So these are all myths and I have written about these myths over and over again. They all occur because people engage in these kind of processes out of romanticism and goodwill without any substantive knowledge or theoretical background, so that is why these myths keep reappearing.

12.7 A New Role for Schools of Planning and Design?

Did visual storytelling work? By shifting the film from the question of "why" to "how", were architects more willing to engage in discussions about participation? Yes. Upon completion of the film I have been invited to screen it in various design offices, in addition to other venues. I discovered that architects shifted their critique from the film, which they indicated demonstrated high-quality practice, to design schools. The new critiques focused on a lack of knowledge held by architecture professionals about soft communications skills – facilitation, mediation, negotiation, quality note-taking, plain language communication, group skills, listening skills and the ability to translate planning and architecture knowledge to a broader public (Blake, 2006b). Planners and designers who practice participation often believe it is sufficient to draw out experiential knowledge. Few are skilled in the ability to demystify planning and design decision-making processes. Another common critique from architects who view the film has focused on a lack of knowledge in architecture schools about creative engagement strategies, including tools, techniques and intent. More importantly, planners and designers need to give up their fear of losing control, try to be flexible and give up their ego a little, which implies a shift in power relations between designers and stakeholders.

Sherry Arnstein (1969), the first to develop a ladder of participation, believes that participation without redistribution of power is an empty and frustrating process for those without power. The reality is that even with citizen control, there may be power struggles within a neighbourhood, between residents, within an organization and between organizations. I would argue that you have to go further; that you should not simply be trying to redistribute power but also working to break down hierarchy, in order for participation to be effective. During the making of the film, Dan Pitera described it best: true collaboration is when the project, not a person, is at the top of the pyramid.

Architecture in film often focuses on historic, sacred or secular architecture, signature buildings, architecture as backdrop for psychological thrillers, visions of urban futures, science-fiction architecture and cities, super-hero architecture or film as a way to explore space. The primary focus is on film as art, propaganda or the spirit of place. Rarely is the focus on film as communication, exploring ways of practice and place-making. Film has the ability to document and demonstrate good proactive practice and place-making in action – as a tool for education as well as a tool for engagement with professional designers, community-based organizations and related stakeholders.

As I discovered in the process of editing the film, architects are more willing to engage in discussions about alternative practices in design when you bring the message forward simply as an example of "how" rather than as a critique of conventional practice. It is best to avoid "why" altogether. Subsequently, as I discovered in teaching, students are willing to engage in conversations about participation when they have a quality example to draw from and discuss, rather than simply reading about the theory of practice. As well, community-based organizations and local stakeholders are willing to test the waters and engage in participatory design when they have an example on film they can view in advance. Testing this in practice, I have found that community stakeholders, after viewing the film, are willing to engage in community design studios and to recruit other stakeholders. They feel more comfortable knowing that mutual knowledge sharing will enhance their ability to participate effectively and that design decision-making is not solely the purview of the architect.

I would caution that visual storytelling is not necessarily superior to words, or more importantly, to practice. Although this film helps introduce the participatory design practice and processes of the Design Center, it is only a start. Sol Worth, in "The Uses of Film in Education and Communication", explains that the release of a film is "a public and social [act]; it is a symbolic form available for participation in a communication process" (Worth, 1981, p. 121). However, Worth expresses concerns that teaching through film (in contrast to teaching about film) sometimes becomes a preferred method, even though film as an effective teaching device is still in question. "Film is one mode in which people can record image-events, organize them to imply meaning, and through them communicate to others" (Worth, 1981, p. 123)...but only one mode. The film about the Design Center must be combined with other forms of communication, written theory, an understanding of the broad skill set necessary for good practice, other examples of tools, techniques and processes, and an opportunity to test the waters in a real context.

Fig. 12.7 Detroit has experienced several race riots since the first one in 1863, resulting in extensive abandonment and decay. Sound House is one of several of DCDC's Firebreak projects in Detroit's inner city, intended to act as a catalyst for community organizing/building, and to encourage the City to demolish unsafe structures. Photograph by Detroit Collaborative Design Center

Worth defines education as "a process by which we not only learn to take in an environment, but in which we develop ways to communicate about it to others by choice and by intention" (Worth, 1981, p. 122). In this instance, visual storytelling is an excellent educational tool to infer, by intention, that integrating literacy building in design and development with local experiential knowledge leads to mutual knowledge sharing among all participants, including architects. It can demonstrate the relationship between collaborative development of a programme and quality design decision-making. As well, it can clarify that engaging for the purposes of romanticism and goodwill, as Sanoff (2006) noted above, is not only inappropriate but dangerous when an architect (or planner) walks a community-based organization or other relevant stakeholders in over their heads. The architect, described by Cuff (1991), does not only need to develop a better understanding of Muslim culture (and possibly language) but also needs a more comprehensive understanding of participatory design practices and the extensive range of communication skills that facilitate the creation of really great building and planning programmes, and therefore quality designs and plans.

References

Arnstein, S. (1969). A ladder of citizen participation. *Journal of the American Institute of Planners, 34,* 216–224.

Blake, S. dir. (2006a). *Detroit collaborative design center. . .amplifying the diminished voice.* Winnipeg (DVD): Sou International Ltd.

Blake, S. (2006b). Knowledge, skills and attitudes needed by community designers. *Plan Canada, 11*(12), 43–45.

Comerio, M. C. (1984). Community design: Idealism and entrepreneurship. *Architecture and Planning Research, 1,* 227–243.

Cuff, D. (1991). *Architecture: The story of practice.* Boston: MIT.

De Carlo, G. (2005). Architecture's public. In P. B. Jones, D. Petrescu, & J. Till (Eds.), *Architecture and participation.* Oxford: Spon.

Francis, M. (1983, Fall). Community design. *Journal of Architectural Education,* 14–19.

Hester, R. T. (1983). Process can be style: Participation and conservation in landscape architecture. *Landscape Architecture, 5,* 49–55.

Hochachka, G. (2005). *Developing sustainability, developing the self: An integral approach to international and community development.* Victoria: University of Victoria.

Mehrhoff, A. W. (1999). *Community design: A team approach to dynamic community systems.* Thousand Oaks: Sage.

Peikoff, L. (1993). Afterword. In A. Rand (1943) (Ed.), *The fountainhead.* New York: Signet.

Sanoff, H. (2006). Personal interview.

Sanoff, H. (2000). *Community participation methods in design and planning.* New York: Wiley.

Till, J. (2005). The negotiation of hope. In P. B. Jones, Petrescu D, & J. Till (Eds.), *Architecture and participation.* Oxford: Spon.

Towers, G. (1995). *Building democracy: Community architecture in the inner cities.* London: UCL.

Wates, N. & Knevitt, C. (1987). *Community architecture: How people are creating their own environment.* Sulfolk: Penguin.

Worth, S. (1981). *Studying visual communication.* Philadelphia: Pennsylvania Press.

Chapter 13
Learning as an Aesthetic Experience: Digital Pedagogies in Planning Didactics

Lidia Decandia

13.1 Making Theory and Practice Interact: The Laboratory as the Context of the Experience

I teach regional planning in the Faculty of Architecture of Alghero where I coordinate a "didactic block"[1] whose theme is "planning in the social context". The particular organization of the course recalls the idea of an "active school" and it is based on the Deweyian concept of "learning by doing". Its didactic structure is substantially interactive and deeply focused on a workshop process where different disciplines' contributions work in synergy. These characteristics led me to reflect on the effectiveness of learning contexts, on the teacher's role, on the relationships between students and teacher and, more significantly, on the languages and the indispensable tools that are needed in order to create real spaces of knowledge production.

The main goal of the course, where theory and practice are deeply interwoven in the tangible experience of field work rooted in a local context, is to discuss the paradigms which constitute the premises of a certain way of conceiving planning. My first assumption is that the territory under investigation cannot be thought of as a neutral surface which exists beyond sense making and appropriation networks. Moreover, the research project cannot be thought about as something entirely conceived by an external mind and dropped on the territory from above. It cannot be seen as something to lower on a territory that is conceived without life and history.

Starting from this perspective, the course workshop wants to offer tools and methodologies which are able to build perceptive and delicate interpretations of the uniqueness of the different local realities. By reconsidering the territory as the complex outcome of an interactive process which involves people, society and environment, the course wants to rethink the very notion of a territorial project. In order to achieve this goal, a detailed and in-depth analysis of the territorial context and of its invisible and temporal dimensions is crucial.

L. Decandia (✉)
Department of Architecture and Planning, University of Sassari, Alghero, SS, Italy
e-mail: decandia@uniss.it

L. Sandercock, G. Attili (eds.), *Multimedia Explorations in Urban Policy and Planning*, Urban and Landscape Perspectives 7, DOI 10.1007/978-90-481-3209-6_13, © Springer Science+Business Media B.V. 2010

There is a thread which connects Kropotkin's approach to Geddes' experiences and to some relevant Italian figures such as Olivetti, Doglio and De Carlo.[2] The course follows this thread and tries to present these historical teachings in contemporary terms. It aims at building collective and learning environments through which students could intercept "condensed" territorial memories, elaborate new occasions of territory construction, interlacing traditions and innovations in ways that are able to meet the needs of contemporary men and women. This is an approach which necessarily requires an exploration of symbolic and expressive languages.

13.2 Taking Care of Contexts

The programme of the course is based on the idea of active learning, which is essential to develop practical planning skills in local contexts. Because of it, the course goes beyond the traditional lecture delivery format. The fundamental idea is to put students in the condition of developing a "caring" or somehow involved attitude towards local territorial contexts. From this perspective it is important not to teach abstract and normative theories that would simply be acquired like "an honey produced by others and to be passively tasted in the perfect resting of body and spirit" (Proust cit. in Abruzzese, 1996, p. 2); rather it is necessary to educate students to develop more perceptive and refined ways of knowing which require an active and participatory involvement.

In order to comprehend and capture the peculiarity of a place or of a territory, it is important to acquire a complex range of skills which are able to detect the differences (Decandia, 2004). This form of knowledge cannot be rooted in deductive or axiomatic reasoning: rather, it implies a way of thinking that draws on measures, relations and qualities, a creative and imaginative approach which cannot be based on a method that is separated from the content. This approach can be built only through a progressive immersion in the context, where it is possible to get in touch and appreciate the passing of time and the potentialities which are inscribed in the peculiarities of the contexts.

It is a way of knowing which requires discernment and judgment skills, imagination and the capability of catching vividly and deeply those intervention principles which can be applied in specific realities and in specific time. It is a form of deep and penetrating rationality, a *poetic* and multidimensional knowledge which implies comprehension and listening ability, empathic desire and immersion willingness. It is not easy to acquire such a rationality because, as Pascal suggests, it requires considerable subtlety and a perspicuous and delicate sense which is nurtured by sensitiveness and fantasy (Pascal, 1670, p. 6).[3]

This is a knowledge formed from immersion and participation: a lived and perceptive comprehension that implies a bodily involvement, not just a mental one. It is a knowledge which speaks both to the intellect and to the senses, which is nurtured by ideas and models as well as by the existential concreteness of the encounter with territories, peoples, passions and emotions.

13.3 Learning as a "Pilgrim's Journey" Towards Knowledge

Starting from this perspective, I decided to rethink the articulation of the class, imagining a complex sequence of didactic steps, rather than simply a lecture format. I imagined the class as an "experiential journey" or, using a stronger metaphor, as a "pilgrim's journey" towards knowledge.

The pilgrim suggests the idea of a person who is walking and inhabiting the space, someone who, along his path, not only sees other worlds but meets things and starts knowing them. He considers things not as objects but as tools "for being in the world" (in the Heideggerian sense): a way to make his own experience more intense. The pilgrim conveys the world and its elements into his life project and because of this he learns how to deeply interconnect with different places (Moreddu, 2008, p. 27).

The way he closely connects with territories and places cannot be interpreted as a declaration of ownership. Rather he lives this relationship as an existential proximity, as a hermeneutical commitment/involvement and as an interpretative act which transforms itself into an artistic and creative process. He experiences places not only through his mind but also through his body and because of this he cannot consider territories just as physical spaces but rather as a stratified interlacement of places and bodies which ooze with sounds, memories, myths, events, faces with voices, glances and gestures with whom it is possible to be in contact.

Through this process of participation and interpenetration, which is spiritual and physical at the same time, the pilgrim reaches a knowledge which is able to disclose new horizons of sense and to destabilize his perceptual stereotypes. These stereotypes are more difficult to change than ideas, because they are rooted in the body (Diodato, 2010). What the pilgrim faces is an in-depth knowledge, which allows him to relocate himself in the change experience and to go through unpredictable experiences which could not have been captured with a distanced, sedate and abstract view (ibid).

The image of the pilgrim and the metaphor of the trip analogously helped me to rethink learning contexts in which it could be possible to go beyond the dualistic opposition between theory and practice: contexts in which it could be possible to rebuild the connections, "the subterranean veining that, despite abstract borders and rigid barricades, always links body and thought" (Melandri, 2008, p. 73), spirit and material. Therefore I tried to imagine a path through which it was possible to reconnect these different dimensions of experience. To give an example, my goal was not to make students passively acquire the work of Geddes, rather to make them live, experience and socialize Geddes' words. What I wanted to build was an interactive trip in which "words could finally become flesh" revealing, through a lived comprehension, new knowledge horizons.

13.4 Maps to Travel

Anyone who starts exploring new territories needs a map to travel. It is necessary to understand what you're leaving and the direction you want to follow in order to achieve an authentic knowledge path. Everyone needs a suitcase of tools to face possible adversities and vicissitudes, but even the pleasures, which constitute the act of travelling.

Food is needed to nourish and a compass is necessary to re-orient ourselves and to find the coordinates, in order not to lose ourselves. But these things are not enough if we don't have the desire and the will to leave, if we are not open to a spirit of adventure. For these reasons it is important to give students the tools which will help them in building the solid ground of their path. At the same time it is crucial to imagine learning contexts which could stimulate their involvement and induce them to plan their own trip.

These are the premises which helped me in reshaping the theoretical part of the course. My conviction is that theory cannot be considered as the basis from which people can deduce pre-established models to duplicate during their action; rather, it is the occasion to express and contextualize a chosen approach. So I thought that the theoretical basis of the class could be imagined as the roots of a tree which go into the soil to find nourishment in the deepest layers. From this perspective, to teach theory meant to make students understand where my roots were: my landmarks, my sources and therefore my peculiar research perspective. The idea was to anchor the map and the trip to a specific theoretical tradition, to a framework to be reinterpreted creatively.

From this starting point, I developed a course in which theory was taught as a sort of story in which I had to select some threads and significant cases which could help me contextualize a journey. My idea was to shape a theoretical teaching following Klee's image: roots and trunk, which are able to "get and transmit what comes from the depth" (Klee, 1959, p. 82); a knowledge which comes from far away; a knowledge that I chose and customized through my own experiential path. Students didn't have to duplicate this passively. Rather they could draw nourishment from it in order to give birth to new creations. Just as in a tree, where the foliage has a mirror-like relationship with the roots but never replicates that model, I intended to give students nutriment and precious juices.

In order to reach this goal, besides communicating this "experiential knowledge", I worked in shaping frameworks and contexts, which could potentially allow students to develop their own autonomous and personal research paths. So I imagined a teaching rhythm which is articulated in lectures interwoven with more complex dialogical and interactive moments: moments in which students are considered not as passive spectators but as people willing to speak out and shape their own destiny. I worked to build an interactive and authentic communication arena in which people could concentrate not only on ideas but on human relationships: a space in which unique and concrete subjects (with a story and a body) could interact, think and feel emotions.

In these kinds of contexts, the role of digital technologies is crucial. The use of these tools allows me to assemble together diverse languages, to use words and voices, images and sounds, films and papers, numbers and poetry. Digital languages are potentially able to create involving situations and environments in which it is possible to produce vital and expressive knowledges that are intended as sensory resources, generating energy and motivation.

The interactive lesson format becomes the occasion to develop a germinative knowledge, which transgresses a simple passive learning. The occasion to experiment with the communicative and cognitive role of aesthetic pleasure, intended not as an accessory but rather as a crucial element which characterizes every communicative process (Gargani, 1995). The occasion to emphasize the powerful role of artistic and poetic languages, which are able to give a "corporeal foundation and a sensuous nature to the same mental representations" (Moreddu, 2008, p. 19). It is the occasion to legitimize the role of sensory knowledges in comparison with the traditional primacy of conceptual knowledge. It is the occasion to reinterpret, even through digital languages, the function of metaphors: those images which were well known in the past and that were able to provoke imaginative processes and to produce resonance through a sensory and emotional fascination. They were able to make people touch, feel and perceive sounds, fragrances and smells. Those images were able to transmit energy, to make sentiments and emotions vibrate and to awaken aspirations and buried knowledges. Like some rituals, tales, myths or frescos that were painted inside cathedrals and municipal buildings, those images were able to awaken a sense of belonging and identity; they were capable of inspiring creativity and making people participate in the construction of some shared values on which the idea of community was based (Decandia, 2000).

13.5 Toolkit

The theoretical framework of the class helped me in contextualizing and outlining the genealogy of the chosen approach. But I needed to give students the tools to develop their own field research.

The actual forms of the territory embed time and the co-evolving story, which connects humans with their living environment. So I tried to emphasize the role of the classical environmental, morphological and cartographic analyses, which are well established in urban planning practice.

At the same time, I gave them the tools and the analytical framework to reconstruct the stratification process through which different communities have reinterpreted their living context over time. I taught how to read signs, morphologies and forms: in other terms, how to read the footprints left on the territory. Moreover, I tried to induce them to interrogate those traces: to make those traces speak through the reconstruction of people's stories and practices from which the same traces were produced.

I believe that the past cannot be thought of as separate from the present. So the ability to read the signs of the past leads inevitably to a reading of the contemporary: the new forms of using space and time, new lifestyles through which people shape their space, giving it always new meanings.

Together with the classical urban planning and historiographical analytical tools, I suggested to the students other tools which could allow them to transgress a simply zenithal or cartographical view: a view which has always privileged the "eye" as the major knowledge tool; a perspectival view that has always privileged, in the analysis of cities and regions, the exterior disposition of volumes, draining from them the life, the visible and invisible relationships which built them.

In order to get in touch with this invisible dimension whose analysis is crucial to determine the uniqueness of a place, I pushed my students to "adopt a lens that could help them to penetrate the living body of the city" (Attili, 2007, p. 10), to immerse themselves in the voices, in the biographies, in the life stories which sediment in the territory. In other words, to adopt those same qualitative methodologies which were already used, in our disciplinary field, by those "fathers" I chose as my reference teachers (Attili, 2008).

13.6 Travelling: "Words Become Flesh"

Maps, theories and tools are not enough to guarantee a real knowledge trip. It is necessary to experience, to go through territories, to live the space so that words could become flesh and learning could become part of an existential project. To meet things and to be with things to know them (Heidegger cit. in Moreddu, 2008, p. 27). It is necessary to abandon that fixed and distanced view, to start moving and wander around them. Students are invited to immerse themselves in the territory, to take a reconnaissance journey from within, to itinerantly explore it step by step.

In order to learn through mind and body it is necessary to experience an existential closeness to places, to discover a "knowledge eroticism", to start to feel and "know the space by perceiving and even touching it" (Bruno, 2006, p. 91), reconnecting touch and sight, gaining back a tactile function that has been traditionally abandoned in favour of a perspectival view.

The students' journey takes place in space and time. So they learn how to sink with their body in the memory basements of men and women, in the deepest archives and layers, to give light to buried documents and papers, neglected pictures, hidden archaeologies. They have to learn to move through the emotional spaces of living bodies, transgressing frameworks and borders, following moving trajectories which draw living, itinerant and palpitating spaces: spaces which are made of relationships and invisible threads that connect affections and places (Bruno, 2006, pp. 188–189). Moreover, they have to learn how to let themselves down into the folds, interstices where light condenses, in order to get in touch with palpitating things, with appearing and disappearing events. Only through this approach can students get at what a territory communicates without saying, what a territory shows without showing. They have to cultivate a curiosity towards what is apparently without a form or a meaning and remains confined in the limbo of the indefinable.

In order to access those sense vibrations which are not quite accessible, in order to read the silence of territories, students have, first of all, to learn how to listen. Listening means to go beyond that knowledge approach based on visual identification in order to give legitimacy to what doesn't show its visual evidence, to what is not immediately accessible but shows its presence only through constantly deferred reverberations.

This presence is never caught "in front of" or "through the act of seeing"; rather, it is a coming and going, a stretching and penetrating, an appearing and disappearing. A presence which cannot be depicted as an absolute identity. "Sound takes away the shape. It doesn't dissolve it, rather it enlarges it, it gives it a width, a thickness, a vibration and an undulation which are not catchable in a drawing" (Nancy, 2004, p. 6). Listening means to "penetrate in that spatiality which penetrates me in the same moment" (Nancy, 2004, p. 23): to open oneself to that "vibrant transitivity", which recalls uncontrollable deferments which are inscribed in the movements of life (ibid). But above all, listening means to build a relationship, to open oneself to other people, without being able to anticipate them or transform them into an object. To open oneself to the resonance of another being.

So I make students experience the territory, urging them to go beyond appearances and to build relationships with the people who move across and inhabit it. Using this approach, students should be able to experiment with the deepest forms of communication in order to awaken resonances in the interlocutors. They should be able to discover words, sounds of the body and voices that build interactive spaces. They should be able to mobilize sensory languages, which encourage the willingness to remember and to tell a story, to enter into a relationship. To animate a potential knowledge space. To reveal memories, life experiences and scattered knowledges.

13.7 To Tell the Story of a Journey: Completing an Experience

In order to make sense of a journey, it is necessary to transform the experience into a story. Anyone who travels knows that sometimes you have to stop and take a breath. If you want your journey to become something more than a simple wandering from one experience to another, you should stop and go back into yourself. You have to comprehend, rethink, make sense of what you met along the trip. You have to go back to the initial theories you learned before the journey, to the novelties and clues you discovered through the travelling. You have to analyse the limits as well as opportunities of your journey. But above all you should learn how to make sense of and give coherence to the different materials you encountered through the journey. As Maltese says, commenting on Dewei's thought, you can fully make sense of something only when the different materials you experience flow into a comprehensible whole (Maltese in Dewey, 1934, p. IX).

If a learning process remains an unconnected sequence of meaningless acts, it cannot produce an authentic knowledge (Maltese in Dewey, 1934, p. X). It is not enough to pick up and enumerate the rough materials taken from your experience and collect them in a simple sequence of information. Rather it is necessary to embrace an interpretive and creative practice to give a shape to these different elements. As in the aesthetic experience analysed by Dewei, in a learning process students should ingest and digest the rough materials they experience according to their cognitive structure, with the foregoing theoretical frameworks, with their perceptual stereotypes.

Students should be able to connect what they encountered along the journey with their deepest emotional core, with their "stone of night" that lies in the deepest layers of their being (Agamben, 2008). As is now commonly accepted in philosophical and scientific debate, our deepest grammar is determined by pre-verbal materials, passions and emotions, which represent the foundational dimension of every cognitive orientation (Bodei, 1991, p. 10), discourses and thoughts. Only forms of knowledge that are capable of self-examination, that can capture what is not told or thinkable, can produce something new. Only through this deep reworking process can the raw fragments which students experienced during the trip be expressively shaped.

Unlike ants, which accumulate materials from others, or spiders, which secrete ideas from their own mouths, bees work to elaborate what they pick up in order to produce honey. In the same way, I teach students to put together the information they collected, the voices they listened to, the documents they read, the explorations they did. I help them, with a steady but sensitive and careful direction, to build their own autonomous narrative path in which they could merge intuition and reasoning, rigour and imagination.

I push them not only to use their cold and detached minds but also to play with their subjectivity, their bodies, their hearts and their passions. What I try to do is to make them organize and communicate their own experience in their specific way (Moreddu, 2008, p. 28). I try to push them to assemble different forms of knowledge, empirical studies and abstract formulation, selecting the materials they think are significant.

Knowledge has to be produced as an act of re-elaboration, an interpretative personal and creative act, not a passive acceptance of others' points of view. It is "a lived, intelligent and sensitive comprehension act" (Diodato, 2010); it is the moment in which the world and objects are not external, rather they start to be incorporated into an existential project. It is an active work in which the apparently distinct opposites of theory and practice, mind and body, spirit and material interweave in the concreteness of an existential fabric and these opposites relate one to the other in the same sense unity (Diodato, 2010).

13.8 Digital Technologies and the Pilgrim's Journey

Starting from this idea of knowledge, digital technologies play a really crucial role in two specific moments: when students start their own knowledge journey and when they need to tell the story of that experience.

Before starting their own journey, students learn to put those tools in their suitcase. They know that those digital tools have great potentialities in giving them the codes to read the world, to enlarge their perception of different environments, to multiply different points of view. They could help them to use particular filters, sound amplifiers to revisit what exists, to see with new eyes what is already there (Branzi, 2006, p. 107); to get the differences, the qualities, the variations; to catch the little clues, the humming; to record sounds or voices; to widen a detail; to follow an itinerant and moving path. Moreover, they know that at a certain moment they will have to tell what they experienced. So they can take advantage of digital tools that allow them to assemble, interconnect, hybridize diverse languages and a wide variety of expressive codes such as texts, films, graphic animations, statistics, sounds, cartographies, contemporary and historical pictures, etc. (Attili, 2008, p. 177). From this point of view, digital technologies have the capability of making students build fluid narrations, not necessarily linear, through which they can give expression to their own creativity.

The use of different languages can make students connect visible and invisible dimensions: the world of things and objects with the immaterial layers, the images, the voices and the life which generated them. Through these technologies every student can potentially give space to the depth of the territory, destabilizing two assumptions: that reality is only the visible and that the contemporary is contained only in the moments of the present.

Digital representations are able to transgress the perspectival and cartographic views that are traditionally adopted in our discipline. They produce fissures and collapses, which enlarge the limits of the space, recalling original and unpredictable dimensions (Rosa in http://www.studioazzurro.com). They make walls and stones speak; they give life to monuments and to those signs which today we are not able to interrogate. They evoke that past which is embedded in the territory: that past which constantly evolves and lives in the present. They recall a sort of "placenta of shadow" (Zambrano cited in Prezzo, 2006, p. 49) made of endless forms, remembrances, different modalities of belonging to spaces, meanings, events and qualities; even of dreams, unsatisfied expectations, undeveloped possibilities and unrealized projects. Moreover, inspired by some interesting examples of contemporary art productions, students need not limit themselves to telling "closed stories". Rather they could develop digital "sensory and interactive" environments through which it is possible to narrate "open stories": frameworks which are able to make further stories proliferate. These environments can be thought of as "lazy engines" which require a lot of collaboration from the user-reader who will be potentially put in the situation of exploring those machines not only discursively but through sensory modalities, through meaningful associations and paths (Levy, 1995, p. 10). Those digital spaces are events through which the same inhabitants could go on enriching a knowledge process, implementing new expressive, narrative and imaginative adventures. These are methods that require the active involvement of users, animating knowledge spaces in which ongoing processes of collective learning can take place.

13.9 The Story of a Journey: The Experience of Santu Lussurgiu

The teaching laboratory found the subject for an experiment in a concrete action research experience. The chance was offered by Santu Lussurgiu Municipality: a small town in Sardinia located in the Montiferru region. Emilio Chessa, an enlightened mayor, suggested we take part in building the initial foundations of the Chirros Project. A project to recuperate the historic centre that was not meant to be limited to an operation exclusively conserving the "wrappings" of buildings or exterior forms of the landscapes, but to trigger an opportunity to re-weave a deep, creative relationship, not ossified, with the past of the places deposited on the territory in signs, spaces, facades and the stones of the town. To start the project off we set up a workshop of collective remembrance in the town, with the students and tutors of the course (Francesca Bua, Cristian Cannaos, Giuseppe Onni, Bruno Palmas and Anna Uttaro): an authentic Memory workshop. We wanted in this way to "go back to letting the walls and stones speak", constructing forms of narration able to open up again, have re-emerge, enter into circulation and socialize, the dispersed knowledges, voices, memories, the life from which the town was actually created.

By building this workshop we wanted to transform the heart of this small town not into a museum of empty carcasses no longer animated by life, but rather into a real laboratory for collective learning where, through narration and working together, it would be possible to later produce new forms of sociality, weave new forms of space appropriation and provide new rules for use of the territory.

We built up the fundamental lines of this action research project in our university classrooms. Through lectures and seminar work, using various language registers, we constructed the initial maps to start out on our journey and packed a case with equipment to tackle the research in the field.

The first evening we introduced ourselves to the town with a lecture event by various speakers at which, together with the singers of Santu Lussurgiu Choir, we explained, using the "choir" metaphor, to which the community was particularly sensitive, what the aim of our laboratory was. During the course of the event, several of us painted the laboratory sign on canvas in colour, in a joint effort. Following a short walk through the town streets, the large coloured fabric was raised onto the faÁade of Montegranatico Hall, situated in the heart of the historic

Fig. 13.1 Studio Azzurro, *Il Mnemonista* (The Mnemonist), taken from Studio Azzurro 2005

Fig. 13.2 Jean Fouquet, *Il cantiere di una cattedrale, XV secolo* (A Cathedral Workshop, 15th century), taken from Bertelli, Briganti, Giuliano 1986, photos and images from the archive of "Matrica: Laboratory of Urban Fermentation"

centre. This large hall, equipped with tape recorders, cameras, video cameras, computers, papers and drawings, became the reference point for our large collective workshop.

We collected archive material, the historic and cartographic sources that would enable us to create an initial outline for interaction with the inhabitants. In this way, by creating our workshop we would, on the one hand, contribute our wealth of technical knowledge and our interactive work method, while they would help us to acquire the documentary material, the old photos they had, but above all, would put

Fig. 13.3 The classroom, photos and images from the archive of "Matrica: Laboratory of Urban Fermentation"

Fig. 13.4 Collecting materials, photos and images from the archive of "Matrica: Laboratory of Urban Fermentation"

to work the knowledges dispersed, their memories and reminiscences and, at the same time, have the ideas, visions emerge that animated the territory.

After preparing the context through detailed, extensive work consisting of meetings and encounters, with two local inhabitants – Giuseppe Onni and Serafina Are – leading the way, we started on our journey to Santu Lussurgiu and finally immersed ourselves in the territory.

The people, who welcomed us with generosity and enthusiasm, immediately showed themselves willing to take part in the operation. It was at this point that the detailed work of listening to each other began. The shepherds, farmers, cattle farmers, artisans, the oldest bricklayers, an old saddler, the women of the town accompanied us, like authentic local experts, along the streets of the town and on the territory, leading us to discover, through their memories and emotions, the dimensions of "inhabiting" and space "lived", the organization of the landscape and the strong ties entwined between town and territory. We realized straightaway that we were dealing with authentic hidden seams of knowledges and memories we needed to bring to the light, enquire into, enhance and, above all, link up to construct genuine "collecting basins". Our work was to be the fine weaving and linking up of these diverse voices. Finally, our technical knowledge, our capacity to read and interpret the sources and documents, could hybridize and mix with those knowledges of experience, those memories and remembrances that "inhabited" the town and the territory. On the days we were in Santu Lussurgiu, the work of reconstructing memory alternated with intense moments of meeting, socialization, discussion and exchange. We often had a party together. A blog, set up on the municipal website, like a sort of log-book, gave notice of the day's programmes, enabling abundant interaction with the local population.

Fig. 13.5 Immersions, photos and images from the archive of "Matrica: Laboratory of Urban Fermentation"

Fig. 13.6 The first evening, photos and images from the archive of "Matrica: Laboratory of Urban Fermentation"

Fig. 13.7 Montegranatico Hall, photos and images from the archive of "Matrica: Laboratory of Urban Fermentation"

Fig. 13.8 Cameras at work, photos and images from the archive of "Matrica: Laboratory of Urban Fermentation"

When we got back to our university classrooms, the students worked on the archive documents, papers, video and sound material collected during the course of the week, experimenting with different forms of replaying and recounting. Through the interweaving and hybridization of different types of language and expressive codes – texts, films, graphic and sound animation, cartography, historic and

Fig. 13.9 Reconstructing memory, photos and images from the archive of "Matrica: Laboratory of Urban Fermentation"

Fig. 13.10 Digital recounting, photos and images from the archive of "Matrica: Laboratory of Urban Fermentation"

Fig. 13.11 Screening of student's videos, photos and images from the archive of "Matrica: Laboratory of Urban Fermentation"

contemporary photos, etc. – made possible by the new techologies, they tried to link up visible and invisible, the morphologies of the town, the world of objects and things with immaterial dimensions, voices and sounds, the life from which they were produced.

This work was taken back and dealt with in a social manner with the inhabitants. The week before Carnival, on the day of the rehearsal for sa carrela e' nanti – a particular horse race that takes place exactly in one of those streets we had specifically analysed   we organized a conference and itinerant exhibition in the town all together. While the students of the faculty told the inhabitants about the work done and explained the papers and drawings displayed in the streets, in the cellars of Via Roma (the street where the race was held) and in the country culture museum, the videos yielded the voices collected, matched with the cartography, pictures and material from the archives. At the same time researchers of national and international fame reflected, at an authentic "jam session" begun the day before at the Faculty of Architecture in Alghero, on the sense of the work done. In weaving the links between Santu Lussurgiu and the world, all together, in the heart of the community, indeed in that workshop that had accommodated us during the Workshop Week in Santu Lussurgiu, we discussed the potential that might be offered by sensitive and metaphorical languages in the renewal of urban construction practices. The event ended with a "transhumance duet": a shepherd and a woman historian accompanied us along an ancient sheep-track crossing municipal territory, used for centuries by shepherds of central Sardinia to take their flocks to spend winter near the sea. The knowledge of experience and the knowledge of science, by hybridizing and mingling together, helped us to discover and look with new eyes at a territory we had no longer been able to enquire into.

Fig. 13.12 The itinerant exhibition and the conference, photos and images from the archive of "Matrica: laboratory of urban fermentation"

Notes

1. The "didactic block" is a didactic unit where different courses work in synergy around a planning workshop.
2. The course tries to investigate the history of an anarchical and participatory planning thread, which, despite the predominant rationalist tendencies, is continuously present in our discipline since its origins. For a further widening of an inquiry on its contents and methodologies, see Choay (1973) and Lanzani (1996). In the last decade, in Italy we are facing a renewed interest in this disciplinary thread (see Ferraro, 1995, 1998; Mazzoleni, 1995; Ventura, 1997; De Carlo, 1999; Olmo, 2001; Buncuga, 2001; Gruccione & Vittoriani, 2005).

3. The "care" (or empathic) knowledge – as it emerges in different disciplinary fields, from economy to natural science, from cognitive to social science – aims at giving importance to creative reasoning, which has been inhibited by the 200-year history of the predominance of the scientific rationality. Today, many scholars are incisively exploring rationalities that are more complex and refined compared with the linear and deductive reasoning. These other rationalities are not a contemporary invention. If we historically look back, we can find, in the folds of the dominant calculating rationality, a thread that connects other forms of knowledge and action. From the "ingenium" of Vico to the "ésprit de finesse" of Pascal and from the "phronesis" of Aristotle to the judgment art of Kant, we can find a wide range of eminent figures who highlighted the fecundity, the rigour and the legitimacy of an approach, which privileges reasoning instead of deductive calculations, deliberation and argumentation instead of proof or verification and comprehension instead of rigid formula (see Le Moigne, 1997). An important debate around the traditional critique of the rational planning approach is taking place even inside our specific disciplinary field (see Belli, 2004; Giusti, 1995; Pasqui, 1995; Pizziolo & Micarelli, 2003). Inside this debate I find interesting the positions of people like Ferrara who – following Dewey's theories – is interested in investigating the themes of the aesthetic rationality in the interpretations of and in the relationship with the local contexts. Like Ferrara, I think that the aesthetic rationality represents the prominent example of a rationality, which is not based on abstract and universalizing principles: rather it is rooted in the uniqueness of the unrepeatable (see Ferrara, 1992; Dewei, 1951; Decandia, 2000, pp. 175–217).

References

Abruzzese, A. (1996). *Analfabeti di tutto il mondo uniamoci*. Genova: Costa & Nolan.

Agamben, G. (2008). *Signatura Rerum. Sul metodo*. Torino: Bollati Boringhieri.

Attili, G. (2007). Narrare l'urbano. In G. Attili, L. Decandia, & E. Scandurra (Eds.), *Storie di città. Verso un'urbanistica del quotidiano*. Roma, Edizioni Interculturali.

Attili, G. (2008). *Rappresentare la città dei migranti. Storie di vita e pianificazione urbana*. Milano: Jaca Book.

Belli, A. (2004). *Come un valore d'ombra. Urbanistica oltre la ragione* Milano: Franco Angeli.

Bodei, R. (1991). *Geometria delle passioni. Paura, speranza, felicità: filosofia e uso politico*. Milano: Feltrinelli.

Branzi, A. (2006). *Modernità debole e diffusa. Il mondo del progetto all'inizio del XXI secolo*. Milano: Skira.

Bruno, G. (2006). *Atlante delle emozioni. In viaggio tra arte, architettura e cinema* (M. Nadottitrans, Trans.). Milano: Mondadori.

Buncuga, F. (2001). *Architettura e libertà. Conversazioni con Giancarlo De Carlo*. Milano: Eleuthera.

Choay, F. (1973). *La città utopie e realtà*. Torino: Einaudi.

Decandia, L. (2000). *Dell'identità. Saggio sui luoghi. Per una critica della razionalità urbanistica*. Soveria Mannelli: Rubettino.

Decandia, L. (2004). *Anime di luoghi*. Milano: FrancoAngeli.

De Carlo, G. (1999). *Gli spiriti dell'architettura*. In L. Schirollo (Eds.). Roma: Editori riuniti.

Dewey, J. (1934). *Art as experience*. New York: Minton, Balch & Company. *L'arte come esperienza* (C. Maltese, Trans.). La Nuova Italia, Firenze, 1951.

Diodato, R. (2010). Museo come esperienza: il luogo virtuale-relazionale. In Studio Azzurro (Ed.), *I musei dell'invisibile*. Milano: Silvana Editoriale (in press).

Ferrara, A. (1992). *L'eudaimonia postmoderna. Mutamento culturale e modelli di razionalità*. Napoli: Liguori.

Ferraro, G. (1995). Il gioco del piano. Patrick Geddes in India 1914–1924. *Urbanistica, 103*.

Ferraro, G. (1998). *Rieducare alla speranza. Patrick Geddes Planner in India, 1914–1924*. Milano: Jaca Book.

Gargani, A. G. (1995). Transizioni tra codici e intrecci testuali. *Pluriverso, 1.*

Giusti, M. (1995). Sapere professionale del pianificatore e forme di conoscenza locale. *Urbanistica, 103.*

Gruccione, M. & Vittoriani, A. (Eds.). (2005). *Giancarlo De Carlo. Le ragioni dell'architettura.* Milano: Skira.

Klee, P. (1959). *Teoria della forma e della figurazione, Milano,* pref. di G. C. Argan. Milano: Feltrinelli.

Lanzani, A. (1996). *Immagini del territorio e idee di piano 1943–1963. Dagli approcci generalizzanti all'interpretazione dei contesti locali.* Milano: Franco Angeli.

Le Moigne, J. L. (1997). Sulla capacità della ragione di discernere. *Pluriverso, 1.*

Lévy, P. (1995). *L'intelligence collective: pour une anthropologie du cyberspace,* Paris, La Decouvert; it. tr. 2002, *L'intelligenza collettiva. Per un'antropologia del cyber spazio.* Milano: Feltrinelli.

Mazzoleni, C., & Doglio, C. (Eds.). (1995). *Per prova ed errore.* Genova: Le Mani.

Melandri, L. (2008). Postfazione. In M. Fraire, R. Rossanda, & L. Melandri (Eds.), *La perdita.* Torino: Bollati Boringhieri.

Moreddu, E. (2008). *In prossimità dei luoghi. Villaggi di cumbessias, gioco dell'arte e un modo particolare dell'indugiare.* Milano: Franco Angeli.

Nancy, J. L. (2002). *À l'écoute. Paris, Éditions Galilée;* tr. it. 2004, *All'ascolto.* Milano: Raffaello Cortina.

Olmo, C. (Ed.). (2001). *Costruire la Città dell'uomo. Adriano Olivetti e l'urbanistica.* Torino: Edizioni Comunità.

Pascal, B. (1670). *Pensèès de M. Pascal sur la Religione et sur quelques aures sujet, Port Royale,* Paris; tr. it., (1962), *Pensieri.* Torino: Einaudi.

Pasqui, G. (1995). La teoria e le pratiche della pianificazione. Per un ripensamento del nesso tra le forme del fare e i modi del sapere nel campo dell'urbanistica, CRU – *Critica della Razionalità Urbanistica, 4.*

Pizziolo, G., & Micarelli, R. (2003). *Il pensiero progettante. L'arte delle relazioni.* Firenze: Alinea.

Prezzo, R. (2006). *Pensare in un'altra luce. L'opera aperta di Maria Zambrano.* Milano: Raffaello Cortina.

Studio Azzurro. (2005). *Immagini vive.* Milano: Electa.

Ventura, F. (Ed.). (1997). *Alle radici della città contemporanea. Il pensiero di Lewis Mumford.* Milano: Città Studi Edizioni.

Chapter 14
Cinema and the "City of the Mind": Using Motion Pictures to Explore Human-Environment Transactions in Planning Education

Michael Dudley

14.1 Introduction

The use of film analysis in teaching has become popular in recent years, especially in theology (see Kozlovic, 2005). It has taken on new importance because "film offers students an opportunity to connect the theoretical discourses we engage in classes to a range of social issues represented through the lens of Hollywood movies" (Giroux, 2001, p. 589).

This chapter examines the pedagogical use of film in planning education, specifically as it relates to the teaching of environmental psychology. The intersections between film, theory, and pedagogy are important because film is herein invested with the power to represent – and more importantly interpret and challenge – our understandings of human-environment transactions. I further suggest that planning students may be undereducated in the nature of these transactions and that the medium of the motion picture – combined with the neglected body of theory represented by environmental psychology – offers an excellent synthesis to address this need.

Planning as a field of study attracts students from across a wide range of disciplines, which lends it a certain intellectual diversity and hence resiliency. However beneficial, this interdisciplinarity often means planning theory instructors must assist students who lack a basic grounding in a number of theoretical areas, such as urban sociology and theories of urban morphological change.

Another major body of theory with which many planning students may be unfamiliar is that relating to human-environment transactions. Known variously as Environmental Psychology, Architectural Psychology, or Environment and Behavior Research (EBR[1]), theories and research concerning human spatial behavior have been evolving and maturing for more than 40 years and are highly germane to land-use planning as they relate to multiple levels of social and spatial scales and organization.

M. Dudley (✉)
Institute of Urban Studies, University of Winnipeg, Winnipeg, MB, Canada
e-mail: m.dudley@uwinnipeg.ca

L. Sandercock, G. Attili (eds.), *Multimedia Explorations in Urban Policy and Planning*, Urban and Landscape Perspectives 7, DOI 10.1007/978-90-481-3209-6_14, © Springer Science+Business Media B.V. 2010

Yet, the literature shows that EBR approaches are rarely taken into account in planning research and practice (Manzo & Perkins, 2006) and are also a neglected body of theory in the academy (White & Mayo, 2005). Apart from classic readings such as those of Lynch (1960) or Whyte (1988), little emphasis is paid to EBR in planning programs. Moreover, the leading organization of researchers in this field, the Environmental Design Research Association (EDRA), attracts few urban planners to its conferences (Sandercock & Sarkissian, personal communication).

In spite of this relative lack of exposure to EBR theory, I find that planning students routinely find themselves either involved in or proposing for their graduate work, studies that concern how environments affect users; how to design urban environments that better meet psychological needs; how to promote more sustainable behavior in the built environment; or how behavior can affect environments. All of these themes fall within the purview of EBR. However, owing to a lack of attention in the curriculum to EBR, students may lack the necessary understanding and theoretical vocabulary with which to undertake such research.

The general premise of this chapter is that a greater emphasis should be placed on EBR in planning curricula. Its primary purpose, however, is to offer one possible means with which to do this: through the use of popular film as a pedagogical tool.

This chapter reports on the use of popular film as a medium to impart EBR theory in a classroom setting. It sets out the rationale for this approach, focusing on hermeneutic analysis as a pedagogic technique. Then it will illustrate these potentialities through hermeneutic film readings based on my experiences using film in teaching, incorporating both my analyses and those of my students.

The method I will follow is therefore not only interdisciplinary and integrative but collaborative. The interpretations I developed as an instructor to initially select the films and theoretical readings for the course will be augmented and elaborated upon in Section 14.6 below by students' insights, which shall be indicated with indented italics. My own reflections served as a foundation for theorizing on the part of my students. As Giroux (2001, p. 594) points out from his own teaching experiences, "my analyses of films are necessarily partial, incomplete and open to revision and contestation. Rather than closing down student participation, my own interpretations are meant to be strategic and positional."

The chapter will show how, through the use of film, the theoretical domains in question may be synthesized and taught. It will set out the practical, pedagogical, and theoretical bases for the use of film in a planning context, showing how motion pictures can present profound – and potentially radicalizing – insights into the human spatial experience.

14.2 Background

Between 2002 and 2008, I taught EBR in the context of a required undergraduate theory course in Environmental Design in the Faculty of Architecture at the University of Manitoba. Under the designation Theory of Design 3, the course follows upon two previous theory courses in general formal design concepts.

In their final year of the undergraduate program, Environmental Design students can elect to focus on architecture, landscape architecture, interiors, or city planning. If they apply, city planning ED students are then often seen as strong candidates for the graduate program in city planning.

It was apparent during my first offering of Theory 3 that the course content would prove challenging to teach. Social science theory is a dramatic departure for most of the design students, many of whom have yet to write a major theory paper. Also, traditional outcome measures for social sciences education (i.e., exams) proved quite ineffective. My students informed me that, as visual thinkers, they were not interested in memorizing and repeating back facts and concepts.

In 2003, I added a film analysis to the curriculum as a seminar presentation, with no written submission required. I matched a selection of popular films with what I felt were appropriate readings and the students were asked to identify the concepts from the literature in the films.

The results were, I thought, very positive: the students were engaged in the assignment and appeared to enjoy conducting and attending the seminar much more than had been the case in earlier classes, when the seminar was concerned solely with the presentation of readings.

Based on this early success, in subsequent years I expanded the assignment to become the core of the course: in addition to a site investigation and the keeping of a theory journal, the students were tasked with not just presenting their findings on the film analysis, but to then submit their report as their group's final theory paper. The film analysis assignment appears to be an effective combination for the Environmental Design students, as it appeals to their visual learning orientations and allows them to assimilate and apply EBR theory in creative ways.

As stated, some of these students go on to the graduate program in city planning. In general, though, very few planning students at the University of Manitoba are acquainted with this body of theory.

The shortcoming this educational gap represents in planning education has become apparent to me for several years. Since 2001, I have acted as the librarian at the Institute of Urban Studies at the University of Winnipeg, where I have assisted many students with their thesis/practicum research. In addition, during 2007–2008 I also taught the department of city planning's required course in thesis/practicum preparation. In both of these capacities I have seen repeated cases of planning students who wish to engage in research that turns out to hinge on an understanding of human spatial behavior, but who were not even aware that such a field existed, to say nothing of the specific theories or methods involved.

In my opinion and experience, EBR constitutes an important substantive component of planning knowledge, but as will be seen below it is neglected both in planning education and in practice.

14.3 Environmental Psychology and Planning Knowledge

The integration of EBR into planning knowledge rests on the recognition – developed over the past four decades – that any attempt to construct a more appropriate and healthy built environment must proceed from some understanding of the psychological needs of those who will use it and shape it. Stephen Carr, in his seminal article "The City of the Mind" (1970), wrote:

> Perceiving and representing the environment, acting in it, and reviewing the consequences are the processes by which we create our personal city of the mind – our own "life space" as it has been called. The form of the environment can help to make that space narrow and confined or broad and open, constantly growing. By organizing our environment properly we can make ordinary city-using tasks simpler to accomplish. We can increase the scope of possible actions for any individual as well as his [sic] sense of competence in carrying them out. And we can increase his [sic] sense of meaning and esthetic pleasure (Carr, 1970, p. 528).

EBR researchers have spent decades trying to understand the nature of these human–environment transactions as well as developing ways to put this knowledge to use in a practical way that can benefit human societies. According to Robert Gifford (2007), Environmental Psychology is

> the study of transactions between individuals and their physical settings. In these transactions, individuals change the environment and their behavior and experiences are changed by the environment...it includes theory, research and practice aimed at making buildings more humane and improving our relationship with the natural environment (Gifford, 2007, p. 1).

Domains of interest to environmental psychologists include attachment to place (Altman & Low, 1992); place and self-concept (Twigger-Ross & Uzzell, 1996); the psychology of home as well as antecedents/effects of homelessness (Rivlin, 1990; Marcus, 2007); the effects of environment on privacy, personal space, territoriality, and crowding (Sommer, 1969; see summary in Gifford, 2007); built environments and crime (Taylor, 2002); the ways in which natural environments can promote health (Kuo, 2001) and community building (Coley, Kuo, & Sullivan, 1997); environmental perception, cognition, and wayfinding (Downs & Stea, 1977); effects of natural landscapes (Kaplan & Kaplan, 1989; Kaplan, Ryan, & Ryan, 1998); diverse environmental needs across the lifespan and cultures (Gifford, 2007); conservation and sustainable behaviors (Geller, 2002); sacred places (Hester, 1985, 2006); how people cope with and plan for disasters (Peek & Mileti, 2002); environmental conflict (d'Estree, Dukes, & Navarrete-Romero, 2002); and how to encourage and nurture public participation in design processes (Sommer, 1983). All of these themes are consistent with planning knowledge.

What is also particularly interesting for our purposes are the very similar disciplinary trajectories between EBR and planning. Both literatures (for example, Beauregard, 1989; Sommer, 1983) reveal that during the 1970s in particular, both planning and EBR researchers began to question or reject their modernist assumptions, positivist epistemologies and comprehensive rationality. Faced with a host of social justice and environmental problems, some planners and psychologists sought to define new parameters for their respective disciplines and to take a more active role outside the academy. Just as architects and planners in the later post-war era realized that an emphasis on formalism was resulting in inhumane built environments, for their part, leaders in what would become known as environmental psychology became interested in situating their discipline in real-world settings and in applying their knowledge to solving real-world problems (Sommer, 1983).

Some of the leading writers in EBR also come from city planning backgrounds: Clare Cooper Marcus, who worked as a planner in England and studied City and Regional Planning at Berkeley and has written extensively about the role of the home in the formation of personal identities (Marcus, 2007); Kevin Lynch, who taught city planning at MIT and wrote the seminal "The Image of the City" (1960); Donald Appleyard, an urban designer best known for writing about "Livable Streets" (1981); and Randolph Hester, who teaches urban design at University of California Berkeley and writes about place, meaning, and citizen involvement in planning processes (2006).

Environmental psychologists were also instrumental in institutionalizing that core postmodern planning practice, public participation, in design processes (Dean, 1994 and Chapter 12). Robert Sommer, in particular, promoted "social design":

> Social design is working with people rather than for them; involving people in the planning and management of the spaces around them; educating them to use the environment wisely and creatively to achieve a harmonious balance between the social, physical, and natural environment...social designers cannot achieve these objectives working by themselves. The goals can be realized only within the structures of larger organizations, which include the people for whom a given project is planned (Sommer, 1983, p. 7).

This connection between people and place-making is key to environmental psychology. As Evans (1996) puts it:

> A conceptual topic of continuing interest within environmental psychology is the concept of place. How are places developed, how do they acquire meaning to people, how are they related to people's plans of action, their preferences, and even to their emotional reactions and well being? And what does the concept mean across generations or across cultures? Place making and the development and sustainability of community has been the subject of several recent books in the field (paragraph 21).

Given planning's own strong identification with place-making processes (see Schneekloth & Shibley, 1995; there are many other examples), the linkages between these disciplines would seem inherent and obvious. Yet, as Lucy (1994) demonstrates, there has long been a gap between planning practice and considerations of human psychology. To address this, Lucy (1994) called upon planners to adopt more interdisciplinary cooperation with other "nourishing" fields. Recent scholarship in planning practice and education also confirms that the legacy of this long-standing disconnect is being reinforced in the academy, where little attention is being paid to EBR in planning pedagogy.

In their examination of knowledge in planning, Ozawa and Seltzer (1999) consulted with planning educators to create a classified list of planning skills and knowledge areas, which was subsequently mailed to over 270 planning practitioners. The list was strongly oriented to competencies, rather than theory. What theory was recorded, again, related to spatial processes in the macroenvironment, with only a general reference to "social forces."

While EBR as such is not referred to in this and other studies in planning knowledge considered for this chapter (e.g., Friedmann, 1996), it was incorporated in

White and Mayo's (2005) survey of 66 planning educators, which found that not only did educators place a low priority on EBR but it also rated lower in the academic realm than it did in practice.

Of course, the gulf between environmental psychology and all of the design professions – not just planning – has been a continual struggle. In 1973, Donald Appleyard looked at these professional and disciplinary barriers, noting that design professionals may not understand why social science approaches are needed, when only "common sense" is required. They may even see such approaches as a threat to their control over decision-making and the project's financial viability. The "future orientation" of designers is also a barrier to understanding, as psychological research is rarely so. And design professionals often eschew social science research published in psychological journals, which in any case is often "obscurely written" (Appleyard, 1973).

Schneekloth and Shibley (1995) speak of this gap as "fragmentation":

> [T]he practice of placemaking is fragmented, and some practices belong to different domains and groups of professionals. There is an ongoing attempt to create boundaries that separate and differentiate the work on many levels revealing a world more concerned with distinction and division than with connection and relationship. Professors and professionals collectively differentiate themselves from "laypeople", even as professors and practitioners seek to differentiate themselves from each other into separate academic and practice domains (Schneekloth & Shibley, 1995, p. 194).

This is, I submit, the case with city planning and environmental psychology. Commonality of purpose, goals, and means would seem clear. What is needed are ways of crossing disciplinary barriers and translating theories considered outside the domain of planning into forms that can intuitively situate the universality of "being-in-place." I propose that this pedagogical problem may be addressed through the use of hermeneutic film analysis.

14.4 "Hollywood Hermeneutics" and "Being-in-the-World"

It bears pointing out that, given their mutual concern with the phenomenology of place, EBR theory and Heidegger's (1962) conception of "Being-in-the-world" or *Dasein* (literally "there-being") share some basic similarities. For Heidegger, humans are not just self-aware of their own Being, but live purposeful, self-directed lives while interacting with other self-aware Beings. But there is an explicit spatiality to *Dasein*: the experience of *Dasein* occurs only as part of a totality within and including the "world." By "world," however, Heidegger is not referring to the physical, objectively measurable Nature all around us, but rather as a function of the process of Dasein's own "world-forming" capacities or the creation of a "complex of reference and relations...a wholly insubstantial horizon of meaning, a whole of reference in which we always move with so much familiarity that we do not even notice it" (King, 2001, p. 55).

Without going overmuch into the profoundly complex philosophy of Heidegger's formulation of Dasein,[2] we can see many parallels with the EBR theory. Ittelson,

Proshansky, Rivlin, and Winkel, (1974), in their early formulation of EBR principles, echo Heidegger when they state that every environment is perceived as unique
by each individual. Rapoport (1990), too, has written extensively on the construction
of environmental meaning. Furthermore, just as Altman and Rogoff (1987) viewed
people and their environments as an indivisible and temporally located totality, so
too did Heidegger view Dasein as a single unitary whole:

> Self and world belong together in the single entity, the Dasein. Self and world are not two
> beings, like subject and object. . .[instead] self and world are the basic determination of the
> Dasein itself in the unity of the structure of being-in-the-world (quoted in Guignon, 1993,
> p. 13).

For the purposes of the analysis to follow, I am concerned with locating in the
films and readings insights into this understanding of "Being-in-the-world": how
humans make sense of their identities in space, create meaningful "worlds" spatially,
and relate to other beings as part of an active human–environment totality.

To undertake such readings, the overall framework for both this chapter and that
of the academic assignment on which it reports is that of hermeneutical inquiry. We
shall be dealing with the interpretation of "texts" both theoretical and cinematic, and
in particular how the interpretation of certain texts informs us in our understanding
of other texts. Through this hermeneutic, new insights not possible otherwise create
new opportunities for learning. Hermeneutic approaches allow us to recognize these
through the discernment of metaphors. Ricoeur (following Aristotle) calls this the
discernment of resemblances, or the

> rapprochement, the bringing closer together of terms that, previously "remote" suddenly
> appear "close." Resemblance thus consists in a change of distance in logical space. It is
> nothing other than this emergence of a new generic kinship between heterogeneous ideas.
> It is here that the productive imagination comes into play as the schematization of this
> synthetic operation of bringing closer together (Ricoeur, 1991, p. 9).

We are therefore going to be undertaking hermeneutic readings to "bring closer
together" planning theory and EBR and also bringing closer together lived and
cinematic understandings of human–environment transactions. Cinema in this case
is considered for its power to metaphorically understand the human condition, in
the world. In his own search for psychological metaphors, Sullivan (1990) noted
that

> the world itself and people within it are relational. By this we mean that to know or identify
> person, things or events, we have to identify or contrast them with other persons, things, or
> events. In order to come to know and understand something we usually attempt to identify
> and contrast it with something which we already find familiar (Sullivan, 1990, pp. 1–2).

Motion pictures are, of course, so very familiar they almost constitute a universal
language and thus offer a uniquely significant pedagogical platform for engaging
with representations of society, and social and power relations:

> [T]he growing popularity of film as a compelling mode of communication and form of
> public pedagogy – a visual technology that functions as a powerful teaching machine that
> intentionally tries to influence the production of meaning. . .suggests how important it has
> become as a site of cultural politics (Giroux, 2001, p. 587).

In the view of Giroux, film analysis in the classroom should be "part of a broader circuit of power relations [and] expand the possibilities of multiple readings of texts while making visible how representations work" (p. 53). Activist bell hooks concurs, having found that her students were made more aware of discourses on race, sex, and class through watching films than they had gained from the readings she'd assigned (cited in Giroux, 2001).

Film allows access to an almost endless array of potential "texts" with which to appraise a wide range of human experiences. All films are redolent with such possibilities. As Lau (1991) puts it,

> My starting point is to take a film as a text [which] is an inscription of a discourse in which both meaning and intersubjective exchange take place. That is, a text has a double world. As an inscription, the text has a "world of its own" that can be analyzed structurally or semiotically. As a discourse, there is the meaning of an experience being transferred from one sphere of life to another. The text, as a dialectic of the two, can be analyzed not only semiotically for structure but also semantically for meaning that transcends the text itself and points toward a vision of the world (Lau, 1991, p. 4).

What is of interest, then, is what carefully selected intertextual readings – Kozlovic's "Hollywood Hermeneutic" (2005) – can tell us about human-environment transactions, and thus, as Lau puts it, "transfer meaning from one sphere of life to another" – to enrich planning education and praxis with EBR theory. We are looking at filmed depictions for their ability to illuminate, metaphorically, the human-environment nexus and how best to plan for it.

Before we can undertake such an analysis, however, we will become more acquainted with the theoretical basis for this exercise: the use of film as a window for understanding human spatial behavior.

14.5 "Begin with the Screen and Move Outward to the City"

The tenuousness of the line between cinema and reality has long been noted by viewers and film theorists alike. French philosopher Baudrillard (1989), for example, viewed the American cityscape as a screenscape:

> Where is the cinema? It is all around you outside, all over the city, that marvelous, continuous performance of films and scenarios...The American city seems to have stepped right out of the movies. To grasp its secret you should not, then, begin with the city and move inward to the screen; you should begin with the screen and move outwards to the city (Baudrillard, 1989, p. 56).

Just as EBR researchers have sought to understand diverse human environmental experiences, so too were early film theorists curious about the psychology of the film-viewing experience. The viewing of projected light in darkened quarters was at the turn of the last century a new form of stimulus and audiences experienced a host of unexpected responses. In his seminal 1916 study of the psychology of film, Munsterberg (1916/1970) reported that audiences were reporting a variety of sensory hallucinations and illusions. . .neurasthenic persons are especially inclined to experience touch or temperature or smell or sound impressions from what they see on the screen. The associations become as vivid as realities, because the mind is so completely given up to the moving pictures (Munsterberg, 1970, p. 221).

This immersive empathy is especially relevant when contemplating the narrative and meanings embedded in fictional films. Andrew (1984, p. 45) describes how viewers "are asked to swim in a time stream, and. . .cannot look away without the fiction threatening to disappear;" and filmmakers, knowing this, rely "on some substratum of spectator understanding of the type of world that becomes the subject of the film." As a result we are "given over to the world" created by the filmmaker (ibid, p. 44) and the boundaries between our own and that on the screen, for a time, dissolve. This experience is not, of course, categorically the same as awakened consciousness but is more akin to dreaming:

> [F]ilm has been compared to the mind. . .with human perception, dreams or the subconscious. . .In a sense, film offers us our first experience of an other experience. Thus our understanding of our world can be informed and changed by this other way of experiencing a world, this other view of a similar world (Frampton, 2006, p. 15).

These understandings extend to more, in the view of Kracauer (1968), than just perceiving the world in new ways, but to seeing elements of the world – and our psychological relationship with it – that would otherwise have been hidden from us. "Film renders visible what we did not, or perhaps even could not, see before its advent. It effectively assists us in discovering the material world with its psychophysical correspondences" (Kracauer, 1968, p. 300).

As discussed, environmental psychology is premised on the notion that all of us negotiate meaning in the environment and that no two people will experience the environment in the same way (Ittelson et al., 1974); this corresponds to a major tenet of film studies, which holds that all audiences negotiate meaning in film. As Frampton (2006) observes:

> The mix of film and filmgoer is always an original journey – the filmgoer adds the *filmind's* film-thinking to their own, naturally or subconsciously reconfiguring it in the process. . .we remake the film via our concepts, and the film remakes our vision (Frampton, 2006, p. 163).

In this way, films do not represent reality, but rather are an interpretation of reality, a creation on the part of the filmmakers, one with which the viewer negotiates meaning. As such this interpretive and creative context represents an extra analytical layer that would otherwise not be available were the students only studying written theory or observing public behavior. Each student – and group of students – will interpret a film (and the reading) in different ways, so this makes every film a potentially new learning environment for each session of a theory course.

As we can see, then, there is ample theoretical support for approaching the study of environmental psychology through the use of film. What follows now are some examples of the potentialities this approach affords us.

14.6 EBR Theory Goes to the Movies

Resonances of EBR theories key to understanding "Being-in-the-world" are surprisingly common in the so-called fish-out-of-water movies, where characters familiar with one environment (or time) are thrown into another. This struggle to make sense of and use unfamiliar environments – indeed to establish the nature of reality itself – drives the narrative of *The Matrix* (Silver, 1999), in which we learn that everything we know as reality is in fact a simulation into which we are all "jacked." Neo, a hacker (played by Keanu Reeves), has become aware that there is something "wrong" with his environment and learns that it is actually a simulation. With the help of his mentor, Morpheus (Lawrence Fishburn), Neo is then "born" into the "real world" – which is in fact a burned-out wasteland centuries into a future dominated by machines. However, Morpheus trains Neo to utilize that environment which he once knew as reality in entirely new ways: to move through, act in, and manipulate the environment before becoming "the One" who can be a total master over it.

Throughout the movie, we must be constantly aware of the need to distinguish between reality and illusion. Egon Brunswik's ideas on "probabilistic functionalism" (1947/2001) are highly relevant here, as they suggest that we are always determining from one moment to the next through an interpretation of distal (objective) and proximal (subjective) cues the extent to which our senses are discerning reality. Ittelson (1973) further proposes that our beliefs about the world determine our perceptions: as he puts it, *believing is seeing*. One can almost hear Lawrence Fishburne's Morpheus when Ittelson (1973, p. 10) writes, "Perception mirrored our innermost values and produced a world which we saw precisely because we wanted to believe in it." But we are urged not to take our perceptions for granted: Carr (1970, p. 518) would have said that Neo, "perhaps sensing that there may be a way to escape [his] bondage...begins to ask, 'why?' "

However, once this question is asked – and the "red pill" taken – Neo begins an irrevocable journey, the course of which is described fairly coherently by Stephen Carr's "phases of man-environment interaction process" (1970, pp. 521–529): Neo first engages in what Carr calls the Directive Phase, in which our needs become such that they direct us to new courses of action

> *[Neo's] directive phase began with his search for Morpheus...Although his perception of the information he had gathered up to this point was confusing and almost absurd, Neo attempted to make sense of the environment...both as a source of essentials and as a ground for action.*

An *Intelligence Phase*, in which we search for new relevant information from the environment and organize it to be retained:

> *Neo...follow[s] the "white rabbit" which represented a path to the truth of the Matrix provided by Trinity.*
> *In order for Neo to control his environment, it was crucial for him to first recognize and understand it. [His] preconceived limitation[s] of his "self" then became apparent through his subsequent behaviors. [Once] Neo began to adapt and break down his previous cognitive notions of the physical limitations he was...able to "free his mind".*

A *Planning Phase*, in which appropriate information is retrieved and transformed to be used in the generation, evaluation, and selection of sets of possible action:

Neo struggles with this phase for the majority of the film. He is aware of the concept of the matrix, and what is possible within the alternate environment. It is his ability to "free his mind", and transform his existing models of what is possible within [the real] environment, into what is possible within the matrix environment. From training within the matrix simulators, and retaining new information from first hand experiences, and Morpheus' teachings, Neo was able to plan his use of. . .the matrix.

An *Action Phase*, in which the plan is executed in a particular environmental context:

This newly acquired information allows Neo to achieve superhuman feats of strength and agility. . .People who are unaware of such possibilities are unable to accomplish or even comprehend these superhuman actions within the matrix. Neo is able to carry out his superhuman stunts because of his knowledge of the supports and constraints of the computer programmed environment.

Having thus integrated new knowledge – and more importantly, new beliefs about his Being-in-the-world – Neo is capable of formulating and putting into action a plan for rescuing Morpheus after he is captured by Agent Smith (Hugo Weaving).

A *Review Phase*, in which the effectiveness of the particular course of action is assessed in order to correct further action and to assign value and meaning to the experience:

The meanings and values of reality and existence are drastically shaken over the course of the film. Neo views the matrix upon re-entering for the first time as fake. [Then] Neo sees what he thought of as reality, the matrix environment, for what it truly is [and elements in the] environment gain new meanings. Telephones don't exist as a simple communication device anymore; they are. . .critical points of exit and entry into the matrix environment. As Neo ventures through Stephen Carr's five phases. . .he is able to comprehend the matrix environment for what it truly is. As a result, he is "enlightened" at the climax of the film, becoming "the One", an unstoppable entity manipulating the matrix. . .however he sees fit, rendering him invincible within the simulated reality.

What we see in *The Matrix* is that, whether we live within an environment with which we are quite familiar or must adjust to a radically new one, we are continually engaging in these transactional phases, with the ultimate goal of seeking environmental meaning. And, like the film itself, these meanings can take religious or quasi-religious forms.

Traditionally, humans have sought for supernatural explanations for their spatial transactions. Such cultures, according to religious historian Mircea Eliade, believed that "space is not homogenous; [they] experienc[e] interruptions, breaks in it; some parts of space are qualitatively different from others" (1959, p. 20). These spaces are considered sacred.

Sacred space acts as a wayfinding tool while also providing an element of mystery, adding interest to every day life. For religious man, these sacred spaces are shared with a like-minded group of people, forming a community (ibid, p. 2).

In our more rationalist era, we are less disposed to find this meaning in God or gods, and our urban settings are replete with "homogenous," "neutral," and profane environments. However, as Eliade explains (1959), our contemporary spatial experiences are nonetheless "crypto-religious" in nature – that is, responses to

> ...privileged spaces, qualitatively different from all others – a man's birthplace, or the scenes of his first love, or certain places in the first foreign city he visited in youth. Even for the most frankly non-religious, all these places still retain an exceptional, a unique quality; they are the "holy places" of his private universe, as if it were in such spots that he had received the revelation of a reality other than that in which he participates in his ordinary daily life (Eliade, 1959, p. 24).

Such spatial behaviors dominate *Falling Down* (Harris, Kopelson, Weingrod, & Schumacher, 1993). Michael Douglas' character William Foster, a laid-off defense worker, is estranged from his wife and daughter and stuck in traffic on his way to his daughter's birthday party. As the heat and his existential frustrations boil over, he abandons his car and embarks on a pilgrimage across a profane and brutal Los Angeles, one in which his personal cosmogony (Eliade, 1959) crashes up against contemporary America. Calling himself D-FENS (after his license plate), Foster makes his way across a landscape of "chaos" – a profane world – in which there is no moral center and no myths, only nonsensical "rules." As one film reviewer put it,

> The deterioration of American society is in evidence everywhere. From the decaying buildings and lousy service, to the liars and cheats who panhandle rather than work – everywhere Foster goes, he's confronted by the rot, the anarchy, the spiritual malaise (Russell, 1999, paragraph 12).

The only place that matters to D-FENS is his former home, where his estranged wife and daughter live. This is his *axis mundi* or "center of the world," what Eliade would call the "holy place of his private universe". To reach it Foster is willing to violate any number of privileged places along the way – places that others have made "sacred" in a crypto-religious fashion (a gang and their hillside, a neo-nazi and his shrine to fascism, elderly duffers and their golf course). What drives his pilgrimage is not just his longing for his *axis mundi* but his feelings of betrayal against an America that he no longer recognizes.

> *William Foster's ideal America is to him what a cosmogony is to sacred man. A cosmogony is an account of the creation of the world, or a set of ideal beliefs. William Foster has... essentially been cast from the paradise ideal of his American dream. Just like Satan in the Christian cosmogony had been cast from heaven to the profane environs of Hell, so has William Foster been cast into the profane environment of south-central Los Angeles... [And just as] Satan function[s] in the Christian cosmogony... as punishment for those sinning against what is ideal within the Christian cosmogony, William Foster punishe[s] those who sinned against his individual cosmogony.*
>
> *There are hints throughout the film as to William Foster's ideas of the perfect life, which is what can be further defined as the American dream. The American dream to William Foster appears to be the ideals from the 1950's through to the 60's; a nice loving family, a house with a yard, a steady nine to five job, a booming economy that encourages low market prices, predominantly white citizens and a general attitude of respect amongst everyone.*

This "cosmogony" is, of course, hardly confined to disgruntled film characters, but key elements within it underlie the presumptive conservative metanarrative driving a huge range of public policy debates, from immigration to day care to welfare. Just as D-FENS rails against immigrant shopkeepers and gang members for having changed his country, so too are our spatial interrelations becoming ever more problematized by polarizing and fearful discourses on immigration, which portray newcomers as a threat (Sandercock, 2003). Distrust and animosities born of prejudices are surely to follow.

These forces are portrayed to devastating effect in the Paul Haggis film *Crash* (Cheadle, Haggis, Moresco, Schulman, & Yari 2004), which peels back the layers of a society steeped in racism – but subtly shows how this pathology is exacerbated by the built environment. The characters in the film are often sealed in their cars – or their respective nodes of wealth and poverty – and as a consequence are unable to engage in the kinds of casual interactions necessary for a functioning society.

> *Dispersed, relatively isolated [urban] nodes create physical distance...which in turn demands the necessity for constant [commuting] throughout the city. Vectors, which serve as the links between these nodes are usually dominated by private transportation (Phillips and Smith 2004). As [automobiles are] essentially private nodes within public vectors – a "home on the road" (Fraine et al., 2007) – an ambiguity of spatial usage materializes.*
>
> *The automobile then becomes an extension of the skin and insulates the senses from environmental details and stimuli. This desensitization does not only exist between man and environment, but also among city dwellers. As [Don Cheadle's character, Detective Graham Waters] says, "it's the sense of touch ... in a real city, you walk, you brush past people, people bump into you. In L.A. nobody touches you. People are always behind this metal and glass, I think we miss that touch so much that we crash into each other just so we can feel something."*

Research into such negotiation of interpersonal space as a form of nonverbal communication can tell us a lot about what we seen in the film. Edward Hall's early work in intercultural spatial relations (1966) explored how Anglo-American standards and expectations concerning personal space and crowding (i.e., in a "noncontact" culture) were pronouncedly different from people from "contact" cultures. Research since then has shown strong confirmation of his observations not just for broad national groups, but for urban subcultures as well. Studies have shown, for instance, that Mexican-Americans maintain much closer interpersonal distances than do Anglo-Americans or Afro-Americans (summarized in Aiello & Thompson, 1990). Findings such as these suggest that miscommunication between such groups is quite likely in ever more multiethnic, multicultural countries:

Different perceptions of space may often lead to different definitions of what constitutes an inappropriate interaction distance...consequently miscommunication can occur when individuals from different cultures attempt to interpret each other's spatial behavior (Aiello & Thompson, 1990, p. 109).

A key element of such miscommunication relates to attribution/expectancy, or what people assume strangers will do, which in intercultural contexts can often be based on stereotypical assumptions (Burgoon & Hubbard, 2004). We see this throughout the film: Jean Cabot (Sandra Bullock), upon seeing two black youths approaching her and her husband (Brendan Fraser), reacts visibly and fearfully; she later distrusts Daniel Ruiz, the Latino locksmith (Michael Pena), as does Iranian shopkeeper Farad (Shaun Toub); Officer Hansen (Ryan Phillipe) picks up Peter Waters (who is black) in his car and, believing (mistakenly) that Waters has a concealed weapon, shoots him.

The personal space implications peculiar to L.A. were also not lost on at least one of the film's actors. In preparing for the film, Ryan Phillipe told reporters,

> When I first moved to L.A. from the East, I thought it was the strangest place on Earth because people didn't interact and mix the way they do in New York and Philly where I spent my youth... There is something oddly segregated about L.A., even though it is the most liberal, leftist, flaky, New Agey, forward-thinking city in the U.S. [Los Angelinos] cling to their personal space. They protect their personal space like nowhere I've seen in this country (Hobson, 2005).

When groups of varying socioeconomic capacities are spatially segregated or ghettoized, and when public spaces capable of encouraging social mixing are not available, people of diverse cultures and ethnicities will only encounter the "other" in unusual circumstances rather than in everyday encounters (Leadbeater, n.d.). Unfortunately, the interactions most of the characters in the movie do have are profoundly racist and what Phillips and Smith (2006) would call "uncivil."

Urban incivilities, prejudice, and hostility toward immigrant "Others" are no longer strictly interpersonal but have become practically institutionalized in the twenty-first century London in *Children of Men* (Abraham et al., 2006). In the year 2027, humanity is decades away from extinction. No babies have been born for 18 years, and civilization is undergoing slow collapse.

> *[The London of 2027 is] a chaotic, dense [and] polluted metropolis where the government instills fear in the general public and exercises force to rid the country of its problematic illegal immigrant population in an almost Naziesque manner. Police rampage through apartment buildings that house foreigners and rob, beat, deport or kill any immigrants they may capture; armed guards restrict refugee access into Britain and control them by any means possible, while the Government is responsible for a series of planned bombings... posed as terrorist attacks.*
>
> *Sustainable design is non-existent because people don't care about the future of the world anymore. Everyone seems obsessed in finding out why there is infertility not at trying to [heal nature], which could be the formal cause of the disaster.*

The global psychic trauma of the certainty of extinction has rendered purposeless almost all human activity. Yet, as Macy (1995) would argue, this is hardly the stuff of science fiction:

> Until the late twentieth century, every generation throughout history lived with the tacit certainty that there would be generations to follow. Each assumed without questioning that its children and children's children would walk the same Earth, under the same sky. Hardships, failures and personal death were encompassed in that vaster assurance of continuity. That certainty is now lost to us, whatever our politics. That loss, unmeasured and immeasurable, is the pivotal psychological reality of our time (Macy, 1995, p. 240).

It is also of course the pivotal psychological reality of the main characters in the film. Years ago, Theo (Clive Owen) and his wife Julian (Juliana Moore) lost their son in a pandemic, and the grief ended their marriage; now universal sterility and accompanying grief are tearing apart civilization. People try to carry on but the futility is so open that the government has issued suicide kits called "Quietus."

In Macy's (1995) view, our repressed grief and terror are holding us back from taking action; for Theo – like most everyone else in the film – this repression and accompanying psychological numbness are the only ways he can carry on.

> Upon the loss of his son Theo transitioned from someone who lived a largely empowered life. . . to someone who led a double life and lived constantly in [what Macy calls the] "fear of pain."
> Theo is held captive by many fears [and has] many numbing devices [e.g., alcohol] that he uses as a response to his fears. . . He continues to live his life as if nothing has changed. He goes to work and continues to live in his apartment using these numbing devices to deal with the pain and fear that he feels. The energy that his repression is taking out of him is making him unable to feel any emotion.

Like many of us, Theo is suffering from what Macy (1995) calls environmental despair. But – and consistent with the EBR theory concerning the restorative capacities of natural settings (Kaplan, 1995) – the extent to which Theo experiences such despair is sensitive to his exposure to natural settings:

> When in the. . . controlled. . . built environments of London. . . Theo [is] extremely introverted, impersonal and rude as he is only concerned for his own personal well-being and safety. When placed into the comfort of [his friend Jasper's cottage in the forest] we are shown the side of Theo that allows us to believe he was once capable of being someone who stood up for that which he believed in and having a family, which he loved and in return loved him. It is this environment that we are shown the truest representation of who Theo was, is and can be as a person.

It is not until Theo is abducted by the underground rebel group, the Fishes, and hired to escort a young pregnant woman named Kee (Clare-Hope Ashitey) to the secretive Human Project that Theo becomes engaged and is able to act. What has happened to him? Theo breaks out of this trance when he realizes that Kee is pregnant – and he experiences what Macy (1995) calls a *catharsis*:

> . . . his repressed emotions are all refocused on getting in and out of Bexhill to the Human Project ship alive. He has meaning and purpose in his life again and he no longer simply moves through the environments he encounters along the way, but thinks about and reacts to them to ensure survival.
> Slowly throughout the movie as Theo helps finish the task he has been charged with we are able to witness his personal transformation from a person suffering from "environmental despair" and a loss of "empowerment" back into someone who is. . . becoming empowered again and standing up for what it is he believes in.

He becomes "empowered with" (Macy, 1995) Kee – and by extension, the rest of humanity – and realizes that the fate of his species rests with him. He escapes with Kee and they make their way to the coast. He delivers her baby in the most horrible of conditions and leads her through a hellish battle scene – becoming fatally wounded in the process – but is still sufficiently "empowered with" her to coach her in parenting, and as he dies takes joy in seeing her rock her baby as he cared for his own lost boy.

Theo's sacrifice of himself, when [he] essentially puts the good of humanity ahead of his own, demonstrates [the] interconnectedness of all people.

That Theo breaks through his despair and is "empowered with" others shows us that hope is not some thoughtlessly optimistic state of mind but rather the result of honestly facing one's own grief and recognizing our interconnections with others.

14.7 Discussion

It has been tempting in the classroom setting to remark on the very close associations between the chosen films and readings, almost to the extent that it is hard to imagine how the filmmakers could have made these films without having read – or become familiar with – the theories in question. Needless to say, such familiarity on the part of the filmmakers is quite unnecessary. Instead what we see in these intersections is surely an indication of the universality of the human experience expressed in diverse ways. As Geoffrey Hill shows in his *Illuminating Shadows: The Mythic Power of Film*, the films he examines "are largely mythicized at the subconscious level. While [filmmakers] might not be aware of their mythic participation, they nonetheless convey significant mythic import" (Hill, 1992, p. 17). Through this engagement with myth, we are faced at a very fundamental level with the complexities of the human experience and with new understandings of spatial power relations.

We can see how the EBR theory may be very effectively illustrated through film analyses. What is more significant though is how these readings can also challenge existing social structures and can therefore be radicalizing. Giroux (2001, p. 589) concurs:

[M]any students see in the public issues addressed by film culture a connection to public life that revitalizes their sense of agency and resonates with this sense of the importance of the cultural terrain as both an important source of knowledge and of critical dialogue.

Critical dialog and the knowledge that results are essential to engaging contemporary crises. We all have the potential to enrich our collective experience of Heidegger's *Dasein*, but only if we, as Carr (1970) suggests, ask "why"? Questioning and challenging what we assume to be immutable realities are the beginning of liberation.

Such interrogations of existing structures must begin with a reflexive posture, to question the role of the designer in society, and motion pictures were especially useful for starting this conversation in the classroom. Oftentimes – as in *Falling Down* and *Crash* – we see how the choices made by design professionals as a part of the political economy of real estate have resulted in dehumanizing, alienating urbanism. Other times, blatantly oppressive settings (like the prison camp in *Children of Men*) are presumed to have had designers, who knew exactly what these places would be used for.

A most compelling example of this latter portrait is the science fiction/horror film *Cube* (Meh & Natali, 1997). Five strangers awaken in a six-sided room, with a hatch on each wall, floor, and ceiling. They realize that each hatch leads to an almost identical room – identical save for the color and the fact that some might be lethally booby-trapped. One of the characters, Worth (played by David Hewlett), is revealed to have been an architect who worked on the design of the vast structure. He says that it was a top-secret military project – a prison – and that his role in the project as a designer was very minor and compartmentalized: all he was required to do was come up with the exterior parameters.

What the film suggests about environmental design is both subversive and disturbing: that oppression must be spatially situated, requiring as it does a particular stage that must be envisioned, designed, and built according to the specifications of a dominant power. The prison of *The Matrix* may have been virtual, but it is no less a designed environment than that of Bexhill in *Children of Men* or the *Cube*. That Worth didn't know the ultimate purpose of the project does not relieve him of his share of responsibility he holds for the violence that follows.

The students in the Theory of Design 3 course were eager to engage with these (and other) ethical dilemmas and the film seminars often revolved around direct questions to fellow students about what decisions they would make or what role they felt designers needed to take to change present conditions, injustices, and crises. This reflexiveness was particularly poignant in one of the reflections on *Children of Men:*

> What's most startling about the movie is that [the people in the film] who did not react in time to prevent [their] crisis are the people of today. The film is set in the year 2027, Theo is maybe in his late 30 s to mid 40 s – the age range our classmates [will be] in that year.

These students were aware of their own vulnerability to what Macy (1995) calls the "fears that hold us captive":

> Each fear is directly related to a set of thought patterns that... can be directly attributed to their stance and action, or lack of, regarding environmental issues. "Fear of Causing Pain"... relates to our desire... to bring as little trouble and worry possible upon those we care for. The "Fear of Appearing Stupid" stems from... not [wanting] to complain about a problem that we are unable to provide an immediate solution for in fear of being called out by our peers as nothing more than a whining bleeding heart environmentalist with no real solutions to our stated problems. The "Fear of Feeling Powerless" is the most realistic and commonly experienced of the bunch that is presented. Many people do not like to feel as if they have no control over the situation in which they are in as this feeling of helplessness is contradictory to the environmental responses of control and safety that have been programmed into us over time. The problem with this however is that this helplessness is the largest problem [related to] "environmental despair," as many people have taken the stance of "I don't think about that because there is nothing I can do about it." The perception held in this fear is that which is most in need of change in order for us as a society to break through this "Environmental Despair" and begin to exact positive change on the whole.

The films and readings sampled in this chapter played a formative role in engaging students in a critical discussion about environments, users, and designers and in challenging assumptions about all of them so as to be better able to participate in bringing about these positive changes.

14.8 Conclusions

More than three decades have passed since Appleyard's (1973) call for more integration between the social sciences and design professions. Yet we see that there are still significant gaps between planning and environmental psychology – gaps in understandings that, if mended, could contribute to making more humane places. I propose that the place to start is in planning education, which continues to be focused on macro socio-spatial processes to the detriment of understanding more intimate human-environment transactions.

I suggest that an engaging and illuminating way to address this gap is through the integration of hermeneutic film readings into planning education, concentrating on readings of environmental psychology theories in cinema. The hermeneutical interpretations gleaned from such a synthesis can enrich planning discourse and provide the basis for more interdisciplinary approaches.

What do we stand to gain?

Instead of talking in general terms about "planning with" publics, planners need to understand first of all *how people engage with their environments.* These are fundamentally individual psychological processes that, while they can be experienced collectively, cannot be fully studied at a macro level. The interpretations above, however, shed some light on the "world forming" (Heidegger, 1962) in which we all engage. Neo in *The Matrix* is deeply involved in learning about, interpreting and furthermore shaping his environment, and his ability to question his assumptions about his environmental transactions is the foundation for his evolution.

Instead of talking in general terms about "place-making" and "encouraging a sense of place" planners need to understand the *processes by which places acquire meaning for people.* Places are the foundation for our sense of self, our identity, our "Being-in-the-world". Our preferences and love for certain places may be rooted in conceptions of the sacred or in more crypto-religious terms, as we see in *Falling Down.* Regardless, our beliefs – our personal cosmogonies – about ourselves in space are also situated in widely held ideologies that contribute to social and power relations.

If planners are going to be able to understand – and hopefully transform – these relations, then they need a better sense of the *psychological dimensions of our socio-spatial relations.* Our interpersonal relations are always spatially situated and subject to the dynamic interplay of our collective efforts to negotiate interpersonal distances, territoriality, and privacy (Altman, 1975). The incivilities in *Crash* show us that, when denied the opportunity to actually carry out these functions with one another in space, people retreat into physical and psychological enclaves that only deepen already entrenched racial and class divides.

Such social and economic inequities are but one of many of the seemingly intractable challenges planners face, along with urban sprawl, climate change, environmental degradation, and energy depletion. Portents of dystopic futures surround our work and can make our efforts seem insignificant to the task at hand. If we are to have confidence that our interventions can make a difference and to continue engaging in these efforts, then planners need to move beyond simplistic notions of hope, optimism – or worse, despair and futility. We need to attain and maintain the strength to question and transform our present spatial arrangements. To do so, we must – like Theo in *Children of Men* – learn to *move beyond despair* (Macy, 1995) and be "empowered with" our fellow citizens, nonhuman species, and habitats.

The immediacy and immersive nature of cinema provides us with a window into these and other potentialities. When matched thoughtfully with relevant environmental psychology theory, motion pictures can offer the planning student an incredibly rich learning environment. These are but a few examples: thousands of possible film/reading combinations and interpretations are out there that can yield even more profound insights for planning scholarship, education, and practice.

Acknowledgements I thank the Environmental Design Program at the University of Manitoba for its cooperation with this project, especially the program's Chair, Associate Professor Eduard Epp. As well, thanks are owed to Dr. Jino Distasio, Director of the Institute of Urban Studies at the University of Winnipeg, for his support in the preparation of this chapter. Thanks as well to my Teaching Assistant Jennifer Lim. Finally and most significantly, I am especially indebted to the students from the 2008 class of students of EVDS 2610, Theory of Design 3 at the Environmental Design program at the University of Manitoba. Your enthusiasm for the project – and the course – was most gratifying. I thank the following students in particular for allowing me to incorporate some of their eloquent insights, observations and ideas into this chapter: Miranda Adam, David Burns, Michael Chan, Billy Chung, Matt Cibinel, Tom Fougere, James Frank, Ashley Laing, Kaley Lawrence, Darci Madlung, Bret Mack, Mumtaz Mirza, Phan Tu Ngoc, Devin Segal, Aiden Stothers, Nils Vik, Zephyra Vun, and Taren Wan. Thank you so much for all of your contributions!

Notes

1. The preferred term in this paper.
2. A fuller explication of Dasein is far beyond the scope of this paper. For excellent introductions to these ideas, see Guignon (1993), King (2001), and Mulhall (2005).

Films Discussed in this Paper

Abraham, M., Newman, E., Smith, I., Shor, H., Smith, T., Bliss, T. A., Bernstein, A. (Producers), & Cuarón, A. (Director). (2006). *Children of men*. [Motion Picture]. United States: Universal Pictures.

Cheadle, D., Haggis, P., Moresco, R., Schulman, C., Yari, B. (Producers), & Haggis, P. (Director) (2004). *Crash* [Motion Picture]. United States: Lions Gate Films.

Harris, T., Kopelson, A., Weingrod, H. (Producers), & Schumacher, J. (Director). (1993). *Falling down* [Motion Picture]. United States: Warner Brothers.

Meh, M. (Producer), & Natali, V. (Director). (1997). *Cube* [Motion Picture] Canada: Cineplex-Odeon Films.

Silver, J. (Producer), Wachowski, A., & Wachowski, L. (Writers/Directors). (1999). *The matrix* [Motion Picture] United States: Warner Brothers.

References

Aiello, J., & Thompson, D. (1990). Personal space, crowding and spatial behavior in a cultural context. In I. Altman, A. Rapoport, & J. F. Wohlwill (Eds.), *Environment and culture. Environment and behavior* (Vol. 4). New York: Plenum Press.

Altman, I. (1975). *The environment and social behaviour: Privacy, personal space, territoriality and crowding*. Monterey CA: Brooks/Cole.

Altman, I., & Low, S. M. (1992). *Place attachment*. New York: Plenum Press.

Altman, I., & Rogoff, B. (1987). World views in psychology: Trait, organismic and transactional approaches. In D. Stokols, & I. Altman (Eds.), *The handbook of environmental psychology* (Vol. 1). New York: Wiley.

Andrew, D. (1984). *Concepts in film theory*. New York: Oxford University Press.

Appleyard, D. (1973). *Environmental planning and social science: Strategies for environmental decision making*. Institute of Urban and Regional Development, University of California, Berkeley, CA, Working Paper issue: 1973, 217.

Appleyard, D. (1981). *Livable streets*. Berkeley, CA: University of California Press.

Baudrillard, J. (1989). *America*. C. Turner (trans). New York: Verso.

Beauregard, R. A. (1989). Between modernity and postmodernity: The ambiguous position of US Planning. *Environment and Planning D: Society and Space, 7*, 381–395.

Brunswik, E. (2001). *The essential brunswik: Beginnings, explications, applications*. K. R. Hammond & T. R. Stewart (Eds.). New York: Oxford University Press.

Burgoon, J., & Hubbard, A. S. E. (2004). Cross-cultural and intercultural applications of Expectancy Violations Theory and Interactions Adaptation Theory. In W. B. Gudykunst (Ed.), *Theorizing about intercultural communication*. Thousand Oaks, CA: Sage Publications.

Carr, S. (1970). The city of the mind. In H. Proshansky, W. H. Ittelson, & L. G. Rivlin (Eds.), *Environmental psychology: Man and his physical setting*. New York: Holt, Rinehart & Winston.

Coley, R. L., Kuo, F. E., & Sullivan, W. C. (1997). Where does community grow? *Environment and Behavior n, 29*, 468–494.

Dean, A. (1994). Socially motivated architecture. In W. Lillyman, M. F. Moriarty, & D. J. Neuman (Eds.), *Critical architecture and contemporary culture*. New York: Oxford University Press.

D'Estree, T. P., Dukes, E. F., & Navarrete-Romero, J. (2002). Environmental conflict and its resolution. In R. Bechtel, & A. Churchman (Eds.). *The handbook of environmental psychology* (2nd ed.). New York: John Wiley & Sons.

Downs, R. M., & Stea, D. (1977). *Maps in minds: Reflections on cognitive mapping*. New York: Harper & Row.

Eliade, M. (1959). *The sacred and the profane: The nature of religion*. New York: Harper & Row.

Evans, G. (1996). *Environmental psychology as a field within psychology*. Retrieved July 13, 2008, from http://www.ucm.es/info/Psyap/iaap/evans.htm

Frampton, D. (2006). *Filmosophy*. London: Wallflower Press.

Fraine, G., Smith, S., Zinkiewics, L., Chapman, R., & Sheehan, M. (2007). At home on the road? Can drivers' relationships with their cars be associated with territoriality? *Journal of Environmental Psychology, 27*, 204–214.

Friedmann, J. (1996). The core curriculum in planning revisited. *Journal of Planning Education and Research, 15*, 89–104.

Geller, E. S. (2002). The challenge of increasing proenvironmental behavior. In R. Bechtel & A. Churchman (Eds.), *Handbook of environmental psychology* (2nd ed.). New York: JohnWiley & Sons.

Gifford, R. (2007). *Environmental psychology: Principles and practice* (4th ed.). Colville, WA: Optimal Books.

Giroux, H. (2001). Breaking into the movies: Pedagogy and the politics of film. *JAC: A Journal of Composition Theory, 21*, 583–98.

Guignon, C. B. (1993). *Cambridge companion to Heidegger*. Cambridge: Cambridge University Press.

Hall, E. (1966). *The hidden dimension*. Garden City, NY: Doubleday.

Heidegger, M. (1962). *Being and Time*. J Macquarrie, E Robinson (trans.). New York: Harper and Row.

Hester, R. (1985). Subconscious landscapes of the heart. *Places, 2*(3), 10–22.

Hester, R. (2006). *Design for ecological democracy*. Cambridge, MA: MIT Press.

Hill, G. (1992). *Illuminating shadows: The mythic power of film*. Boston: Shambhala.

Hobson, L. (2005). Matt, Ryan team up as L.A. Cops. The Calgari sun, May 1st 2005. Retrieved April 8, 2008, from http://r-phillippe.com/calgarysun2005.php

Ittelson, W. H. (1973). Environment, perception, and contemporary perceptual theory. In W. Ittelson (Ed.), *Environment and cognition*. New York: Seminar Press.

Ittelson, W., Proshansky, H., Rivlin, L., & Winkel, G. (1974). *An introduction to environmental psychology*. New York: Holt, Rinehart & Winston, Inc.

Kaplan, S. (1995). The restorative benefits of nature: Toward an integrative framework. *Journal of Environmental Psychology, 15*, 169–182.

Kaplan, R., & Kaplan, S. (1989). *The experience of nature: A psychological perspective*. New York: Cambridge University Press.

Kaplan, R., Ryan, R., & Kaplan, S. (1998). With people in mind: Design and management of everyday nature. Washington: Island Press.

King, M. (2001). *A guide to Heidegger's being and time*. Albany: State University of New York Press.

Kozlovic, A. K. (2005). Hollywood hermeneutics: A religion-and-film genre for the 21st century. *Film Journal, 11*. Retrieved March 26, 2008, from http://www.thefilmjournal.com/issue11/religion.html

Kracauer, S. (1968). *Theory of film: The redemption of physical reality*. London: Oxford University Press.

Kuo, F. (2001). Environment and crime in the inner city: Does vegetation reduce crime? *Environment and Behavior n, 33*(3), 343–367.

Lau, J. K. W. (1991). "Judou": A hermeneutical reading of cross-cultural cinema. *Film Quarterly, 45*, 2–10.

Leadbeater, C. (n.d.). *Remixing cities. CEOs for cities, Chicago*. Retrieved April 24, 2008, from http://www.ceosforcities.org/rethink/research/files/RemixingCities.pdf AU

Lucy, W. (1994). If planning includes too much, maybe it should include more. *Journal of the American Planning Association, 60*, 305–318.

Lynch, K. (1960). *The image of the city*. Cambridge: MIT Press.

Macy, J. (1995). Working through environmental despair. In T. Roszak, M. E. Gomes, & A. D. Kanner (Eds.), *Ecopsychology: Restoring the earth, healing the mind*. San Francisco: Sierra Club.

Manzo, L. C., & Perkins, D. (2006). Finding common ground: The importance of place attachment to community participation and planning. *Journal of Planning Literature, 20*, 335–350.

Marcus, C. C. (2007). *House as a mirror of self*. Newburyport, MA: Red Wheel.

Mulhall, S. (Ed.). (2005). *Routledge philosophy guidebook to heidegger and being and time*. London: Routledge.

Munsterberg, H. (1916/1970). *The photoplay: A psychological study*. New York: Arno Press & The New York Times.

Ozawa, P., & Seltze,r E. (1999). Taking our bearings: Mapping a relationship among planning practice, theory and education. *Journal of Planning Education and Research, 18*, 257–266.

Phillips, T., & Smith, P. (2006). Rethinking urban incivility research: Strangers, bodies and circulations. *Urban Studies, 43*, 879–901.

Peek, L. A., & Mileti, D. S. (2002). The history and future of disaster research. In R. Bechtel & A. Churchman (Eds.), *Handbook of environmental psychology* (2nd ed.). New York: JohnWiley & Sons.

Rapoport, A. (1990). *The meaning of the built environment: A nonverbal communication approach*. Tucson: University of Arizona Press.

Ricoeur, P. (1991). *From text to action: Essays in Hermeneutics, II* (K. Blamey & J. B. Thompson, Trans.). Evanston, Il: Northwestern University Press.

Rivlin, L. G. (1990). The significance of home and homelessness. *Marriage and Family Review, 15*, 39–56.

Russell, L. (1999). *Falling down*. Filmcourt. Retrieved April 23, 2008, from http://www.culturecourt.com/F/Hollywood/FallDown.htm

Sandercock, L. (2003). *Cosmopolis II: Mongrel cities in the 21st century*. London: Continuum.

Schneekloth, L. H., & Shibley, R. G. (1995). *Placemaking: The art and practice of building communities*. New York: Wiley.

Sommer, R. (1969). *Personal space: The behavioral basis of design*. New York: Prentice Hall.

Sommer, R. (1983). *Social design: Creating buildings with people in mind*. Eaglewood Cliffs, NJ: Prentice-Hall.

Sullivan, E. (1990). *Critical psychology and pedagogy: Interpretation of the personal world*. Toronto: The Ontario Institute for the Study of Education Press.

Taylor, R. (2002). Crime prevention through environmental design (CPTED): Yes, no, maybe, unknowable, and all of the above. In R. Bechtel, & A. Churchman (Eds.), *Handbook of environmental psychology*. New York: John Wiley & Sons.

Twigger-Ross, C. L., & Uzzell, D. L. (1996). Place and identity processes. *Journal of Environmental Psychology, 16*, 205–220.

White, S. S., & Mayo, J. M. (2005). Environmental education in graduate professional degrees: The case of urban planning. *The Journal of Environmental Education, 36*, 31–38.

Whyte, W. H. (1988). *City: Rediscovering the center*. New York: Doubleday.

Chapter 15
Stinging Real! Four Essays on the Transformative Power of Films and Storytelling in Planning Education

Andrew Isserman, Anuttama Dasgupta, Susy Hemphill, and Mallory Rahe

> *Why don't you let go and tell everything you know about being who you are from where you are? All sorts of little subjects must lie buried in your being a New England Italian of a family of farmers who haven't altogether forgotten Italy. Probably you aren't desperate enough to be bold yet. But bold you've got to be with the realities or with the analogies or with both before you will prevail in writing. Tell us something so stinging real that we wouldn't think you'd dare to tell it. . . . Tell us something about your life and surroundings that no newspaperman could imagine – that I couldn't imagine. Inside stuff.* Robert Frost, 1933, letter to his student Hugh Saglio, Amherst College
> (Frost, 1993, p. 19)

15.1 Essay One

The plan is simple. Every Tuesday night we watch two films, every week you write a one-page essay, and Mondays and Wednesdays we meet in seminar. Through the films, essays, and discussions with your classmates, you learn about the United States, yourself, and your values. You become a more complete human being, better writer, and better planner. (Course syllabus 2008)

15.1.1 On the Road with Buddy and Philbert

Four weeks into the course, I still felt like a disoriented tourist who had boarded the wrong bus and was now traveling to an unknown destination, too embarrassed by her audacity to draw attention to herself by asking to get off. What was I, the only non-American person in that room, doing in a class that promised to "rediscover the

A. Isserman (✉)
University of Illinois, Urbana, IL, USA
e-mail: isserman@illinois.edu

L. Sandercock, G. Attili (eds.), *Multimedia Explorations in Urban Policy and Planning*, Urban and Landscape Perspectives 7, DOI 10.1007/978-90-481-3209-6_15, © Springer Science+Business Media B.V. 2010

landscapes, histories, and economies of America through film"? I was still shocked by my impulsiveness at having chosen to do four credit hours of a film-watching course with a professor of economics instead of something more practical that I could apply to my future planning career. Had I traveled half-way across the world and persevered through three grueling semesters of the masters' program, only to be so self-indulgent as to be lured in by the promise of arm chair travel? I could watch the movies anywhere, anytime I wished. In fact, some of the movies listed in the schedule I already had seen. Yet, the idea of furthering my planning education through films and discussions was such a novel concept that I wanted to see for myself how it would play out. The writing component of the course intrigued me, too. My curiosity and sense of adventure got the better of me, and I enrolled myself in this course.

I trudged to class thinking to myself that I don't really belong here, I have no a priori knowledge or intuitive understanding of what makes the people of this country who they are. What I know is based on second-hand information gathered through books that I have read, the music that I listen to, and the movies that I have seen, many of which have to be discounted for being larger than life Hollywood productions about Superheroes saving the world. Of course, there were always the media, molding and tempering my impressions of the United States, and the stories that family and friends carried back from their travels here. But there was no denying that I was on unfamiliar territory. The only thing I could bring to the class was my objectivity. This class is not about me, I decided.

Total darkness. If not for the creaks, groans, and shuffles of my classmates settling into their seats, I would not have been able to tell where I was. As the momentary blindness began to give way, 19 Armory gradually emerged out of the dark. I could now make out Professor Isserman silhouetted against the fluorescent white screen with the LEDs of the DVD player glowing softly into his glasses. A few clicks and a triumphant chuckle later, the screen suddenly sprang to life and we were on our way. The opening titles announced the night's first movie, *Powwow Highway,* and I got ready to meet the Cheyenne tribesmen, Philbert Bono and Buddy Red Bow, who, I had learned from Roger Ebert's review, would be taking me on a road trip from an Indian reservation in Montana to Santa Fe, New Mexico. Just like in earlier movie-viewing sessions, a window would soon open up, offering glimpses into another unfamiliar world that I could experience vicariously for the duration of the film. Once more, I would leave with a story imprinted on my mind, coloring my thoughts for days to come. I settled deeper into my seat in anticipation of the long journey ahead. On the screen, Philbert Bono was looking out of a broken window at a junkyard full of dilapidated rusty old cars and imagining a team of galloping horses. Life is full of surprises, I told myself. You never know what you will discover till you risk taking on the great wide Unknown.

Eventually in the course of the semester's movie watching, discussions, and essay writing, I came to realize why I wanted to travel with Philbert and Buddy. Their journey gave them the unintended discovery of a sense of pride for their lost heritage. Their transformation conjured up my own lifelong quest for a sense of belonging and my earnest hope that it would suddenly spring upon me.

A long, lonely stretch of highway opened up somewhere in the middle of nowhere for Buddy and Philbert to pass through on their journey to New Mexico. The landscape rolled past in a series of snapshots caught by the windows of their car. I had read somewhere that what we perceive as reality is a fictionalized version of the impressions that we accumulate in our minds over time and that we all have a unique compendium of stories we lug around with us wherever we go, constantly adding to our stock. If cinema is a surrogate for life, then the movies of my mind had merged with the movie I was watching. Buddy was ranting about the injustices his people faced on the reservation, and I shared his outrage and resentment. I was now a part of his story and he was a friend with whom I empathized. I had found an alternative way of experiencing the world of strangers. Slowly this conclusion emerged: if we see the world as an anthology of personal narratives, we might be less inclined to fear, hate, and act unjustly.

After the movie sessions I would head back home through a quiet night made blurry by softly falling snow, replaying in my mind scenes from the movies I had just watched and mulling over the questions that they led me to ask. If I were lucky enough to catch a bus, I would look around at the tired faces peering out of scarves and drawn-up coat collars to wonder what their stories are and if they could guess mine, but they would all be looking outside at the cold night with unseeing eyes, the way we often look at people without really seeing them. I thought of the data tables that I worked with in my planning courses and how each number in a column was made up of living, breathing people whom I would never meet or who would pass me by indifferently on a bus. The characters that we so deeply identify with or empathize with on screen would go unnoticed if we happened to pass them on the street, given our tendency to generalize, label, and negate individuals. I realize the impossibility of solving any of the world's planning problems if we approach them on a person-by-person basis. Yet, not realizing that ultimately any planning decision plays itself out at the level of individuals can be very myopic and insensitive. I can decide to abandon all the Philberts and Buddies on their reservation and leave them to their own means, but when Philbert tells me a personal story about the injustices he has suffered, I empathize and want to help.

15.1.2 *An Ensemble Cast, an Unscripted Drama*

It's one thing to talk about issues in the context of planning and movies, but it's a totally different exercise to have to write a personal essay about the same issues and read it out loud in seminar. Like the ensemble cast of *Crash*, we were gathered around a wooden table and a large glass jar improvised as a teapot ready to discuss the previous evening's movies and our essays. I found the total lack of defined roles rather unsettling. There was no script or screenplay to hang on to. As Professor Isserman enthusiastically explained, though not in these words, the class was an unscripted drama and the narrative was ready to follow us wherever we wanted to take it. Instead of looking at the professor, we sat there looking at each other. I felt totally at sea, especially because my first essay, which I had e-mailed in, had been a total disaster. Professor Isserman's comments still ring in my ears, "This is a great piece of academic writing, but what I asked of you is an essay that is stinging real. This is not it." I was disappointed, but at the same time happy to learn that at least there was a clearly discernable plot. Though the subject of our pursuit was uncharted territory, we had a clearly defined goal.

Our class discussions often strayed from the starting point, a movie or an essay, and wandered into wayside fields and ditches. Every digression was well worth the time spent in the search for the "stinging real." As we delved deeper, we were rewarded by a thousand new ways of looking at and saying the same thing. Philbert told us the best way to reach a chosen destination was not necessarily to travel along the shortest straight path between the start and the finish. If the journey was the "destination," rushing headlong for the finish without pausing to savor the sights and smells along the way would be denying ourselves the true spiritual essence of the journey. The quest for experiences may take us along a circuitous route but that would make it even more worthwhile.

For a few weeks, I continued to be inhibited by my self-consciousness at bringing to the table stories that I suspected the others could not relate to. I remember staring at one of my essays and wondering why anyone would care. But then again, I had no choice but to go with it because this was the only story I could write convincingly. This was my story, and I knew no other. So I would have to brave it. I had to remind myself countless times that in a room full of strangers, it's a matter of relative strangeness. Getting past the fear of being judged was the first hurdle, but my fear was dispelled when I realized that the others were in the same boat. A sense of community grew among strangers and allowed us to relax and open up.

I found myself in the hallowed company of the painfully self-conscious and introverted Ben, quiet and sensitive Mallory, emotionally high-strung Morgan, enigmatic Michael, acutely observant Sang, and the deeply insightful conductor, Professor Isserman, who orchestrated lively discussions by skillfully drawing out reactions from a group of people who by themselves might have been happier keeping their opinions to themselves. Every step was like a window opening into a parallel universe, each perspective uniquely distinct. Strangers turned into fascinating characters. Their secrets peep tentatively from between the lines as they tell stories about personal triumphs and failures. They make me wonder secretly if I had the courage to go so far as Mallory had gone in her story about her inability to transcend racial prejudices in the pursuit of a romantic relationship. This was a window of rare insight, as was the essay that Michael began with the words, "The summer I was homeless...," as if it was a kind of regular everyday occurrence that most people deal with on occasion.

I am not sure whether the situation in the classroom reflected the world we saw through the movies or the movies led us to the discovery that, in a sense, everyone is an Outsider in one way or another. I think it was a bit of both, but it came to light through the reading of each other's weekly essays. In every movie we watched, the settings and background issues changed, but what recurred through all the stories was protagonists in situations where they were the odd one out and plots that told us how they worked their way through.

15.1.3 Stories

Initially, both the stories and the stinging real proved to be elusive. We caught glimpses of it now and then, but as the semester progressed we warmed up to the idea and to each other, enough so that we could let our stories flow. From Morgan's complicated genealogy to Michael's experiences working with Amtrak, from the strength that Mallory and Sang drew from their fathers, a Midwestern farmer with a love for travel and a convenience store owner of Korean origin with an indomitable entrepreneurial spirit, we collected snapshots of the people and experiences that cumulatively make up the human face of America that we were trying to discover through the movies. Free of generalizations and full of personal quirk and insight, the stories that I heard in class pointed to a depth and richness of human experience that left me profoundly moved.

However, even until this point I saw myself as the outsider, the only person in the class who told stories about distant places that nobody really related to. Then Professor Isserman arranged for us to watch *The Namesake* at the Boardman's Art Theater in downtown Champaign. I was totally unprepared for the reactions that the movie would draw from me. *The Namesake,* the story of an immigrant Bengali family's struggle in adapting to life in America, made me desperately homesick. The sari-clad women made me want to run and burrow my face in the sweet soft cotton of my grandmother's lap. The family's conversations created in me an irresistible urge to roll Bangla limericks off my multilingual tongue. The references to food made me hungry for my mother's cooking. Curiously enough, I felt not the sad longing that an immigrant experiences for things left behind but the pride and joy of ownership with which a native looks at familiar things. I also identified with Gogol. Just like him, I also had an identity crisis, struggling to find a common ground between multiple cultures that I straddle. The *sari* was not an exotic garment to me but something I could easily slip into and be as comfortable in as I was in my faded jeans and T-shirt. I could sculpt the perfect *samosa* from scratch with the same matter-of-factness that I could amble into the Art Institute and identify the works of all the Impressionists.

How could I be on both sides at the same time? Suddenly without warning, the deep and intense sense of alienation I was secretly suffering from welled up in my throat. The movies of my mind were running wild, wreaking havoc. The mosaic of seemingly disconnected images that my memories were made of made me feel like a rudderless boat cut adrift on an unforgiving ocean, looking for the nearest shore. Where was home? In the almost mythical home of my ancestors in Dacca abandoned by the grandparents during the Partition of Bengal, my parents' sea-facing third-floor apartment in Chennai, southern India, the tiny townhouse I shared with another Illinois student on Lincoln Avenue in Urbana, or some future location where I would eventually wind up?

My life suddenly seemed to be made of endless comings and goings without ever arriving anywhere. Impatient and restless, I had willingly put on migrant shoes but at the same time I was wary of my "brain being drained" in any way. I found it demeaning to think of myself as part of a mindless herd, like swarms of African buffaloes migrating across a sweltering African Savannah. Why couldn't I just pass through the places I was discovering on my journey without having to pledge my affiliation with one place or the other? Why did I have to leave anything behind?

The Namesake brought it all home, the futility of resistance, the absurdity of deciding that people could be only of one culture and place, and the irrational, self-defeating notion that I was an outsider and didn't really belong. There was simply no denying the fact that by undertaking this journey, I had willfully thrown myself into the melting pot of cultures that the world is today and had opened myself up to being transformed into someone whose identity is not defined by narrow generalizations. There are millions of people like me who are drifting along smitten by wanderlust, passing through, trying to build composite lives and finding parallel footholds in strange new worlds. The people who are lucky (or unlucky) enough not to have to physically uproot themselves are constantly finding themselves having to redefine their own identity. Or, like Philbert and Buddy, they are finding an imperative to unearth their own heritage buried under a borrowed identity. The issue is universal and, contrary to what I thought before, this class is about me and stories like mine. I realized that in my essays what I really have been documenting is a personal account of someone who is experiencing the birth pangs of a new world first hand. Am I going to clutch all my stories to myself like a bundle of relics from a distant planet, or am I going to be a medium of exchange, sonorous and resonant?

15.1.4 Expecting a Window, Finding a Door

Nothing expands the mind like travel. After graduating from Illinois, I purposefully traveled a lot, from the blue ridges of the Smoky Mountains to the sunny climes of the California coast. I drove through many a highway similar to the ones Buddy and Philbert traveled. On each of these journeys, I stopped my car, got out, and walked around in the scenery just to prove to myself that the world is real and I am a part of it. As I pondered the many unfamiliar landscapes and unknown neighborhoods, I wondered if I could spot a Maria (*Maria Full of Grace*), Maryam (*Maryam*), or Danny Vinyard (*American History X*). I didn't see anyone I personally recognized, but I felt less lost and less alienated than before, owing to the thousands of miles I have traveled with all the real and fictional characters from the class. Josey Aimes (*North Country*) and Tre Styles (*Boyz N the Hood*) are as real to me as the moonlit room in Oregon that Ben looked out of in one of his essays and the abandoned Midwestern farm that I saw through the viewfinder of Mallory's literary camera. I am not a passive spectator to the world anymore. I have learned to look beyond the immediate field of vision, past tangible and familiar images to the unarticulated realm of histories, economies, and cultures made up of the personal stories of the people who inhabit them.

Stories speak to people. Stories transcend superficial differences of culture, race, ethnicity, nationality, and gender, to bring everyone to a common humanity. And what we learned through this class, both as planning students and as people, is that shorn of external baggage, most people have similar concerns and aspirations. Stories have the ability to haunt us, resonate in our hearts, and cling to our minds like water to a malleable pallet of mud. We can all deny the cold indifference of factual information, but few of us can resist the warm embrace of a story told in first person and not be transformed by its cathartic power.

As a planning student, I learned that the world was a composite of individual lives and unique experiences. As a writer, I acquired a growing confidence that there is a greater need for storytellers today than ever before to give a voice to contemporary stories. I have learned to listen and observe with a planner's objectivity and an artist's sensitivity. There seem to be fewer strangers in my world from whom I feel I need to withdraw. All around me is an interesting gallery of familiar portraits animated by the widest spectrum of human emotion and experience, waiting to be drawn out into stories.

Who I am has also begun to matter. My mongrel/hybrid identity is no longer a burden to be cast aside and has taken on a new relevance. I am not the only outsider trying to fit into an unfamiliar world, dealing with the notion that I appear "strange" to the people around me. I have realized that strangeness is not a problem peculiar to people moving to a different place. People encounter it all the time. In finding their own niche in the world (Mallory and Ben), in creating a private space for themselves within the communal space of a family (Morgan), reinventing and reinstating their identity among peers (Sang and Michael), and in claiming the right to take the "road less traveled" and stretching the boundaries of planning pedagogy (Professor Isserman), we are all in the company of strangeness. That is why the end titles of our semester-long drama have refused to fade away from my mind. Every day my conviction grows that I am part of something really important.

This class is not just a window that I can look out of. It is a door that I, as a planner and writer, can hold open for others to pass through. The course made me realize that we resist all things strange and unfamiliar because they challenge the stories of our isolated personal worlds. If we can overcome this disconnect, we will start to remodel our stories to accommodate the common truths of our collective humanity. The door I hold open will lead to this landscape of shared human aspirations that planners are yet to map. As more common stories are discovered, I will be a part of an exciting new narrative.

15.2 Essay Two

Your essays are an essential part of the course, as important as the films in helping you and your classmates discover the USA. Robert Frost, Leo Tolstoy, and leading contemporary writers and artists will help you write. You will revise your essays in response to the comments, class discussions, and your growing sense of good writing and what you are trying to say. When the course is finished, you will have a wonderful self-portrait for you and your descendents to treasure decades from now. (Course syllabus 2008)

15.2.1 Heritage

Write! Don't just stare at the empty page. Write! You know you don't need to read the prompt again either. You have it memorized and there are no secrets hiding between the lines. *I can't write I need to go outside for awhile and think in the sunshine.* Don't even consider going out there to take a nap, you have had your distractions. Do you feel better now that you have finished that romance novel you were reading? *Shhh!!!! That was for me, I needed to do that.* Will you stop lying and work!

I pushed back from the computer table and rubbed my eyes irritably. Today was not going well. Snippets of conversation and flashes of details cluttered my mind. My first attempt had so many names and details everyone missed the message. Throwing it aside to create something with less confusion, I lost what I loved so much in the first attempt. Starting from scratch again seemed an interminable task, but not completing this essay seemed to say more. *What you have no heritage?* I set my fingers to the keys again. "I grew up on a farm, and I was taught to work hard." Wow, that is uninspiring and boring. I have written many of my essays this way. I begin by laying out a fact pattern, details, and statements. These sentences may combine to tell the reader an interesting story or a new perspective, but their form is uninspiring. Make the story come alive, don't say "I was taught to work hard," show the reader what that means.

Let them feel the sweat running down my back before 9 am, the calluses that develop on my palms after cutting thistles all day by hand, and the comforting aches in my calves and back after clearing a newly baled field of hay. Make it so vibrant that the man who has never left Fifth Avenue will cry and laugh and be shaken with an understanding of my rural inheritance. Surely he and all the others will see that my experiences have made me a handyman, but this is not my point. Now I must show them how spending the day carrying a pointed shovel and walking the hills of the pasture in search for thistles has affected my relationships, my goals, and how I feel when I wake up. But don't merely list these items as if preparing to make a trip to the store. No! Make the items speak for themselves. Let integrity show the reader how it handled a friend's betrayal. Let respect reverently recount how it felt to watch my father stand for something he believed in. Now you have what you need. Write!

Her deep steady breaths are calming as I talk to her about my problems. Sitting in the straw, I press my cheek into Ruby's soft supple neck. She doesn't flinch, and her skin merely ripples beneath my hand in a slow twitch as I stretch an arm over her back. Chewing her cud, she takes a moment to exhale deeply. Her hair is soft and clean from my recent grooming. I stretch out my legs and let my body lean into hers. She is warm and her subtle smell mingles with the sweet clover hay. I grew up thriving on being outdoors, working with my father or playing alone on the farm. I loved my rural childhood and all of the independence and responsibility it carried.

Showing cattle is not profitable, even for the most successful people, but it is more than ribbons and prize money. Showing cattle formed a special bond between a father and his daughters. As a wrangling cowboy, dad won everywhere. His success made a name for the family and paved the way for his brothers. He also made a living from selling cattle, fitting show cattle, and working cattle sales. Unfortunately, during the 1980s cattle preferences changed from purebreds to crossbreds, and the cost of changing genetics was high. Dad took some risk but couldn't afford to buy the hottest Italian Chianina cattle imports and chose to focus on his young family instead. When I started showing in the early 1990s, we still had good breeding stock and competitive cattle, but it wasn't the same and neither was he. He wasn't the swanky, handsome wrangler who used to smoke in tight jeans and boots. He was the father of a little blonde with braces. He was more concerned with making sure I enjoyed myself and stayed safe than competing and maintaining his reputation.

In 2001, I was showing Mauriette, a home-raised May heifer, without the benefit of the expensive feeds, fake hair, or the steroids that my competitors used. The ring was filled with entrants, and the sun beat through the plate glass windows illuminating the sweat and the airborne sawdust. The judge was pacing. My heifer stood at attention, and we walked together in a circle with long precise strides. Tensions were high. I took another deep breath and straightened my chin. Making quick adjustments to the heifer's feet I concentrated on the judge while I stroked the heifer's belly with my showstick so she would stay relaxed. This was the Angus show at the Illinois State Fair and winning here would be the pinnacle of some people's lives. Dad still likes to win, but as we were getting things ready that morning he had stressed what he always does, "Go out there and have some fun. We are probably going to get our butts waxed, but that's okay." Mauriette and I won our class and the division, and he was back in the limelight and incredibly proud of me. For him it was a great moment, something he always wanted me to experience and something he himself had wanted to do again. That night we walked up the street for a ribeye sandwich and sat in the Coliseum watching the horses. We talked briefly about the win, but then dad started asking again about college and careers.

15.2.2 University

My dorm was mostly from the Chicago suburbs. My new friends joked about my occasional accent and often poor pronunciation of words I had read in books but had not heard in conversation. They couldn't relate to my stories about the farm and my livestock, so I kept them to myself. My roommate took me to buy "stylish" jeans, and I stopped wearing my boots and beltbuckle. Paired too often with my flannel shirts, they marked me, "this one's from the country." I didn't really need them, now that I walked everywhere on a concrete sidewalk.

I became more certain I would not return to the farm. My parents tense conversations about the daily gambles with the weather and the markets were too hard, and treating our animals as a business was too painful. Dad added businesses and went back for auctioneering and appraisal training to support the life we love. My classmates in agricultural economics, faced with similar situations, focused on working in agriculture without returning to rural areas. They saw their future in larger agribusiness companies. I have always believed that people should be able to choose to stay in rural areas, and, after reading about poverty and distress in mystical places like the Mississippi Delta and Appalachia, I was drawn to work in challenged communities. Feeling untrained and unprepared for a real job as graduation approached, I applied to two planning programs. Instead of attending an Ivy League school far away, I chose to stay in central Illinois.

I began learning about the history of cities and planning, and I felt a new world was being opened. When a class offered the chance to apply skills to a real setting, I eagerly signed up. Nothing had prepared me for the broken streets and overgrown yards of the Lower Ninth Ward in New Orleans. Painted plywood struggled to provide some order in a place without street signs. Driving through deserted neighborhoods, watching people work to tear down their toxic, damaged homes, I felt overwhelmed. How could I say anything meaningful in this situation? What did I know of the people, their housing needs and preferences, their culture and heritage? Absolutely nothing. I decided I was not cut out for planning or for cities.

Spending five years at a university turns your hands very soft. Over the years, dad had adjusted to working alone, and I, once his constant shadow, had lost some of my knack at tightly winding baling wire around a gate to keep the cattle in. No longer do I brazenly walk among the herd to separate calves for weaning or corral a bull to be moved to another pasture. The thin rubber of my last pair of overshoes, perfect for wading through mud and manure, had become cracked in the corner of the garage and were eventually thrown out. Mom and dad were more interested in sitting at the table and listening to my stories about school than having me disappear outside to walk our pastures cutting thistles.

My parents had kept me blissfully ignorant of their continued financial struggles with up and down markets and rising costs. My sister called to say that calving had gone worse than usual. Dad had lost three calves and four cows in two weeks to birthing complications from internal bleeding and twisted and prolapsed guts. One calf fell into the creek and froze. Another was breached. Dad worked with the cow, helping her to deliver the baby as fast as possible. Pulling it free, he pounded on the baby's lungs, furiously clearing its nostrils and mouth and willing it to breathe. It didn't.

I was drifting. My brief urban experiment had failed. Conversations about school became awkward. Dad couldn't understand why I wasn't working in agriculture. "You're throwing away a gift," he would say when mom wasn't around.

When my advisor offered a new class, I thought it might let me get to know him and then maybe I could ask for his advice. From the course description, it sounded like one of my guilty pleasure electives from undergrad. I wasn't convinced I would learn something about planning, but a drifting person is open to suggestion. I wasn't prepared for the power movies would have in recalling strong memories of a culture and heritage I thought I had to abandon.

I finally met Appalachia. The immersion into another part of rural America conjured up memories of my own neighbors. I watched people working hard for their families, cooking in kitchens without the latest appliances, and visiting with family on my grandparents' flowery couches. This was me. Appalachia was not some backward, completely impoverished, foreign, and mystical place. Parts of this story could have been set in my hometown. These people could have been my neighbors, but my classmates were callous, "Why don't those people just move? Why do they keep choosing to work in the coal mines?" Why does my family continue to raise cattle and spend time showing them at county fairs? We don't make money showing and for years we have been losing money with the livestock. That's why dad has taken on two extra non-farming jobs. We do it because it is what we love to do, it is who we are and how we like to spend our time together, and I can't imagine my parents' life or my childhood without it. I felt an old familiar rise of anger driven by my classmates' innocent but completely misinformed comments. *You don't know what you are talking about, and you just don't understand.* I was screaming inside, but I chose not to speak out. From the course I was learning that it is far more convincing to show someone rather than tell them. I would write.

In my weekly writings, I had tackled issues of race and worked through some of the more insidious things about small communities. Now I turned to the positive sides of rural life, family, and values. Watching *Tully* I saw the strength of a father and felt the sometimes destructive qualities of the desire to shoulder your burdens alone. The sweeping views of country landscape and small communities pulled at me. Why can't people understand why we work so hard for this? I doggedly pursued Frost's goal of "so stinging real that we wouldn't think you'd dare to tell it." I would spend hours remembering my past, analyzing it with new perspectives, and asking the questions that lay in previously unspoken conversations. Each week brought a new assignment to uncover another piece of my value and belief system. It was hard, but each week I found a new piece of me, and I labored to understand it and to convey it to others. I was desperate not to see my home misrepresented and misunderstood.

I rediscovered my passion for rural people. In *Country* I watched a farm family repeat similar conversations my own family used to have. How bad will the harvest be, will we be able to pay off our loans? I have left, but my roots are deeply buried in a white clay soil on a hill in central Illinois. I have traveled abroad, made friends with people from glamorous evil Chicago, discovered opera, and played water polo. Still my favorite memories, the place I turn when things are not going well, are about the farm and the peace that comes from doing physical labor.

Taking this course has taught me to understand my dad's warnings. My rural experiences are a gift. I can now understand why some rural students at Illinois develop farm-only social circles. They know that the majority of people outside of home don't understand and don't even want to try. We rural people are an easy target for stereotypes, and outsiders feel justified in disparaging rural actions, choices, and values. As I learn about sundown towns, resentment of Hispanic immigration to rural areas, and the lasting effects of segregation, I find myself in an odd position. I grew up in these places. My school district had one black family. One town to the north has a slaughtering plant that started hiring Hispanics in the early 1990s. I know the people who act and speak out of ignorance, fear, and confusion. I could have been one of them. I have not yet learned what my contribution can be, but I know I can no longer avoid my rural experiences. I have found and appreciate my story.

15.2.3 Home

A lace curtain blew in and out against the upstairs window of the dilapidated house on the edge of town. *Click*. Flinging its fringes in the breeze it will make a great black and white still. So will the antique upright piano that sits in the front room through an open door. *Click*. Its dark finish, once polished every Sunday, has cracked and bubbled from years of summer heat. A century farm sign is grounded at an angle in the front yard. Instead of snapping the camera I stop to read. In 1977 the Abernathys were awarded the sign for 100 years of tenure on this soil. The peeling paint and propped open front door indicate that the Abernathys are long gone. This farmhouse is now only one piece of another farmer's much larger farming spread. The new owners do not want to live in this house or to bother to rent it out. So it sits alone. The deep sigh coming from my grandma settles inside of me. The resignation in her voice that recounts visiting this house to taste fresh blackberry pie does not. She is an excellent guide to this sprawling rural region, and she remembers who used to live in all of these abandoned houses. Her stories bring these structures alive as I follow her to the back of the house. My eyes settle on the delightful twisted, gnarled hedge cornerstones of the faded red outbuildings. *Click*. As I pull away the camera I am offended as I notice their state of neglect. She continues with memories of watching the men in the community build these barns. Their size and height now make them good for little more than storing junk. Glancing at my grandmother in confusion, I realize that this strong and often opinionated woman has accepted this, but I refuse to. Unexpressed indignation grows inside of me as we get back into the car. My grandmother reminds me that there are many more places to visit today in my quest to photograph a neglected past.

My grandpa's one-room schoolhouse still sits near the highway, but the weeds and brush have disguised it well. *Click*. Through the camera lens it is impossible not to enjoy the tree-covered hills and steep valleys that stretch on behind this tiny building. The smooth expanse of paved surface is mercifully still. With no houses in sight and the sound of swaying grasses drowning in the soft howls of the wind, this decaying building looks peaceful. But in my search for the history of my own past, the serenity of the landscape seems desolate and leaves me overwhelmed by sadness. Taking another glance at the sinking roof and weathered walls, I follow my grandma to the car.

I think of our farm and my grandparent's farm. What will happen to the land in a family without boys? My sister is going into public relations and, while I love the farm, I don't like the inherent risk of farming.

We drive past the school my father attended. It has a new life, but a compromised one. Torn down but for a few rooms, the two-story brick building has been converted to a gas station.

This rural area that I am photographing for its wealth of abandoned structures has no development pressures. It hasn't added a new house in the past 20 years, and the three-story Victorian home that would be worth a fortune elsewhere brought only $75,000. I can't imagine ever worrying about large-scale development flattening the hills I grew up on. Instead of comforting me, this thought causes me to brood over the alternative of neglect and my parent's mortality. My heart beats faster as I realize how fiercely I love this rural area that I am photographing. This is my home, and I must save it.

15.3 Essay Three

We invite you to contribute to this project by writing and submitting your own statement of personal belief *about Planning*. We understand how challenging this is – it requires such intimacy that no one else can do it for you. To guide you through this process, we offer these suggestions: Tell a story: Be specific. Take your belief out of the ether and ground it in the events of your life. Consider moments when belief was formed or tested or changed. Think of your own experience, work, and family, and tell of the things you know that no one else does. Your story need not be heart-warming or gut-wrenching – it can even be funny – but it should be real. Make sure your story ties to the essence of your daily life philosophy and the shaping of your beliefs. Be brief: Your statement should be between 350 and 500 words. That's about three minutes when read aloud at your natural pace [National Public Radio, Writing Instructions, This I Believe (two italicized words added)]

15.3.1 Planning, What Might I Believe?

I venture into the nook in my apartment when I'm forced to produce something. I sidestep the wall-mounted table and plop down onto the loveseat tightly jammed between two walls. I open my laptop in front of me. One lone overhead light shines down onto my laptop as if to say, "This is your purpose, nothing else. Please cooperate." The rest of the apartment sits silent and dark. The nook leaves me with few distractions. I settle in and begin to work.

Each week I found myself in the nook writing reflective pieces about my relationship with various topics. Each week I struggled to share a glimpse of myself. I was forced to explore difficult topics by myself, using my own experiences as sources of authority. I was uncomfortable relying on my own voice and experiences. It's scary to trace out your own beliefs in writing without following the path of others. There's less room to dodge or hide behind someone else's beliefs.

Sharing and discussing the papers during class was another adventure in self-discovery. At times I was thankful for the anonymity. Other times it felt ridiculous. I laid myself bare in the essay, why try to cover it up in class? At times the critiques stung, how could my classmates misconstrue my words? Other times the class discussions motivated me to revise, clarify, and strengthen the paper. I would leave class and run to the Funk library to stow away between the third-floor book stacks, put in my headphones, and write. Reading my classmates' work inspired me to create more compelling stories. Their stories filled my head with ideas, storylines to play off of, and emotions to evoke.

I spent the week contemplating what I might believe in. I lay awake at night, shocked by the struggle to clarify my convictions. I'd previously articulated and acted upon my feminist beliefs in equality, opportunity, and access. Why was saying what I believed suddenly so difficult? Because I was being asked to express my own beliefs, not align with a movement. Now I was vulnerable, asked to stand alone, and explain myself. My academic experience in developing complicated arguments based in slight differentiations resisted the assignment's simple instructions. After eight weeks of writing I found myself back at square one, sandwiched in my nook, alone with a laptop and my thoughts. I anxiously drum the keys on my laptop, hoping my beliefs will spring forth onto the screen.

I begin by exploring my planning beliefs. I recall travels in South India, noting the vivid details and insightful lessons in sustainability and humility. I begin another version about the importance of community and my mother's neighborhood superiority complex. She's convinced that all neighborhoods strive to be like ours, Beaverdale. It's naive and endearing. She doesn't know about the tax increment financing that helped promote development, the movement to preserve the green space, or the spreading gentrification. She just likes Beaverdale. Unable to relay sufficiently my mother's love for quaint brick homes, hardwood floors, and tree-lined streets, I discard the writing.

Frustrated, I begin to recall the energy I feel in some of my favorite places. I begin crafting an essay about the two years I lived chaotically alongside a thousand freshmen transitioning to college. I loved driving by the building at night, seeing hundreds of windows lit up, and wondering about the mini-sagas unfolding behind each window. Each room contained its own drama, heartache, homesickness, and joy that spilled out into the hallway, seeped under doorframes, through thin walls, and out into the night air. Each room was connected by common space yet completely absorbed in its own friends, classes, and social circles. It was beautiful. I struggled to pinpoint my belief in the building and communal living. My thoughts turned to the summer flooding and a clear theme emerged – we should have known better. I revisited a familiar topic, writing about the waters that ravished my community.

As I recalled the details, I wrote without knowing where I was going. I crafted my beliefs on paper, unsure of what I believed. I struggled, hiding behind vague descriptions. I initially used empty descriptions, hoping that readers would accept the damages as devastating, horrific, and unimaginable. I told readers about the devastation, but I didn't show them. I told readers I felt overwhelmed, but I didn't invite readers in to share my sorrow. I walked a tight line between my personal experience and the larger planning story. I finished the piece late at night and sent it off to a friend for advice. I awoke the next morning rejuvenated and ready to work. With feedback from my friend, I worked to eliminate background details and focus on the main story: we hadn't planned for the eventuality of another flooding disaster.

In the end I was pleased with the piece and my planning belief. After brainstorming for a week, writing several different essays, and finishing a compelling story about flooding, I still struggled to articulate my belief. I was shocked by my inability to state a planning-related belief in a sentence. It was a powerful exercise and made me reconsider how planners communicate.

15.3.2 Planning, This I Believe

Hi, my name is Susy Hemphill and I believe in planning for that which is unimaginable, but inevitable. For 4 years I lived along the Iowa River. I watched it course through the city and appreciated its beauty, but gave little thought to its potential. Last summer all that changed. Winter snow left the ground wet, heavy spring rains inundated the area, and increased flow from upstream forced the river to the edge of its banks.

In early June the Army Corps of Engineers announced the spillway was reaching capacity; more water would be released to prevent large-scale flooding. Under police orders hundreds of homes along the river were to be evacuated. The water had been rising for weeks – discussed in hushed, reserved tones at the farmers market, its growing appetite accommodated by closing portions of City Park – yet the orders felt sudden. The Iowa City community braced for the impact as the unthinkable began to happen, yet again.

Adamant to save what we could, sandbag stations appeared across town. I joined my neighbors and co-workers. We were optimistic that the mountain of sand looming before us would save our building. We worked side by side as the rain poured down our backs. I lunged at the sand, digging in deep, filling my shovel with anger, only to turn and neatly drop the contents into a bag, soon tied off and distributed. My back ached with the repetitive motion; the gritty sand coated my arms and legs. We were a machine, slowing only to avoid swinging shovels as the pile shrank and we moved in for the kill. Initially the plan was to protect only the most vulnerable areas. As days passed, we saw that the entire structure was vulnerable. We hastily began to move furniture and records to higher ground. Confident that the water wouldn't penetrate the sandbags, we unplugged computers, leaving them vulnerable on the first floor. After a week of sandbagging, the structure was fortified. As I rode up the hill away from the floodwaters, I looked back at the six-foot wall now surrounding the building, sure that it would hold.

The floodwaters penetrated the city indiscriminately. The waters entered our homes, business, and schools, seeping into basements, crawling up the drywall, and contaminating entire structures. The wall that I'd spent hours constructing, built of sand and filled with hope, sprung leaks and caved under the water's pressure. When I toured the damage, I saw three feet of water flowing through my building. The computer cords we unplugged, furniture we deemed too bulky to move, and photos that just didn't seem important at the time now swam in the murky, polluted water. My best efforts did little to counter the force of the water.

The community had been through this before, just 15 years earlier, but they said it wouldn't happen, not again in our lifetime. So what do I believe? I believe we placed our bets on technology and human innovation without thinking about the inevitability of another flood. We sought to control and dominate, but the river refused to yield.

15.3.3 Why Planners Need Storytelling

Convince me that watching movies and reading and writing stories have contributed to your planning education. (Final paper assignment 2008)

Last fall I attended a preliminary strategic planning meeting for the University of Illinois's East St. Louis Action Research Project (ESLARP). Facing an uncertain future, ESLARP staffers sought to begin discussions on restructuring and re-envisioning the organization's work. The meeting was with key stakeholders, including representatives from local businesses, neighborhood groups, local schools, churches, fraternities, sororities, and community members.

Early Saturday morning we pulled off the interstate and into East St. Louis. Despite prior visits I find myself continually surprised by the deterioration that greets me. I jostled around in the back of the van as we drove over the potholes and shoddy repair jobs. Driving toward the Mary Brown Community Center, we passed abandoned lots, overgrown with weeds, occupied by decrepit structures. Out the back window I saw homes once loved and well maintained, their roofs now caved-in under neglect and disrepair. We arrived and I hopped eagerly out of the van to begin working. We completed the preparations. The tables were neatly arranged to promote discussion, food was set, coffee prepared, and scripts decided upon. Community members started to filter in and discussions began. Each table was given two questions and 15 minutes. The tables were asked to submit a top five list, which would be posted at the front of the room for large group discussion. We were so calculated, so coordinated. When the meeting began, we knew what we wanted: the top challenges and suggested priorities for the partnership over the next five years.

The residents, however, knew what they wanted: a place to network, room to talk, and time to share stories. As University members with critical schedules and goals to achieve, we rushed in with our scratch-and-sniff markers, color-coordinated paper, and poster-sized post-it notes. We had goals and a consensus to reach.

I was charged with leading a small group discussion to ensure that five ideas emerged at the end. My table consisted of young, enthusiastic community members with limited experience and enormous ideas. They disregarded my specific, well-structured introduction and began a free-flowing dialogue about their interests and work in East St. Louis. Oh, no, I thought, looking down at my schedule, we'd passed the Introductions period. The group was talking through the Brainstorm Silently time slot. I gently nudged, trying to steer the group back to our agenda and break their conversation down into sound bites for the larger discussion.

The residents shared stories about their work. One fraternity member discussed participating in afterschool programs and mentoring for East St. Louis youth. Another's eyes lit up as he talked about igniting the entrepreneurial spirit in teenagers. "You see, we give them the tools, we teach them to repair computers," he said clapping his hands together, "and then, the kids are able to sell the electronics for a profit. And boy, once they see that they can do this, it's unstoppable." The table nodded with agreement, recalling their own adolescent struggles to earn spending money.

I seized the moment, asking the group to identify issues in the community that the partnership might be able to address. One man mentioned East St. Louis' dilapidated downtown. As soon as the idea left his lips, the group attacked the problem, throwing out ideas until the downtown was reconstructed into a vision surpassing anything I could imagine. They sought to transform the buildings that once announced East St. Louis' prosperity and thriving jazz scene. They did not see a return to the glory days of the 1950s but a new haven for green jobs, restored infrastructure, and potential in a place where few previously saw it. They sought green jobs, redevelopment in abandoned factories, and new computer training programs.

I listened to their ideas and took notes. On my mind was the list we were expected to generate; we needed five challenges. The group moved onto another issue, East St. Louis' lack of local jobs. One member began listing physical assets – extensive rail lines, access to the Mississippi River, and interstates at their doorway – all providing means to manufacture and distribute across the United States. Someone suggested the City begin encouraging local artisans who could utilize the inexpensive, empty warehouse space to craft beautiful pieces to be shipped across the United States. They would make plates or other goods handcrafted by skilled, native East St. Louis artisans, marked with a Made in ESL sticker for all Americans to see. But their vision was beyond creating goods; they wanted to ship small packages of joy, crafted locally, announcing a message of hope and prosperity in East St. Louis. "East St. Louis would be back," they said, "and the country would know it."

Our hour of discussion time ticked away. I looked through my notes, hoping to harvest five issues and areas for collaboration. I began chipping away at their stories and struggles. When we wrote down jobs, the story of teaching middle school students to refurbish computers was lost, and East St. Louis artisans were overlooked. We generated our list: jobs, connections, funding, economic development, and blighted properties. Removed from context, the list was lifeless. Our goal-oriented meeting left little room for personal narratives. We needed the stories to tell each other about the list, to tell each other why the jobs and restoring the downtown mattered. The community members' beautiful vision for downtown was condensed into two words, downtown revitalization.

Stories are important. They challenge us to articulate our beliefs, share emotion, and become vulnerable. As I sat at the table taking notes, Don Peters, the head of a local nonprofit, began talking about East St. Louis. "I don't know what it is," he said, "there must be something in the water that happens to these kids." My mind began racing, I didn't understand where he was going. Was he referring to the process whereby promising young children are led astray and discouraged by the lack of opportunity in their community? "East St. Louis just keeps pumping out very talented people, Miles Davis, Jackie Joyner-Kersee, Katherine Dunham, Dick Durbin, they just keep coming. Where else can say that?" he said smiling ear to ear. He spoke with pride and joy. People should hear this, I thought, startled by my initial reaction. People should meet Don and everyone else in this room and see how much they care about their community. Their stories should be told.

As we drove back to Champaign-Urbana the following day, I couldn't help but think that we got it wrong. Our structured meeting inhibited discussion. What was meant to generate ideas instead stifled brainstorming. We sought broad ideas for East St. Louis and ESLARP. We wanted objective goals that would translate well to the University and prospective donors. We spent too much time translating and not enough time listening.

The University frequently takes undergraduate students down to East St. Louis for outreach weekends. Students are able to volunteer and interact with community members. During one such weekend we'd completed laying down gravel for a park walkway and were heading back to the hotel after a hard day's work. My driving companion turned to me and asked, "Hey, why don't they just tear this down and build homes?" "What do you mean? There are homes all around us," I replied. "I know," he said, "but they should build nice houses like in my hometown." "You want them to tear these homes down and build suburbia?" I asked. "Well, wouldn't it be better?" he responded. "Daniel, I think the people are what make East St. Louis special. If you tear down their homes and community, what are you left with? Let alone all of the issues with stagnant property values and the inability to recapture development costs . . ." I trailed off. We arrived back at the hotel, and I was left alone in the driver's seat with my thoughts, "What have we done wrong?"

I went to work in East St. Louis because I valued the community and wanted to learn how to work in cities of decline. Like the student volunteers on the outreach weekends, I heard the stories of tragic shootings, lives cut short by gang- and drug-related violence. When Don Peters spoke, I saw the limitations in my understanding of the community: I knew we saw different communities. Without stories, I saw only the potholes, the shootings, and the poverty. I didn't see the joy and hope and belief in their community. Without knowing the stories, it's easy to suggest tearing down the neighborhood.

This spring ESLARP will continue to re-envision the program and the work it does in East St. Louis. Like all programs on campus, it will continue to market itself and advocate for increased funding. Hopefully ESLARP can find a compromise between meeting campus goals and being responsive to residents. At the meeting we overlooked the stories behind job promotion and economic development. We overlooked the reasons we chose to work in communities like East St. Louis and the reasons we choose to work as planners.

I came to planning frustrated. I spent two years acting out my ideals at a women's health clinic. Little changed, and I craved change. I was exhausted from arguing for access to basic reproductive health care. I saw planning as a means to address equity, working from within. I hoped that planning would provide an efficient, practical way to act on my beliefs. Throughout my first semester I heard lectures on the built environment, read about development, and studied the origins of humanity. In classes we talked about systems and inefficient allocations, but we forgot the people. Maybe they were there all along, between the surveys and regression analyses, but I lost track. Just like in East St. Louis, we lost track of the people behind the plans.

This course and my classmates took me to places I didn't think planning went. We discussed race, heritage, and, above all, ourselves. We talked about water policy, good places, and the urban/rural divide, but only through the eyes of the characters we interacted with in weekly movies and our own experiences. Instead of planning for people we talked about people. It's a momentous shift to approach an issue from the vantage point of a story. Together we brought the people back into our planning education. Toward the end of the semester I began researching federal flood policy.

As I started to tell my personal story from the summer Midwest flooding, the lines began to connect. Describing federal flood policy is meaningless without personal accounts of devastation, confusion, and anger. The policy failings quantified in billions of dollars, graphed in increasing inefficiencies, and mapped in color-coded flood plains are far less powerful than the stories of individual homes and dreams washed away. I was pleased to see personal narratives come back into my research and, again, think about planning for people. I'm looking forward to finding more stories as I begin my planning career.

15.4 Essay Four

So here you have it, Leonie, the course in the words of three students. I hope people will feel the magic of the course and enjoy reading the chapter like a collection of good short stories. I have opted to be very quiet myself. What treasures we get and how much we can learn when we allow our students to tell their stories and think about their educations! How about that!

Wow, Andy! "How about that," indeed. I love how you have woven this together, it is very polished, very moving, and very provocative, pedagogically speaking. It's almost perfect. Yet even as I write that, and as much as I respect your silent voice in all of this, I really would love an Epilogue from you, maybe 500 words. Put yourself and your emotions and desires into this mix. After all, you are obviously really tough with them about being "stinging real." SO now I am performing your role, in asking you to do the same, as an Epilogue to this piece.

But what is there to add, Leonie, and pray tell why? The students have already touched you, you already have my experience, stinging real, in that you, like me, smile inside in wonder and joy at what the students have done. Can a teacher ask for anything more? Calling it an Epilogue, not an intrinsic part of the work itself, you share, I sense, my concern about not detracting from or marring the students work.

Yes, the Epilogue idea is precisely to set it aside from the students' stories and give that its proper space. What's of particular interest to me is the back story: how did an economics professor in planning come to this idea, how you struggled to implement and refine it, and what do you get out of it.

15.4.1 *Becoming That Crazy English Teacher*

"Russ, babe, it did not go down that way. The way you said. . . . It wasn't art that made you lose your job at the bookstore. It was a broad. . . . Artists are a lot like gangsters. They both know the official version, the one everyone else believes, is a lie" (Banks, 2001, p. 25).

Did you hear me, Noah? I would have liked to have met more of your friends last night. Noah had walked over to his computer and was typing. Wait a few minutes, Mom, he replied. What did you do? she asked. I sent some friends a message to come meet my parents and help finish the champagne from Avi's birthday party. Soon 15 people were in his dorm room. Sitting on a sofa in the corner, I happily absorbed the rapidly flying banter. I liked these kids, sharp, scintillating, lively, engaged, funny, white, yellow, brown, black, teasing, and enjoying each other. As we walked down the dorm stairs that night, I said ruefully to Ellen, I guess it is too late in my career to become a liberal arts college professor. Brunch the next morning, a restaurant I had visited with my father graduation weekend three dozen years ago, plates piled high by 10 hungry students at a crowded table, I so enjoyed the conversations that I resolved to return from Family Weekend and figure out how I could teach such undergraduates. And what could I teach? For over a quarter century I had taught only research skills to masters' students in planning and doctoral students in economics and geography, but I have gotten ahead of the story.

Maybe it really started with the farm boy I met when conducting exit interviews with graduating seniors. Why did he have to take French literature or any humanities course, he asked, to be a farm manager? A total waste of time! What good would humanities do him? How about a course on the farm in American novels? I replied, thinking *Grapes of Wrath* and *A Thousand Acres.* Sounds better, he said. How about rural America in movies? Even better, he nodded. As department head of Agricultural and Consumer Economics, I passed the idea on to the associate dean of Agriculture. Consider a college-wide humanities course focused on the rural experience, help students see the humanities as a life-enriching and reaffirming opportunity, not as an obstacle or useless requirement.

A year later, no longer department head, I started designing a new course. On my mind was the conclusion of a committee I had convened, asking six economists who had graduated from small liberal arts colleges how we might bring the best of our educational experiences to our huge university. We had 600 undergraduates majoring in our department, and budget cuts from 42 to 36 faculty members had us worrying about the quality of undergraduate education. Honors courses, the committee had recommended, that provide "memorable interaction with a stimulating professor; the challenge to think critically, write clearly, and debate issues that do not have a right or wrong answer; and internship opportunities that broaden horizons". Picking up the exit interview idea again, I sent around an e-mail: "Can you recommend some good novels or films with rural themes? The novels and films lead us to think and write about economics and government action and inaction that affect rural folks. Hence, my working title is something like Films, Fiction, Feds, and Folks."

Bit by bit, my colleagues weaned me from the notion that the course would blend social science, film, and writing. I had imagined a course in which I would lecture Wednesdays for half the class on the economics and public policy behind what we had seen in the Tuesday movies, say, at Indian reservations or the Mississippi Delta. I would contribute my analysis as a Professor of Regional Economics, Planning, and Policy. No, said Fred Hoxie, Swanland Professor of History and expert in American Indian studies. No, said John Unsworth, Professor of English and Dean of the Graduate School of Library and Information Science. Let the films speak for themselves, they urged. Two emeritus planning professors, Al Guttenberg and Len Heumann, liked that idea. Teach this film course to retired professors, they said, and we will take it. Hmm, I was on to something.

Jacob and Noah, our two sons, were invaluable guides throughout. Drawing on their own college experiences, they independently counseled me to drop initial plans for a novels-oriented course and focus on films. You are fooling yourself, Dad, if you think even good students will read more than 100 pages a week, and you will not know from the class discussion who has done the reading and who has not. That settles that, I concluded, the 601 pages of *East of Eden* in my hand. Films, it is, and my hunt for movies became more urgent. I insisted that the University treat this course like a laboratory science. We would need four hours of scheduled lab time to watch films together plus three hours of class time each week. Also, my wise sons advised, don't lecture a lot. Students like to discuss ideas with one another.

Upon my return from Family Weekend, enthusiastic to find a way to teach honors students, I spoke again with Kirby Barrick, the associate dean of Agriculture. How about a writing professor with whom I might co-teach a film and literature course? Contact the Campus Honors Program, he replied, they are very good at helping people design innovative, interdisciplinary courses. I learned that those courses are limited to 18 Chancellor's Scholars, 125 students chosen campuswide from among the 7,000 matriculating each year. Promising. I outlined my course idea in an e-mail and scheduled a meeting with Bruce Michelson, Professor of English and Program Director. You know how to write, he said, you do not need a co-teacher. He warned me, though, to be allowed to teach in this program, professors have to apply and submit a complete course proposal that is evaluated by a committee chaired by an associate provost. Only a few interdisciplinary seminars are offered each year.

Now I was on my own. I had to find movies and figure out how to teach writing. I can teach writing, he had said. Research papers, theses, dissertations, sure. I had been a journal editor for 25 years, but creative writing? My last creative writing class was as a freshman at Amherst College in 1964. I pulled out my old file: a required course, three short essays a week, drawing on our own experiences, selected essays to be anonymously discussed in class, 33 essays and a longer paper during the semester, comments written on the essays and returned within two days, no essay grades. That was it. I adopted this pedagogy, modified to an essay a week, and started learning about it. My old essays seemed very lame, and they were, consistent with my recollection that I had done okay, a 78 for the semester, midway in the grade distribution; the high was a 90, and the low, earned by a young fellow who is now a dean at a major university, was a 67.

In short, I was preparing to teach outstanding students something in which I was decidedly mediocre. Not until our 25th college reunion had I even understood that the course had something to do with showing readers, instead of telling them. I make it easier on my students and myself by handing out Frost's letter the first week. Stinging real, something only you could write, he had instructed in 1933.

I studied the old course. I read a doctoral dissertation written about it. I read essays and memoirs of faculty members who had taught it, including Theodore Baird, a Shakespeare scholar, the force behind this course required of all freshmen from 1938 to 1966, and William Pritchard, a Robert Frost biographer, who took the course as an undergraduate in 1949 and returned to teach it nine years later. Pritchard (1995, p. 115) described the course as "totally consuming," which turns out to be right, even without his two sections, six class meetings a week, and 1,320 essays to grade per semester. New links to that old course continue to surprise me. Today I learned that my section instructor, Kim Townsend, went on to write books on manhood and friendship and teach a course on community, topics eerily similar to ones I have chosen for this course. Perhaps there resides in us both a residue of the old course, its emphasis on discovering what we really mean by the words we use.

I read writers on writing to help my students and me understand what we are doing. In addition to the Frost letter, I brought them Leo Tolstoi (1899) on art (if only the reader can feel what you felt, then it is art), which was the focus of one of my English 1 assignments. I discovered that National Public Radio's *This I Believe* offered similar instructions and had made story telling its explicit focus. Pulitzer Prize winners Michael Chabon, Richard Russo, and Robert Olen Butler are at my side, ready to join the class when I think their insights will help students break through. This year the late David Foster Wallace led me to *Dragon Slayers*, a moving essay on African-American studies by Jerald Walker (2007, p. 286). The writing professor, James Alan McPherson, a Pulitzer Prize winner, explains, "You have to show them what's real." "What's real?" asks Walker, the student. "You," McPherson replies. Last year I added Judith Jamison (2007), Artistic Director of the Alvin Ailey American Dance Theater: "A dancer can have all the right physical moves, but that doesn't mean he'll knock your socks off. He has to find his truth in what he wants to say, and show us who he is as a person."

You get the picture. I went from a know nothing, know nobody, to a person who eagerly reads short stories and other literature, both for pleasure and in search of gems to strengthen the course. The same holds true for motion pictures. Starting from knowing only a handful of films that combine a strong sense of place with a policy issue, wondering whether I could find enough for a semester's course, I now have over 300 DVDs relevant to the course and have watched over 200. I also bought a top-rated treadmill and a 50-inch plasma high-definition TV. My purchasing was fueled when I overheard Ellen's best friend mention how much her professor husband spent on golfing fees in one weekend. Done! I was liberated to start collecting, freed of a sense of extravagance. My treadmill and movies are an improvement over the campus recreation center, and I have a healthy new hobby. I ran my way through *Silkwood* in two sessions.

My first and best film mentor was Roger Ebert, an Illinois alumnus. His website allowed me to spend hours searching for movies, for instance, specifying at least three stars with the word coal or mining in the review. Fewer than six weeks after meeting with the honors program director, I had compiled a database of 138 Ebert-recommended movies and a 150-page booklet of his reviews, organizing them under topics such as Industrial Towns or Asian Diaspora. Ebert is enamored of movies with a strong sense of place and stinging real people, and he led me to potential movies by descriptions such as "In *Thunderheart* we get a real visual sense of the reservation, of the beauty of the rolling prairie and the way it is interrupted by deep gorges, but also of the omnipresent rusting automobiles and the subsistence level of some of the housing. We feel that we're really there, and that the people in the story really occupy land they stand on" (Ebert, 1992). More recently, I began monitoring the *New York Times* movie section, paying particular attention to Critics' Picks. The original Ebert list started me eagerly collecting, much like the boy I was with a checklist of baseball cards. It was a big day when I found *Margaret's Museum* through a Canadian distributor, almost as good as when I traded Ricky Rodriguez for a 1951 Mickey Mantle.

Melding together films, novels, and essay assignments, I prepared the course proposal. The initial title was *Road Trip! Rural Regions in the American Imagination.* Several course elements would not survive, including the title. *Road Trip* lacked gravitas, I was told. Each student was to read one novel from a list I had prepared, write a review of the book, and select an excerpt to be included with the review in an anthology compiled by the class for next year's students to read. It's still a good idea, but the first time I taught the course we were so swept up in the films and writing and revising that the students and I did not want to take time out for a novel. The proposal also had my last tether to the research world I know so well, writing and presenting an extended research paper, "an opportunity to learn the story behind the story about something that has caught your eye in a film." By mid-semester, when I learned the course would qualify for the University's advanced composition requirement without the research paper because of the oft-revised essays, we were doing so well that even I had no desire to keep the research paper. I substituted the final paper, convince me that watching movies and writing essays has contributed to your education, and added an essay, what have you learned thus far about writing, to accompany the first four revised essays.

The course title is critical, Noah and Jacob had stressed. Film is a good word, they said. They mulled various possibilities and tried some out on their friends. Cultures is good, too. It will get you one set of students, and economies will get you another who might think cultures signals a soft course, not for them. You need a word to make clear you are not showing old movies students saw in high school. We launched as US Cultures and Economies in Contemporary Film. Within two hours of registration opening, the course was fully enrolled and had a waiting list. Our journey was on!

When the class started four months later, I was ready. Before our first session, I pointed the students to the National Public Radio website to listen to *This I Believe* essays and required them to write one "about a core belief you hold regarding the United States." That essay was followed by (1) Have you ever been a stranger? What does it mean to be a stranger? (2) Have you forgiven someone, been forgiven, or are unable to forgive? What does it mean to forgive? (3) What thing in life is sacred to you? What does it mean to be sacred? What responsibilities, if any, do you have toward things in life you consider sacred? and (4) Have you ever pursued justice, failed to pursue justice, or been denied justice? What does it mean to pursue justice? What responsibilities, if any, do you accept to pursue justice? The films dealt with the themes of the essays, for instance, *Maria Full of Grace* and *The Brother from Another Planet* for being a stranger, but the essay instructions made clear: You are not expected to refer to the movies we watched, but you may do so if you wish. The films served to loosen tongues and provide vivid examples of stinging real. The essays are the students' movies. Like the filmmakers, the students become artists, showing their classmates American lives and dilemmas, as Anu, Mallory, and Susy have done.

End of back story? No, so far we have only the undergraduate course. The planning course started after planning students expressed dissatisfaction over relations among themselves – too little communication among groups, be it by race, ethnicity, domestic, and international, and too little sensitivity toward stereotyping in assignments for group projects, such as a Chinese student doing the calculations. Maybe the film course could help. In 2007, the second time I taught the honors course, I opened a section for planning graduate students, and six planning students enrolled, including Anu and Mallory. In 2008 I designed a version specifically for planning graduate students, and Susy was among the 11 students enrolled, 6 from planning, 2 from landscape architecture, 2 from education, and 1 from theater. As Anu and Mallory illustrate, graduate students may feel a guilty reluctance to take a film and writing course instead of building more conventional skills. Maybe these essays will convince others that watching films and writing stories can contribute importantly to planning education.

So now you have an official back story, but maybe the real root is Jack Nicholson and a darker story. I rarely went to movies in pre-course days, but Ellen loves to laugh and does it easily and well, so I agreed to accompany her to his new comedy. Not funny. Even Ellen did not laugh. In *About Schmidt*, Nicholson plays a man who has nothing after he retires and no one after his wife dies. That struck a nerve. What would I do if I were cut off from family and couldn't be a professor? I have a good answer now. I can be the old guy who shows Tuesday movies in the retirement home. With movies, literature, and stories to invite, I will always have something good to do and always be part of a close-knit learning community. Read Ebert (2002) on *About Schmidt*: "Most teenagers will probably not be drawn to this movie, but they should attend. Let it be a lesson to them. If they define their lives only in terms of a good job, a good paycheck, and a comfortable suburban existence, they could end up like Schmidt, dead in the water. They should start paying attention to that crazy English teacher." I have become that crazy English teacher, and all is well.

15.4.2 Achieving These Results

Andy Isserman's role as a guide and facilitator must have been crucial in getting his students to produce such intimate narratives. It takes a special kind of person to do that, but perhaps having him write an afterword to the stories in which he talks about himself and what he did to achieve these results would be useful. An altogether remarkable experiment. (John Friedmann, Professor Emeritus of Planning, UCLA, and American Collegiate Schools of Planning Distinguished Planning Educator)

Loved your chapter. The kids wrote wonderfully – if I could get that quality – wow. (Robert Begg, Professor of Geography and Regional Planning, Indiana University of Pennsylvania)

You can get that quality. I never know from week to week which students' essays will amaze me next. John Friedmann has it right. Good teachers, like you, that is, good guides and facilitators, can help students achieve these results. Here are some thoughts about what is important to do and not do.

Commenting on the students' essays in considerable detail is crucial, and so are the multiple rounds of revisions to help the stories emerge. My goal is not great stories, although they come every semester. More important is that the writing helps students discover important things about themselves, be it gaining a better understanding of what concepts like heritage, forgiveness, and sacred mean to them, their relationships to land, water, community, the economy, government, the drug world, and other planning foci, or their experiences and perceptions of good places and people of other races, immigrants, women, men, rich and poor, city and country folk. What I do might look like editing, but really I am helping the self-discovery process.

As you read your students' essays, you will start recognizing some tendencies. Their first paragraph is often just throat clearing, and the essay does not really begin until the second or third paragraph. Sometimes the author does not discover the true beginning of the story until the very last paragraph. Other times the last paragraph or two might be irrelevant to the story. You will notice an abrupt change of voice; maybe the storyteller suddenly morphs into an op-ed writer leaving personal experience behind to tell people what to think, a bogus social scientist weaving a great generalization about what we all believe, a term paper writer quoting several readings from another class to explain how we act, or something else to avoid leaving the bottom of the page blank. You'll see the disconnect and the move away from stinging real.

Often authors avert their eyes. They squirm away from the story, finishing the paper with words anyone could have written. Up to the brink they go, and then a commercial break, a soliloquy, anything to avoid facing whatever made them look away. Certain words may be telltale signs of a tale untold. Clearly and obviously often mean the opposite, not clear, not obvious. They signal you that a gentle prod could be productive. More generally, keep alert for what is not in the story but might be important. Sometimes the whole essay is a smokescreen, a circling about, but it will contain a hint, a few words, a sentence or two, that are clues a real story exists. Sometimes authors hide entirely. They are nowhere in sight anywhere in their essay as they write on and finish the page, perhaps reporting on something they saw but without any personal engagement.

With a class of 20, expect to spend 10 hours a week writing comments. Every Saturday night the 700-word essays arrive by e-mail. I look forward to them, eagerly reading each the moment it arrives. Then the work begins. Although they are only one page, the serious reading averages 20 or 30 minutes per essay. I turn on track changes and write comments, move portions around, make suggestions, delete paragraphs, and ask questions. I give reactions like your paper really starts here or point out where they wiggled out of the light and the story. Sometimes I chop their essays up and put them together again differently to show how they might breathe life into their writing. I also do some editing to delete unnecessary words, correct punctuation or grammar, straight Strunk and White things. They learn from the examples and improve over the weeks. I e-mail the papers back to the authors before Monday's class, no grade, just all the comments and edits. The revisions of all previous essays, with due dates three times in the semester, continue until students submit their final portfolios of revised and replacement essays.

Kurt Vonnegut (2001, pp. 242–244) explains why planners can teach a course like this: "Listen, there were creative writing teachers long before there were creative writing courses, and they were called and continue to be called editors. ... The best creative writing teachers, like the best editors, excel at teaching, not necessarily at writing." I find that very comforting. I know I am a good editor, and that is what I think is necessary to "get that quality" from your students. Read carefully. Be sensitive and alert. See where the authors might be trying to go and help them draw it out of themselves. One helpful device is to ask, in paper or class, how might the author do these sentences as a screenplay or what would you show in the film version, and suddenly the author comes alive and sees and tells the story vividly.

The whole class will join you in helping authors find their voices and stories. Each week I print copies of all the essays and bring them to class. We read the first essay, and the students discuss its substance and writing. Like an auctioneer seeking one more bid, I ask is there anything more for this author. I distribute the essays anonymously because the conversation is much more candid and helpful when the students do not know who the author is. The class with only six graduate students, when anonymity was impossible, reinforced this conviction. One day in the undergraduate course, a student began hesitantly and apologetically, I hate to say this, but this essay is the worst one we have read all semester. Others proceeded to explain vigorously why it failed. That particular essay was written by a Harvard professor. I had inserted it anonymously into the week's packet on a pedagogic whim because it was not stinging real and there was no person in sight. Under different circumstances in a different course, students might have read the essay as an authoritative style to be emulated. Here it provided an opportunity to review what the students had learned about writing. I doubt the attack would have been as frank and the suggestions as crisp without anonymity.

Students can join conversations about their own essays without revealing their identity as the author, and many do. One might say, I think the author meant such-and-such, to which classmates reply, no way, how could you think that, and one more author will have learned a great lesson in communication, how easily one can be misunderstood. Commentators often get the gender of the anonymous author wrong. A woman in the course wrote a splendid essay as a man explaining what generations of the men in her Irish family have been taught about being a man, and then she was able to be herself and respond to those notions with others in the lively class conversation.

Another very important role you must play is a non-role. Realize that this course is not about you and your views. No matter how self-evident they might be to you, how strongly you hold them, or how passionately you want the students to understand and see the light, stifle it. Help your students think and speak as clearly as they can, listen closely, and ask questions for clarification if their classmates do not.

In a discussion sparked by a movie I might say fewer than 10 sentences in 80 minutes. We had watched *North Country* the night before, a movie about the first sexual harassment case. Who wants to start? I asked. A woman began, I was ready to slug the first man I saw after the movie, and the conversation was on. Forty minutes later, it had gotten quiet. I pointed out that only women had spoken thus far. Did they want to know anything from the men? Did any man want to say anything? And they were off again, until we had to vacate the room. Four sentences in a class. Their essays on what it means to be a woman continued the discussion in the next class. The students taught each other, and me, far more than I could by lecturing about sexual harassment or dominating their discussion of what they had seen and what it meant.

Like the rest of society, members of your class will have different views on every topic from abortion to the role of government or what makes a good place. Keep your views to yourself, lest you interfere with a student's search and self-expression. Judge neither right nor wrong, neither foolish nor wise, the student who writes about sleeping drunkenly with a loved one's friend or the one who writes of celibacy and the marital bed as sacred. Your role is to create a safe environment for discussion. Do it well, and students will hear their peers discussing and questioning their values and experiences, not their teacher lecturing them on what their values should be and, thereby, silencing them. You will learn, too.

Your role also is to promote participation, to be a good moderator. Be alert to who has not spoken and ask them what they think and draw them in. As the class begins to read the next essay, you might say, Emily and Molly, please start the discussion when the class has finished reading. Let no one hide in your seminar. When you sense an essay discussion was unbalanced or too discouraging, ask the class what did you like about this essay, what did it do well, or what can the author do, so the author leaves encouraged and prepared to revise or write anew.

The structure of the course, the films and the emphasis on active learning through writing and discussion, seems to work very well. All four times I have taught the course, I have been on The List of Teachers Ranked as Excellent by their Students. This course should succeed in the hands of any reasonably sensitive, caring professor who can edit. You can help your students write wonderfully. Try teaching this course, and your own students will amaze you.

15.4.3 Enabling One's Soul to Grow

I teach this course because the students do such good work. What teacher could walk away from a course that results in insights and beautiful essays like Anu, Mallory, and Susy have created? This course is the best teaching I have done since coaching kid's soccer. Palpable learning occurs every day right before my eyes. I have been on the Excellent List for methods and policy courses, too, but this course is magical. I see the joy and sense of achievement in students' faces when they finally get it right and know they have learned something very important to themselves, very powerful, even transformative, maybe linking them in a new way to their own family and heritage or their goals. Somehow this course lives up to the bold promise of its syllabus: You become a more complete human being, better writer, and better planner.

Almost every student who takes this course gains a deeper appreciation of their power and worth. I teach this course in awe of what the students do. I am certain that they and their ancestors and descendents will treasure their writing portfolios, their self-portraits, in the decades ahead. The university of today, someone has said, allows students to study everything except themselves. In this course students learn about themselves and their relationships to others. The journey is well worth taking.

I treasure the connections this course gives me to the arts and life. I watch movies and read short stories as course preparation. I read essays about writing by writers and insightful film reviews, all a joyful part of enhancing the course. Like a butterfly collector seeking something new, I look for new essay topics, new movies, newspaper articles, and thoughtful quotations, anything that might be captured in my net to bring the class something interesting, to take us somewhere new and spark new explorations. I make connections among things in this world that would elude me if I were not seeing them through the lens of this course. I gain new interests. My learning is palpable, too.

The power of storytelling has captured me. Through the movies and the student stories, I meet new people and gain new understanding of lives and life. I feel more a part of the world around me. I know many more human beings in the peculiar way of knowing that relies on images on the screen and made-up stories that somehow become real and bring people closer together. The students' writing is often more authentic than movies. One student made stinging real the conflicted thoughts and actions of a sorority girl during rush week, gathered amass with her sisters on the house steps singing to potential pledges. Another made stinging real a family of Korean grocers and their relationships to the community around them. Movies usually reduce the former to female body photo-ops and the latter to scenery props for urban violence or butts of language jokes. Another student, adopted from Asia as a child, poignantly labeled herself as one whose face does not match her name. Yes, the students' essays change how I see the world around me.

When I turned 60, I found it oddly exhilarating. I made up a theory to understand why. Our first 30 years we devote to Becoming, from learning to control our bowels to attending kindergarten and beyond. Son Jacob has just completed Becoming. Married a week ago, graduating for the final time two weeks earlier, with a wife, a profession, and a job, he enters three decades of Being, being a husband, being a father, being a professional, and more. At age 60 begins Bonus, a period that can be as long as the other two, but one for which our society has not delineated roles, expectations, and growth paths as clearly as for Becoming or Being. This course makes me suspect that Bonus can be full of adventure just like the first two periods. I can reprise favorites from Becoming and Being and discover new ones. I expect another exhilarating ride. I am seeing new things and old ones anew. To conclude with Vonnegut (2001, p. 244), "The primary benefit of practicing any art, whether well or badly, is that it enables one's soul to grow." This course is an art. Here I grow.

References

Banks, R. (2001). A novelist's vivid memory spins fiction of its own. In *Writers on writing: Collected essays from the New York times*. New York: Henry Holt and Company (first published New York Times. Available December 6, 1999, from http://www.nytimes.com).

Ebert, R. (1992). *Thunderheart*. Chicago Sun-Times. Available April 3, from http://rogerebert.suntimes.com.

Ebert, R. (2002). *About Schmidt*. Chicago Sun-Times. Available December 20, from http://rogerebert.suntimes.com.

Frost, R. (1933). Letter to Hugh Saglio. In *Your success is my success. Robert Frost to Hugh Saglio*. Amherst, MA: The Friends of the Amherst College Library, 2004.

Jamison, J. (2007). *This I believe: To thine own self be true*. Heard on National Public Radio's All Things Considered. Available April 2, from, http://www.thisibelieve.com.

Pritchard, W. H. (1995). *English papers: A teaching life*. St. Paul, MN: Graywolf Press.

Tolstoi, L. N. (1899). *What is art?* (A. Maude, Trans. from the Russian Original). New York: Thomas Y. Crowell and Company.

Vonnegut, K., Jr. (2001). Despite tough guys, life is not the only school for real novelists. In *Writers on writing: Collected essays from the New York Times*. New York: Henry Holt and Company (first published New York Times. Available May 24, 1999, from http://www.nytimes.com).

Walker, J. (2007). Dragon slayers. In D. F. Wallace (Ed.), *The Best American Essays 2007*. Boston: Houghton Mifflin Company (first published The Iowa Review, Fall, 2006).

Chapter 16
Conclusions

An Infant Forum: The Rewards and Risks of Multimedia in Urban Interventions

Leonie Sandercock and Giovanni Attili

This book originated with our personal journeys, 'beyond the Flatlands', in search of more expressive languages for the field; ways of being more attuned to the embodied nature of urban social experience; ways of capturing the multiple stories and polyphonies of urban life. To give attention to the hidden life of objects and places and of invisible inhabitants. To point to those things which cannot be said, to listen for those things that are muted. To develop a sensitivity to, a window on and a respect for the uncelebrated. To search for remarkable things that are otherwise not remarked on. To listen to the city with a third ear. To observe with a fresh gaze that can make our capacity for astonishment come alive again. To make the familiar strange and to investigate the self-evident. To offer an alternative story to the glossy official accounts. To show the implications of the past in the present. And to link individual biographies with larger social and historical forces. All of which led us to 'thinking in pictures' and 'thinking with all five senses'.

We also start from a theoretical position critical of the dominant forms of representation of the city (the cartographic anxiety) and the kinds of knowledge and experience regarded as legitimate, and thus to questions of exclusion and silencing. It is in silences and absences that inequitable relations and gross political complicities are hidden. We each feel an urgency to invent new descriptive and analytical tools which can give centrality to people, focusing not only on individual practices but also on the collective practices through which inhabitants create their own meaningful life spaces in the face of large social and historical forces. From this perspective, we decided to explore tools which not only capture such everyday experiences of meaning making but also give citizens more opportunities to participate in conversations about their cities and communities and more influence in shaping, improving and protecting them.

Our own collaborative investigations and evolving experiments with multimedia have in turn led us in search of a network of like-minded folks. The resulting book unabashedly reflects our own and others' excitement about the ways in

L. Sandercock (✉)
School of Community and Regional Planning, The University of British Columbia, Vancouver, BC, Canada
e-mail: leonies@interchange.ubc.ca

L. Sandercock, G. Attili (eds.), *Multimedia Explorations in Urban Policy and Planning*, Urban and Landscape Perspectives 7, DOI 10.1007/978-90-481-3209-6_16,
© Springer Science+Business Media B.V. 2010

which multimedia can be used by activists, NGOs, immigrant and indigenous communities, planning scholars and educators, wherever urban policies and planning strategies are being debated and communities are struggling to shape, improve or protect their life spaces. The book is an exploration of a new frontier in the urban planning and policy fields, a frontier 'beyond the flatlands'. It displays a new set of tools and diverse ways to use them.

In presenting our collective efforts in this book we are not offering a 'how to' manual or a typology of best practices: we are not providing an atlas or an encyclopaedia. We are exploring, with both the excitement and the trepidation of children in a forest or at the beach for the first time, a forum in its infancy: diverse applications of multimedia tools in the fields of urban planning research, teaching and practice. In this concluding chapter we look for the gifts and insights, the rewards of this treasure hunt and at the same time we watch out for the rogue wave that might pound us into the sand or even the monster lurking behind the trees. In other words, we go beyond enthusiasm for the new, incorporating a critical stance about the power relations embedded in these new information and communication technologies as well as the limitations of each of the applications we have showcased.

Many social theorists have examined the ways in which observation and scrutiny (the methods, actually, of social research) are tied to government, control and power. As Foucault, especially, has explained, the power of Jeremy Bentham's model prison was based on total surveillance in what he called a panopticon, an all-seeing structure. Here the prisoner is constantly aware of being open to scrutiny. Nowadays though, in the digital age, as the Norwegian criminologist Thomas Mathiesen has suggested (in Back, 2007, p. 13), Bentham and Foucault's powerful metaphor of surveillance coincides with an historic turning of the tables. It is not just 'the few' who are observing, taping and keeping records on 'the many', but 'the many' that now watch and scrutinize 'the few'. It is not only that Big Brother is watching us, but that we are watching Big Brother. From the citizen bystander who captured on video the Los Angeles police officers beating Rodney King in 1992 to Filippino activists using cell phones to mobilize people in the streets, to those Iranian citizens using social chat networks to communicate and spread dissent after apparently manipulated election results in 2009, digital media have made possible this historic reversal of the one-way flow of power.

In an analogous way, the advent of digital media in the field of planning has begun to reverse the one-way *flow of power*, from experts to their clients, from governments to their 'subjects', opening the possibilities of democratizing the field and empowering the marginalized. In Rubin's video experiment in Oakland, California, the potential of video-making for reasserting the primacy of the street and street life was revealed. Beyond transportation planning's traditional modelling tools, controlled always by the expert, video became an invitation to urban sociability and a means of producing counter-data, qualitative representations of streets and their hidden faces and uses. In Wagner's account of post-disaster recovery planning in New Orleans, digital communication tools provided a forum for critique of and opposition to the state-driven recovery planning process. The recovery activism that

Wagner describes could not have happened without the Internet, websites, blogs, data bases, list serves, online surveys, mapping programs and discussion groups that brought residents together in cyberspace when they were scattered across the country and unable to return home. Digital technologies provided a critical forum for oppositional planning and for the creation of a meaningful and hopeful recovery process in the face of disaster and uncertainty. Hallenbeck's collaborative video project with students and street-oriented youth in Canada's poorest postal code empowered youths and other residents through a process of utopian imagining and visual appropriation. Sarkissian's use of video in planning practice has empowered (created the space for and given legitimacy to the voices of) children, low-income residents and diverse users of public facilities. Attili and Sandercock's film about the Collingwood Neighbourhood House in Vancouver has energized and further empowered that local institution and the many residents involved in it, as well as leading to changes in government policies regarding the social integration of immigrants, recognizing the importance of neighbourhood-based approaches.

In a somewhat different way, new planning *pedagogies* have led to a profound self-empowerment of students. Isserman's use of film in the education of planners results in them discovering more about themselves and their values and what they want to fight for, while Decandia's teaching of urban social research through the application of digital technologies is overturning the supremacy of intellectual and rational learning and replacing it with a learning based on the five senses. In diverse ways, then, these applications of multimedia are overturning established power relations, challenging long-standing pedagogies, creating more possibilities for the democratizing of planning practices.

In terms of *representing the city*, our contributors have all sought ways to expand the language, the expressive qualities and the range of voices heard in planning research and practices. Attili's hypermedia experiment in working with Afghani refugees gives attention to the hidden life of objects and places and of invisible inhabitants. It points to those things which cannot be said, and listens for those things that are muted. Attili and Sandercock's documentary about the Collingwood neighbourhood develops a sensitivity to, a window on and a respect for the uncelebrated. It searches for remarkable things that are otherwise not remarked on. Decandia and her students' immersion in the life of the village of Santu Lussurgiu is listening to the city with a third ear (Berendt, 1985). Ciacci's use of film to research changes in the Veneto region is very much a case of observing with a fresh gaze that can make our capacity for astonishment come alive again. By investigating what appeared to be self-evident (the countryside becoming the city), he actually made the familiar strange and revealed a more complex reality than what was assumed to be the case. Hallenbeck's use of audio collages rather than video interviews to overcome pre-existing stereotypes about residents with addictions and disabilities, produced astonishment in some viewers, who thought they were listening to middle class commentators and then had to re-think their prejudgements.

Our capacity for *astonishment* comes alive again through many of these chapters, not only in the content but in how this content is portrayed. When we see in Attili and Sandercock's documentary six thousand low-income and immigrant residents reclaiming a neighbourhood park from drug dealers and youth gangs through a participatory planning process; when we see children designing their ideal house and neighbourhood in one of Sarkissian's videos or low-income residents of an outer suburban municipality working with a community artist to transform derelict public spaces in another; when the struggles and courage and hope of Afghani refugees or disaster victims in New Orleans are made visible; when transportation planners, policemen and bureaucrats dress as Greek gods in a role-playing exercise designed by Sarkissian to create a dialogue about alternatives to road transportation; and many more instances in which creativity, flamboyance and humour create new spaces for dialogue, and memorable moments such as a children's lantern parade or the ritual burning of a neighbourhood stigma are captured on video.

In the Preface we described a moment of epistemological crisis in the 1980s when Leonie was unable to connect a macro-political economy research framework with a set of biographical field data, to combine individual stories with the larger social and economic forces shaping those lives. Twenty years later, through multimedia, we have the tools to achieve this combination of storytelling and analysis. Attili and Sandercock's documentary, 'Where strangers become neighbours', does precisely this in the intersecting life stories and images of immigrants alongside a narrative of the age of migration, an account of a community-building process and an analysis of an innovative planning culture in the City of Vancouver. Attili's hypermedia of the Esquilino links individual biographies with larger social and historical forces, as does Isserman's use of film in teaching US Economies and Cultures to planning students.

These then are some of the gifts, rewards and insights delivered by multimedia. Lest all of this start to sound too collectively self-congratulatory, though, we need to acknowledge some of the pitfalls, shortcomings and limitations of multimedia projects: the rogue waves and monsters lurking in the forest. The dark side. This involves a discussion of intended audiences and the challenges of cost and distribution; questions of ethics and power relations; inclusion and exclusion; authorship and ownership; advocacy and propaganda; and the importance of personal and organizational reflexivity.

One of the more obvious pitfalls for the multimedia enthusiast is the question of *audience*. For whom is a particular multimedia product intended? Is the chosen format the most suitable (in terms of length and style)? And how will it reach its intended audience? Each of these needs to be thought through before launching into a project. For example, Attili spent several years working on his hypermedia of the situation of transient migrants in the Esquilino district in Rome. When a member of the City Council saw it, he was impressed and wanted to make it available to the public through placing small digital screens in the park inhabited by the migrants, showing the stories of their struggles and dreams. This idea was never realized, in part because that municipal council was not re-elected, but also because there was an ethical issue of protecting the identities of the interviewees. As a result, this hypermedia has had very little exposure, limited to academic settings.

Rubin's video experiment had an immediate audience in a presentation to a State Assembly member (who had her own agenda for the street) and was also intended to engage more broadly with the city, region and state over the development and planning of San Pablo Avenue in the East Bay of San Francisco. But apart from the single planned screening for the Assembly Member, Rubin had no strategy for disseminating the video as a way of starting a local and regional conversation or of returning it to the street for feedback from his interviewees.

Attili and Sandercock had at least three intended audiences when they began their documentary about the work of the Collingwood Neighbourhood House (CNH) and the integration of immigrants. One was potential fund raisers, who might be persuaded by the film to contribute more money to the CNH program budget for immigrant and refugee settlement services. A second was the wider policy community in other Canadian cities who might be inspired by the CNH story. And a third was cities in European and Asian countries now experiencing significant levels of immigration and associated social unrest, who might also learn from CNH how strangers can become neighbours, through a community development approach. As it turned out, the length of the film (50 minutes) prevented it from being used in instrumental meetings with potential funders. When CNH asked the film makers if they could make a shorter version, Attili and Sandercock were denied permission by the distributor, the National Film Board of Canada, which viewed this as competition with their commercial product. In this case, solving the distribution question through the NFB created another problem, lack of flexibility in helping the community organization. Similarly the search for a distributor for the film beyond North America led to a contract with the publisher, Springer, for a book and DVD package. The authors/film makers then had no control over the pricing of the resulting product (100 euros), which mitigates against a wide distribution. Reaching their desired Canadian audience has been more successful, thanks to a research grant that financed workshops in four cities and the production of a Manual to accompany the film, to be left with local communities. The learning in this experience, for Attili and Sandercock, has been to think more carefully for their next project about the questions of ownership and distribution and to attempt to retain more control so that any profits can be ploughed back into the community whose story is being told.

Audience became a very tricky question for Hallenbecks' project. Her video, *Wishlist*, was one of three short videos which were intended to be screened together, as part of a participatory video project about a street redesign, involving collaboration between students and street-oriented youth. One target audience was to be urban professionals and activists attending the World Urban Forum and the World Planning Congress, both in Vancouver in 2006. But the more important immediate audience was the City of Vancouver, whose planning department was rethinking and redesigning this particular street in the Downtown Eastside of Vancouver, a marginalized neighbourhood under threat of gentrification. Initially intended to feed into the public consultation process, the video was partly funded by the City of Vancouver. But by the time other funding had been secured, and the videos planned and executed, the planning department had already decided on the physical redesign of the street. A more troubling issue arose when one of the three videos used a particular editing technique to ridicule some city planners and designers as well as local politicians and developers. In an ethically flawed feedback process, the film makers had not taken the trouble to ensure that all of their interviewees had seen the rough cut footage and given final approval for the use of their interviews. When one senior planner with the City saw this footage and deemed it to be inappropriate, the sponsors of the project (the university, a private consulting firm and an NGO) agreed to withdraw all three films from circulation until the controversy was resolved. This decision meant that *Wishlist* could have no further input into the planning process for Carrall Street. There are two lessons here. One has to do with patronage (pleasing a sponsor) and the other with ethical protocols, each of which will be discussed shortly.

One final example about audience is a more positive story. Ciacci's film research into regional changes in the Veneto was initially sponsored by the National Institute of Planners in Italy for screening at their national conference in 2000. Ciacci himself envisaged the film as an instrument for stimulating public debate about changes that were happening in the region and consciously set out to make a non-didactic film which would hold up a mirror to planners and politicians as well as residents of the region. After an initial modest distribution of one hundred video cassettes, the reception of the film was such that Ciacci was commissioned by the regional government of the Veneto to make a new edition for distribution among local politicians and the general public. This time, five thousand copies were made, seemingly indicative of the success of Ciacci's non-didactic, non-demonising approach.

Gurstein's overview (Chapter 11) addresses this question of audience and argues that if multimedia is to be effective as a change agent, it must proceed with protocols in place that commit stakeholders not only to engage in meaningful dialogue but also to act on its outcome. While this admonition is important, it is not pertinent to all film/video makers, some of whom do not set out to secure the participation of 'all stakeholders', preferring rather to make a more oppositional, provocative or advocacy piece.

In fact, the *political intentions* of multimedia producers occupy a spectrum from allegedly descriptive and non-didactic to advocacy and even 'propaganda'. As Ciacci (Chapter 1) has argued with regard to the early 'Town Planners' Cinema', the product was a 'kind of filmed propaganda'. In other words, the intent was not to open a conversation about a range of alternatives but rather to present a solution already arrived at by 'urban experts'. Ciacci raises the question of whether film necessarily serves the purposes of those in power or whether it can extend participation in the project for urban change to the largest possible number of people. The range of film and multimedia projects discussed in this book confirms a positive answer to this question. Ciacci's own film on regional changes in the Veneto is one example of a non-didactic approach, which seeks first to draw attention to certain changes in the built environment and then to ask audiences to think about the desirability of such changes. Likewise Gurstein's documentary about outsourcing chose to present the multiple arguments for and against, rather than to take an advocacy position. Rubin approached his video about San Pablo Avenue 'without a preconceived agenda, regardless of the expectations of the film's patron', and Hallenbeck and her collaborators sought to elicit the dreams of local residents and convey them to city planners, rather than starting with a preconceived position. On the other hand, Blake's film sought to present a particular point of view, advocating the merits of participatory design through the telling of one inspiring example of such a practice. Likewise, our film about the Collingwood Neighbourhood House evolved, during the research, into more of an advocacy film than we had originally intended. We were always conscious of walking a tightrope between being critical observer/researchers and becoming sympathetic insiders. We had to keep stepping back and asking whether we were missing something, whether there was a dark side to our story that we were reluctant to excavate. We continued to ask critical questions about inclusion and exclusion.

What our collection of cases depicts then, is a range of political intentions and roles for multimedia, from documenting meetings and workshops for various purposes such as information or training (Sarkissian's examples in Chapter 8), to presenting key policy issues in a dispassionate manner (Gurstein's video), to launching an open-ended exploration with the intent of stimulating dialogue (Ciacci, Rubin, Hallenbeck), to advocacy (Attili and Sandercock, Blake). Surely there is a place for all these types of film making and what is essential to all of them is *self-reflexivity* and transparency about purposes. All film and multimedia production involves editing, and the editing process is always already an editorial (that is, *interpretive*) process, in that it involves choices of what to use, what not to use, how to shape a story for a desired effect (see Attili's Chapter 3 on 'the power to narrate'). As Rubin writes, 'acknowledging the patronage and intended audience of a city planning video is the first step in adopting a reflexive approach' (Chapter 5).

Recognizing and portraying multiple points of view can, in theory, also foster reflexivity. In practice, it can equally lead to confusion or the diluting of a message, as Gurstein notes. Multimedia can encourage the practice of reflexivity in communities, through the dialogue it generates, even when a film adopts an advocacy approach, as we have experienced in the many workshops and discussions that have used our film as a catalyst (Sandercock, Chapter 4). But for multimedia to be effective in community building or as an agent for change the individual reflexivity of the film maker is not enough. Without organizational reflexivity – a willingness to examine the collective assumptions and culture that inform practice – responsiveness to dialogical processes is unlikely. This suggests the importance of a clear commitment by government agencies, NGOs and other decision-makers to enter into the dialogue that a multimedia project generates. That, in turn, poses challenges for institutions and communities to develop their capacity to incorporate video and other forms of multimedia into their governance structures (see Chapters 7 and 11).

Self-reflexivity and critical thinking are as essential to multimedia production as they are to any other research process. That means being clear about our own inherent biases and situatedness, and our power, as the person with the camera and the budget (Attili, Chapter 3). It also means thinking critically about how and when multimedia can be most effective and for what purposes (from influencing policy to opening a dialogue to stimulating community development); who are the appropriate participants in the research design, production and analysis; and how multimedia might offer the opportunity for social learning, through a well-designed iterative process of feedback and multiple screenings and workshops during the making of the product. In other words, as with any other planning approach, the process can be as important as the output.

Reflexivity is also at the heart of an *ethical process*. The question of ethics has been central to ethnographic film making for many decades (see Asch, 1992; Banks, 2001; Barbash & Taylor, 1997; Geertz, 1979; Ruby, 1995, 2000) and is equally pertinent to multimedia projects in planning. Typical ethics reviews in university research settings cover such formal and universalized issues as inclusion and exclusion, potential risks to interviewees and protocols for feedback with interviewees. Attili challenges this universalizing approach in his detailed discussion in Chapter 3 of situational ethics, which we will not repeat here. Instead, we add two further dimensions of special significance to multimedia producers: the politics of voice (the dilemma of speaking for others) and the issue of authorship/ownership (the copyright dilemma).

The self-conscious framing of a research product helps readers/viewers to perceive what is beyond the visible part of the project: the process and the involved subjectivities. It's the means through which it is possible to measure the credibility of the research, its situational ethics and its 'asymmetrical reciprocity' (Attili, Chapter 3). In this respect there is a further consideration that needs to be developed: namely, the ethical complexity of the very idea as well as the act of advocating for someone else. That is traditionally seen (and condemned) as the act of *speaking for others*. Planning is historically imbued with this sense of assuming the needs of others, of claiming to understand others. Advocacy planners exalted this mission, traditionally working for marginalized communities and expressing their needs 'in a language understandable to his client and to the decision-makers he seeks to convince' (Davidoff, 1996, p. 307).

This assumption is now widely challenged. Feminist and postcolonial critic bell hooks makes the argument:

> No need to hear your voice when I can talk about you better than you can speak about yourself. No need to hear your voice. Only tell me about your pain. I want to know your story. And then I will tell it back to you in a new way. Tell it to you in such a way that it becomes mine, my own. Rewriting you, I write myself anew. I am still author, authority. I am still colonizer, the speaking subject, and you are now at the center of my talk (Hooks, 1990, p. 343).

Speaking for others is not a straightforward exercise. First of all it requires a definition of *other* versus *self*: a definition that constantly shifts according to the position of the central subject. Moreover the *other* and the *self* are changed in the mutual knowing process. Secondly, the act of speaking and listening is 'politically constituted by power relations of domination, exploitation, and subordination. Who is speaking, who is spoken of, and who listens is a result as well as an act of a political struggle' (Alcoff, 1995, p. 105).

One way to avoid this is for the planner to be part of the community he/she wants to speak for. But this solution cannot be the answer because there is no way to change the 'outsider-ness' of most planners. As Stieglitz (1999) acutely observed, what needs to be transformed is the patronizing role traditionally embodied by advocacy planners, looking for a more balanced relationship between community and planners: 'a strategic game between power liberties' (Foucault in Hindess, 1996, p. 99).

Multimedia, however, offers other ways of addressing this dilemma through critical reflection on the politics of voice. Chapters by Hallenbeck, Rubin, Attili and Sandercock, all offer alternatives to the problem posed by bell hooks.

These considerations have important implications in the planning theory realm: the advocacy planning paradigm signifies a historically disruptive shift which was able to make visible and integrate the inevitably political dimension of the work planners do. Nevertheless it appeared shackled by a certain naïvety in failing to address classic distributional and power issues as well as the core of the relationship between the so-called planners and the planned. Assuming a heightened ethical awareness connected with the concept of asymmetrical reciprocity, nowadays advocacy planning practice can define itself in new ways: as a contextualized and situational practice in which planners and communities co-develop strategies to address shared values and needs.

The oft-repeated charge against classical anthropology and ethnography was that its practitioners were amoral plunderers of the stories of 'Others', typically those with little power, for personal as well as 'scientific' aggrandizement and without any accompanying sense of reciprocity. Eventually an auto-critique developed within anthropology and a lot more emphasis has been placed on thinking through what constitutes an ethical relationship in terms of research design and methods, *authorship and ownership*, trust and reciprocity. All of these issues are germane to multimedia productions.

From the perspective of a situational ethics, outlined in Chapter 3, researchers need to talk through all of these questions before a project begins and establish protocols collaboratively. If an individual, organization or community is willing to have their story told by an outsider/researcher, a collaborative partnership of understanding needs to be developed. Extended dialogue needs to occur around the following questions: What's in it for those whose story is being told? What do they hope to get out of it and will the project be designed in such a way as to ensure their needs are likely to be realized? What control will they have over how their interviews are used? How will they be consulted or involved throughout the production process? Will authorship be shared? Will ownership of the multimedia product be shared, including any potential profits? What's in it for the researcher/producer? Will there be an ongoing relationship after the production is finished? Is the researcher prepared to acknowledge the gift of this story and what can s/he offer in return?

While it's unlikely that such a collaborative approach can ever be a perfectly symmetrical power relationship, researchers can make an effort in this direction by openly discussing the questions identified above and co-creating both a process and an outcome that address a shared sense of purpose and meaning making. This was our intent throughout the 3-year action research project with the Collingwood Neighbourhood House (see Chapter 4). We co-authored a book (with shared royalties) and co-produced a Manual with them, co-designed community workshops and did many joint presentations of the documentary to diverse audiences. We have an ongoing relationship with CNH in assisting with the establishment of a social enterprise. We discussed and agreed on a distribution plan for the documentary, successfully approaching the National Film Board of Canada. What we did not foresee until it was too late, until we (Attili and Sandercock) as producers signed the contract with the NFB, was that this would preclude us and CNH from doing anything else with our footage and that the NFB would devour the lion's share of royalties – money that we felt should be being ploughed back into the CNH's programmes and services. There was a certain naivety on the part of ourselves and CNH in thinking mainly about the 'prestige' of having one's story told by this legendary (in Canada, anyway) organization, which had been known in previous decades for sponsoring and promoting films with a social change agenda. Lesson learned the costly way. The intention is to reclaim the copyright when the contract expires and hand over the full copyright to CNH so that they can use the film as part of their social enterprise. And the lesson for our present and future projects is to find ways to distribute the product that retain as much profit as possible for the community or organization whose story it is.

We have just been discussing the power relationships between multimedia producers/researchers and those whose stories they are telling. But there is also a broader *context of power* that needs to be considered in both the planning and the evaluating of multimedia projects. Multimedia tools are created within societal processes and as such are entwined with dynamics of power and control in *specific contexts*. Wagner's account of the digital mediation of recovery planning in post-disaster New Orleans is a salutary reminder of the complexity of these inevitable power dynamics. On the one hand, he demonstrates that digital communication tools definitely contributed to the empowerment of local citizens as they developed collective responses to the disaster and its mediation by three levels of government. In particular, web-based tools provided important venues for the development of counter-narratives to the 'official' story of the recovery process and these counter-narratives in turn enabled social learning processes that helped empower local residents and NGOs. But, in the absence of a responsive planning process and open dialogue with elected officials, the recovery process overall has continued to suffer in spite of residents' ability to produce their own critical feedback and propose alternatives through digital technologies. In Wagner's words, 'digital communication tools have not replaced the streets, the council chambers, or Capitol Hill as venues for political action ... Marches on City Hall still matter and the politics of recovery are unfolding on every block' (Chapter 6).

In a political sense, then, the digital city cannot replace the physical city. And yet, it can help to transform the power dynamics of traditional urban politics. Multimedia undoubtedly has an oppositional power/knowledge that would have delighted Foucault. This power resides both in its ability to uncover and persuasively portray countervailing stories that challenge dominant discourses *and* in its ever-evolving ways of providing communication channels beyond the control even of authoritarian regimes.

Reflecting on the legendary sociologist Max Weber, Paul Rabinow wrote that 'the calling of science must include a sense of passionate commitment, combined with methodical labor and a kind of almost mystical passivity or openness' (Rabinow, 2003, p. 99). If we substituted in this quote 'the calling of planning', the result would ring equally true, at least for the contributors to this book. Our explorers in the fields of multimedia in planning have each displayed a passionate commitment to its liberatory and enriching potential. Each has laboured methodically through the chores and challenges of film and video making, of constructing hypermedia and of negotiating digitally mediated planning processes. And each has revealed moments of almost mystical passivity or, perhaps more accurately, an openness to unsettling dialogues with humility and uncertainty.

The end result is that these contributions demonstrate the rich potential, through multimedia, for layered, complex and open-ended representations of urban life as well as enabling multiple forms of voice, participation and empowerment. These chapters have shown the potential, too (in the form of persuasive storytelling), for stimulating dialogue, opening a public conversation and influencing policy. There are diverse ways in which multimedia can nurture community engagement and community development as well as oppositional forms of planning. Multimedia tools create the opportunity for urban researchers to discover new realities, to expand the horizons of qualitative and quantitative research and to represent the city in multidimensional and polyphonic ways. And multimedia products can offer transformative learning experiences, 'educating the heart' through creating access to a democracy of the senses.

References

Alcoff, L. M. (1995). The problem of speaking for others. In J. Roof & R. Wiegman (Eds.), *Who can speak? Authority and critical identity*. Urbana: University of Illinois Press.

Asch, T. (1992). The ethics of ethnographic film making. In P. I. Crawford & D. Turton (Eds.), *Film as ethnography*. Manchester: Manchester University Press.

Back, L. (2007). *The art of listening*. Oxford and New York: Berg.

Banks, M. (2001). *Visual methods in social research*. London: Sage.

Barbash, I., & Taylor, L. (1997). *Cross-cultural film making: A handbook for making documentary and ethnographic films and videos*. Berkeley: University of California Press.

Berendt, J. E. (1985). *The third ear: On listening to the world*. New York: Henry Holt.

Davidoff, P. (1996) [1965]. Advocacy and pluralism in planning. In S. Campbell & S. Fainstein (Eds.), *Readings in planning theory*. Malden, MA: Blackwell.

Geertz, C. (1979). From the native's point of view: On the nature of anthropological understanding. In P. Rabinow & W. M. Sullivan (Eds.), *Interpretive social science: A reader*. Berkeley: University of California Press.

Hindess, B. (1996). *Discourses of power: From Hobbes to Foucault*. Cambridge, MA: Blackwell.

Hooks, B. (1990). Marginality as site of resistance. In R. Ferguson et al. (Eds.), *Out there: Marginalization and contemporary cultures*. Cambridge, MA: MIT Press.

Rabinow, P. (2003). *Anthropos today: Reflections on modern equipment*. Princeton, NJ: Princeton University Press.

Ruby, J. (1995). The moral burden of authorship in ethnographic film. *Visual Anthropology Review, 11*(2), 77–82.

Ruby, J. (2000). *Picturing culture: Explorations of film and anthropology*. Chicago: University of Chicago Press.

Stieglitz, O. (1999, Spring). Advocacy Planning and the question of the Self and the Other. *Critical Planning, 6*.

Name Index

L. Sandercock, G. Attili (eds.), *Multimedia Explorations in Urban Policy and Planning*, Urban and Landscape Perspectives 7, DOI 10.1007/978-90-481-3209-6,
© Springer Science+Business Media B.V. 2010

Subject Index